OF 9

A POLITICAL BIOGRAPHY OF
DELARIVIER MANLEY

EIGHTEENTH-CENTURY
POLITICAL BIOGRAPHIES

Series Editor: J. A. Downie

TITLES IN THIS SERIES

Daniel Defoe
P. N. Furbank & W. R. Owens

Jonathan Swift
David Oakleaf

FORTHCOMING TITLES

Alexander Pope
Pat Rogers

Henry Fielding
J. A. Downie

Richard Steele
Charles Knight

John Toland
Michael Brown

www.pickeringchatto.com/politicalbiographies

A POLITICAL BIOGRAPHY OF DELARIVIER MANLEY

BY

Rachel Carnell

LONDON
PICKERING & CHATTO
2008

Published by Pickering & Chatto (Publishers) Limited
21 Bloomsbury Way, London WC1A 2TH

2252 Ridge Road, Brookfield, Vermont 05036-9704, USA

www.pickeringchatto.com

BRITISH LIBRARY CATALOGUING IN PUBLICATION DATA

Carnell, Rachel
A political biography of Delarivier Manley. –
(Eighteenth-century political biographies)
1. Manley, Mrs (Mary de la Riviere), 1663–1724 2. Satirists, English – 18th century – Biography 3. Women authors, English – 18th century – Biography 4. Authors, English – 18th century – Biography 5. Great Britain – Politics and government – 1702–1714 6. Great Britain – Politics and government – 1714–1727
I. Title
828.5'09

ISBN-13: 9781851968572

Typeset by Pickering & Chatto (Publishers) Limited
Printed in the United Kingdom by Athenaeum Press Ltd., Gateshead

CONTENTS

THE AUTHOR

Rachel Carnell is Professor of English at Cleveland State University. She is the author of *Partisan Politics, Narrative Realism, and the Rise of the British Novel* (2006) and co-editor (with Ruth Herman) of the five-volume *Selected Works of Delarivier Manley* (2005). Her articles have appeared in *Eighteenth-Century Studies, Eighteenth-Century Fiction, Nineteenth-Century Literature* and *Studies in the Novel.*

For Alison and Greg

ACKNOWLEDGEMENTS

I must first thank Ruth Herman and Chris Mounsey for bringing me into the world of Manley studies. I am also infinitely indebted to the National Endowment for the Humanities for the year-long fellowship that has allowed me to write this book. (Any views, findings, conclusions, or recommendations expressed in this publication do not necessarily reflect those of the National Endowment for the Humanities.) Bob Owens and Catherine Ingrassia are due particular thanks for their kindness in writing the letters of recommendation that helped me secure that fellowship (and Bob offered timely advice about a political pamphlet once ascribed to Defoe).

Alan Downie read every chapter of the manuscript and offered crucial corrections and suggestions. Roger Manning kindly read my second chapter and provided incisive counsel about seventeenth-century Anglo-Dutch military history. Gary Dyer offered invaluable advice about the legal history of seditious libel and careful comments on my seventh chapter. Joyce Mastboom kindly translated one of Roger Manley's letters written in Dutch. Ros Ballaster helpfully answered a last-minute query. Lee Zickel and Alan Cliffe offered superb editorial suggestions and improvements to every chapter. Cleveland State University offered support and assistance throughout the project. Any remaining errors are my own.

One of the pleasures of writing this biography was that it required me to seek assistance from a broad range of persons outside of my usual sphere of literary history. The Duke of Beaufort generously allowed me access to the archives at Badminton House and permission to cite from material I discovered there. Clive Cheesman, Rouge Dragon Pursuivant at the College of Arms, provided delightful conversation and invaluable information about Roger Manley and the Manley family tree. Anna Baghiani of the Société Jersiase kindly offered all the resources she could find about Roger Manley's experiences on Jersey. Joy Thomas, of the Wrexham Local Studies Archives, was likewise extremely helpful. Margaret Edwards, of the Priaulx library, on Guernsey, generously made a search of birth records for me and explained a key detail about ecclesiastical record-keeping in the Channel Islands.

Paul Pattison, senior properties historian at English Heritage, generously responded to my email query about the architectural history of Landguard Fort with pdf scans of his sketches of the probable buildings on the site in the 1680s. Elaine Milsom, at the Badminton archive, kindly assisted with my research there. I am also indebted to the assistance I received from local records offices in Hertford, Exeter, Truro, Portsmouth, Ipswich, Chester, Wrexham and Jersey. The staff at the London Metropolitan Archive, the National Archives (UK), the British Library, Case Western Reserve's Kelvin Smith Library, the George Peabody Library at the Johns Hopkins University, the Cleveland Public Library's History Department and Cleveland State University library were unfailingly helpful.

I could not have completed this study of Manley's life and family without crucial assistance from my own extended family. Gwen, John and Elysia Harrison offered hospitality in East Molesey during three separate research trips to London. Joyce and Chris Mounsey provided a warm welcome and delicious meals during every trip that took me into Hampshire. My mother-in-law, Margaret Lupton, looked after our daughter for a week in Warrington when I was doing research in London and Jersey. On another occasion, my mother took care of our daughter in Cleveland when I was away in London. Henry and Rachel Lupton provided hospitality during my research stint in the West Country – and valuable assistance in tracking down theatre history in Devon and Cornwall.

My parents, Sue and John Carnell, have been enthusiastic supporters of this project from its inception. My husband, Greg Lupton, has provided every possible assistance both at home and on research trips abroad. Our daughter, Alison Carnell Lupton, cheerfully helped search out the name 'Manley' in graveyards all over Britain, and has been unfailingly patient while 'mommy finishes her book', although she is extremely relieved that it is now done.

A NOTE ON DATES

In general, the dates in this book are Old Style, except that the year is taken to start on 1 January, rather than on 25 March. The only exceptions to this rule are the dates on the letters that Roger Manley wrote when in exile on the Continent. Following the conventions of previous editors of his letters, I have kept the New Style Continental dating on those.

Dates given for the publication of Manley's works reflect information from newspaper advertisements about the actual publication date, rather than the date on the printed title page. Thus, *The Remaining Part of the Unknown Lady's Pacquet of Letters*, which appeared in September 1707 (as advertised in *The Post Man and the Historical Account* for Thursday, 11 September 1707), is given as 1707, rather than 1708. *The Power of Love*, which was published in late December 1719 (as advertised in *The Daily Courant* for 21 December 1719), reflects that date, rather than 1720. The fourth edition of *The Adventures of Rivella* appeared not in 1725, but in October 1724 (as advertised in *The Daily Post* for Wednesday, 14 October 1724), under the title *Mrs. Manley's History of Her Own Life and Times*. The posthumous 'seventh' edition of *The New Atalantis* appeared in August 1740 (as advertised in *The London Evening Post* for Saturday, 2 August 1740), although its title page lists the date of 1741. Since this information is newly discovered (with the aid of a recently available electronic resource), these dates are different than the dates listed for these works in *The Selected Works of Delarivier Manley* (2005).

Manley Family Tree

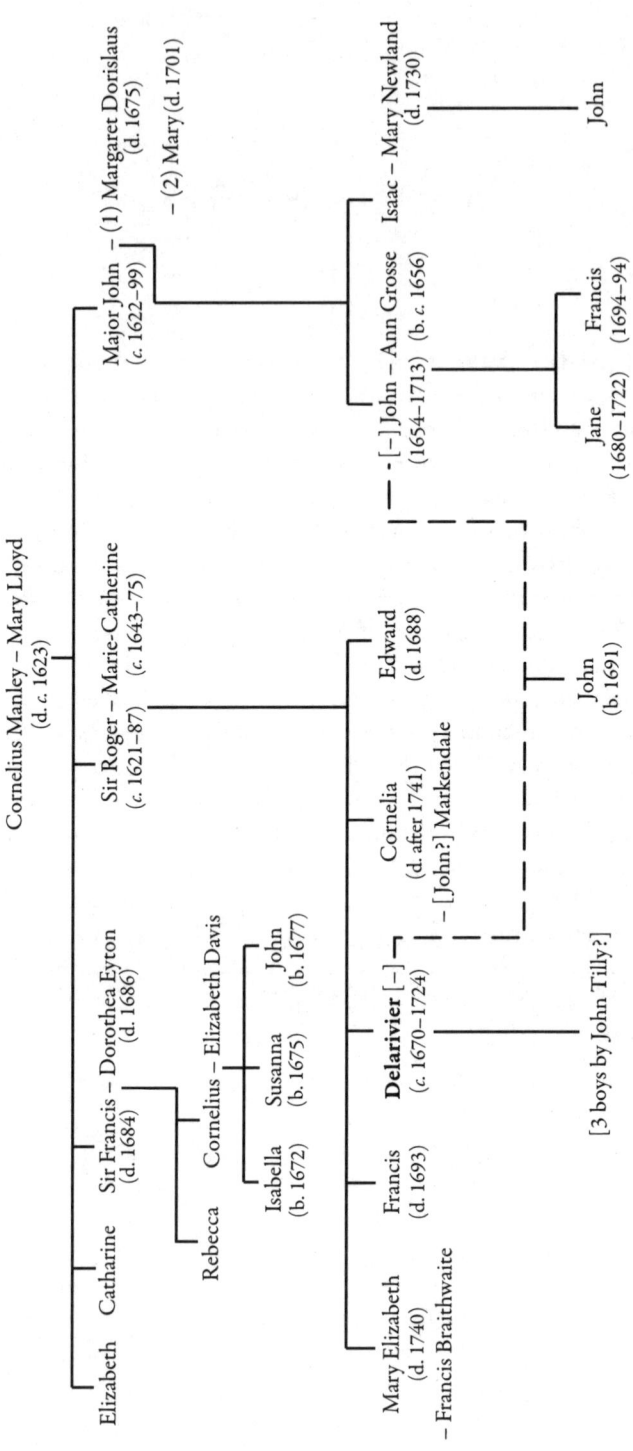

INTRODUCTION

Delarivier Manley (*c.* 1670–1724) was a satirist for the Tories during the reign of Queen Anne (1665–1714) and an important member of Robert Harley's propaganda team from 1711 to 1714 when Harley (1661–1724) was Chancellor of the Exchequer and Lord Treasurer, in essence, 'prime minister' of Great Britain. In 1711 Manley replaced Jonathan Swift as editor of the Tory periodical the *Examiner*. Moreover, her best-selling political scandal chronicle, *Secret Memoirs and Manners of Several Persons of Quality, of Both Sexes. From the New Atalantis, an Island in the Mediterranean* (1709), probably helped bring down the Whig government in 1710 and influenced the development of the novel in Britain. Despite these achievements, Manley has been both neglected and misunderstood by subsequent generations.

Modern readers who know of Manley may have heard of her through a passage in Alexander Pope's *The Rape of the Lock* (1712, 1714), in which Pope (1688–1744) uses the sustained popularity of Manley's *The New Atalantis* as an ironic measure for time immemorial. The thief of Belinda's lock proclaims: 'Let Wreaths of Triumph now my Temples twine, / .... As long as *Atalantis* shall be read'.[1] This line at once acknowledges the immense popularity of Manley's most famous work five years after its initial publication and, through its mock heroic tone, conveys ironic scepticism about its future popularity. In fact, readers in later decades did lose touch with the court and society scandals from Anne's reign, and Manley's works were largely out of print by the end of the eighteenth century. However, rather than dismissing Manley's importance because her political satire stayed in print for less than a century, we might instead be impressed that a work of satire as topical as *The New Atalantis* was not only translated into several languages within the first few years of its publication but was issued in new editions in 1735 and 1740, the last one over three decades after its initial publication and a decade and a half after Manley's death.

There was clearly something about Manley's innovative approach to political satire that resonated with the public long after its immediate topicality had faded. Moreover, her reinvention of 'Varonian' satire (as she terms it in a preface to the second volume of *The New Atalantis*),[2] may well have influenced the author of

Gulliver's Travels (1726), her friend and fellow Tory pamphleteer Jonathan Swift (1667–1745). Even the ironically dismissive Alexander Pope may not have withstood her stylistic influence: some of the satirical cataloguing and the personal attacks of *The Dunciad* (1728–9) seem to share the spirit of Manley's political scandal chronicles.

The vehemence with which Manley attacked the leading Whigs of her day marginalized her professionally once the Whigs took control of government after Queen Anne's death in 1714. Moreover, the fact that her political satire mockingly recounted often lascivious scandals in the lives of well-known court and society figures tarnished her reputation with many contemporaries. Furthermore, Manley's irregular personal life left her vulnerable to the slanderous insinuations of her political enemies. A clergyman acquainted with Mary, Lady Cowper (1685–1724), wife of the Whig High Chancellor William, first Earl Cowper (1665–1723), one of the objects of some of Manley's most pointed satire in *The New Atalantis*, described Manley (inaccurately) as the 'Daughter of an apple woman' and (perhaps accurately), as the mother of '3 bastards'.[3]

Shortly after her father's death in 1687, Manley irregularly 'married' her already-married cousin, John Manley (1654–1713), who would later become a Tory MP; their son, John Manley, was born in June 1691.[4] In 1694, after John Manley had either abandoned or was abandoned by her, Manley lived for six months as a companion to Barbara Palmer (bap. 1640, d. 1709), Duchess of Cleveland, a former mistress of Charles II (1630–85). In 1696 Manley was actively involved in the not yet respectable world of the theatre, as she attempted to make a name for herself as a playwright. She was subsequently involved in an adulterous relationship with the married governor of Fleet Prison, John Tilly, by whom she may have had three illegitimate children.[5] Manley lived out the last decade of her life with the Tory printer John Barber (bap. 1675, d. 1741), possibly as his mistress during part of that period. Such a personal history inevitably damaged her posthumous reputation, already at risk in the hands of Whig historiographers. Like the slanderous gossip spread by Lady Cowper's clergyman friend, posthumous political attacks on Manley were frequently couched in personal terms. For example, when defending his Tory ancestor John Churchill (1650–1722), first Duke of Marlborough (whom Manley had pointedly satirized for his frequent support of Whig political and military policies), the twentieth-century statesman Winston Churchill (1874–1965) deftly dismissed Manley as 'notorious' and as 'a woman of disreputable character'.[6]

Despite such dismissive posthumous treatment, 'Mrs. Manley' (the name under which she published) has never been entirely forgotten. Because her bestselling political scandal chronicle *The New Atalantis* recounts anecdotes about a broad range of society figures, scholars and historians have long relied on it for information about her contemporaries.[7] Scholars have also generally taken

Manley's quasi-fictional autobiography, *The Adventures of Rivella; or, The History of the Author of the Atalantis* (1714), as well as her two epistolary prose works, *Letters Writen [sic] by Mrs. Manley* (1696) and *The Unknown Lady's Pacquet of Letters* (1707), as literal statements of 'facts' about her life as if they were transparent accounts of reality rather than literary creations. Although these texts certainly do supply crucial (if not always reliable or verifiable) information about her life, her fictional autobiography appears to have been shaped by the political exigencies Manley faced during the spring of 1714, when she was writing the work; it certainly does not serve as an 'objective' or comprehensive biographical account. Furthermore, all of Manley's works demonstrate her skill at modifying and manipulating popular literary genres of her era. Nevertheless, the critical tendency to treat Manley's writings merely as raw data, rather than as innovative literary and political creations, has meant that literary historians have not taken Manley as seriously as a writer as they have other (male) satirists of her era, such as Jonathan Swift, Alexander Pope or Richard Steele (bap. 1672, d. 1729).

Paradoxically, the literary critics who have kept her name alive – i.e. those interested in the origins of the British novel – have also rendered Manley a marginal figure in their literary trajectories, by misconstruing her stylistically innovative political scandal chronicles (sometimes referred to as 'secret histories' or *romans-à-clef*) as failed attempts at novel-writing, rather than as highly original works of political satire.[8] Only recently has Manley been understood within the tradition of neo-classical satire, probably because her own 'Varonian' style of satire, as she describes it, has been less familiar to modern readers than the Juvenalian and Horatian forms of her male contemporaries.[9]

In short, Manley's life and works have been misunderstood because they have been interpreted through lenses inappropriate to discerning who she was and what she was writing. Since no one has ever published a full biography of Manley, scholars have also routinely repeated mistakes made in secondary sources, so that inaccurate or uncertain material has long been accepted as fact. Manley is still listed in most archival catalogues as 'Mary Delariviere Manley b. 1663' although there is no tangible evidence to assume that the birth of a Mary Manley, noted in a scrap of paper in the Sloane Collection of the British Library, should be taken as the birth record for someone listed in her own will as 'Delarivier Manley', on her own gravestone as 'Mrs. Delarivier Manley' and in her father's will as 'De la Riviere'.[10] Furthermore, although recent scholarship has addressed the political and historical circumstances of the persons and events that Manley was satirizing in her political scandal chronicles,[11] there is very little scholarship on her plays, her verse or her epistolary writings, nor has anyone thoroughly analysed her development as a political thinker and literary stylist across the three decades of her career as a writer. To observe that she was a loyal Tory, the daughter of an exiled royalist military commander, which is about as far as analysis of her political development has progressed, does not address, for example, the more subtle questions of why she dedicated an early publication to a well-known Whig peer, or what her attitude might have been to the Jacobite cause.

Certain passages in her fictional autobiography suggest that Manley was not sympathetic to the exiled Stuarts because of their Catholicism. However, scholars who have taken these comments at face value have not recognized that she was writing her autobiography in 1714, at a time when the Tories and Whigs alike were anticipating a change of government. She thus would have felt a need to present herself as a moderate and flexible Tory, rather than as a partisan Jacobite. However, archival evidence suggests that members of influential Jacobite families, including relations of Henry Somerset (1684–1714), second Duke of Beaufort (to whom Manley dedicated *The New Atalantis*), seemed to take for granted that Manley's publications were sympathetic to the Jacobite cause.[12] Furthermore, both her bigamous husband, John Manley, and her later companion, the Tory printer John Barber, were at various times staunch Jacobite sympathizers, although we should by no means assume that Manley's own politics were always or inevitably aligned with those of the men in her life. In order to make sense of her as a thinker and a writer in her own right, we must carefully identify where her political and intellectual ideas follow and where they diverge from those of the family members and friends who influenced her.

In order to understand Manley's political development, we must also acknowledge that she probably did not write the predictably anti-Whig *The Secret History of Queen Zarah and the Zarazians* (1705), a work long attributed to her, but whose attribution careful scholarship has recently cast into doubt.[13] Furthermore, although there is no more reason to doubt Manley's loyalty to the Church of England than there is to doubt her Toryism, Manley's attitude towards the religious controversies of her day – to which she alludes knowingly in her epistolary writings – also needs to be examined in detail. Moving beyond the traditional view of her as a disreputable gossip, failed novelist, or mere political hack, this study will tease out the nuances of her development as an intellectually engaged political thinker and a writer who was always fully conscious of the political tides of the publishing world around her.

Critically appreciated by her contemporaries for her sophisticated satirical political pamphlets and remembered centuries later for her popular political scandal chronicles (even if they were often misread as novels), Manley, in fact, should be understood as a stylistic innovator in a wide variety of literary and political genres, including occasional verse, post-Restoration drama, epistolary travel narratives, political secret histories, fictional autobiography and novellas in the style of sixteenth-century Continental tales.

As the author of four plays produced during her lifetime, Manley saw the works of John Dryden (1631–1700) and Aphra Behn (*c.* 1640–89) as models, although she clearly was interested in pushing the boundaries of familiar dramatic genres: in her first heroic tragedy, she gives her tragic heroine not the usual two scenes of ranting familiar to the Restoration stage, but six occasions for a tragic rant.[14] Similarly, while the popular epistolary histories and travelogues of Marie-Catherine Le Jumel de Barneville, comtesse d'Aulnoy (1650–1705), obviously inspired Manley's early writings, Manley's briefer, more humorous epistolary works – *Letters Writen by Mrs. Manley* and *The Lady's Pacquet of Letters* – have an entirely different feel than d'Aulnoy's lengthy epistolary histories. Manley's epistolary works are shorter and more pointedly humorous; they might be described as abbreviated and satirical amalgams of d'Aulnoy's style and the styles of other now forgotten collections of fictional letters such as Charles Gildon's, *The Post-Boy Robb'd of his Mail* (1692–3).

We could see Manley's satirical political scandal chronicles – *The New Atalantis* and its sequel *Memoirs of Europe towards the Close of the Eighth Century* (1710) – and her final set of novellas, *The Power of Love in Seven Novels* (1719), as stylistic precursors to the eighteenth-century novel. Such works certainly render political issues and controversies in personal and anecdotal terms, as do many subsequent eighteenth-century novels. However, to view such works simply as precursors to the later 'realist' novel, or else – as they so often have been seen – merely as raw biographical source material, is severely limiting. Such a view prevents our understanding the literary innovations Manley offered either in direct response to, or at least with the awareness of, the publications of her contemporaries.

In short, Manley has been marginalized not only because her anti-Whig narratives would contradict subsequent Whig versions of history but because the genres in which she was working – such as prose satire, anecdotal political secret histories and quasi-fictional epistolary history – have become overshadowed by the subsequent dominance of prose fiction and in particular by what Margaret Anne Doody has termed 'Whig prescriptive realism'.[15] Rather than attempting to understand Manley within the social, political and literary contexts of nineteenth- or twentieth-century British or American culture, this political biography will situate her life and her work as much as possible within the context of her own era.

In the chapters that follow, I shall trace Manley's development as a writer and thinker through an analysis of how she modified the style and structure of the literary and political genres with which she was familiar, including Classical and Continental literature and Restoration drama, as well as the often ephemeral political and literary outpourings of her own era. Only through such a detailed analysis of her stylistic innovations can we begin to understand and make sense of the range of her intellect, the flexibility of her political thought, and the emergence of her own voice as distinct not only from that of the other writers of her era but also from the powerful influences of her father, her bigamous husband and her other intimate friends, as well as her political allies, former friends and enemies.

1 'A LONG UNTAINTED DESCENT': HER FATHER'S DAUGHTER?

Delarivier Manley was the daughter of the royalist military officer and historian Sir Roger Manley (*c*. 1621–87) and a French-speaking noblewoman from the Spanish Netherlands, Marie-Catherine (*c*. 1643–75). Manley was proud of her descent and her royalist heritage; she describes her family as 'Ancient' in her quasi-fictional autobiography, *The Adventures of Rivella*, presumably referring to the fact that the Manleys of Chester had held a coat of arms (a black left hand on a white background) since at least the thirteenth century.[1] The influence of her father's royalist politics and the transformative experiences of his years in exile undoubtedly shaped Delarivier Manley's own life and political work. In fact, it has been taken for granted by most scholars that Manley was to some extent a 'chip off the old block', her own work as a Tory satirist representing the logical next generation of her father's staunch royalism, as both a military officer and a historian. An early twentieth-century dissertation on Manley underscored the presumed significance of Manley's father to her own development by its subtitle 'A Cavalier's Daughter in Grub Street'.[2]

If we actually examine Roger Manley's extensive published works, we notice an obvious difference between them and his daughter's publications. While his histories are dry, chronological, and somewhat predictable products of an often obsequious royalist seeking patronage, his daughter's works are satirical and anecdotal, full of colourful gossip designed to tarnish the reputations of her enemies. A closer look at her father's rhetorical style, however, suggests a literary flair and a political flexibility in his letters that he might not always have been able to fully express in his official writings or his published histories. Moreover, his published histories themselves demonstrate a talent for partisan propaganda that his daughter would both inherit and develop with satiric panache.

In the preface to the original Latin version of his *Commentariorum de Rebellione Anglicana* (1686), subsequently published (without this preface) as *The History of the Rebellions in England, Scotland and Ireland* (1691), Roger Manley cites Juvenal's well-known quip 'Difficile est Satyram non scribere' (it is difficult not to write satire), in order to remind his readers that the events of the

Revolution (or 'rebellions', in royalist parlance) would be easy for him to satirize, although he is attempting to write an objective account, in which he neither 'courts' the reader, nor 'holds him at a distance'.[3] What Roger Manley suggests is an entirely objective account, of course, is an unmistakably royalist narrative of the 'rebellions', although the style itself is factual and dry, with almost no personalized observations or interjections.

Roger Manley's letters to friends at court, family members and employers offer a more nuanced and colourful portrait of a royalist whose years in exile necessarily obliged him to make choices more complicated than simply deciding 'for' or 'against' the house of Stuart. As a military officer in exile, Manley found employment, like many English, Scottish or Irish officers abroad, as a paid soldier in the Dutch forces; forces that, between 1646 and 1665, were sometimes allied with the English, and sometimes at war with them. When employed by the Dutch, or the United Provinces, Manley also seems to have played a role as a secret agent, offering military information about the Dutch and European military operations to a Parliamentarian family member responsible for collecting intelligence for Cromwell's government. Although Manley's daughter never expresses any doubt about Roger Manley's fundamental royalism, we do not know for certain whether this decision to work as a secret agent for Cromwell stemmed from an *amor patriae* stronger than his loyalty to the house of Stuart or simply from his need to earn a living.

Delarivier Manley invariably describes her father as full of integrity and royalist loyalty. Her perspective, however, was that of someone who was not born until after the Restoration and did not begin writing until after the Revolution of 1688–9. Roger Manley's own letters show a soldier in the mid-seventeenth century making decisions about which army to fight for and to which country to offer his military and investigative talents without the benefit that hindsight would provide to others looking back on his decisions. His letters nevertheless offer probably the most significant point of similarity between father and daughter: their parallel capacities to define and redefine themselves rhetorically in order to survive the shifting political turmoil of their own eras.

This talent for self definition and redefinition shared by Manley *père* and *fille* might be likened to the efforts of modern-day celebrities and politicians to package and repackage their own media images.[4] For Roger and Delarivier Manley, however, such rhetorical skills were not developed out of a mere desire for popularity, but stemmed from a fundamental need to survive. We might first imagine Roger Manley as a young man seizing the musket and the password of his captors and bluffing his way through the enemy ranks to escape from Powys Castle, then subsequently and painstakingly crafting a military career both on the Continent and at home, with few resources other than the power of his epistolary style. We then might imagine by what verbal powers Delarivier Manley – scarred by smallpox, bigamously married, mother of at least one and possibly four illegitimate children, and, by 1705, abandoned by her lover of five years and incarcerated in Fleet Prison – would emerge from this nadir and not only survive to tell her own tale, but become both feared and respected as a political satirist and secure a quasi-respectable place for herself in the household of a future mayor of London. The daughter, like the father, seems never to have lacked courage, certainty in her own worth, or confidence in her own powers of persuasion.

Exiled Royalist and Second Son

As she suggests in her description of her family as 'Ancient', Delarivier Manley came from a family of established pedigree, certain of its own social position. Delarivier suggests in an autobiographical passage in *The New Atalantis* that her family suffered materially because of the civil war, which she credits as leaving her 'Grandfather's Possessions in its Ruins'.[5] We do not know the exact extent of the family possessions that may have been sacrificed or forfeited. The home of Roger Manley's older brother, Francis Manley (d. 1684), was 'taken' in 1645, although it may have been restored, either when he made peace with Parliament in 1655, or else after the Restoration.[6] In his will Roger Manley bequeaths to his children 'certain houses ... at Wrexam', which he himself may have inherited from his older brother.[7] Manley Hall, an estate in Erbistock just south of Wrexham, stayed in the Manley family until the nineteenth century.[8]

Despite the national political circumstances that clearly shaped his life, Roger Manley would, as a second son, not have expected to inherit the family landholdings in Denbighshire or Cheshire, whatever their exact extent before the Revolution. It would also appear that even before the start of the Revolution the family landholdings were not so extensive that the eldest son necessarily expected to earn his living merely from the rents from his land: Francis Manley became a member of Gray's Inn in 1642,[9] and eventually embarked on a successful career as a judge in northern Wales. Roger Manley's own life's path, by contrast, seems to have been more complicated partly because he was a second son and partly because war broke out before he could finish his education.

Delarivier Manley asserts in *The Adventures of Rivella* that her father, whom she describes as a 'Scholar in the Midst of a Camp', 'left the University at Sixteen Years of Age to follow the Fortunes of K. *Charles* the First'.[10] Although there is no official record of his matriculation at Oxford or Cambridge, Roger Manley might well have begun his studies with a private tutor at either university, or he might have considered following in the footsteps of his elder brother at Gray's Inn, had the Revolution not intervened. He became a captain in Lord Byron's regiment, which was formed in August 1642, its first task to secure Oxford (which, if Manley had been studying there, may explain why he 'left the University' and joined the regiment).[11] After being taken prisoner at Powys Castle in 1644, then probably helping to defend Denbigh Castle in 1646, Roger Manley fled to the Continent and spent almost two decades in exile, employed during much of this period as soldier for the United Provinces (the political union of northern states of the Netherlands). Following the Restoration in 1660 Manley began a career in the English military, serving first as a captain in an English regiment in the United Provinces, then as captain of a regiment in Portsmouth, then from 1667–71 as lieutenant governor of the royal forts and castles on Jersey, where several of his five or more children, probably including Delarivier, were born. He was subsequently captain of a royal regiment of footguards and posted to various locations, including Portsmouth, where he served as deputy governor between 1675 and 1680 and where he was knighted by Charles II in 1675.[12] In 1680, by which time his daughters were of an age to be married, Roger Manley had been appointed governor of Landguard Fort in Suffolk, where he served until his death in 1687.

Roger Manley was, in other words, modestly successful as a career military officer; he was also modestly successful as a military historian, having translated several works from Dutch and written several detailed histories of foreign and domestic tumults, including *A History of the Late Warres in Denmark* (1670), *The Russian Imposter: or, The History of Muskovie, under the Usurpation of Boris and the Imposture of Demetrius, Late Emperors of Muskovy* (1674), 'The History of the Turkish Empire continued from the Year 1676 to the year 1686' (which was published as a final section in Paul Rycaut's *History of the Turkish Empire from the Year 1623 to the year 1677* (1687)),[13] and his *Commentariorum de Rebellione Anglicana*, for which he may also have written the English translation, which was published after his death.[14] His historical works have been of use to subsequent military historians (his *Warres in Denmark*, for example, was for a long time the only English work to treat the Dano-Swedish war of 1657–60), but they did not make him any remarkable fame or fortune. At his death in 1687, Roger Manley's fortune amounted to slightly less than £600, as well as a share in various family houses, not an insignificant fortune but not a great sum with which to launch the careers of two sons or provide dowries for two unmarried daughters.

Survivor and Satirist

Scarred by childhood smallpox and with little provision for a dowry, Delarivier Manley seems to have been seduced shortly after her father's death, by her first cousin, John Manley, who was about fifteen years her senior. He had been educated at least in part by Roger Manley, and was probably one of Delarivier's legal guardians. Manley claims in an autobiographical sequence in *The New Atalantis* that John Manley married her bigamously by persuading her (falsely) that his first wife Ann, née Grosse (b. *c.* 1656), had recently died. As Manley explains in this passage, she was in short order, 'marry'd, possess'd, and ruin'd'.[15] In the summer of 1691, their child, John, son of 'John and Dela Manley' was born and christened at St Martin-in-the-Fields, Westminster.[16] This early bigamous union with her first cousin seems to have ruined Manley's prospects for any subsequent, legal marriage; it also shut her out from most polite society. However, this move to London with her cousin John Manley, who would later become a Tory MP for various boroughs in Cornwall, probably helped determine Manley's subsequent career as a writer.

Delarivier Manley seems to have stayed in London for about three years, living first with John Manley. During the first six months of 1694, after she either left him or was left by him, she lived in the household of Barbara Villiers, Duchess of Cleveland. Subsequently, for reasons that are not well understood, she left for the west of England, taking a stagecoach to Exeter in the summer of 1694. Manley had returned to London by the spring of 1696 and oversaw the production and publication of her first two plays: *The Lost Lover; or, The Jealous Husband: A Comedy* (1696) and *The Royal Mischief: A Tragedy* (1696). A short epistolary work, one in which she began her career-long attempt at rhetorical self-definition, *Letters Writen by Mrs. Manley*, was also published that year.

Having already met with some limited success at playwriting and epistolary prose, Manley tried her hand at poetry. Two of her poems were published in *The Nine Muses* (1700), a collection of poems by women writers, in honour of the recently deceased Tory playwright John Dryden. The collection, which Manley helped plan and execute, was obviously intended to position strategically these female 'muses' in the literary-political publishing world of their day. Between 1697 and 1702, Manley was the mistress of John Tilly, governor of Fleet Prison, and was involved with him in an attempt to intervene in the famous Bath-Albemarle lawsuit, an attempt they hoped would produce a financial reward for themselves, although the suit was not resolved to their advantage. Manley was briefly imprisoned in November 1705, possibly for debt. In late 1706, her third play, *Almyna: or, The Arabian Vow. A Tragedy* (1707), was produced on stage. In 1707 Manley also brought out another epistolary miscellany, *The Unknown Lady's Pacquet of Letters*, which appeared in two parts, published in January and September. In this work she recounts gossip about others with whom she was once friends, including Richard Steele and the Duchess of Cleveland, and narrates, as amusing fictionalized vignettes, certain events in her own life.

By 1709, Manley had launched her career as a Tory political satirist. Her *New Atalantis* appeared in two parts, the first in May and the second in September or October of 1709. This is a work in which she both inaugurates her version of 'Varonian' political satire and continues to define herself rhetorically by including fictionalized third-person anecdotes about events in her own life, always narrated in such a way as to lend a sympathetic spin to her situation. In October

1709, Manley was arrested and interrogated as the author of this work, on what appears to have been a charge of libel. She was subsequently released and charges were dropped a few months later. This arrest did not deter her from bringing out in short order *Memoirs of Europe*, which was just as strongly critical of the Whig-controlled administration as its predecessor.

From 1711 to 1713, Manley worked actively as part of Robert Harley's Tory propaganda team, writing pointedly satirical pamphlets critiquing a range of Whig policies. She was especially critical of governmental strategy in the War of Spanish Succession, which she and other Tories felt was being unnecessarily prolonged by the military leader John Churchill, Duke of Marlborough. In the summer of 1711, she replaced her friend Jonathan Swift as author of the Tory periodical the *Examiner*, writing the final six issues that year. Extant letters to Robert Harley from this period reveal Manley's sense of herself as a professional pamphleteer, and party loyalist.

In June 1714, Manley brought out her quasi-fictional autobiography, *The Adventures of Rivella*, which appeared shortly before the death of Queen Anne (1 August 1714). With the Whigs back in power in the autumn of 1714, Harley under investigation, and Jonathan Swift back in Ireland, Manley's opportunities for writing Tory propaganda were greatly diminished. For her most successful play, *Lucius, the First Christian King of Britain. A Tragedy* (1717), her former friend and subsequent political opponent in pamphlet wars, Richard Steele, then governor of the Theatre Royal in Drury Lane, reputedly paid her the generous sum of 600 guineas. In late 1719, shortly after Eliza Haywood's debut as a novelist with the first two volumes of her phenomenally popular *Love in Excess* (the third volume was published in 1720), Manley turned back to early Continental sources to produce *The Power of Love*. This is a work with which she may have tried to capture some of Haywood's success and by which she was clearly once again attempting to redefine her own narrative voice and style.

In looking at this varied mixture of publications across two and a half decades, it is easy to see the difficulty faced by subsequent generations in understanding Manley's place in literary history. While she wrote some successful plays, Manley never established herself as her generation's Aphra Behn. While she wrote some fascinating epistolary miscellanies, these short, highly innovative pieces are not easily classed in the same genre as the lengthy epistolary travelogues with which Marie d'Aulnoy made her name as a writer. While Manley did excel at political propaganda, the genre for which she was best known in her own time – the political secret history – has not been granted as much importance by modern literary historians as the satirical essays of Jonathan Swift or the satirical couplets of Alexander Pope. Manley is perhaps best understood as a liminal figure, one who helped rupture and update seventeenth-century and neoclassical traditions, replacing them with more accessible prose designed both to critique earlier traditions and rewrite them for the early eighteenth-century literary marketplace.

As a satirical and stylistic innovator, Delarivier Manley did not shy away from taking risks. In *The New Atalantis*, in a satirical retelling of James II's abdication, she turns James II (1633–1701) into a young woman (Princess Ormia), demonstrating a political and literary verve that stood out even in an era of sharp-tongued Grub-Street journalists. Manley also produced some stunning narrative innovations in the structure of her less satirical prose: she frames her 'autobiography' as a conversation about her between two male courtiers in a dialogue possibly spoken in English (although this detail is not made clear), translated into French, ostensibly recounted and transcribed in French, and then translated into English for publication. Were we to define Manley in terms of her difference from her own father, we might oppose the serious royalist historian to the flippant Tory satirist daughter. However, defining either the daughter or the father through such a facile opposition would obscure both the nuances of their very different life experiences and the stylistic complexity of their written works.

A 'Perfect Bigot'?

In *The Adventures of Rivella*, when explaining why she is 'immoveable' in her desire to 'serve her Country, and the ancient Constitution', Delarivier Manley describes herself as 'a perfect *Bigot* from a long untainted Descent of Loyal Ancestors'.[17] At first glance, this comment appears to do little more than inform us of something that most readers of Manley have taken for granted: that she was a staunch Tory, descended from a proud royalist family. However, simply taking this comment at its face value overlooks the textual sophistication of Manley's quasi-autobiographical, quasi-political, quasi-fictional narrative.

First of all, we must remember that Manley does not narrate her autobiography in the first person; rather she tells her story through the voice of the fictitious Sir Charles Lovemore, ostensibly a long-time admirer of Manley. Lovemore is identified in the key published with the second and subsequent editions of the novel as Sir John Tidcomb (1642–1713), a general in the British army, who had died the year before *Rivella* appeared in print. It is not known whether Tidcomb was ever in love with Manley, or whether in fact he knew her at all.[18] However, unlike Manley's husband, the bigamous John Manley, or her subsequent companion, the printer John Barber, Tidcomb was a Whig. He was a member of the Kit-Cat Club, whose other members included the satirist Richard Steele, Manley's one-time friend and subsequent political opponent. Tidcomb had once been a protégé of James Butler (1665–1745), second Duke of Ormond, a Tory military leader and ally of Marlborough, whom Manley had satirized, along with

Marlborough, in *The New Atalantis*, the political scandal chronicle for which she was apprehended in October 1709.

Manley suggests in *Rivella* that Lovemore's family estate was near to where her father was stationed while on Landguard Fort. In fact, the Tidcomb estate was in Wiltshire, while Landguard Fort is on the Sussex coast, on the opposite side of the country. Suggesting that he was a friend of the family puts a respectable spin on a connection (if they were in fact acquainted) that might have begun in less respectable circumstances. Manley could, more plausibly, have met Tidcomb in London through her cousin-husband or else when she accompanied the Duchess of Cleveland to gambling evenings at Madame de Mazarin's lodgings, as is suggested by a scene in *Rivella* in which the two discuss her life and prospects. In this scene, Lovemore (Tidcomb), as a long-time admirer, ostensibly offers Manley the refuge of taking up residence with him at his country estate. Whether or not the offer was ever made and whether or not Manley refused it (as she claims), she might well have considered him an ally and a supporter, despite their political differences, since in the introduction to *Rivella* she characterizes him as 'a Person of admirable good Sense and Knowledge'.[19]

Manley's comment (in Lovemore's voice) about her 'untainted Descent of Loyal Ancestors' occurs in a scene that presumably took place in the winter of 1710, after the charges of libel against her had been dropped. According to Lovemore's account (in Manley's autobiography), Manley and the printers and booksellers involved in selling *The New Atalantis* were happy to have avoided conviction for what he (she) describes as the 'heinious Offence, and the notorious Indiscretion of which they had been guilty'.[20] According to this version of events, after Manley had been released on bail but before the charges against her were dropped, Lovemore had offered to help Manley escape to France and seek the protection of 'the Queen, that was once to have been her Mistress', i.e. Mary of Modena (1658–1718), for whom Manley claims she would have been a maid of honour at court had James II not been forced off the throne in 1688. In Lovemore's (Manley's) version of the story, Manley then protests that she could not consider going to France (to the exiled Stuart court at St Germain en laye) because James's wife, Mary of Modena, was 'the greatest Bigot in Nature to the *Roman* Church', whereas Manley herself 'was, and ever would be, a *Protestant*, a Name sufficient to destroy the greatest Merit in that Court'.[21]

Writing *Rivella* in the spring of 1714, when Queen Anne's health had deteriorated so badly that the Hanoverian succession would have been seen as imminent by many, Manley was probably distancing herself from the conspiracies that would eventually lead to the Jacobite risings of 1715, following George I's accession to the throne. Nevertheless, several decades earlier, in the mid to late 1680s when Manley and her family had been hoping (even expecting) a place at court for the adolescent Delarivier, they apparently were not overly bothered by the Catholicism of James II and his wife. In other words, although there is no reason to doubt Manley's own loyalty to the Church of England, her staunch anti-Catholic stance in a text written in the spring of 1714, when the Whigs' imminent return to power was widely anticipated, might be explained by her desire to position herself as both strongly anti-Catholic and anti-Jacobite. We should thus probably view this 'autobiographical' detail, one that scholars have hitherto taken as historical fact, as instead an instance of Manley's sophisticated political manoeuvring at a time of dynastic transition.

It is also important to remember that Manley apparently composed the text of *Rivella* hastily in order to prevent Edmund Curll (d. 1747) from publishing a very different version of her life story, to be written by Charles Gildon (*c.* 1665–1724), a hack writer and political opponent of Manley, whose patron, the Whig MP Arthur Maynwaring (1668–1712), served as political secretary to Sarah Churchill (1660–1744), Duchess of Marlborough, the target of some of Manley's most pointed political satire. In a posthumous preface to the fourth edition of *Rivella*, which appeared shortly after Manley's death under the title *Mrs. Manley's History of Her Own Life and Times*, Edmund Curll, the probable publisher of *Rivella*, explains how Manley heard of Gildon's plans for writing 'The History of *Rivella*, Author of the *Atalantis*' as '*A severe Invective upon some Part*' of Manley's '*Conduct*'.[22] Such a publication would obviously have provided a Whig smear on one of the Tory's best known propagandists. Had Gildon written the work himself it certainly would have been critical probably not only of Manley but of the politicians and policies her own satire favoured. In order to prevent the appearance of this not-yet-completed work, Manley then ostensibly went to Curll and asked if she could write the piece herself, using the same title. According to his 1724 preface, he agreed, probably on the assumption that something written by Manley, as author of the *Atalantis*, would sell better than whatever Gildon would write.

In fact, we cannot be sure that the writing and publication of this work occurred exactly as Curll attests in this preface. No publisher is listed on the title page for the first edition, published in June 1714; however, recently discovered advertisements for the second edition of the work, which appeared in September 1714, indicate that it was published for 'J. Roberts in Warwick Lane'.[23] Before we summarily discard Curll's account, however, we should remember that Roberts was a well-known 'trade publisher', i.e. one who worked for a fee and did not own the works he published but was often employed by authors or other booksellers for works that might have been deemed risky.[24] Given that the advertisement for the work indicates that it is 'interspersed with Memoirs and Characters of several Persons Cotemporary with the said Author' and that no publisher was printed on the title page of the first two editions, it is reasonable to assume that Curll may have considered the work somewhat dangerous (in light of Manley's own arrest for *The New Atalantis*) and employed Roberts – a trade publisher he used regularly for such items[25] – to publish it for him. Third and fourth editions were advertised for both Roberts and Curll (in notices with almost identical wording), and Curll's name appears on the title page of his fourth edition, to which he adds the posthumous preface.[26] Assuming that his account in that preface is not far from the truth – which would explain why the work was not printed for John Morphew, Manley's usual trade publisher – the very genesis of *Rivella*, as well as the timing of appearance in the summer of 1714, indicates the charged political context in which Manley was writing her own life story.

Lovemore (as Manley's narrator) tells us that once the charges against her were dropped, he did not congratulate Manley as her other friends had done, but persuaded her against feeling satisfied with her '*Success*' in having avoided punishment. Moreover, he (she) claims that in the course of the conversation, he eventually 'brought her to be asham'd of her Writings, saving that Part by which she pretended to serve her Country, and the ancient Constitution'. It is at this point that he (she) then mentions parenthetically that 'there' (presumably referring to her support of 'the ancient Constitution') 'she is a perfect *Bigot* from a long untainted Descent'.[27] The emphasis here on her family's political immovability is consistent with her description (in Lovemore's voice) of her father's having died of disappointment after James II's abdication.[28] While Roger Manley spent almost twenty years in exile for his support of the Stuarts during the Civil Wars, this passage lengthens his lifespan for political effect: he died in the spring of 1687, about eighteen months before William of Orange's invasion of England.

In considering how Manley frames her discussion of her party loyalty, it is significant that she narrates it in the voice someone identified in the keys as a Whig army officer, and that she has *him* describe *The New Atalantis* as 'heinious' and it is *he* who asserts her 'immoveable' loyalty, not to the Tory party *per se*, but to the 'ancient Constitution', itself not a written document but an ideal of nationhood and old-fashioned English liberty, often used by Whigs to refer to the principles of 1688, but to which either party could and did allude as a patriotic gesture. As the quasi-legal and estranged wife of a Tory lawyer and MP and the former lover of the cunning governor of Fleet Prison, a barrister, and as someone who had herself attempted to help mediate in the most famous lawsuit of her age and had once secured a fraudulent witness in a palimony suit, Manley here demonstrates her skill at the art of verbal deniability. Should the Tories regain control of government in her lifetime, Manley could appease her professional allies, such as Robert Harley and Jonathan Swift, by noting that it was Lovemore, i.e. the deceased (and Whig) Tidcomb, who used the word 'heinious' to describe her most popular anti-Whig satire. Manley's narrative also describes her own and her family's Tory loyalty in no uncertain terms. Should the Whigs regain and retain control of government, however (as they in fact would after 1714), Manley could point out that her own autobiography describes her famously anti-Whig *New Atalantis* as 'a notorious Indiscretion'.[29]

In the summer of 1714 Manley may even have been trying to position herself as someone who might be willing to write satire or propaganda for the new government. In pointing to the 'Part' of her writings that promote loyalty to the traditional English notion of the 'ancient Constitution', she is presumably referring to the satirical pamphlets that she wrote in 1711 in opposition to the Whig administration's and Marlborough's policies concerning the War of Spanish Succession. Marlborough's own removal from office in late 1711 and subsequent fall from favour with many Tories and Whigs alike could be seen as having vindicated Manley's warning about the risk to the country's well-being that she and ultimately many others believed his policies posed.

Another indication of the double-edged partisan resonance of *Rivella* is Manley's observation, in a passage in which she (in Lovemore's voice) berates the Tories, whom she describes as 'most Supine, and forgetful of such who served them', for not coming to her aid during her imprisonment. Her narrator explains: 'as to Gratitude or Generosity, the *Tories* did not come up to the *Whigs*'. The passage continues, however, offering a snide remark about certain Whig journalists even while apparently valuing the Whigs for 'never suffer[ing] any Man to want Incouragement and Rewards if he were never so dull, vicious or insignificant, provided he declar'd himself to be for them'.[30] Manley's narrator observes that 'the *Whigs* were so unforgiving they would not advance one Step towards a *Coalition* with any Muse that had once been so indiscreet to declare against them,'[31] suggesting that, despite her 'untainted Descent' she may have at least considered the possibility of seeking Whig patronage so that she could continue writing political pamphlets, a genre of writing for which she showed particular talent.

Manley concludes *Rivella* with the observation that she is no longer interested in writing about politics. Of course, this claim is not made directly, but in the voice of Lovemore, who does not suggest that Rivella (Manley) volunteered this opinion of her own accord, but rather that she has now come to share *his* opinion: 'She now agrees with me that Politicks is not the Business of a Woman, especially of one that can so well delight and entertain her Readers with more gentle pleasing Theams'.[32] Judging from the popularity of *The New Atalantis*, however, Manley pleased readers not when she was depicting innocent romantic scenes, but when the seductive portraits of familiar figures turned unexpectedly into stinging satire. Moreover, the 'Tragedy for the Stage' that Lovemore informs us that she is planning to write – i.e. *Lucius, the First Christian King of Britain* – would recount the restoration of the true heir to the English throne,[33] hardly an apolitical 'Theam' two years after the accession of the Hanoverian elector George I (1660–1727) as king of Great Britain.

The double-edged language in *Rivella*, Manley's slippery, political self-portrait, indicates that Manley, like almost every other politically connected person of her time, was obliged to be ready, at every change of monarch or government, to change if not her political principles, then at least her manner of representing them. The self-portrait in *Rivella* also demonstrates Manley's attachment to the foundational narratives that her father must have imparted to her of their family's importance, loyalty and merit.

That 'Ancient Family'

In understanding Manley's family background and social position, it is helpful to use as a point of comparison the families of John and Sarah (née Jenyns) Churchill, Duke and Duchess of Marlborough. Powerful and wealthy, and intimate confidants of Queen Anne, the Marlboroughs were frequent targets of Manley's satire for their support of political and military policies that Manley opposed. Sarah Churchill, as matriarch of a family that would retain political and social prestige into the twenty-first century, eventually had control of a fortune worth over £4,000,000, while Delarivier Manley died with an estate of less than £400 and no fully legitimate progeny. In the mid-twentieth century, as has already been mentioned, the Marlboroughs' descendant Winston Churchill would dismiss Manley as 'a woman of disreputable character'.[34] Despite the eventual differences in their wealth and station, however, Manley and the Churchills came from similar family backgrounds: royalist gentry of modest means with aspirations to succeed at court.

Like Manley, both Sarah Jenyns and John Churchill were born into relatively impoverished gentry families, and John Churchill's father, Sir Winston Churchill (bap. 1620, d. 1688), had, like Manley's father, fought on the royalist side. Both Jenyns and Churchill began their careers as attendants at court – Churchill as page to James Duke of York and Jenyns as maid of honour to James's wife, Mary of Modena. Delarivier Manley, two decades younger than Churchill and about a decade younger than Jenyns, claims, in *Rivella*, that she would have been offered the next vacant position as maid of honour to the same queen. Such a promise could have certainly been made, since Manley's father was in frequent correspondence during the 1680s with a cousin, Robert Francis, who was at court and might have attempted to arrange a court post for one of Roger's children. Had she gone to court, Delarivier Manley, rather than being tricked into a bigamous marriage with her cousin, might either have made an advantageous marriage, as did Sarah Churchill, or perhaps become a mistress to a powerful courtier or someone in the royal family, as did John Churchill's sister Arabella (1649–1730), who became mistress to James, Duke of York (subsequently James II), a liaison often credited with launching John Churchill's impressive career.

The success of the royalist branch of the Churchill family certainly stemmed in part from the fact that Winston Churchill (John Churchill's father) was able to stay in England after the success of the Parliamentary forces by taking sanctuary with his wife's family, who had supported Cromwell. By contrast, the royalist Roger Manley left England in about 1646 and spent the next fourteen years in political exile on the Continent, serving in Dutch forces during various campaigns and writing military histories. As aware as she was of the personal and political achievements of John and Sarah Churchill, Delarivier Manley must have been deeply conscious of the differences between the opportunities available to the offspring of royalist families who had managed to survive the Revolution in England and immediately claim positions at court and the very much more limited opportunities available to a family like hers, where the loyalty and courage of a father resulted in political exile from England, followed by a frustrating career in the English military always at a significant distance (in postings in the United Provinces, on Jersey, in Portsmouth and in Suffolk) from court.

It is arguable that the future Duke of Marlborough might have acquired his much vaunted political and diplomatic skills during the childhood years spent in the impoverished household of his Cromwellian maternal grandmother, in which family members of both political parties lived side by side in cramped quarters and frugal circumstances.[35] Moreover, having had the advantages of staying in England and developing relationships at court, the Churchills were able to amass wealth and acquire property that not only restored but improved the family circumstances. By contrast, the experience of exile and sacrifice for the sake of loyalty to the crown and a subsequent feeling of neglect after the Restoration were clearly defining experiences for Roger Manley and his children. Nor was the contrast between the Churchill and the Manley families lost on Delarivier Manley, who would pointedly satirize John Churchill for his disloyalty to James II in 1688.

Delarivier Manley was probably born on the isle of Jersey about ten years after the Restoration; thus she did not share her father's years in exile. Nevertheless, her father's loyalty, and the personal sacrifices he made for the crown, were, according to her own account, an informing theme of her childhood years. In *Rivella*, she describes her father as 'he term'd himself, truly loyal'.[36] In a short autobiographical sketch in *The New Atalantis*, Manley describes her family story as she must have heard it throughout her childhood:

The inhuman Civil Wars, that rent asunder the Kingdom of *Atalantis* [England], involv'd my Grandfather's Possessions in its Ruins; and when afterwards that a Calm succeeded, and the Royal Line was restor'd, unhappy *Counsels* prevail'd. Those that had been Sufferers were the least regarded, thro' a *dangerous* wise Maxim of the then *Minister*, who told the *young unthinking* Monarch, He must encourage and employ his *Enemies*, to try to make them his *Friends*: For as to those that were so out of

Principle, they wou'd be his Friends still, without other Incouragement. Thus the suffering Loyalty of our Family, like Virtue, met little else but it self for a Reward. My
Father had, indeed, a Military Employment, which, tho' not of half the Value of that
paternal Estate which was lavish'd in the Royal Service; yet upon his Decease, we were
sensible of the Loss of it.[37]

Manley focuses here on the suffering endured by the royalists, a suffering that,
in her family's view, Charles II did not adequately redress financially. The view
that Charles did not do enough to compensate them for their suffering was
shared by many other returning royalists. However, Delarivier Manley's complaint (made forty-nine years after the Restoration in a work of political satire)
nevertheless demonstrates the predictable linguistic turns of someone raised
in a royalist household: she is careful to blame the advice given by Charles II's
minister for her family's suffering rather than the monarch himself. It is likely
that whatever strains of complaint Roger Manley made familiar to his children
as they were growing up, he would have framed them in terms of the mistakes
of other courtiers, rather than the mistakes of the monarch himself. Even if his
own rhetoric had not always been so punctilious, his daughter's careful choice of
phrasing here would help to demonstrate the tradition of royalism she claims as
her inheritance.

Despite the echoes we hear here of her father's laments, it is important to
remember that while Manley may have grown up listening to royalist complaints,
she hardly spent her life feeling sorry for herself. Her Toryism was vigorous, and
she certainly was familiar with her father's refrain of loyalist martyrdom, but
her own partisanship more often takes the form of witty satire than lamenting
complaint. Here again, her father probably provided an example: he clearly had
mastered the rhetoric of royalist lament, but his letters also reveal a sense of
humour, and his approach to his career and his own writing offered the example
of persistence and perseverance.

Roger Manley had to wait until he was about sixty before he was promoted
from captain to major (in part, no doubt, because of the cost involved in pur-
chasing such a position when one was offered), and he was clearly dissatisfied
with his continual postings to remote military fortifications. However, he never
gave up his attempts to persuade his friends at court to press for yet another
preferment; nor did he give up his efforts at writing laboriously detailed military histories whose dedications indicate a persistent hope for royal patronage or
favour. In other words, the sense of injustice behind his laments may have been
real enough, but the laments themselves were also rhetorical constructs; whatever sense of injustice he felt seems not to have prevented him from enjoying life
or from continually pursuing further honour, preferment or reward.

As we tease out Delarivier Manley's vision of her self and her 'Descent', it is
important to understand how her father's own narratives, which clearly shaped

her sense of her own family background and political tradition, were themselves skilful rhetorical constructs. We need to look carefully at the language her father uses, both in his letters written back to England while he was in exile and in his letters written to friends at court, after the Restoration, when he was seeking favour for what he had suffered. In the next chapter, we will come to understand how Roger Manley's predictable royalist laments and dry chronological narratives reveal a talent for literary rhetoric and political self-fashioning, a talent that his daughter would subsequently develop in even more imaginative ways.

2 ROGER MANLEY: 'A SCHOLAR IN THE MIDST OF A CAMP'

Delarivier Manley writes of her father: 'none could be more *Brave*, more *Loyal*, more *Virtuous*'.[1] Certainly her father, whom she describes as 'a Scholar in the Midst of a Camp'[2] must have been courageous; he also clearly enjoyed sharing the narratives of his adventures. As an officer in Lord Byron's regiment during the Civil War, while still a young man,[3] Roger Manley was taken prisoner at the capture of Powys Castle in early October 1644, but made a daring solitary escape, which he describes in a letter to his commanding officer. He begins by describing how the enemy 'possessed themselves of the whole Castell' and then offered 'faire quarter to our Men which they gladly received'. Manley, however, fared better than the rest, in part because he was captured early in the fray and then 'comitted to the custody of one of their musketeers'. Manley managed to get the advantage of this musketeer, and 'sorted his Musket from him with their word' – presumably their password – 'by which helpes' he 'passed through their Guards and soe escaped'. As he describes to Lord Byron, there were 'none escaping but myself that I heare of'.[4]

Manley appears to have been daring and clever, but also lucky, in his escape from this 'castle' (more accurately described as a fortified country house when compared with the forts and castles Manley would subsequently administer). Without questioning his actual courage, we might observe that he plays up his bravery in his description of what happened to him after his escape. In his narrative to Byron, Manley describes his subsequent 'flight in the countrey' where, he writes, he 'mett at least with a hundred of the country people ... some of them suspecting mee'. Those 'country people' that he believes suspected him, he then asserts, 'would have laid hands upon mee and soe have conveyd mee to Middleton' – i.e. John Middleton (1608–74), a major-general in the Parliamentary army. Whether or not anyone in fact intended him harm or did lay hands on him is unclear. Roger Manley nevertheless sums up, in writing from Bala on his way to Chester, that 'with much adoe I escaped them all'.[5]

Even if we discount the bravado in the above passages, Roger Manley was clearly a staunch enough royalist to fight bravely for Charles I (1600–49) and spend fourteen years in exile.[6] Nevertheless the 'Untainted Descent' his daughter would later claim as her Tory inheritance may have described the royalism of Roger Manley and his older brother, Sir Francis Manley, but did not extend to their Parliamentarian younger brother. This brother, John Manley (*c.* 1622–99), married Margaret Dorislaus (d. 1675), daughter of the Dutch philosopher and diplomat Isaac Dorislaus (1595–1649), whose 1627 Cambridge lectures on the tyranny of Junius Brutus resulted in complaints that his analysis supported republicanism and regicide.

During most of the 1650s, Manley was not only probably employed as a military officer for the United Provinces but was in regular correspondence with and apparently paid as an intelligence agent by his brother John's brother-in-law, Isaac Dorislaus (d. 1688), a Parliamentarian like his father as well as solicitor to the court of admiralty from 1653 to 1660. Manley began sending letters of intelligence to Dorislaus as early as 1653, at a point when the United Provinces was still at war with England. Although in his letters to Dorislaus he suggests that his loyalty to England is greater than his loyalty to Charles Stuart, Roger Manley may nevertheless have been in correspondence with Charles Stuart, or his agents, during some part of the 1650s, as will be discussed later in this chapter. Moreover, in 1657 or 1658, he might conceivably have been in correspondence with another 'captain Manley', possibly a cousin, who was helping to recruit soldiers for Charles Stuart's planned invasion of England. Manley's letters to Dorislaus from the 1650s reveal an enthusiasm for working for Cromwell's government belied by the royalist laments in his post-Restoration letters to court. By examining the differences in Roger Manley's epistolary discourses from these two eras, we will see the rhetorical skill required of a royalist trying first to survive twenty years of exile and then to gain preferment from a Restoration court deluged with similar requests. Through the example of her father's rhetorical shifts, we also gain an important perspective on Delarivier Manley's talent for tailoring her rhetoric to the different political ideologies she would confront in subsequent decades.

The Plight of Defeated Royalists

When Roger Manley left England for the Continent in the mid to late 1640s, the United Provinces was concluding a war with Spain and negotiating the treaty of Westphalia (1648). This treaty would secure independence for the United Provinces while the southern provinces of the Netherlands would remain under Spanish control. Although the province of Holland, economically the most powerful of the northern United Provinces, was happy with the terms of the treaty and the ensuing peace settlement, the House of Orange and its political supporters would have preferred to continue the war against Spain. The House of Orange wanted to pursue control of the Spanish Netherlands in order to secure a unified Netherlands with tolerance for both Protestants and Catholics. In 1642, just before the outbreak of the English Civil War, Frederick Henry, Prince of Orange, had arranged a marriage for his son, William II (1626–50), with Princess Mary Stuart (1631–60), daughter of Charles I and sister of the future Charles II. This marriage allied the House of Orange to the Stuart monarchy. William II became Prince of Orange upon his father's death.

In 1649, after his father-in-law, Charles I, was executed by the English, William II negotiated a secret treaty with the French to declare war against England and recommence the war against Spain. These plans were never carried out, since William died suddenly of smallpox in November 1650, and after his death the United Provinces functioned without a stadholder from 1650–72, governed largely by anti-Orange republicans in Holland. Although the leadership in Holland during the 1650s was wary of the house of Orange, it nevertheless remained fiercely independent, resisting the English Commonwealth's desire to bring a political union against the Stuarts and the House of Orange. This disagreement and continuing commercial rivalry, as well as England's passing of the Navigation Act of 1651, ultimately resulted in the first Anglo-Dutch War (1652–4).

Most biographical sources indicate that Roger Manley left England in 1646.[7] However, if we follow Manley's own reference to 'fourteen years in exile' in the preface to his translation of *A True Description of the Mighty Kingdoms of Japan and Siam*, which was approved for publication by Whitehall in November 1662, we might infer that Manley left England in 1648.[8] However, it also seems plausible that Manley would have left England at the same time as his commanding officer, John, first Baron Byron.[9] After the defeat at Chester in February 1646, which followed a string of military miscalculations and disappointments, Byron retreated with his soldiers to Caernarfon Castle, from which he intended to command the royalist operations in northern Wales. Byron's contemptuous and authoritarian management style, however, caused a revolt among the locals: in March the gentry of Anglesey rejected his authority, and when he crossed the Menai Strait, which separates Anglesey from the mainland, in order to reassert his authority, he was met by gunmen who tried to assassinate him. Byron returned to Caernarfon, where he was soon facing a siege by a Parliamentarian force. In June he surrendered, gave up his command, and left for France, where he found refuge at the palace of St Germain, in the household of Charles I's wife, Queen Henrietta Maria (1609–69).

After an unsuccessful attempt to return to his military command on Anglesey in 1648, Byron spent the rest of his career abroad, eventually becoming superintendent of the Duke of York's household.[10] However, what happened in 1646 to the officers under Byron's command, including Roger Manley, is not so clear. Whether Roger Manley left England in 1646 or 1648, he is usually believed to have landed in Holland (as opposed to any other province in the

United Provinces) and to have begun working immediately for Isaac Dorislaus, the father-in-law of Manley's younger brother John.[11] However, the sources usually provided for this information do not include any letters between Manley and the older Isaac Dorislaus, who was first sent by Oliver Cromwell (1599–1658) on a diplomatic mission to the United Provinces in 1648 and was murdered in 1649. There are likewise no extant letters to or from the younger Isaac Dorislaus (who did not begin working in intelligence until the 1650s) before 1653.[12] It is perhaps conceivable that Manley was working as an agent for Isaac Dorislaus senior while the latter was employed by Cromwell on a diplomatic mission in 1648, although Manley's experience as a royalist captain under a consistently unsuccessful commanding colonel would hardly have given him any credentials for such a mission.

It is also possible that after Byron's departure for St Germain Manley found employment with another regiment and continued fighting under a different commanding colonel. He asserts in a letter to Isaac Dorislaus dated 15 July [1654], that his 'coming out of Denbigh-castle' was his last action in support of the Stuarts.[13] This would suggest that he was fighting at Denbigh (possibly alongside his brother Francis) when it was defeated by the Parliamentarian forces in October 1646. If he were taken prisoner at this time, he might have been sent into exile, although during this first English civil war royalist officers were not routinely sent into exile but generally only required to give their word that they would not take up arms against Parliament.[14] However, it is conceivable that in June 1646, with King Charles I himself held prisoner by the Scots, Manley accompanied or followed John Byron to St Germain to seek refuge with the other defeated royalists at the exiled court of Queen Henrietta Maria, Charles I's wife.

If Roger Manley did not seek refuge at St Germain in the summer of 1646, and if he did not end up on the Continent in the autumn of 1646, he might have sought refuge elsewhere, perhaps with Parliamentarian members of his own family in Wales. He might also have made his own way to The Hague or to some other port in the United Provinces where, as an English royalist, he might have found a welcome with the supporters of the House of Orange. Many of these supporters were also sympathetic to the English royal family because of William II's marriage to Charles I's daughter, Mary Stuart. If he did find refuge with the Orangists, Manley might not have settled in the province of Holland, as has been assumed by previous scholars, since the ruling forces in that province generally opposed the Orangist party.

Another possible scenario, since we have no concrete evidence of Manley's whereabouts from 1646 to 1653, is that when Manley first left England, he neither sought refuge with the Orangists nor patronage from Dorislaus, but went to the Spanish Netherlands. In 1656 Spain would offer refuge to Charles

II (who had fled England for France in 1651), after the French and the Dutch United Provinces were closed to him by diplomatic arrangements negotiated by Cromwell. Spain would also employ various regiments of Anglo-Irish troops during this period (some of whom would eventually be under the command of the future Charles II and James II), and Manley himself would eventually marry a noblewoman from the Spanish Netherlands. However, he probably did not marry Marie-Catherine before the late 1650s or early 1660s (since she would have been too young);[15] we thus have no reason to assume that Manley was in the Spanish Netherlands before the late 1650s.

Returning to our initial assumption that Manley found employment in the Dutch United Provinces or else refuge at St Germain, he probably would have neither sought employment with nor been employed by the elder Isaac Dorislaus on a mission for Cromwell in 1648. Further evidence that Manley found refuge in the United Provinces is the fact that he was employed by the States General (the governing body of the republic of the United Provinces), as a lieutenant in the army stationed in Maastricht from 1653–4, during the first Anglo-Dutch War.[16] This war was provoked by Cromwell's passing of the 1651 Navigation Act (attempting to bar Dutch involvement in English trade). It began after the death of William II, when the United Provinces were under the control of the anti-Orangist Holland party, having been originally planned by William II to take revenge against the forces that had executed his father-in-law, King Charles I. Roger Manley would probably have been sympathetic to this campaign, despite whatever oath he had taken not to fight against Parliament following his regiment's defeat at Denbigh Castle in 1646; he was also apparently content to be employed by the Dutch army, even if someone other than William II was going to lead the war against England, since he accepted the post of lieutenant in the garrison at Maastricht.

It is worth noting that, as an exiled royalist, Manley took employment with the Dutch in the first Anglo-Dutch War, but that after the Restoration, during the second Anglo-Dutch War (1665–7), when he was an ensign in Colonel Sidney's regiment in Dutch service (during a period of alliance between England and the United Provinces), he was among those officers who refused to swear allegiance to the States General in 1665. Of course, one interpretation of that second war was that it was an attempt by 'unreconciled English republicans in exile to revive the English civil wars', and so Manley would have been signalling his opposition to such factions to the restored monarch.[17] It is also significant that the States General did not employ Manley directly in the naval campaign against England during the first Anglo-Dutch War, but placed him at the garrison in Maastricht, which at the time was an isolated holding of the United Provinces located within the Spanish Netherlands. This garrison would have served as a defence against the Spanish (with whom the United Provinces had been at peace since 1648) and against the French (who, during the third Anglo-Dutch War would capture Maastricht as an initial foothold against the Dutch). Thus Manley's employment in this inland garrison would not have required him to fight directly against his own countrymen.

Nevertheless, given England's shifting military and diplomatic relations with the Dutch during the second half of the seventeenth century, it makes sense that either side would have been reluctant to employ a native of the other if the strategic position was a particularly sensitive one. Manley's letters of intelligence to England, written while he was employed in the Dutch campaigns against Sweden in the early 1650s, also remind us that Manley was always treading carefully between loyalty to his native country (and to his extended family and networks of potential patronage at home) and loyalty to the country where he was currently finding refuge and employment. There is also some evidence to suggest that Roger Manley may not merely have been employed simultaneously by the United Provinces as a soldier and by Cromwell's government as a spy: he may also at the same time have been in contact with other exiled royalists who in 1667 or 1668 were attempting to aid the efforts of Charles Stuart, in exile in Bruges, in his plans to regain the English throne.

What remains of Roger Manley's correspondence from the 1650s suggests that he was juggling conflicting loyalties and also attempting to keep open simultaneously a variety of future options for employment with various Dutch, Parliamentarian, European and possibly Stuart contacts. His situation seems in some ways similar to the situation his daughter Delarivier would experience in the spring of 1714 when she was facing the reality that were she to continue her career as a political pamphleteer under a Whig government, she would need to soften her tone towards a party for which she might conceivably decide to write. In the end, both father and daughter seem to have maintained their royalist and Tory loyalties: Roger Manley eventually enjoyed a respectable, if unremarkable, military career in the decades after the Restoration, and Delarivier Manley was able to continue writing, in different forms and different genres, after the Whigs returned in 1714. However, there were clearly periods in the lives of both father and daughter when each saw the need to keep as many options open as possible, and both were certainly skilled at preparing for the next shift of the political wind by crafting their narrative personae in rhetorically flexible ways.

'It Seems My Frends Have Forgot Me'

By April 1654, the Dutch had lost the first Anglo-Dutch War and were forced to accept peace on English terms. However, in the wake of this defeat, Johan de Witt (1625–72), the young councillor pensionary of the province of Holland, rose to power in the United Provinces as a brilliant leader in both domestic and military policy. De Witt restored the financial position of the States General and rebuilt the republic's prestige in Europe. He avoided further strife with England and intimidated the French in a naval dispute. De Witt also supported both Poland and Denmark in their fight against Sweden's attempted conquest during the First Northern War (1655–60). Although Roger Manley would probably have been more sympathetic to a Dutch government under the control of the pro-Stuart House of Orange, he nevertheless served the United Provinces in the garrison at Maastricht. However, as early as August 1653 (the date of the earliest known letter of intelligence from Manley to London), Manley also seems to have been in the employ of Isaac Dorislaus, offering information about Dutch and European military positions to Cromwell's government.

In late summer 1655, Manley apparently accompanied two Dutch envoys to Sweden.[18] In 1656 and 1657 he was serving the United Provinces at their garrison in Danzig, Poland, commanding a regiment of foot soldiers. He was regularly writing letters of intelligence from Danzig about this European conflict to officials in London. Exactly where Manley's personal sympathies lay during this conflict is not entirely clear. As has already been explained, however, if any vestiges of his royalist sympathies were still intact at this juncture, Manley probably would have felt less loyalty to de Witt's government than he would have felt had the United Provinces been led by William II of Orange. In fact, Manley's likely royalist leanings make us wonder why he would have been writing letters of intelligence to Cromwell's government, which did not want either the Danes or the Swedes to control the Baltic entirely but which nevertheless took Sweden's side in 1658 when the Dutch joined the Danes in order to prevent the Swedes from taking Copenhagen.[19]

As a royalist (if he still considered himself one after ten years or more of exile), Manley may in fact have felt some sympathy for Sweden, which had in 1649 shown support for the Stuart cause. He also probably felt a loyalty to the English nation and England's naval power, whether or not the Stuarts were currently ruling England. Such an *amor patriae* might also have encouraged Manley to cultivate a family connection in Cromwell's ruling elite, even if such a connection might seem inconsistent with the royalist principles he expresses so eloquently in both his published works and his letters to court after the Restoration. As some of his letters to Dorislaus suggest, Manley may also, at certain periods in the mid 1650s, have genuinely given up hope that Charles Stuart could muster the forces necessary to return to England, and he may genuinely have wished for employment with Cromwell's government, a desire at which he hints in one of his letters to Dorislaus.

Roger Manley's letters of intelligence appear to begin in about 1653, when England was still fighting against the United Provinces in the first Anglo-Dutch War. The letters, many of which were collected and catalogued with the papers of John Thurloe (bap. 1616, d. 1668), are usually addressed to 'Antony Rogers at the Post Office', but are understood by the editors and cataloguers of Thurloe's papers to have been intended for the younger Isaac Dorislaus, who was employed in intelligence work for John Thurloe. Thurloe, a trusted councillor of state under Cromwell, was director of intelligence and (from 1655-9) postmaster general, a position he purchased from Roger Manley's brother John.[20] In sending intelligence to Dorislaus (a.k.a. Rogers), Manley was aiding the comprehensive intelligence operation being run by Thurloe, who viewed the Dutch, even in times of peace, with extreme caution.[21] In portions of these letters Manley openly describes the location of his regiment and the movements of various European forces. Nevertheless, he often refers to an enclosed cipher, presumably containing information that was sensitive enough to indicate that he was walking a fine line between his loyalty to his current employers and his loyalty to his native country and his extended family.

The earliest extant letter from Manley to his Parliamentarian relation is presumed to be from Maastricht, 23 August [1653]. In this letter, as in future letters, Manley's assigned task appears to have been to report weekly to Dorislaus whatever news he has seen or read. His letters generally recount what he knows of Dutch and European military movements and any rumours he may have heard about any of these countries' political or military plans. In this letter, Manley describes the Dutch effort at recruiting soldiers, and the costs involved: 'Wee take on men as fast as wee can; but they cost dear.'[22] It would appear that Dorislaus has asked Manley not to send more than what might normally be reported in newspapers or periodicals, but to be 'carefull in his intelligence', presumably in order not to give the impression of active spying, should the correspondence be intercepted. Dorislaus might also have been wary of Roger Manley's probable tendency to offer up his own theories and speculations, since Manley responds in this letter, which appears to have been written relatively early in their correspondence: 'You wish mee to be careful in my intelligence, and I promised you nothing but newes; though I doe not remember, that I have wrote any thing yet to you; nay I am not sure of it, that was not very true.'[23]

Manley was also apparently expected to convey any other strategic information he learned about and to send copies of the newspaper and periodicals to which he had access. In this first extant letter, he refers to 'the inclosed Courant of the 16th of August', which covers 'the substance of all our letters relating to the last fight'.[24] In a letter from April 1654, he shares his information about a likely accord between the French and Spanish monarchs, which he has gleaned through letters he has seen 'from good hands' from 'Paris & Brussells'. Manley also notes that the Spanish are levying troops at Cologne and that he hears that England will be offered 'half the charge of the war & a Million coutant' (amounting to a substantial subsidy) if they will 'brake with the Dutch'. Manley's own personal response to this seems to be revealed when he adds, 'giving us cause of new apprehensions'.[25]

In return for the news and the European perspective he provided to Dorislaus, Roger Manley clearly expected to be kept informed by Dorislaus about political developments in England and France. In the letter from April 1654, Manley reminds Dorislaus to 'fayle not' to send a copy of the 'Articles',[26] presumably referring to the Anglo-Dutch peace treaty to be signed that month. Manley requests, in the 23 August letter, because of the excessive costs of postage due on them, that Dorislaus send (presumably in a single package) 'the French gazetts with *politicus* weekly'.[27] This habit of sharing news information may have served as a means of making acceptable to his Dutch employers (in case his mail was opened) his own epistolary sharing of news with Dorislaus, but Manley was also clearly hungry for English news himself. By 1657, Manley was occasionally expressing frustration with the exchange: 'I see there is no way to oblige you to write, but by being silent; yet when your letters, like my rent-dayes come, 'tis so slowly, and such a huge way about, that I dare not show them for newes'.[28]

The epistolary relationship between Manley and Dorislaus seems to have been somewhat strained at times. Dorislaus apparently complained if Manley were not regular enough, or detailed enough in his reports. In a letter of 20 September 1653, probably from Maastricht, Manley complains to Dorislaus: 'Yow grumble every weeke at mee for particulars, whilest yow deale with mee yourself only in generalls'.[29] Manley is concerned, for example, that in a previous letter Dorislaus 'sayd the Scots were quashed' while 'wee make them here very considerable and numerous'. In his letter from Brussells, dated 15 July [1654], Manley anticipates Dorislaus's complaints and adopts a defensive posture: 'For feare you should grumble, although it bee in the beginning of the week, I would not fail to write to you'.[30]

The letter from July 1654 also offers us some insight into Manley's tricky political situation. Four decades after the Restoration his daughter would insist on her lineage of 'Untainted' royalism, but it would appear that after eight years of exile, and with the eventual restoration of the Stuarts probably seeming unlikely, Manley was careful in how he represented his political sympathies to his Parliamentarian employers. He explains in this letter to Dorislaus that he will not visit the resort at Spa, although he had 'purposed to have taken the waters', because Charles Stuart, whom he cautiously describes with the politically neutral epithet of 'the Scots king', was on his way there. Manley claims that he is concerned that should he visit Spa while Charles Stuart and his sister were there, he would 'thereby to render [him]selfe obnoxious in England'. While this may be only a convenient posturing intended to improve his relations with his employer, Manley seems serious in his request that Dorislaus procure him 'a passeport from his highnesse' which would facilitate his visit to England and, as Manley explains, 'give me the content of seeing you'.[31]

Manley concludes the July 1654 letter with his claim, already discussed, that he had 'acted nothing directly nor indirectly' for the Stuarts since he left Denbigh-castle.[32] Despite his concern about giving the wrong impression by visiting Spa while Charles Stuart was there, Manley nevertheless seems to have gone, presumably with Dorislaus's consent, and to have observed Charles Stuart's 'court'. Manley reports to Dorislaus on 21 August [1654] that 'the king's trayne is not great, but in very good equipage'; he also describes the retinue of exiled courtiers as, for the most part 'slaves of as little magnitude as influence', who 'rather wish then contribute to the doing of their master's businesse'. Manley also reports that this court has now removed to Aachen, 'under pretence of bathing' and then probably 'to Collen' [Cologne] for '50,000 l. of the German moneys ... and then doubtlesse for Scotland'.[33]

In a letter dated November 1656, Manley reports to Dorislaus on his progress in learning languages, particularly Latin and Dutch, which he would presumably need for his espionage work. In the same letter, Manley expresses interest in the 'money of mine' that Dorislaus apparently mentioned in one of his previous letters. It seems likely that this refers to money Dorislaus was paying Manley for his letters of intelligence. An extant piece of evidence of subsequent payment for Manley's espionage work ('£20 To Mr. Dorislaus for Roger Manly, for the public service, 6 May [1659]') suggests that Manley might have been receiving such payments regularly.[34] It is also possible that either of his brothers might sometimes have been sending Roger Manley money, or that they were entrusted with some of his properties or assets (if he had any) that sometimes yielded income. Whether or not Dorislaus was regularly paying Manley, by 1657 he at least seems to have expressed satisfaction with Manley's performance as an intelligence agent. Manley responds to Dorislaus's letter from 2 January 1657: 'I ... am glad to heare ... that my endeavours are pleasing to our frends'.[35]

The extant letters to Dorislaus provide, in their entirety, a fairly nuanced portrait of Roger Manley as an individual – although they may provide only partial insight into his political leanings since Manley would necessarily have remained silent about whatever lingering royalist sympathies or hopes he may have harboured, buried under the cynical assessment he offered Dorislaus of Charles Stuart's 'court' in exile. Although Manley and Dorislaus may have grumbled at each other and may not have entirely trusted each other, Dorislaus was clearly Manley's main contact with England and with his own family. Roger Manley does not seem to have been receiving regular letters from either of his brothers, and he seems not always to have been certain of their whereabouts. Thus, even though Dorislaus was not a blood relation, nor necessarily of a sympathetic mind politically or philosophically, Manley, in his exile, was clearly grateful to have been in contact with him. In the letter of September 1653, Manley asks to be remembered to 'our sister' – i.e. Margaret, née Dorislaus, sister of Isaac and wife of Manley's younger brother John. It would appear that John himself was apparently too busy, as a major in Cromwell's army, to be in direct contact with his exiled brother, and Francis Manley, having made his peace with the Parliamentarians in 1655, was busy as a judge. Roger Manley grumbles to Dorislaus, 'As for Jack, I shall no more expect the favour of his thoughts, till he be Jack out of office; but 'tis not matter, whilest you retayne mee in your good graces'.[36] In a letter from early November 1656, Manley repeats his frequent complaint of being 'far from friends'.[37] By December 1656, he was feeling neglected by his family: 'It seems my frends have forgot me'.[38]

By early 1657, Roger Manley seems to have had some infrequent communication from his brother John, although he was still relying on Isaac Dorislaus to keep alive the links between himself and his own brothers. In January he writes: 'I suppose br. M. to be gon agayne, or hugely employed, that he does not performe his promise, which was to give mee an accompt of himselfe and our friends. Pray put him in mind of it, and let me at least every moone here from you too, else shall feare mee neglected.'[39] John seems at some point seems to have promised to send a fur coat, probably a necessary protection against the Polish winter, but Roger was obliged to rely on Dorislaus to remind John to provide it, and neither John Manley nor Isaac Dorislaus seem to have been in any hurry to assist Roger Manley with his sartorial needs. In April 1657, Manley writes:

> I desired you in my last to send me so much cloth as will make mee a complete suit of cloth of the finest gray, let there bee a paire or two of silk half stockings added to it of what color you please & a good demy Caster with the other things I sent for. Let them bee sent with the very first shipping to Danzick to set Corse for mee & if Jack will adde the promised fur Coat hee will adde to the obligations I owe him.[40]

A week later, Manley was still trying to determine whether Dorislaus intended to help him replenish his wardrobe: 'Those things I sent for pray let them come with the very first shipping or let me know to the contrarie that I may make my provisions otherwise'.[41] In early May, Manley expresses his continued frustration at his brothers' neglect: 'If I were sure Jacke was in towne, he should hare from me, but neither hee nor Frank are kind'. He then pleads for better treatment from Dorislaus: 'Bee not you soe [unkind like his brothers], but love always, deare sir, Your most affectionate and faythfull servant'.[42]

By late May, Manley seems to have had no response about the clothes, since he again demands that Dorislaus 'Send mee the things I wrote to you for with the first'. Here, Manley also requests that Dorislaus 'add a dozen pair of women's white and coloured gloves'.[43] This last request, to which Dorislaus seems not to have responded to in any haste (if at all), is the only hint we have of Roger

Manley's romantic life. This request for gloves (which may never have been sent) may indicate a dalliance (or preparations for one). Since Marie-Catherine (the future Lady Manley) was only about fourteen years old in 1657, and since she was a native of the Spanish Netherlands, not Poland, this request for ladies gloves had nothing to do with her. By June 1657, Manley seems to have given up hope that Dorislaus would send the ladies gloves or the promised fur coat from his brother John, but he was still pressing for the grey fabric for his new suit: 'let me ... know what is become of the cloth, which I much want'.[44] A month later, he was still wondering whether he should expect 'those things' or not.[45]

Roger Manley's Epistolary Style

In addition to offering some insights about his personal life, his loneliness in exile, and his relations with his family, the extant letters from Roger Manley also give evidence of his developing literary style. Even in a fairly routine cover for an enclosed cipher, Manley displays a literary turn that we find in many of his subsequent letters and historical writings, an epistolary style that may have marked his conversational manner and shaped his daughter's flair for wit. After explaining to Dorislaus in a letter, dated 13 September 1656, that he will 'omit nothing wherein I can imagine your interest and advantage may be concerned', he begins his description with a dramatic bravado: 'Poland is the stage, whereupon the sad tragedie of this north-east part of the world is acted'.[46] He subsequently describes the players in the conflict ('Swedes, Poles, Muscoes, Tartars, Cossacs, Brandenburgers, Danes, and Hollanders') and gives the location of the Swedish king. He also significantly frames the position of the alliance for which he is fighting in sympathetic terms, placing Sweden (whose side England will later join) in an unsympathetic light: 'wee ... doubt not but by our league guarantee with such powerful allies to be secure from the intolerable yoake of the usurping Swede'. Although this information is not in cipher, and probably reveals little that Thurloe would not already know from other sources, Manley nevertheless closes with the possibly unnecessary flourish in his postscript: 'Pray lett not this newes be published in the prints'.[47]

Roger Manley's next letters are briefer, with fewer linguistic flourishes. He informs his correspondent of what little is known for certain about the fight over Riga between Sweden, Poland and Russia: 'Some say, that the Muscovite have raised the siege, being forced thence by the pest and ill weather; and there are that say, that he is got close to the wall. The truth is uncertain [as] ... no post can come from these quarters.'[48] In another letter, which he signs with the pseudonym Lockhart, he describes – in the third-person – his own military position and employment: three hundred of the foot soldiers at the Danzig garrison are 'under the command of one capt. Manly, an Englishman'.[49] In a letter in which he has actual news to report – the death of the Swedish chancellor – Manley seems pleased that he has something concrete to offer. Having related this news, Manley then confidently presents his own interpretation of events and predictions of what is to come: 'This blow may decide the fate of Prussia and Pomerania: if the Sweade be beaten (which I cannot believe, if providence be neutral), they may happily loose [i.e. lose] not only Pomerania, but what else they hould in the empire, for they cannot possibly recruit in these countreyes'. Manley easily contradicts others' predictions, offering his own strategic analysis when he considers it superior to that of others: 'The king of Poland is expected in Dantzik every day, being within seven Dutch miles of the place; but I cannot believe, that he will leave his army, the enemie being so nere him'.[50]

The tone of confidence evident in Manley's analysis of military strategy and foreign policy certainly anticipates the confident tone which his daughter will later adopt in her bold satires of the Whig ministry during the reign of Queen Anne. Whichever side Roger Manley was working for, his prose suggests that he felt himself superior to those around him. We see this same tone two years later in a letter to Johan de Witt, one of the most powerful politicians in the United Provinces during the late 1650s. Although no one has been able to decipher the precise services Manley was offering to de Witt – some sort of secret political manoeuvre for which Manley insists he would require only one company of men – Manley's confidence in his own superior capacity to carry out this tricky assignment is perfectly clear, despite his somewhat inelegant (if perfectly fluent) French: 'puisque je me flatte que j'ay quelque chose plus que les autres, qui me pourra rendre recommendable partout' (since I flatter myself that I have some-thing more than the others that could recommend me everywhere).[51]

As I have already suggested, Roger Manley, as an exiled royalist, would probably have been more politically sympathetic to the Orangist rather than the de Wittian faction; he also seems to have willingly offered intelligence to Cromwell's government. We might well ask why he was suddenly offering secret services to de Witt himself, services that apparently would put Manley in de Witt's power: 'le maistre du secret sera obligé de demeurer touious dans vos-tre puissance' ('the owner of the secret would be obliged to live always in your power').[52] The answer may be that he simply needed the employment. In a letter dated June 1657, Manley explains to his correspondent in England that he has just been dismissed and replaced by 'other officers being come from Holland to take possession of our vyneard'. He suggests that he 'will take a turne into Prus-sia, to see the country and the Swedes milicia', and he expresses his desire to 'be further serviceable to you' since "twill be time I were employed".[53]

Expressing a similar concern about employment in his April 1658 letter to de Witt, Manley explains that he has to earn his living ('mais il faut aussy que j'y trouve mon compte').[54] Whatever occasional payment Dorislaus might have been able to provide for Manley's letters of intelligence to him, these payments would presumably not have been enough to live on. On the other hand, his need for employment one year earlier did not seem so urgent as his letter to de Witt suggests, since in the letter of 6 June 1657, while awaiting the replacements that will put him out of a job, Manley observes to Dorislaus that he does not lack for 'invitations to stay here [at Danzig] in the towne-service'.[55] Such offers of employment may genuinely have evaporated by April 1658. However, his royalist politics, latent though they might have been at times, may also have played a role in Manley's decisions at this time. In the letter to Dorislaus of 6 June 1657, Manley suggests that he would prefer to find employment with the 'Swedes or Danes' (rather than stay in the town service at Danzig), but he would like to know the preference of Dorislaus as to where 'you would have me to goe'.[56] However, by November 1657, Manley seems not yet to have accepted any definite situation or necessarily been given any advice from Dorislaus. He writes from Wismar seeking advice and employment from his Parliamentarian relation: 'I am offered faire conditions here: I would rather serve my country. Lett me know your advice'.[57] From this and earlier letters to Dorislaus we might assume that Manley was eager to serve Cromwell's government as long as Charles Stuart seemed incapable of offering any alternative. However, after Richard Cromwell (1626–1712) replaced his father as Protector in September 1657 and as Charles Stuart's support and resources increased, Manley may once again have turned his thoughts to serving the House of Stuart.

That Other Royalist 'Captain Manley'

Despite his own royalist laments after the Restoration and his daughter's subsequent insistence on his unswerving loyalty, in the autumn of 1657 Manley described himself willing, even eager, to be in Cromwell's employ; by the spring of 1658, he appeared ready to negotiate with de Witt's government, for a fair price. These attempts at finding employment, however, may not have prevented him from staying in touch with other royalists or agents of the future Charles II, whose whereabouts Manley routinely reported to Dorislaus. By 1656 Charles Stuart had reached Bruges, then part of the Spanish Netherlands, from whence he was planning an invasion of England with the promise of 6,000 troops from Spain. However, to give Roger Manley's loyalty to England the benefit of the doubt, it is conceivable that the now obscure offer Manley was making to de Witt may have been a ruse to draw de Witt into something that would have been of benefit either to England or to Charles Stuart. If we assume that Manley was a more loyal royalist in exile than his letters to Dorislaus suggest, it is also conceivable that Manley found that his espionage work for Cromwell's government permitted him to stay abreast of England's concerns about international diplomacy, concerns that necessarily would have been of interest to the Stuart camp.

In June 1667, one John Thomson wrote a letter of information to Edward Nicholas (1593–1669), an advisor and 'secretary of state' to Charles Stuart in Bruges, informing Nicholas of two letters from England describing one 'Manley formerly a Capt in the Kings Service but now a colonel by virtue of a commission sent him by Charles Stewart', who was apprehended in London in April 1657, and subsequently questioned again in Vlissingen (Flushing), following his boast that he could send '2,000' men into England to help place the Stuart heir apparent on the throne. Thomson's concern, as an agent of Charles Stuart's 'government' in exile was that this Captain Manley had been indiscreet in bragging about the money (ostensibly £2,000) he had spent 'in the King's business' and seems to have betrayed several 'honest' men who put their trust in him. Meanwhile, according to Thomson's account, this Captain Manley seems to have been interrogated by Cromwell and acquitted in late April or early May. Having interrogated this same Manley himself in Flushing in early June, Thomson concludes that he is either 'an absolute fool' or an 'arrant knave'.[58]

If we judge from Roger and Delarivier Manley's post-Restoration expressions of royalist loyalty, we might assume that this wayward Manley 'formerly a Capt in the Kings Service' could conceivably have been Roger Manley, formerly a captain in Lord Byron's regiment. However, nothing in Roger Manley's politically cautious letters to England from 1653 to 1657 would suggest that he was either an 'arrant knave' or 'an absolute fool'. Moreover, the dating and sequence of Roger Manley's extant letters from Poland, in which Manley frequently expresses his desire to please Dorislaus's contacts in Cromwell's government, also indicates that the Captain Manley interrogated by Cromwell in the spring of 1657 was almost certainly not Roger Manley. During the late spring of 1657, Roger Manley was writing at least every other week from Danzig, frequently pestering Dorislaus to send grey cloth and ladies' gloves. It would not have been possible for this Manley to have left Poland, travelled to England and returned between any two of these tightly sequenced letters. The Captain Manley causing some alarm to John Thomson, however, could conceivably have been the cousin whom Roger Manley mentions as travelling from Rotterdam to London in the autumn of 1654.

In one of his regular letters of intelligence, Roger Manley mentions to Isaac Dorislaus in October 1654 that he hopes 'Capt. Manley is safe arrived with you'. He assures Dorislaus that this Captain Manley will be able 'to give you a particular accompt of our countrey', thus suggesting that this other Manley might also have been a royalist in exile in the United Provinces.[59] In his next letter to Dorislaus, Roger Manley refers to Captain Manley again, still hoping he has safely arrived, and refers to that captain's brother (to whom Roger is sending a bill of exchange from Rotterdam), as 'Cos. A. Man', presumably Arthur Manley, first cousin of Roger and his brothers.[60] In other words, we know that there was another royalist Captain Manley, cousin of Roger, in exile in the Netherlands during the 1650s; this person may well have been the cousin John Manley in whose regiment of foot Manley was subsequently employed. There is no tangible evidence suggesting that this other exiled Manley was in fact the man bragging about his ability to raise forces for Charles II, but it is possible that this Manley, obviously well known to Roger, might have found a welcome with Charles Stuart's court in Bruges in 1656 and been made colonel by one of Stuart's agents in early 1657, while his cousin Roger toiled away in Danzig. If this other Captain Manley were in fact cousin to John, Roger and Francis Manley, he might then have been able to use his well-placed Parliamentarian family connections (John Manley and Isaac Dorislaus) to persuade Cromwell to acquit him, as in fact occurred, according to Thomson's account.

Roger Manley himself, meanwhile, although probably not engaged in the sort of active (albeit bungled) acts of service to Charles Stuart in which the other Captain Manley was engaged, was nevertheless still keenly interested in the English political situation, including the tricky political question of whether or not Cromwell would be named king of England. In May of 1657, when the other Captain Manley was in London being interrogated by the Protector about his royalist intrigues, Roger Manley was expressing concern to Isaac Dorislaus that the latter had been 'silent' about 'the new change the parlament is about to introduce in England', possibly a reference to the rumours that were circulating at about this time that Cromwell might be made king. Presumably such a move would greatly offend those who still considered Charles Stuart the rightful king of England and might help reverse the sympathies of those exiled royalists, such as Roger Manley, who had been working as agents for Cromwell's secret service.

In a letter of 27 April, sent from Brussels, from Sir Edward Hyde (1609–74), subsequently Earl of Clarendon, to Secretary Nicholas there is a possible reference to someone named Manley: 'I do not think Manley? opposed Cromwell's being King, nor that he desired it for other reason than new importunity, to which he will yield at last'.[61] If this reference is to a Manley, it is possibly to the garrulous Captain Manley already mentioned in another letter to Nicholas concerning Cromwell's title. However, the political concerns of this wayward Manley might also have been the concerns of other royalist Manleys.

By June 1657, as he was anticipating being relieved of his duties in Poland by other officers being sent from Holland, Roger Manley describes himself as 'in the crisis of my fortune' and makes reference to a letter from his brother Francis, which he promises Dorislaus he will answer shortly. This 'crisis of fortune' may simply refer to the financial crisis Manley anticipated when he would be relieved of his military employment in Danzig. On the other hand, such a 'crisis of fortune' might have prompted another political or philosophical reversal. Moreover, it would appear that when Manley wrote to Dorislaus asking for a chance to serve his country in November of 1657, such an offer was not forthcoming. After losing his position in Danzig, Manley seems to have found employment accompanying the ambassadors of the United Provinces on their visit to the King of Sweden. By early September he was writing to Dorislaus from Lübeck, by November from Wismar, and by December from Warsaw. By mid-February 1658, Manley seems to have returned to The Hague, from whence he writes to one Harald Oxe, mentioning the difficulty of his recent journey, as well as his desire to serve the King of Sweden.[62] Between February and April, Manley was still sending twice monthly letters to Dorislaus, either from Maastricht or The Hague. However, his final extant letter to Dorislaus is dated 12 April 1658. It may be that Manley continued writing to Dorislaus, and that the letters have not been preserved. Nevertheless, it is also possible that Roger Manley followed in the footsteps of the other exiled royalist Manley and became involved, directly or indirectly, in serving the cause of Charles Stuart, a cause made more plausible as dissatisfaction with Richard Cromwell increased.

Testimony preserved in the *State Papers of John Thurloe* includes a reference to a 'Mr. Manley' who at a tavern in Cheapside on 8 May 1658 'spoke of 200 horse', which he could provide 'at an hower's time' upon Charles Stuart's arrival from 'Oastend, or some other place unknown to the deponent'.[63] The bragging confidence of this person's conversation resembles the tone of the other royalist Captain Manley, possibly Roger's cousin, already apprehended and interrogated in the spring of 1657, more than it does the tone of Manley's letters to Dorislaus. On the other hand, Roger Manley very likely retained at least a latent loyalty to the Stuarts, even if he had expressed cynicism to Dorislaus about the Stuart court in exile after visiting it in 1654. Moreover, Manley was writing to Dorislaus in March 1658 of a planned visit to England. Manley's last extant letter to Dorislaus suggests that he anticipated a delay in that visit. However, since the sequence of letters ends at this point, it is conceivable that Manley was able to go to England in early May. There is one other extant letter from Manley written from Maastricht that spring: this is the letter to de Witt dated 27 April in which Manley offers to provide de Witt a special but unspecified service, but then there is a gap in the extant letters from Manley until October 1658, when he writes again to de Witt from Maastricht, inquiring (in Dutch rather than French this time) about his previous offer. However, the five-month gap in the epistolary sequence certainly allows time for Manley to have travelled to England in late spring of 1658, as he had originally planned.

If Manley did make this visit in May 1658 and if it did involve any service to Charles Stuart (whether or not Roger Manley was the same Manley overheard in a tavern in May), this would explain the lack of subsequent letters to Dorislaus. The 'Mr. Manley' described as drinking wine and making plans in the tavern in Cheapside in early May 1658 was apparently given a commission as 'collonel of horse' from 'the king Charles Stuart' in Bruges on 20 January in 'the 9th yeare of his [Charles II's] reign', i.e. 1658.[64] Roger Manley could probably not have been in Bruges on 20 January 1658, since on 23 January he was still in Bremen (over 160 km east of Bruges), on his way back from Wismar. However, Manley was travelling back and forth regularly between Maastricht and The Hague in February and March, 1658, and it is conceivable that he could have found time to visit Charles Stuart's 'court' at Bruges, about 80 km south of the Hague, during those months – or at least have been in contact with one of Stuart's agents. The imprudent style of conversation itself is not typical of Manley's letters to Dorislaus, nor does it seem likely to reflect the persona of someone recently trusted by the United Provinces to accompany their ambassadors to Poland. On the other hand, the bragging confidence of tone is not dissimilar to the confidence that Manley expressed in his two 1658 letters to Johan de Witt. Moreover, there is further testimony about this incident that makes a possible connection to Roger Manley's experience on the Continent. When this Manley was examined he apparently revealed that he became

> ingaged for Hutchinson to raise a regiment of men for the king of Sweden; but before he [Manley] would be bound, he made him [Hutchinson] swear he would never fight directly or indirectly against the house of Stuarts, else he never became bound; and said, that if this designe went on in London, that Hutchinson with his party would joyne; and that the said Manley told the deponent, that there would be men enough both from cittie and country, that would joyne.[65]

If Manley had been trying to raise men for the King of Sweden, it would have been consistent with his desire to meet with the 'Swedes milicia' during his planned 'turne into Prussia' in the summer or autumn of 1657 and his desire to serve the King of Sweden expressed in his February 1658 letter to Harald Oxe.

Manley's ostensible promise to Hutchinson that whatever he was being asked to do as a mercenary soldier, he not be obliged to fight against the Stuarts, is also consistent with the principles according to which we imagine Manley operated during his years in exile: accept employment as needed, and try to work for the good of his country (even if that meant working for Cromwell's government), but be cautious about doing anything that would ultimately work against the Stuart cause. As his daughter would later intimate in her own nod to the Whigs in *Rivella* (as being generous to those who wrote for them), finding gainful employment sometimes might require a willingness at least to consider softening one's political principles. Just as Roger Manley might have justified the employment he found for Cromwell's government as 'serving' his country if not his monarch, so Delarivier Manley, anticipating a change of government in the spring of 1714, chose to describe her underlying political principles as those of the 'ancient Constitution'.

Whatever Roger Manley might have been doing between May and October 1659, he did nothing that prevented him from receiving in May 1659 the only recorded payment from John Thurloe, via Dorislaus, of £20 for his 'public service'.[66] On the other hand, there are no surviving letters from him to Dorislaus between the letter of October 1658 and the letter of July 1665, in which he describes his being knighted by Charles II. In other words, whatever services Roger Manley may have offered or intended to offer to Charles Stuart in the summer of 1658 and whatever he may have done between 1659 and 1660 to help the Stuart cause, there is no remaining paper trail. However, whatever services he may have rendered for the future Charles II, Manley was offered no reward upon the Restoration. As Manley's post-Restoration letters to friends at court indicate, it would take him six years of pulling strings at court to find a military position back in England.

Post-Restoration Royalist Laments

Whether or not Roger Manley was involved in any schemes to help Charles Stuart between 1658 and 1660, he was certainly active after the Restoration in attempting to gain favour with the new regime for his years in exile. Some time before 1661 (probably about a decade before Delarivier was born), Roger Manley became an ensign in a company of foot in the Low Countries commanded by Captain John Manley, a first cousin from whom Manley may have gained his expertise in military fortification (and possibly the same royalist Captain Manley interrogated by Cromwell in 1657).[67] Manley subsequently served as ensign to Captain Thomas Ogle in Colonel Sidney's Regiment in the Dutch service. In 1665, when the officers in that regiment, including Manley, refused to swear allegiance to the States General, the units were disbanded and became reconfigured in English service as the Holland Regiment; Manley became ensign on 23 June and captain on 19 September 1665.

During this period, Manley wrote a letter seeking patronage from Henry Bennet (*c.* 1618–85), first Earl of Arlington (a privy councillor and secretary of state for the south), that contains the kind of the lament about his exile with which Delarivier and his other children probably became familiar in subsequent years, from the colourful tales of his years in exile Roger Manley almost certainly recounted to his family. Manley's cousin Robert Francis was clerk to Arlington's secretary, Joseph Williamson (1633–1701).[68] It appears that Arlington had 'mentioned' Manley, to Sir George Downing (1623–84), an English diplomat in The Hague, 'which', Manley explains, 'exacts this humble returne of [his] acknowledgment and thanks'. Manley then acknowledges both his own devotion to the king's service and his appreciation for Arlington's previous advice and assistance, even as he begins his complaint about his career having suffered because of his years in exile:

> That I am here in order to the Kings Service is by your direction and commands where I shall also continue in the joy as long as I am judged usefull being my Life is devoted to it and hath always bin employed in it: It is therefore to your L^PPs goodnesse and bountie that I dare addresse myself for protection and patronage humbly desiring that as there hath bin some wrong done mee in the preference of others to my prejudice in my absence so you will be pleased to redresse or repayre it, your L^PP knowing very well how sensible disgraces of that kind are to men of our profession.[69]

The certainty with which Manley asserts the 'wrong' done him suggests that the injustice inflicted by his exile is a familiar narrative. His sufferings in fact are such a familiar story that he declines going into detail about them and focuses instead on Arlington's generosity: 'I will not trouble yr L^PP with the story of my sufferings and exile, for that was but duty'.[70]

Manley finally mentions, in an aside written in the margin next to his signature, what probably should have been the central topic of business in a letter to the secretary of state: informing him that de Witt (with whom Manley had a decade earlier been trying to curry favour) sent him orders 'to be gone' and that Manley subsequently 'excused', or ignored, these orders 'upon communication with Sir George [Downing] and the priviledge of the Embassie'.[71] Here again, Manley's tone of confidence, even arrogance, seems somewhat at odds with the humility he affects when asking for the continued patronage that he very much believes is his due.

With what would seem the most important official piece of business communicated in the margin, Manley then returns to the main topic of this letter: his continued hope for preferment, in particular, it would appear, in the field of fortification. However, rather than setting out his knowledge and expertise in the body of the letter, Manley adds as a postscript a sort of resumé of his employment experience, followed by a refrain of his usual lament about his exile having worked against his preferment:

> If I know any thing it is fortification having employed these 20 years in the speculation and practice of it, so that if his M^tie have occasion for my service I humbly desire y^r L^PPs recommendation. This particular hath bin remonstrated by some of my frends to my Lord Generall who was graciously pleased to give mee hopes of employment, but I fear my absence may have prejudiced mee in this as well as the other.[72]

Roger Manley is probably correct in thinking that his years in exile materially disadvantaged him. Although those who fought for the crown had the advantage over those who had sided with Cromwell, royalist families, such as the Churchills, who remained in England during the Revolution may have been better positioned to begin their careers after the Restoration than those, like Manley, who had spent a decade or more working as mercenaries in foreign employ.

A significant difficulty for those pursuing a career in the military was that England did not maintain a standing army. Even before the civil wars, British soldiers had always sought employment and military experience as paid soldiers on the Continent; their presence was especially sought starting in 1618 when the Thirty Years War began (Roger Manley's uncle Edward was 'a Captain in the Low Countries' who was 'slain at the breach of Mastricht [*sic*]').[73] At the Restoration, once Cromwell's New Model Army had been disbanded and Charles was attempting to reward returning royalists with positions and advancement, he was allowed by Parliament only the number of guards and garrisons he personally could finance.[74] There were simply not as many opportunities for long-term military employment as there were men pursuing military careers. In the early years of the Restoration, cabinet ministers such as Arlington must have been deluged with requests for preferment by royalist soldiers, as Manley no doubt realized. By 1668, when writing another begging letter to Arlington, he enclosed it in a cover letter to his cousin Robert Francis, asking the latter to 'deliver my Lord Arlington the enclosed when he is in a good humour. It is only to beg a continuance of his patronage.'[75]

Although in his published military histories Manley demonstrates a standard royalist distrust of the presumptuous 'ambition' of Cromwell and the Parliamentarians, he was certainly ambitious enough in his attempts to get ahead in his own career. Given the difficulty even for loyal royalists to advance their careers in the military after the Restoration, Manley seems to have certainly progressed, albeit not as quickly or to as high a station as he would have liked. By 1675 Manley was clearly delighted to be knighted by Charles II: in a letter to Isaac Dorislaus, he describes how the King 'knighted y[r] Brother in his bed chamber'.[76] However, his military promotions were slow in coming. Although he had apparently been a captain in King Charles's forces in the 1640s, Manley was only an ensign in the Holland Regiment in June of 1665. He was promoted to captain three months later, in September 1665, but he was still a captain when deputy to the governor of Portsmouth in the late 1670s and in 1680 when he was made governor of Landguard Fort.[77] Part of the problem, of course, was that there were few opportunities for winning a company-grade commission on the battlefield at this time, and the other possible route to promotion would have required capital to purchase a commission. By the time that his position as governor was renewed upon the accession of James II, in February 1685, Manley had apparently attained the rank of 'lieutenant colonel'; such a rank was not permanent, but granted to senior captains in a regiment at the discretion of the commanding colonel.[78]

Furthermore, while Roger Manley had certainly demonstrated that he could command a regiment or a fortification, he was never offered a military position of strategic significance. In the mid 1670s, Samuel Pepys (1633–1703), then secretary of the Admiralty commission, mentions Roger Manley when listing the disappointments he has had to give those many requesting preferment.[79] Mont Orgueil Castle, where Roger Manley was stationed on Jersey, was of strategic military importance from the thirteenth to the fifteenth centuries, but it was mainly used as a prison in the seventeenth century. Similarly, while Landguard Fort had been of central importance during the Anglo-Dutch wars and was important again in the first and second world wars, at the time Roger Manley took command there in 1680, the outpost was not high on the list of English military priorities. In February 1680, just before being granted the governorship of Landguard Fort, Manley had in fact petitioned (unsuccessfully) for the possibly more prestigious, and probably more lucrative, position of the Receiver General of the Duchy of Cornwall.

Roger Manley's trope of royalist lament and his continual pressing for further advancement, however, should not lead us to assume that he carried out his military duties with anything less than full energy and diligence. After four years of being in charge of Landguard Fort, he writes of his desire to 'do the King more service in this retreat than I have been able to do in 43 years' colonelling'.[80] Although Manley reminds his correspondent that he is labouring away in the remote 'solitude' of Suffolk, he nevertheless promises that he is doing his best to improve conditions there. We also see, even in this relatively brief note, a literary allusion: his choice of 'colonelling' echoes the well-known first stanza of Samuel Butler's *Hudibras* (1662–4), when the knight leaves home to seek his fortunes after the manner of Don Quixote.[81] Despite the fatigue signalled by this allusion, Roger Manley's letters indicate, above all, persistence: a persistent focus on the needs of his regiment and a persistence in his continual demands for advancement in his career; we see a similar persistence in his continuing to produce factually-dense military histories until his death, none of which ever became best-sellers or made him famous.

Royalist Military History

Roger Manley's first published work – *A True Description of the Mighty Kingdoms of Japan and Siam* (1663) – was simply a translation of another scholar's account, and his *History of the Late Warres in Denmark* was more valued as a military and naval reference than as a politically partisan history or an emotionally poignant story.[82] In this history, Manley mentions his own eyewitness observations only a handful of times.[83] Manley's subsequent works, however, do demonstrate an appreciation of the power of rhetoric and a willingness to exaggerate with literary flourishes for political purposes.

The Russian Imposter, an account of Boris Godunov and the false Dmitry, a more emotionally engaging narrative than his other publications, was clearly intended for readers interested in topics other than military history. Manley, or his publisher, apparently realized that it was a very different sort of work than his other publications and his name was not listed on the title page in the first edition. However, the story of an imposter, however romanticized, certainly would have particular political resonance for a royalist critical of the Interregnum. Although we do not know for certain that his daughter Delarivier read this work, *The Russian Imposter* nevertheless is probably, of all of Roger Manley's works, the closest in style and approach to his daughter's subsequent political secret histories.

Manley's *De Rebellione Anglicana*, published posthumously in an English translation as *The History of the Rebellions in England, Scotland and Ireland*, is largely a chronological account of battles in the Civil Wars and Monmouth's Rebellion. Following the style of traditional Renaissance war memoirs, Manley offers no more detail about the battles in which he personally fought than others.[84] However, the rhetoric Roger Manley uses, while nothing like the playful political critique and pointed satire that his daughter's works would demonstrate, does suggest that he had a predilection for irony and political satire, even if he did not indulge in it in his published works as often as his daughter would. While the familiar lament of an unsatisfied royalist permeates Roger Manley's letters after the Restoration, whatever resentment he may have harboured against Charles II's government for not rewarding him sufficiently for his years in exile did not mar the tone of his published military histories, which are written from an unabashedly royalist perspective. In his *History of the Rebellions*, as in some of his letters of intelligence describing battles on the Continent, we see life compared to literature, especially tragedy:

> Tragedies will scarce find Credit with Posterity, whilst the Ages to Come, mistrusting the Reports of such enormous Villainies, will look upon our unheard-of Vicissitudes, but as the Fancies of Poetry, and the Decoration of Theatres.[85]

It is clear that Manley appreciated language, as his daughter later would, for its literary qualities as well as its rhetorical power and political effect. Roger Manley does not embroider this level of flowery rhetoric throughout his *History of the Rebellions*; much of it is simply a dry and factual accounting of battles. However, while the publisher claims in the preface that history is written 'with great

Impartiality',[86] Manley's political allegiance is obvious when he describes with disdain the violence of the 'prevailing Faction':

> For how is it possible to believe, that the *Best* of Princes should meet with the *Worst* of Subjects, on whom he had conferred more Graces, than the whole Series of his Ancestors? And that he, who valued his Kingdoms and Life, at a lower Rate than the Happiness of his People, should by a Judicial Parricide, be sacrificed to the ambitious Violence of a prevailing Faction and their Representative.[87]

Manley uses language typical of seventeenth- and eighteenth-century political pamphlets in casting his political opponents as an extreme faction in contrast to the 'Moderation of their Prince'.[88] He also insists on Charles I's 'Reverence for the Laws', a statement that in the mid-1680s, when the *History of the Rebellions* was published, cast a traditional royalist position in terms sympathetic to the Exclusionists, who generally argued that the monarch was not above the rule of law.

Not only does Manley use language with the rhetorical ease of a seasoned political propagandist, he also reflects in a thoughtful way on how the opposing side deployed political rhetoric to its own best advantage. In a discussion of how the Parliamentarians went about recruiting for their army, he observes that 'The Title of *King*, was as yet held in great Veneration by the People'. He then explains that because of this veneration: 'It pleased them, therefore, to entitle their War to the *King and Parliament*, though nothing more contrary to both'.[89] Elsewhere, Manley reflects on the way in which each side in the conflict brought 'God' into the discourse: 'The *Cavaliers* Word was *God and Queen Mary*; the other Side, *God with us*'.[90]

Although Roger Manley's *History* is largely a description of battles, and not a biographical accounting of the major players in the Civil War, Manley does acknowledge the 'loyalty' and 'courage' of those he admires. Moreover, he does not entirely shy away from personal slights for political purposes, slights of the sort his daughter would later put to such effective use in her satire. Manley engagingly recounts an unflattering anecdote about Oliver Cromwell set in 1642, during a period when Cromwell was a Captain of Horse in Essex's regiment. According to a story that was probably already a royalist legend, Cromwell apparently had 'absented himself from the Fight' in the following manner:

> He had observed from the Top of a Steeple in the Neighbourhood, the Disorder of the Right Wing of their Army, wherewith being greatly terrified, he slipp'd down for haste by the Bell-Rope, and taking Horse, ran away with his Troop; for which Crime he had been cashier'd, had it not been for the powerful Mediation of his Friends.

Manley contextualizes this anecdote by claiming that he relates such a story of 'this so famous Chieftain in the following Wars, to shew, how the Temperature of Body and Mind may, by Life and Ambition, be entirely altered'.[91]

In other words, the story about the cowardly Cromwell (possibly one Roger Manley enjoyed recounting to his own children) not only effects a personal slight against a past republican leader (typical of the sorts of personally damaging anecdotes Delarivier Manley would later recount of powerful Whigs of her own and earlier eras) but also ascribes Cromwell's future military courage to his powerful 'Ambition', a character trait that royalist – and in the 1680s, when he was writing this, anti-Exclusionist – propaganda writers would rarely ascribe to their heroes. We see this same Tory distrust of ambition elsewhere in Roger Manley's *History of the Rebellions* when he refers to the 'nefarious Ambition of *Pretended-Reformed Christians*',[92] i.e. those responsible for executing Archbishop William Laud (1573–1645). Assuming that this sceptical attitude towards ambition was familiar from family conversation, it is not surprising that, several decades later, John Churchill's ambition and achievements would become the target of Delarivier Manley's most pointed satire.

Roger Manley's traditional Tory attitude towards distinctions of rank and status are also evident in his *History of the Rebellions*. In discussing those who remained loyal to Charles I in Ireland, Manley returns to the discourse of tragedy:

> some of the principal of the *Nobility*, continued, to their great Honour. Unshaken in their Fidelity to the King; *nor* so bloody, but that some Marks of Humanity, appeared in the very *Actors* in this *Tragedy*, who sheltered, cloathed, fed, and delivered very many from the Barbarities of their Associates.[93]

Manley's sympathies here lie, not surprisingly, with the loyalist nobility and gentry; he also favours traditional landowners over the merchant classes. He describes the City of London (dominated by moneyed interests) as 'the Parent and Nurse of that *nefarious Rebellion* against the King'.[94] By personifying London in this passage, Manley adopts the politically charged metaphor of parenting: in a royalist Tory universe, where the trusted line of authority runs from father, to king, to God, an interfering nursemaid (alluding to the then familiar phrase 'nursery of the rebellion'), who does not adequately respect the traditional hierarchy, becomes the source of rebellion.

Whether or not Delarivier Manley knew this passage in her father's work, she would have been familiar with the politically charged use of the patriarchal family as a model for political obedience, the standard model from High-Church conduct books and from the Bible. Although her father does not seem to have been a tyrannical or dictatorial parent, he nevertheless would almost certainly have taken for granted a hierarchical model of family structure as best in both household and state. Delarivier Manley, of course, would freely rework the analogy for her own political purposes when she re-gendered James II as Princess

Ormia, thus signalling his cowardice, in her satirical retelling of the events of 1688.

In concluding his military history of the Civil War and the Restoration with an account of the Monmouth's 1683 uprising, Roger Manley again returns to the political analogy of the disrespectful member of the domestic family. He describes James Scott (1649–85), Duke of Monmouth, as 'youthfully rash, inconstant, ambitious, and hurried on with the Pretense of vindicating *Liberty* and *Religion*',[95] a characterization typical of how royalists and Tory propagandists would describe Parliamentarians or Whigs. Worse than all this, however, for Manley, is Monmouth's fickleness. After some setbacks in the field in the autumn of 1683, Monmouth apparently wrote letters to his father and his uncle, 'seemingly full of Ingenuity, wherein he acknowledges his Crimes of Unfaithfulness against the King, and of Ingratitude to the *Duke*; bewailing what he had done, and humbly supplicating Pardon for what was past'. However, as Manley notes, 'the unhappy Youth, being bewitched by the Artifices of wicked Men, and his own Ambition, broke that Faith which he had so solemnly promised to preserve inviolable'.[96]

Charles II, whom Manley described as 'the mildest of Princes', was ultimately obliged to banish Monmouth. Manley here observes that 'The King did not long survive this ... being intercepted by a violent *Apopletic* Fit',[97] almost suggesting that his illegitimate son's disloyalty may have helped bring about Charles II's final apoplepsy. This rhetorical conflation is similar to the slight rewriting of history Delarivier Manley will effect in her fictional autobiography, when she suggests that James II's abdication brought about her father's death, from grief for his monarch. As has already been explained, while Roger Manley probably would have been disappointed at James II's abdication, he had died six months before William of Orange invaded England. Whether or not Delarivier Manley had read her father's *History of the Rebellions*, she would certainly have been familiar with Roger Manley's view of the British subjects who took up arms against their sovereign.

The History of the Rebellions, the last of Roger Manley's published works, and his most overtly partisan, was probably written, at least in part, to discredit Exclusionist ideology of the mid-1680s. It is therefore not surprising that Manley deploys certain literary stylistics for partisan effect. He even playfully acknowledges the overlap between political and novelistic rhetoric when he describes the groups attempting to overturn the Restoration in 1663 as '*Novellists*'. The face value of this term here, of course, simply refers to those seeking the *new* (from the French *nouvelle*, piece of news or short story): the 'novellists' are those who 'did dare to buz after a New Change'.[98]

The idea of the *novel*, following the French *nouvelle*, or Italian *novella*, was certainly familiar to European readers, from well-known sixteenth-century collections of such stories by Marguerite de Navarre (1492–1549) and Matteo Bandello (1485–1561), many of which appeared in an English anthology prepared by William Painter (*c.* 1540–95), *The Palace of Pleasure* (1566–7). It would not be surprising if Roger Manley had read either the Painter anthology or other such stories in the original French (a language in which he was fluent and which was the native tongue of his wife). His daughter Delarivier was certainly familiar with such tales: she would translate and adapt several of the stories found in Painter's collection for her publication *The Power of Love in Seven Novels* (1719).

Roger Manley's most evocative acknowledgement of the connections between political and what we would now term novelistic discourse occurs in *The Russian Imposter*. Although this work has nothing to do with English military history, its treatment of a usurping imposter would have had obvious resonance for a nation having so recently restored a monarchy, as Manley points out in his preface. He explains:

> I found so much parallel betwixt these Troubles and those of my Native Country, which by a Providence not many degrees short of a Miracle, is but lately rescued (I may say, uninchanted) from an Imposture of more Artifice and Delicacie, by how much it is more difficult for one person to vary his shapes to the same eyes, than for those eyes to be deceived by a variety of persons, that I have here thought good to present the world with some Observations of the later sort.[99]

Following standard royalist rhetoric, a country's choosing to be ruled by anyone but a monarch from the traditional line of succession could only be explained by enchantment.

Roger Manley's *Russian Imposter* offers an account of ambition and villainy that in some ways gestures towards Aphra Behn's novelistic and romanticized accounts of Whig ambition and Tory martyrdom, *Love Letters Between a Nobleman and his Sister* (1683–5). *The Russian Imposter*'s stylistic connection to the genre of romance, moreover, is accentuated by the decision (whether Manley's own or his publisher's) to include as an appendix to the 1677 reissue an account of 'The Amours of *Demetrius* and *Dorenski*, Rivals in the Affections of Marina, Relating to the foregoing History of Muskovie'.[100] This work demonstrates the political resonance of romantic intrigue and betrayal as would Aphra Behn's and Delarivier Manley's subsequent partisan accounts of ignoble scenes of seduction.

Once we recognize the gossipy romantic overlay of this work by Delarivier Manley's serious military historian father, we are obliged to acknowledge that the traditional (nineteenth- and early twentieth-century) distinction between 'historians' and 'purveyors of gossip' is a false binary.[101] As Delarivier Manley's own works suggest, she herself not only understood how that cultural distinction between (serious) satire and (mere) romance would be used to dismiss her work, but she also knew well how to take advantage of that distinction for her own political and legal purposes. She may have considered herself a satirist in the style of Varro, but when politically prudent – whether defending herself against charges of libel in 1709, or defining her public persona in preparation for the new Whig regime in 1714 – she could also choose to define herself as a writer with 'so peculiar a Genius for [Love]',[102] suggesting that she was merely a writer of diverting 'romance', a genre which, as she well knew, should never be assumed to be apolitical.

3 A 'LIBERAL EDUCATION': YOUTH AND EARLY LIFE IN LONDON

Because Roger Manley spent his career as a military officer, enough of his official correspondence exists for us to obtain a fairly clear sense of where he lived and how he passed his time during the last three decades of his life. Unfortunately, there is no such official paper trail for his daughter Delarivier. A handful of her letters to Robert Harley survive, as does the order for her arrest for libel in November 1709, following the publication of the second volume of *The New Atalantis*; there is also evidence in London's municipal archives about a transfer of debt in the autumn of 1705 and her imprisonment in the Fleet later that year. However, there is much about Manley's life, including basic details such as the year and place of her birth, about which there is no tangible record. Manley requested in her will that most of her personal papers, with the exception of the drafts of several plays, be destroyed after her death. Most of the information we have about her must be sifted out from her fictional autobiography, *The Adventures of Rivella*, and from the presumably somewhat fictionalized anecdotes about her own life and experiences included in her epistolary and satirical works. However, as has already been suggested, Delarivier Manley, like her father, was adept at persuading others to view her as she wished them to; moreover, the way she presented herself often had a political motive behind it.

Birth and Early Childhood

We turn with some caution, therefore, to *The Adventures of Rivella*, in order to tease out a narrative of her life and early years. Through the voice of her admiring male narrator, Lovemore, she informs the reader that she was born 'in *Hampshire*, in one of those Islands, which formerly belong'd to *France*, where her Father was Governour'.[1] Presumably this passage means simply that Manley was born on the Island of Jersey some time between 1667 and 1672, during the period when her father was lieutenant governor of the royal forts and castles on that island. Although the isle of Jersey was never part of Hampshire, the Channel islands

were considered part of the diocese of Winchester, Hampshire (or Sarum), during this era.[2]

Manley's contemporary and fellow author Charles Gildon, who wrote the
entry about her in *The Lives and Characters of the English Dramatick Poets* (1699),
helps corroborate this account of her birth with the statement: 'This Lady was
born on the Isle of Jersey'.[3] Another piece of evidence supporting Manley's having been born on Jersey is that she was probably named after Delariviere, née
Cholmondeley, Morgan (d. 1683), second wife of Sir Thomas Morgan (1604-
79), governor of Jersey and Roger Manley's superior officer when the latter was
stationed on Jersey. Certainly the most plausible reason for Roger Manley to
have given the somewhat unusual name Delarivier (or 'De la Riviere', as it is
written in his will) to one of his daughters would have been to curry favour (or
potential future favour for his daughter) with his commanding officer's wife, a
wealthy woman with an estate in Yorkshire.[4]

The only extant birth record of any child born to Roger and Marie-Catherine
Manley is for a son, Roger Manley (who predeceased his father and may not have
survived childhood), baptized in the parish of Grouville, on Jersey, in September
1672, shortly before Roger Manley left Jersey in the autumn of 1672.[5] As Fidelis
Morgan has pointed out, if we assume that Delarivier was born on Jersey and if
we allow time for the gestation of young Roger, she must have been born no later
than 1671.[6] Assuming, then, that Manley was born between 1667 and 1671,
she would have been 'very young' when her mother died in 1675, as she claims
in *Rivella*.[7] This date range is also consistent with the fact that Manley never
includes any specific details about her mother in any of her work. She clearly
describes her father's personality but never makes any references to her mother
that would suggest that she had any memory of her. A birth between 1667 and
1671 also accords with Jonathan Swift's description of her in a journal entry in
1712 as 'about forty'.[8]

The traditional, but mistaken, scholarly assumption (based on a birth record
for a 'Mary Manley'), that Delarivier Manley was born in 1663 leads one scholar
to conclude that Manley 'consistently reduced her age by ten years, whenever
such deception was possible'.[9] Delarivier Manley, like her father, was certainly
adept at putting the most positive spin possible on her own life, especially in
matters of politics. She suggests in her fictional autobiography that she was
younger than she probably was at the time that she was seduced by ('married'
to) her bigamous cousin and when she wrote her first two (unremarkable) plays.
However, there is little concrete evidence to suggest that, simply for reasons of
personal vanity, Manley regularly attempted to present herself as a full decade
younger than she actually was.

The five children still alive when Roger Manley made his will in February
1687 are mentioned in the following order, presumably from eldest to youngest:

'Mary Elizabeth Brathwaite', 'Francis Manley', 'De la Riviere Manley', 'Cornelia Manley', and 'Edward Manley'. There were certainly other children (including the son born on Jersey in 1672), however, who did not survive their father, but with whom Delarivier may have spent some part of her early childhood. We do not know exactly when Roger Manley married Marie-Catherine, a noblewoman from the Spanish Netherlands, who died at Portsmouth in 1675, aged 32.[10] They were certainly married by 1666, when Roger Manley describes his wife as having been mistakenly identified as a French woman when she arrived at Weymouth.[11] Moreover, they had probably been married at least a year before the start of the second Anglo-Dutch War (1665–7), since in another letter Roger Manley refers to his wife awaiting a favourable wind to sail to France to fetch 'a little boy' they had left at Liège 'before the Dutch War'.[12] Roger Manley also mentions in a letter to his cousin that twin sons were born in 1668.[13] Although one of these three sons might have been Francis, who is listed before Delarivier in Roger Manley's will and so presumably is older than her, two of these three brothers seem to have died young; presuming from the father's will that Edward was younger than Delarivier, he was probably not one of these three.

Edward and Cornelia, the youngest siblings alive when their father wrote his will, were probably born after the birth of young Roger in 1672; it is likely that neither of these was born on Jersey although birth records have not been found there or elsewhere. Delarivier's oldest surviving sister, Mary Elizabeth (d. 1740), may have been born on Jersey, possibly before the twins born in 1668, if we accept as correct the suggestion in *Rivella* that 'Maria' (i.e. Mary Elizabeth, who married Francis Brathwaite in the summer of 1685), was 'six Years elder'.[14] The text of *Rivella* suggests that Mary was eighteen and Delarivier twelve in 1685 (the summer of Monmouth's uprising and the summer that Mary Elizabeth married Braithwaite and Delarivier had a flirtation with an officer stationed at Landguard Fort), but it seems more plausible that Delarivier would have been between fourteen and sixteen (having been born between 1669 and 1671) and Mary between twenty and twenty-two. Mary then might have been born after her parents left Liège (and the young son behind) for Portsmouth in 1665, but before the birth of the twin boys mentioned in a letter as being born in 1668. Manley's younger siblings, Cornelia and Edward, would then have been born some time between 1673 and November 1675, when their mother died. It is possible that Marie-Catherine died in childbed or of complications resulting from the birth of her last child, or else she might have died from the smallpox infection that scarred her middle daughter's face.

Delarivier Manley's very early years then were likely spent on Jersey with her father and mother and various siblings; whether or not the young children actually lived in the family circle or were placed with a wet nurse is not known. Mont Orgueil Castle, the usual residence of the lieutenant governors of Jersey (and often given on Roger Manley's letters as the place from which he was writing), is a rambling medieval fortress, constructed between the thirteenth and sixteenth centuries, built on the rocky edge of the south-east corner of Jersey. At the start of the seventeenth century Queen Elizabeth had intended to have it dismantled and the stone used to build a more modern fortress. When Sir Walter Raleigh was appointed governor of the island in 1600, however, he persuaded Elizabeth to preserve the structure,[15] although it was still in such disrepair by the mid-seventeenth century that it was not considered fit quarters for the future Charles II in 1648 when he took refuge on Jersey. Charles was housed instead during his two years on Jersey in the more modern governor's residence, built in the 1590s within the confines of Elizabeth Castle. By the middle of the seventeenth century, the lieutenant governors on Jersey regularly occupied the sixteenth-century residential apartments in Mont Orgueil, while the governors of the island inhabited the more comfortable residence in Elizabeth Castle.

The Tudor residential apartments at Mont Orgueil, where Roger and his family presumably lived for five years, comprise a small warren of rooms, over four different levels, in one corner of the castle, linked by various narrow staircases. The family's living quarters were situated above crypt-like lower levels, which housed political prisoners and religious dissidents during the seventeenth century (including women accused of being 'witches'). It would not have been an especially comfortable place for a family, especially with the probable noise and stench from the prison making their way up the stairways. It is, of course, possible that the children were placed in the care of a wet nurse nearby – one reason that might explain why the son Roger was baptized in the parish of Grouville, south-west of the castle, rather than in the parish of St Martin in which the castle itself is located. It would also appear that the children may have been sent to boarding school at quite a young age. Roger Manley mentions in a 1669 letter that on his next family visit to England he and his wife and will put their 'eldest daughter' to school.[16] If this daughter, probably Mary Elizabeth, had been born in about 1665 (after the start of the second Anglo-Dutch War, whose outbreak obliged them to leave behind a young son in Liège), then she would have been four years old in 1669, old enough to leave the local wet nurse (if there had been one) and not inconceivably young to be put at school in England rather than endure the daily life at a crumbling military outpost and prison.

Roger Manley was able to visit England several times during his stay on Jersey. He could only visit, however, if his absence from Jersey did not overlap with that of the governor; in 1668, for example, he was obliged to cancel his trip to accommodate Governor Morgan's travel schedule. Manley did manage to visit England (and presumably put his daughter to school) in the summer of 1669. During this trip he seems to have been engaged in a rather bizarre prank (or strange mistake), in which he accused another traveller of being a highwayman's decoy, then subsequently recanted and dropped the charges. Even after having recanted, however, Manley nevertheless referred in a letter to Robert Francis, his cousin at court, to his having 'narrowly escaped being robbed by the highway-men Cassells and Ashenhurst, having eluded them by securing the trepanner in Coventry'. On these occasional visits home, Roger Manley clearly enjoyed him-self. In this same letter in which he ascribes to himself more courage and bravado than was probably merited by his having apparently accused an innocent man, Manley admits to Robert Francis that while in Wrexham with his brother (pre-sumably Francis), he was 'almost drowned with drinking your health'.[17]

During his five years on Jersey Manley also probably made visits to Guern-sey. There is some correspondence between him and Christopher Hatton, the governor there; in one of his letters to Hatton, Roger Manley mentions that his wife intends sending some Mont Orgueil lizards (the castle is home to Britain's largest population of Common Wall lizards) to the 'ladies' on Guernsey.[18] This letter indicates that the wives of the two governors (of two islands only twenty miles apart) might have been acquainted, and so the suggestion in one eight-eenth-century source that Delarivier Manley was born 'at sea between Jersey and Guernsey' may not be entirely implausible,[19] although it seems unlikely that a governor's wife would have been permitted to take a sea voyage, however short, during the period of her pregnancy when gentlewoman of her era were usually in confinement. While it is conceivable that Manley was baptized at sea, extant church records on Guernsey do not indicate any evidence of Manley having been baptized there.[20]

Delarivier Manley herself probably spent at most three years on Jersey and may have been only an infant when the family left the island in late 1672. She offers no description of the place (whether the ambience of the old castle or the shrieks of prisoners) in her later writings. Her father was clearly relieved to return to mainland England; in early 1673, he expresses his gratitude to Joseph Williamson, then an assistant to Secretary of State Arlington, 'for my recall from an irksome exile so near the sun'.[21] Roger Manley, presumably accompanied by his wife and the children not away at school, then moved several times: from Windsor to Brussels then Portsmouth, where he became captain of the Royal Regiment of Foot Guards and deputy to the governor of Portsmouth.

Marie-Catherine Manley died in November 1675, just four months after her husband was knighted by Charles II.[22] Delarivier Manley, who was prob-ably about five when her mother died, was not sent off to school (according to her own account in *Rivella*), and the older daughter, who was sent to school in England while the family was on Jersey, may have been brought back to the household either upon the family's settling in Portsmouth or following their mother's death. It is possible that Roger Manley, who in his daughter's account was very fond of his children, decided that he would like them living in the same house with him after his wife's death. In *Rivella*, Manley's narrator mentions a governess, and it is likely that either when the family was settled in Portsmouth or else after the mother's death a governess was hired to educate the three girls.

Presumably, the father supervised the education of his sons: the fluency of the Latin in his published writing indicates that he would have been capable of giving them a grounding in classics that would prepare them to enter university or to study law, although the elder son seems to have chosen a naval career. Francis was made lieutenant (on the York) in October 1668 and commander of the fire-ship *Roebuck* in January 1691.[23] Were Francis one of the twin boys born in 1688, he would have been twenty at the time he was made lieutenant; if he were the son born before the second Anglo-Dutch War, he would have been about twenty-four. Since becoming a lieutenant required at least two years' prior service as a midshipman or master's mate, Francis presumably would have begun his career no later than 1686 (when he was probably eighteen or twenty-two) and possibly much earlier, since boys often began their naval service quite young during this era.[24] It seems plausible to assume that Francis might have joined a ship as a master's mate (a usual starting point for the sons of gentlemen) some time between 1675 and 1680, during the years when Roger Manley was stationed in Portsmouth; otherwise, he might have joined as late as 1686, just before his father's death, in the event that he chose a naval career only when anticipating his father's demise.

By 1693, Francis Manley was captain of the *Swan* (or the *Sun Prize*), which was assigned to protect the English mackerel fishery; he was mortally wounded when it was taken by the French in June 1693.[25] We have less information about Edward, the younger brother, who died in 1688, possibly at the home of Dr Robert Midgley (1654/5–95), a physician and classicist as well as a family friend. We do not know if Edward (who might have been born between 1673 and 1675) was living with his father and sisters during some portion of father's time as governor of Landguard. In *Rivella*, Manley mentions that her younger brother was 'pension'd' at a Huguenot minister's house not far from Landguard Fort where she was sent for a few months to study French; Edward may have been studying French himself perhaps for the same reason as Delarivier, with the hope of being offered a place as an attendant at court.[26] It is also possible that Edward was studying with Dr Midgley in London, in preparation for a different career (perhaps as a physician), before he died in 1688, or else that he was apprenticed to his uncle Edward Floyd (or Lloyd), for a profession that has not been identified, since he bequeathed money to that Floyd and one of his sons as well as to Floyd's apprentices.[27] However, since Edward refers in his will to expenses occasioned by his 'long Illness' and makes bequests to both his father's former maid as well as the maid that looked after him in London during his illness, he may have been physically unable to prepare for any career before his death.

Robert Midgley was apparently a friend of Roger Manley, and was, according to *Rivella*, 'related to the Family by Marriage';[28] Edward Manley's will indicates that he appreciated Midgely's kindness to him. That friendship, however, which apparently resulted in Midgely's helping to sort Roger Manley's papers after the latter's death, would subsequently prompt Delarivier Manley to suggest that Midgley appropriated one of her father's unpublished works. She asserts that her father was 'the Genuine Author of the first Volume of that admir'd and successful Work', *The Turkish Spy*, which Midgley, 'An Ingenious Physician', 'continu'd ... until the Eighth Volume, both by his own Pen, and the assistance of some others, without ever having the Justice to Name the Author of the First'.[29] In fact, the first volume of this work, *The Eight Volumes of Letters Writ by a Turkish Spy Who Lived Five and Forty Years Undiscover'd at Paris* (1694) is generally believed to have been written by Giovanni Paolo Marana (1642–93), whose name appears on the title page, although the remaining volumes are usually ascribed to William Bradshaw and (or) Robert Midgley. It is difficult to know whether Delarivier Manley, in making this accusation against Midgley (who may have slighted her after her irregular marriage to John Manley) genuinely believed her father wrote this work (and had evidence of his authorship), or whether she was confusing *The Turkish Spy* with *The History of the Turkish Empire*, for which her father's authorship of one section was not acknowledged on the title page.[30] It is also possible that Manley intentionally misstated the title of the work her father wrote about Turkey, as a means to suggest that her father was more of a best-selling author than he actually was.

In *Rivella*, Delarivier Manley mentions her own birth on Jersey and the death of her mother, but begins the central part of her story in her early adolescence, when she first fell in love with 'Lysander' (James Carlisle, d. 1691), a young military officer and sometime actor in London, whose regiment was stationed on Landguard Fort in the summer of 1685. Manley mentions her two sisters and her father (as well as her various suitors) in her portrayal of her life from this period, but makes no specific mention of her brothers. When she describes her father's death (in 1687), she refers to her brothers only as being absent, pursuing their careers, thus leaving her prey to the advances of her older cousin, John Manley.

It seems, from Roger Manley's letters and Delarivier Manley's account in *Rivella*, that Roger Manley spent the late spring, summer and autumn at Landguard from 1680 until his death in 1687, accompanied by his daughters, but spent the winters with them at his house in Kew (where he died in the winter of 1687), returning to Suffolk only after the winter storms had passed. In one March letter, Roger Manley describes the effects on the fortifications of the 'rigour of the winter' that he observes on his return to Landguard.[31] Since he was pursuing a career in the navy, a pursuit boys often started at a young age,

Francis Manley would probably have spent most of these years on board ship, probably only occasionally visiting his father and sisters at the house in Kew or, less frequently, in more remote coastal Suffolk. Edward may have been part of the family circle until his father's death, when he might have moved to London, or he may have moved somewhat earlier to London, where he was living in 1688 when he died (probably about age 12 to 15). Roger Manley was clearly busy both with his writing and with his military command when he was present at Landguard Fort (his letters are full of requests for materials to rebuild the fort and companies of soldiers to staff it), but he seems also to have had time for entertaining his officers and his family. In *Rivella*, the narrator talks about join-ing the Manley sisters in keeping their father company, visiting and 'drinking Chocolate' during his morning 'Toilet'.[32] Manley's narrator also describes scenes at dinners and at the gaming table where Delarivier and her older sister enjoyed the company of the officers.

In *Rivella*, the scenes at Landguard Fort are described as taking place in a 'Castle', which suggests that the governor of the fort might have been housed on site in apartments comfortable enough that his daughters and their governess were also lodged there. Archaeological evidence indicates that there was a gov-ernor's residence within the confines of Landguard Fort in the 1680s. Although it would not have been as comfortable as the more substantial one built in the mid-eighteenth century, the 'governor's house was detached and substan-tial to judge by the plan, facing the main entrance and looking directly across the parade ground'.[33] Delarivier Manley's memories of her father, according to her narrator's account of them in *Rivella*, suggest that he was fond of his chil-dren and probably somewhat indulgent of his daughters. During one evening's entertainment he apparently entrusted Delarivier with the key to his military storeroom so that she could fetch him some coins for his evening at play; she also apparently helped herself to a handful of guineas to assist the ensign with whom she was then infatuated, 'whose Eyes ... spoke him willing to be Grateful'.[34] Her narrator describes her father as 'a wise' man who had the kindness to say noth-ing to his daughter about her obvious infatuation with Carlisle, although in the narrative he takes steps to make certain that the young ensign's regiment is sent away immediately.[35]

In reality, royal warrants dictated the brief stay of the Duke of Norfolk's Regiment (in which James Carlisle was an ensign and Francis Brathwaite, future husband of Mary Elizabeth Manley, was a captain) at Landguard Fort in July 1685 for reasons having nothing to do with Roger Manley's middle daughter.[36] However, in having her narrator recount the story as he does, Manley is able to show her father as both empathetic and chivalrous – a traditional Tory hero who takes responsibility for the vulnerable young women in his care. In *Rivella* Manley follows the conventions of sixteenth- and seventeenth-century heroic romance in beginning her story with her adolescence and in making chivalry a central issue. She contrasts loyal royalists or Tories, like her father, who could be relied on to take care of dependent women; men like her brothers, who were inconveniently absent; and unscrupulous rakes like her cousin and bigamous husband, John Manley, who might have converted to Toryism under her father's influence but who never seems to have understood the basic prerequisite of Tory chivalry as Manley saw it – to take care of those needing protection.

Manley's narrator in *Rivella* describes her as being in 'Awe' of her father, as would befit a Tory daughter, and not usually inclined to help herself to guineas from his storeroom, except when blinded by a youthful infatuation.[37] The rest of the narrative indicates that Roger Manley's middle daughter viewed him with both love and respect and that as a father he was attentive to the children's moral and intellectual development. As Manley's narrator in *Rivella* explains, she was 'much indebted ... to a Liberal Education, and those early Precepts of Vertue taught her and practised in her Father's House'.[38]

Youth and Education

The very choice of the word 'Liberal' has interesting overtones for a future satirist who would make her way in the largely male world of Grub Street. Traditionally defined as the 'arts' or 'sciences' considered 'worthy of a free man',[39] a 'Liberal Education' apparently suggested to Delarivier Manley the education given to a well-read and cultured gentleman not necessarily destined for a single specific profession. Not surprisingly, in her published works Manley usually describes men she admires as liberally educated and those of whom she is critical as lacking such an education. In *The New Atalantis*, when satirizing William, Earl Cowper, Manley states that Cowper's father (whom Manley describes as 'an old *Debauchee*, given to irregular Pleasures'), did *not* bestow 'a liberal Education upon his Son'. Instead, Manley's narrator explains, as if offering the reason for what she considered the latter's moral failings, his father 'bred him to the practice of the *Law*, in that manner that is the least generous, and most corrupt'.[40] By contrast, in *Rivella*, Manley compliments her lover John Tilly, governor of Fleet Prison, as having received, 'a learned and liberal Education', whose 'Taste' was 'delicate, in respect of good Authors'.[41]

William Cowper, who attended private school in St Albans and possibly also Westminster school before entering the Middle Temple in 1682, may have had a similar education to Tilly, who likewise was trained in law but seems not to have attended university. Although little else is known about Tilly's family background or education, he was a member of the Inner Temple and called to the bar in May 1692.[42] Moreover, Tilly's 'Taste' for the works of 'good Authors' does not necessarily indicate something learned in formal studies, since Manley's narrator indicates in *Rivella* that Manley herself first introduced Tilly to the *Moral Reflections* of la Rochefoucault, a copy of which she was apparently carrying with her when they first met.[43] Once he had glanced through it, according to the narrator, 'He form'd an Idea from that Book of the Genius of the Lady, who chose it for her Entertainment'.[44] For Manley, then, a 'Liberal Education' seems to represent the education that her father might have given to her, and that she would help to give to Tilly: sharing books and discussing them together.

The term 'Liberal Education' certainly does not call to mind a typical female education, nor does Manley necessarily align 'those Precepts of Vertue taught her and practised in her Father's House'[45] with simple conduct-book codes for women. By connecting her 'Vertue' to the morality of her liberal education, Manley's narrator suggests that we should judge her according to the moral standards set for a free man, which would be consistent with her desire 'to serve her Country, and the ancient Constitution',[46] a desire expressed in the published works of which her protagonist Rivella claims to be most proud. Such a moral standard would put less emphasis on the chastity emphasized in traditionally strict codes of moral conduct for women, according to which Manley would necessarily fall short. By contrast, the virtue and morality of a free man were linked in such classical works as Plato's *Phaedrus* to friendship and love. Manley ends *Rivella* with the coy suggestion, not inconsistent with classical notions of male virtue, that she is virtuous in part because she is

> the only Person of her Sex that knows how to *Live*, and of whom we may say, in relation to Love, since she has so peculiar a Genius for, and has made such noble Discoveries in that Passion, that it would have been a *Fault in her, not to have been Faulty*.[47]

By contrast to men, for whom love and friendship could be understood as a civic virtue,[48] neoclassical women had to be careful about whom they loved, being especially cautious about falling in love with men who did not understand the precepts of (for Manley, Tory) chivalry. Women of her era also had to be cautious of the dangers of being deemed 'Faulty' by a society quick to judge women for the slightest deviation from the appearance of moral propriety. Manley's quip that not being 'Faulty' would have been a 'Fault' in her offers an interesting reworking of a line from George Savile (1633–95), Marquis of Halifax's *The Lady's New Year's Gift, or Advice to a Daughter* (1688). Discussing dancing, an accomplishment that Halifax believes appropriate to teach young women, he warns that they must be cautious, since

> To Dance sometimes will not be imputed to you as a Fault; but remember that the end of your Learning it, was that you might the better know how to move gracefully. It is only an advantage so far, when it goeth beyond it, one may call it excelling in a Mistake.[49]

Manley had already alluded to this well-known line from Halifax in a section of *The New Atalantis* about a young girl about to be seduced then abandoned by her older guardian, identified in the keys as William Bentinck (1649–1709), first Earl of Portland, a trusted royal advisor during the reign of William III (1650–1702) and a powerful Whig. Manley clearly faults Portland for his apparent breach of promise to a young woman he was understood to be engaged to marry.[50] This section underscores the very real danger for women when the female 'Vertue' of being attractive in public becomes the 'Mistake', or 'Fault', of being seen as prey to someone in a position to take advantage. Manley also uses this story to turn the concept of 'Fault' inside out, satirically ascribing it to those who are obviously victims rather than those who are obviously 'Faulty', such as (in her moral universe) self-serving Whig politicians. In describing, in the final lines of *Rivella*, being 'Faulty' as a virtue in herself, Manley emphasizes her rejection of traditional codes of female virtue. Instead, she judges herself by her knowledge of how to 'Love',[51] in a phrase that suggests that we might view her as an experienced courtesan – someone who has made a career at court (or in the public sphere) through her skill not only at love (or for writing about love), but at politics and wit, a woman, in other words, who has had a 'Liberal Education'.

Manley insists on our judging her according to her ideas of male, therefore classical, learning. However, the sort of classical education she herself received is not entirely clear. Although Manley's father was fluent enough in Latin to write an entire work of military history in it (his account of the English revolution or 'Rebellions', as he terms it), he appears not to have taught the language to her. She was capable of citing the occasional line of Latin, but the classical works to which she alludes were usually available in some convenient English translation. A certain portion of the classical learning Manley displays, especially in *The New Atalantis*, appears to be cited from a late sixteenth-century English handbook of quotations (available in a 1707 edition), from which, judging from its title, many male wits of her day probably also regularly borrowed: *Politeuphuia, Wits Commonwealth. Or a Treasury of Divine, Moral, Historical, and Political Admonitions, Similes, and Sentences.*[52]

Manley's narrator in *Rivella* claims that she learned French at the house of a Huguenot minister, and it has traditionally been assumed that she read and translated from the French (in part because the preface to *Queen Zarah and the Zarazians* was translated and 'borrowed' from an essay by abbé Morvan de Bellegarde).[53] However, since it now appears unlikely that Manley in fact wrote *Queen Zarah*,[54] the borrowings from the French in that work do little to confirm her claim about her fluency in her mother's native tongue. Although Roger Manley was fluent in Dutch and French (as well as Latin) and married to a Francophone noblewoman, Delarivier Manley would not have needed to be sent to the Huguenot minister's house to learn French, as she claims she was in *Rivella*, if she had already learned the language from her parents' conversations in it, an opportunity presumably lost because her mother died when Delarivier was so young.

If Delarivier Manley had been destined, before the abdication of James II, to be a maid of honour to Mary of Modena, as is suggested in *Rivella*, then she would certainly have had to learn French. The narrative of *Rivella* suggests, however, that Manley may have stayed only a few months with this minister's family (probably in Suffolk),[55] where one of her brothers was also lodged, since she concludes that this minister had tried to persuade her father to let her stay longer, with the promise that since young Delarivier had made such swift progress with French, that he was certain that in a year's time, he could have made her 'Mistress of those Four Languages of which he was Master, *viz., Latin, French, Spanish* and *Italian*'.[56] It would appear, however, that Manley was not permitted to stay longer to become 'Mistress' of those other languages, since presumably in her published works she would have demonstrated (and perhaps boasted) of that knowledge rather than merely the hypothetical possibility of it.[57]

Manley probably did speak some French, but the works of the French authors to whom she regularly refers, such as d'Aulnoy and la Rochefoucauld, were available in popular English translations, and her citations from la Rochefoucauld's *Maximes* are often word for word from the standard English translation of her day.[58] It is also worth noting that, despite having published in many of the important literary genres of her day – drama, poetry, epistolary miscellany and political secret history – Manley never tried her hand at a published translation, something she might well have attempted during the years she was struggling to support herself, had she had the necessary language skills.

In addition to citing from classical sources in translation and books of quotations, Manley's works suggest that she cited from memory mythological stories and current works of her day. Her earliest writings, which will be discussed in detail in the next chapter, are sprinkled with quotations from and references to a range of contemporary English and French authors (from English translations) as well as ideas and ostensible quips from classical works, which she may have remembered her father or her more educated friends as citing, or which she may have sought in a copy of *Wits Commonwealth*. While Manley's knowledge of the classics was probably somewhat superficial, she seems to have been a wide and voracious reader, interested in the world of human ideas from philosophy to theatre, science, religion and politics. Her idea of her own 'Liberal Education' probably derived from her appreciation of what she read and the pleasure she apparently took in connecting her observations about daily life to anecdotes and observations from both classical and contemporary authors.

Whatever the precise details of her education might have been, Delarivier Manley clearly was widely read, and she valued her ability to converse with ease on a wide range of topics. Judging from the allusions to other publications in her published works, once Manley moved to London, she seems to have kept abreast of current publications and their references to intellectual and theological debates. She was also clearly versed in seventeenth-century French heroic romances, which were readily available in English translations. In the brief passage in which she tells the story of 'Delia' in *The New Atalantis*, she claims to have read such romances while she and her sister were staying with 'an old out-of-fashion Aunt' after her father's death.[59] The style of Roger Manley's *The Russian Imposter*, the romanticized history of the false Dmitry, suggests that he too was familiar with the genre of historical or heroic romance; some such works may have been on the shelves of her father's library, presumably in addition to various classical works and works of military history.

In *Rivella*, Manley suggests that she regretted not having had the opportunity to go to school with other girls her own age; instead, according to her narrator, she was supervised, at least during her father's tenure at Landguard Fort, by a 'severe *Governante*', described as 'worse than any *Duenna*'. The Manley daughters' governess is described as vigilant: *Rivella*'s narrator complains that 'as young as [he] was' he could 'only be admitted at Dinner or Supper, when our Family visited'.[60] We should remember, of course, that this account of Delarivier's adolescence is being narrated by Lovemore, a fictitious admirer who claims to have been sixteen during the summer when Mary Elizabeth Manley met and married Francis Brathwaite. This narrator claims to be an old family friend with an estate near Landguard Fort, identified in the published keys as Colonel John Tidcomb, at that juncture a forty-year-old military officer. The idea of the middle-aged Tidcomb as an innocent youth when he met Manley offers a curiously double-edged lens to his ostensible complaints about the chaperone's over-severity, as Manley herself was certainly aware.

If he had met Roger Manley's daughters during this period (although it is more likely that he first met Delarivier Manley subsequently in London, if he knew her at all), Tidcomb would have done so as a fellow military officer of Roger Manley who may have had some business with him: Tidcomb was made a captain in the Somerset Regiment in June 1685, at the time that Brathwaite and Carlisle (and Manley's subsequent acquaintance in the theatre, Thomas Skipwith) received their commissions in various regiments. The putative governess's ostensible restriction on Delarivier's (and presumably her sisters') social life does not seem unreasonable for three girls being raised without a mother on a military base, especially if they might be prey to the advances not only of sixteen-year-old ensigns, but also of forty-year-old captains. We should recall that Delarivier herself would be seduced a few years later, after her father's death, by her cousin John Manley, then in his mid-thirties.

Aside from serving as a strict chaperone, exactly what this governess (if there were one) taught the Manley girls is not entirely clear: perhaps dancing, needlework or drawing. Manley's works rarely include scenes of young girls mastering traditional female accomplishments, although she does regularly allude to the dangers of reading too many romances, as well as the dangers of reading some of the more sensually suggestive passages in Ovid and other classical authors.

Having early understood that she was promised to be a maid of honour, Manley's own sense of self was clearly defined less by any governess, or any conduct-book chapter on preparing to be a virtuous and obedient wife, than by her own innate sense of the witty conversations in which she imagined she might partake at court with other liberally educated courtiers. In *Rivella*, Manley is careful to define herself as not merely an intriguing author but also as a conversationalist, thus emphasizing the distinctions she sets up in her analysis of men: between those who master a craft (such as law) and those liberally educated who demonstrate wit and good taste. The Chevalier d'Aumont, to whom Lovemore is ostensibly relating Manley's story, appropriately asks: 'What Humour is she of? ... Has she Wit in her Conversation as well as Her Pen?', allowing Lovemore to offer a short discourse on wit and Manley's claim to it. Lovemore's response presumably sums up Manley's own understanding of her achievements as a writer and as (liberally educated) person:

> What do you call Wit, answer'd *Lovemore*: If by that Word, you mean a Succession of such Things as can bear Repetition, even down to Posterity? How few are there of such Persons, or rather none indeed, that can be always witty? *Rivella* speaks Things pleasantly; her Company is entertaining to the last; no Woman except one's Mistress wearies one so little as her self: Her Knowledge is universal; she discourses well, and agreeably upon all Subjects, bating a little Affectation, which nevertheless becomes her admirably well.[61]

An educated conversationalist such as Manley has more than the technical skill of someone trained for a single profession: she is widely read and able to converse 'agreeably' on many topics.

Significantly, her narrator insists that she does not define herself as a mere '*Author*', thereby distinguishing herself from those satirists or pamphleteers who might be simply technically proficient professionals. Instead, as Lovemore explains: 'I was well pleas'd at the Character a certain Person gave her (who did not mean it much to Her Advantage) that one might discourse Seven Years together with *Rivella*, and never find out from her self, that she was a *Wit*, or an *Author*'.[62] This description sets Manley above the hack political pamphleteers of her time and in the same set as the gentlemen scholars she so admired, such as the playwright and Jacobite politician George Granville (1667–1735). This passage also reminds us that she viewed herself throughout her life as someone destined for life at court, rather than life in Grub Street.

After Her Father's Death

Whatever dreams of and preparation for court life Manley and her family may have made, the Revolution of 1688–9 changed everything. As Manley's narrator explains in *Rivella*, 'the *Abdication* ... came on, the Queen was gone to *France*, and *Rivella* thereby disappointed of going to Court'.[63] The narrator then goes on to describe Roger Manley's demise, adjusting the actual chronology to suggest that James II's departure caused Manley's death. Although Delarivier Manley consistently links her own development and misfortunes to those of her country, her future was probably affected more directly by her father's death than by the change in sovereign. Even if James II had not departed for France in 1688, it is not clear which family member would have continued petitioning for Delarivier's place as maid of honour once her father died. Of course, the Tory romance plot of the innocent orphaned heroine; vulnerable, without the protection of a father, to the advances of unscrupulous men, was already familiar by 1714, and Manley used it herself in her political secret histories. She consistently presents herself as an innocent heroine, vulnerable to the advances of her unscrupulous and self-serving cousin, who might be a Tory (even a Jacobite) in political affiliation but appears Whiggish (i.e. unchivalrous and unreliable, in a Tory moral universe) in temperament.

Roger Manley died late February or early March 1687: his will is dated 26 February, when the governorship of Landguard Fort was given to Lieutenant-Colonel William Eyton. On 19 March 1687, Eyton is described as replacing 'Sir Roger Manby [*sic*], deceased'.[64] At this point, as Manley indicates in *Rivella*, Delarivier and Cornelia were apparently placed in the care of the 'out-of-fashion Aunt' mentioned previously. Their older sister was, according to the text of *Rivella*, 'upon her Marriage' to Francis Brathwaite, captain of the 12th (Suffolk) Regiment, in the summer of 1685 during the brief time when Brathwaite's regiment was stationed at Landguard Fort.[65] At the time of their father's death, Delarivier and Cornelia's brothers were already busy in their careers; moreover, Mary Elizabeth and her husband apparently did not invite her younger sisters to live with them, leaving them, it would appear, vulnerable to the influence of their older cousin John Manley.

In *The New Atalantis*, in the passage in which Delia relates her own story, Manley describes her older sister's husband as 'so ill-natur'd and disobliging, that our Family no longer convers'd with theirs'.[66] Whatever caused this disagreement, there was apparently not a significant breach between Roger Manley and his daughter (and son-in-law) since he left Mary Elizabeth Brathwaite his house at Kew, while the two younger daughters received £200 each and a share of the family houses in Wrexham. As other scholars have suggested, the family breach may have occurred because Brathwaite was Catholic.[67] However, this seems somewhat unlikely. Roger Manley and his children were certainly members of the Church of England, but, as I have already observed, if the Manleys had been hoping for a position for Delarivier as maid of honour to Mary of Modena, they obviously felt comfortable with the possibility of her being influenced by the Catholicism of the Queen and her entourage. The rupture between the Manley sisters, since it was probably not over a matter of religion, may have occurred because of some perceived favouritism in Roger Manley's leaving a house to Mary Elizabeth (who might have had children by 1687 and was probably in need of an adequate place to live).[68] Or, the breach might simply be understood as genuine incompatibility between siblings. Edward Manley, who presumably wrote his will shortly before his death in 1688, left only £10 to Mary Elizabeth but £20 each to 'Dela' and Cornelia (a difference that might also be explained by the difference in the marital status between eldest and younger sisters).

When Francis Manley wrote his will in 1691, he disregarded both Mary Elizabeth (possibly because of this breach) and Delarivier (possibly because of her 'marriage' to her cousin), leaving all of his estate to Cornelia. When Delarivier herself died in 1724, she left most of her estate to Cornelia; her will does not mention her sister Mary Elizabeth, who lived until 1740 and, like the rest of the siblings, left a bequest to Cornelia, who seems to have been the last survivor of Roger Manley's children.[69] In any case, half a decade earlier, Delarivier and Cornelia did not find a home with the Brathwaites after their father's death, according to the account in *The New Atalantis*. As Delia explains, 'the Care of' the two younger Manley daughters was entrusted by their father, on his deathbed, to their older cousin John Manley:

> My Father associated with Don *Marcus* two remote Relations; one immediately after dy'd; the other was old, had gain'd a large Estate in the World, liv'd at the distance of above two hundred Miles from us, lov'd his Ease, and resolv'd to enjoy it; so that he left the Care of us, and our Affairs, wholly in Don *Marcus*'s Hands.[70]

The 'remote Relations' are presumably the executors of Roger Manley's will, Ellis Lloyd and William Eyton. Eyton (who was probably related to Roger Manley's sister-in-law Dorothea, née Eyton, wife of Francis Manley) died less than a year after Roger Manley, in January 1688, having held the office of governor of Landguard Fort (in which he succeeded Manley) for less than nine months.[71] We do not know exactly when Ellis Lloyd (presumably related to Roger Manley's mother, Mary, née Lloyd) died, but if he outlived Eyton, he seems not to have taken any interest in the affairs of the Manley children.[72] The girls were thus sent, apparently at their cousin's discretion, 'into the Country, to an old out-of-fashion Aunt'.[73]

It was previously assumed that the girls were sent to Wrexham or Erbistock, in Wales, and that the 'Aunt' to whose care Delarivier and Cornelia were entrusted was Lady Dorothea, née Eyton, Manley, widow of Sir Francis Manley, Roger Manley's elder brother. However, as Fidelis Morgan has pointed out, the widow Dorothea Manley died in the summer of 1686, at least half a year before Roger Manley.[74] Of course, sending the girls 'into the Country' does not mean that they were sent as far as Wales. They might have been sent to some female relation of Arthur or John Manley perhaps living somewhere near Kew – which would still be 'into the Country'. Otherwise, they might have been sent to Elizabeth or Catharine, née Manley (if either was still living), older sisters to Francis, Roger and John Manley, or else possibly to a sister of Dorothea Manley, née Eyton, or William Eyton, possibly living in Wales.[75] Whoever she was, this 'out-of-fashion Aunt', who was 'full of the *heroick stiffness* of her own *Times*', as Manley explains in *The New Atalantis*, would read to the Manley sisters 'Books of *Chivalry* and *Romances*',[76] a form of literature that Manley suggests made her prey to the subsequent advances of her older cousin, whom she mistakenly viewed as a hero. It was apparently shortly after the death of this female relation that Delarivier was seduced and 'ruined' by her first cousin John and so began her life in London.

Before we turn to that period in her life, however, it is worth considering the possible influences of different family members, and their politics, on Delarivier during her youth. The simple version of the story is that there was a split between the royalist and Cromwellian branches of the family and that Delarivier followed her father in her royalist leanings and then followed the leanings of her Tory first cousin, who was educated in part by her father, according to Delarivier Manley's account of things. The actual narrative is somewhat less clear cut. As we have already observed, Roger Manley may have fought on the royalist side and gone into exile, but he remained in touch with his Cromwellian relations and their friends at the post office, even passing information to them relating to military events on the Continent. Delarivier Manley obviously spent her childhood and youth in a royalist household and knew well the legend of all that the family had sacrificed for its loyalty to King Charles I. However, ties of kinship apparently remained strong despite political differences, as was probably the case in many families – as in the example of John Churchill's royalist relations taking refuge with their Cromwellian family members.[77]

Even while in exile on the Continent, Roger Manley apparently visited England several times; he mentions in his letters to his brother-in-law Isaac Dorislaus the pleasure he will take in seeing him, as well as his brothers, Francis and John. Moreover, the letter Manley sent to Dorislaus in 1675, upon his being knighted by Charles II, indicates that Manley remained in cordial relations with Dorislaus after the Restoration. During Roger Manley's stay on Jersey, he and his wife also apparently made several extended visits to family in England and Wales. How close Roger Manley felt to his Nonconformist, Cromwellian brother John Manley is not known. We know from Roger Manley's correspondence with Dorislaus in the 1650s that he frequently desired to hear from his brother John; however, John Manley is not mentioned in Roger Manley's will (written in 1687). It might have been that John Manley's radical religious beliefs and his political involvement with Exclusionist conspiracies of 1685 had put some distance between the brothers. John Manley's house in Wrexham 'was raided in 1663 and 1665 as an illegal conventicler'; moreover, he was also 'on the fringe of the confused plotting which led to the Rye House conspiracy' and he joined Monmouth's rebellion in 1685.[78] There may have been some distance between the brothers because of Roger Manley's religious and political influence on the younger John Manley, who seems to have become a member of the Church of England (since he married Ann Grosse in Westminster Abbey before 'marrying' Delarivier in a very different sort of ceremony) as well as a staunch Tory.[79]

Whatever ideological distance may have separated Delarivier Manley's uncle John from his brothers, she herself nevertheless recounts a family narrative that is sympathetic to what that side of the family also endured. In describing her family in a passage in *The New Atalantis*, Delarivier Manley observes that both the Parliamentarian and the Royalist branches suffered from the Civil War. In referring to 'a Brother of my Father's', i.e. the elder John Manley, a major in Cromwell's army, she non-judgementally ascribes his political preference for 'the Factious Party' as owing to 'an Error in Education'. She then explains that although he had initially done well for himself, his later somewhat straightened circumstances were a result of his having purchased 'a wrong Title', which 'upon the Restoration of the Royal Line ... reverted back to the former Possessor'.[80] John Manley's situation was further strained in 1666 when the brewery he had purchased after the Restoration was ruined in the fire of London.

Since his brother John was left in these awkward circumstances 'with several small Children', Roger Manley apparently pitched in, to assist the eldest of these. According to Delarivier Manley's account in *The New Atalantis*, Roger Manley 'took care to give' his nephew John Manley 'the Education of a Gentleman, and endeavour'd to tincture him with true *Principles*'.[81] Manley describes her father as 'more like a Father, than an Uncle' to John Manley, taking responsibility for 'all the Expence and Care he had of his Education'. In this passage, Delarivier Manley's larger point is not about any breach between the young John Manley and his own father but about how 'ungratefully' her cousin had 'rewarded' her father for all that care and attention: 'in the ruin of a Daughter, who, but for him, might have flourish'd Fair, an Ornament to his House'.[82] Exactly when or if the younger John Manley visited or lived with Roger Manley's family is not clear, although presumably he did not do so before the Manleys returned from Holland to Portsmouth in 1665, when the boy would have been ten years old. He may have been living with the family when they were in Portsmouth between 1665 and 1667 before Roger Manley's family left for Jersey.

It is conceivable that the younger John Manley lived with Roger Manley's family while they were on Jersey, which might explain why Delia relates that he was, 'as I have often heard him say himself, a *Man*, and with my Father in the next Chamber, when I was born'.[83] The phrase 'Education of a Gentleman' suggests that Roger Manley might have helped train his nephew in classical languages in preparation either for university or for studying law. There is no record of John Manley having attended Oxford or Cambridge; however he became a member of Gray's Inn in 1671 (and would be called to the bar in 1678).[84] When Roger Manley returned from Jersey, his nephew was probably already busy with his legal studies, a pursuit which (according to Delarivier Manley's account) Roger Manley may have helped finance. Roger Manley may also have been influential in persuading his nephew to abandon his Nonconformist upbringing and join the Church of England. From the way that Delarivier Manley describes John Manley's relationship with her father, it would seem likely that John Manley might have visited his uncle's family frequently during the years that he was studying in London and they were living in Portsmouth.

According to the story of Delia in *The New Atalantis*, after the 'out-of-fashion Aunt' died, Manley and her sister were left 'at large without any Controul'. Their cousin John then arrived, in false mourning for his wife, apparently, according to Manley's narrative, with the intent of seducing and ruining her; he would also take control of, and swiftly run through, her modest inheritance (the £200 and the share in the family houses in Wrexham). As Delia explains it, shortly after his arrival, her 'Cosin Guardian immediately declared himself [her] Lover, with such an eagerness, that none can guess at who are not acquainted with the Violence of his Temper'.[85] Her own response she describes as conditioned by what might be described as the illiberal education of heroic romances with which she became absorbed at the home of her elderly aunt.

Although Manley explains that her cousin 'had always had an obliging Fondness that was wonderfully taking with *Girls*', she insists that she herself was never attracted to him: 'I was no otherwise pleased with it [his declaration of love for her] than as he answer'd something to the Character I had found in those Books that had poyson'd and deluded my dawning Reason'.[86] Delia, who is telling her own story in this part of Manley's narrative, further justifies her own behaviour by explaining her chasteness: 'I had the *Honour* and *Cruelty* of a true *Heroin*, and would not permit my Adorer so much as a Kiss from my Hand, without ten thousand times more Intreaty than any thing of that nature cou'd be worth'. Manley also insists on the purity of her motive in marrying her cousin by insist-

ing, 'I had marry'd him only because I thought he lov'd me'.[87] The scene in which
she agrees to marriage is even presented in a plot straight out of heroic romance:
only after her cousin devotedly nurses her back to health during a sudden and
serious illness, does she deign to marry him out the 'Gratitude' in her 'Nature'.[88]

This predictable romance plot of the 'ruin'[89] of a young woman in the absence
of parental protection was important to the Tory (and Jacobite) historiography
depicting the sufferings of the nation after the departure of James II. By exten-
sion, in 1714, with Queen Anne's demise predicted, the same plot would serve
as cautionary comment on the unknown fate of the country under the anticipated succession of George I, the distant German cousin who would scarcely
satisfy the romance plot line of true Stuart heir appearing to protect the country.
Manley's narrator in *Rivella* further plays up the romance motif of lost honour
by observing: 'it would be well for her, that I could say here she dy'd with Honour, as did her Father'. At this point in *Rivella*, the moralizing language of heroic
romance clearly represents a Tory agenda – setting up the parallel between the
'unhappy Country' suffering in the wake of James II's departure, and Rivella's
ruin presented as worse than death.[90]

Even Manley's depiction of her bigamous husband, or her 'Spouse' as she
terms him in *Rivella*,[91] represents not simply a critique of the man who 'ruined'
her, but a political critique of a Tory who, like so many of the politicians she
satirizes in *The New Atalantis* (including, for example, John Churchill, Duke
of Marlborough), does not meet her high standards of personal and political
loyalty. In a passage in *The New Atalantis* about her seducer, Delarivier Manley
describes (in the voice of Delia) the shifting political loyalty of her cousin (Don
Marcus) as emblematic of his lack of moral character:

> Yet can this Man talk of *Honour*, of *Loyalty*, of losing all for his *Duty*, though wholly
> forgetful of it, when he join'd *Henriquez* [William of Orange] with the *Count de
> Grand Monde* [John Grenville, Earl of Bath], securing the strongest Citadel of the
> Kingdom, against the reigning Prince, and naming it the *Glorious Cause*. But not
> succeeding in his first Pretensions (where he put in for being one of the Divan [Parlia-
> ment]) he revolted back to the *Royal* [Tory] Party, and made himself all that Reign,
> a *distinguishing noisy* Tool, only fit to *speak* there, what the Men of Discretion of his
> side, were well enough contented to hear.[92]

To be fair to John Manley, many other Tory gentry – including the Earl of Bath
and John Churchill, subsequently Duke of Marlborough – felt the political
necessity of deserting the floundering (and Catholic) James II in 1688. Also to
be fair to John Manley, he did not originally stand as a Whig in his first attempt
at gaining a parliamentary seat; he was backed by the Tory Lord Bath when he
stood for Truro 1689 (although there was a double return and he was not seated
by the House). However, Delarivier Manley's satirical account here demonstrates the technique she would employ in much of her published work: to use

the genre of romance as a tool for satire and to use anecdotes about disloyalty in love to suggest political unreliability.

The political motif of inadequate chivalry and ruined innocence is so prominent in *Rivella* that it is difficult to be certain how much of the narrative accurately depicts Manley's own life and how much represents her talent at partisan spin. At the same time, however, the text itself, like so many of Manley's other works, manipulates the conventions of the genre of heroic romance even as it deploys them. Manley's narrator suggests that it would have been better if she had 'dy'd with Honour' than follow the path she followed.[93] At the same time, in the very first paragraph of the narrative, this narrator offers an alternative moral frame for viewing Manley, by reminding the readers that he has often heard her say, '*If she had been a Man she had been without Fault*'.[94] In other words, Manley might choose to reiterate motifs of Tory heroic romance when it suited her political purposes, but she would also take the liberty of undercutting the very genre whose conventions she so often borrowed, thus hinting at her potential for embracing different moral or political ideologies and revising the conventions of standard literary genres.

First Years in London

In considering Manley's seduction by her cousin John Manley – the pivotal turning point in her life that may eventually have led to her becoming a writer – we may well wonder to what extent was she was a wholly vulnerable and innocent victim, and to what extent might she have been a knowing and willing participant in the scheme of bigamy. For a young woman without parents, or much of a dowry, and whose prospects for marriage apparently were diminished by the scars of smallpox, it might have been appealing to flee her remote situation with the elderly aunt and explore the vibrant cultural and social life of London. It is easy to believe that her older cousin and guardian seduced and deceived her; there is certainly logic in placing the blame for the situation squarely in the hands of the older and more experienced party. However, in subsequent depictions (her own and others') of herself, there is never any hint of her as vulnerable victim.

By her own account in *Rivella*, as a young adolescent she was not shy about helping herself to some guineas from her father's military storeroom to assist a young officer at the gambling table. By 1694, Manley was clearly confident and smooth talking enough to inveigle herself into the household of the Duchess of Cleveland, and then charming enough to have been dismissed from it, on the ostensible grounds of attempting to seduce the latter's son into marriage. In 1696, shortly after the appearance of her first two plays on the London stage, Manley was mocked in the farcical stage production *The Female Wits* as Marcella, a play-

wright overbearingly confident about her talent as a writer and the charms she
held for the men of the theatre world, as well as men of power, position and family. In the extremely biased account of Manley in Lady Cowper's papers, John
Tilly – after leaving Manley to marry another woman – is said to have warned a
household servant not 'to trust' (the evidently persuasive) Manley.[95]

It is possible that Manley was entirely deceived by her older cousin when he
convinced her that he was marrying her legally. It also seems possible, however,
that Delarivier Manley herself may have been attracted by the life she envisioned
in London and a chance to escape the hospitality of elderly relations. Although
she refers to herself as 'wanting of fourteen'[96] at the time she married her cousin
(in about 1690), she was probably about twenty – not quite as young as the narrative of *Rivella* suggests, although certainly still young enough to be vulnerable
to the blandishments of an experienced seducer. The 'illness' Manley refers to in
The New Atalantis, during the course of which her cousin nursed her to health,
might have been the early stages of a pregnancy.[97] In other words, it is possible that the irregular marriage might have been concocted as a cover for a prior
seduction. Whether John Manley persuaded his cousin into marriage before
or after seducing her is an open question. He could be, apparently, a persuasive
suitor. As Manley relates in *The New Atalantis*, he had previously misrepresented
the extent of his estate to the orphaned Cornish heiress Ann Grosse before marrying her in 1679:

> I had formerly heard Don *Marcus's* Lady repeat, in the violence of her Rage, the base
> Methods he had took to gain her, producing Writings to a good Estate, when he had
> but the expectation of a small one, and that not 'till after the Death of his Father.[98]

Manley herself describes the 'eagerness'[99] and intensity with which her older
cousin had declared himself in love with her, an eagerness that itself might have
been persuasive to a young woman whose prospects for a less clandestine 'marriage' were apparently not wonderful.

As Manley's narrator in *Rivella* recounts, 'I have heard her Friends lament the
Disaster of her having had the Small-pox in such an injurious manner, being a
beautiful Child before that Distemper; but as that Disease has now left her Face,
she has scarce any Pretence to it'.[100] As Lovemore explains, however, although her
face is scarred, Manley still has allure: 'Few, who have only beheld her in Publick,
could be brought to like her; whereas none that became acquainted with her,
could refrain from loving her'. This infatuated narrator continues, 'I have heard
several Wives and Mistresses accuse her of Fascination: They would neither trust
their Husbands, Lovers, Sons, nor Brothers with her'. Lovemore then elaborates
the charms of her lips, arms, feet and other parts – 'Her Neck and Breasts have
an establish'd Reputation for Beauty and Colour' – making clear that he has
never seen 'any of *Rivella*'s hidden Charms'.[101] Although the phrasing here sug-

gests that the narrator himself has never been physically intimate with Manley, his language ascribes to Manley the fascination and sensual allure of a courtesan, not the sort of demure propriety described in eighteenth-century conduct books as appropriate for a wife.

There are no known likenesses of Manley, but her account of herself in *Rivealla* is somewhat consistent with Jonathan Swift's description of her in 1712 as 'very homely and very fat'.[102] The description of Manley in *Rivella* in fact more closely resembles that of Queen Homais in *The Rival Princesses*, the anonymous novel that Manley probably used as a source text for her first tragedy, *The Royal Mischief*. In that earlier novel, the perfection of Homais's lips, teeth, arms and hands are acknowledged and her 'Neck and Breast' are described as having 'so exact a symmetry of Beauty' that 'no Painter' could have drawn them.[103] Queen Homais is also described as 'inclin'd to fat'; Rivella's narrator likewise refers to Rivella having grown 'fat'.[104] Moreover, Homais is described as inciting 'rebellious thoughts in [her] beholders' just as Lovemore will describe Rivella as dangerously fascinating to husbands, sons and lovers.[105] Rivella is also consistently described in terms of her witty and agreeable conversation, echoing the earlier novelist's description of the ambitious and contemptuous Homais: 'yet it was impossible with all these faults for any person not to love her, or desire her conversation'.[106]

Manley's textual self-portrait, of course, was published in 1714, three and a half decades after she was probably seduced by her cousin, a seduction that resulted in her subsequently having to survive sometimes by her own pen and possibly sometimes as a kept mistress. Nevertheless, this description of her as dangerously alluring, or even (following the allusion to Homais) ambitious and usurping, is consistent with her own apparent sense of herself as destined for a life at court, either as a courtier (attendant to Mary of Modena), courtesan (as the above self-portrait suggests) or in some other sense as a public figure, as she would become through the notoriety of her best-known published work. Whether or not Delarivier Manley made a conscious decision to tie her destiny, however irregularly, to that of her persuasive, ambitious cousin, moving with him to London allowed her to escape the confines of a rural solitude where the only diversion was reading out-of-date romances. Moreover, after the death of the elderly aunt, it might have been somewhat unclear where the younger Manley daughters might next find refuge.

The circumstances of the marriage ceremony as Manley describes them – only two witnesses, her sister and her servant – suggest that the persons involved realized there was something irregular about the event. It was apparently not performed under the auspices of the Church of England, to which Manley insists she was loyal (when explaining why she would not have joined Mary of Modena's court in exile). Manley's Anglicanism, it would seem, could serve as a badge of political honour when convenient (as it was in the spring of 1714 when she was writing *Rivella*), but her exposure to the dissenting branch of the Manley family may have provided a more open and flexible attitude towards marriage ceremonies. She and her cousin were wed by someone she describes not as a 'priest' or 'pastor' but simply as 'a Gentleman who had married a Relation of ours'.[107]

We do not know exactly where the marriage between John and Delarivier took place. The elderly aunt with whom Delarivier and Cornelia were staying may have been living in northern Wales, where members of John Manley's extended family were well connected among Nonconformists. The popular dissenting preacher Morgan Llwyd had been allowed to hold clandestine religious gatherings at Bryn y ffynnon, a house leased by Major John Manley (father of the bigamous John Manley) after the Restoration.[108] Major Manley himself was apparently adept at keeping the authorities at bay during illegal religious gatherings; on at least one occasion he opened a window and 'entered into a dilatory dispute' with the authorities about their lack of a search warrant while about 80 to 100 worshippers escaped by the back door of his house.[109] Certain members of the Eyton family also remained staunch Nonconformists after the Restoration.[110]

Given these sorts of family connections in a place like Wrexham, which remained strongly dissenting through the late seventeenth century, it would certainly have been feasible to find a Nonconformist minister to preside over a marriage ceremony if the Manley girls were in fact living in Wales at this time. Major John Manley, who had been living in London since the Restoration, would also have been well connected in the dissenting community there, and his High-Church son might conceivably have made use of family contacts in either location. Such a dissenting ceremony (had it not been bigamous) might or might not have been legally recognized, depending upon how and by whom it was performed and whether it took place before or after the passage of the Toleration Act in 1689. We do not know the exact date of the union of John and Delarivier Manley, although a likely guess would be some time in 1689 or 1690 (a year or so before the birth of their son John in July 1691). Nor do we know whether or not Delarivier actually believed the ceremony was legal. It is possible that John and Delarivier were married by Morgan Llwyd, who had presided over the wedding of Henry Davis of Wrexham to Margaret Manley (John Manley's sister), a ceremony for which he was later granted a pardon from the king.[111] Someone who was as staunch a Nonconformist as Llwyd, however, may not have been interested in marrying two Anglican cousins, one of whom was bigamous, merely for the sake of their convenience. But if he did not, there were certainly other Nonconformist ministers, in both England and Wales, known to the dissenting branch of the Manley family, one of whom John Manley could have persuaded to 'marry' him and his cousin.

Modern readers might wonder why John Manley would have gone to the trouble of tricking his cousin into what for him would be a bigamous and illegal marriage, if all he wanted to do was to seduce her. The promise of marriage must have been an effective seduction line, but John Manley, apparently wanted more from Delarivier. It is true that he had been married to the heiress Ann Grosse since 1679, but he had begun mortgaging her property not long after they were wed. In 1682, John Manley had mortgaged, for about £350, some of the properties Ann and her siblings had inherited from their father; in March 1691 (just a few months before the birth of his and Delarivier's son), John Manley would mortgage another property for £360. By 1702, he would be mortgaging properties for the much smaller sums of £27 and £20, perhaps because there were no larger properties in his wife's estate available for him to mortgage.[112] If, as Delarivier Manley suggests in *The New Atalantis*, her 'Spouse' had little self-restraint in his habits of drinking and gambling, it is not surprising that he should have found his cousin's £200 inheritance convenient, and, as she explains, quickly 'lavish'd' it 'away'.[113]

In 1689, John Manley had not been granted a seat in Parliament, having stood for a seat in Truro for which there was a double return. He would not begin his career in Parliament until 1695,[114] and he had not yet been appointed Lord Bath's steward of the manor. John Manley thus seems to have had leisure time enough to pursue his young cousin, whom he probably found good company, physically attractive (despite the scarring on her face), and possessed of a convenient (if modest) sum of ready cash from her inheritance. He might have liked the idea of a live-in companion (mistress, or 'wife') in London when he was busy with business in town. Or perhaps he had in fact given the matter very little thought until after he seduced his cousin, at which time the clandestine marriage seemed the best way to cover her illegitimate pregnancy.

Whatever Delarivier Manley's actual understanding was about the legality of her marriage when she was either persuaded or obliged to marry her cousin, she soon discovered the extent to which she had been deceived about his personality. According to her own account in *The New Atalantis*, her cousin-husband was cruel and domineering, not allowing her any companions – even at first denying her the visits of friends, family or relations, even that of her own sister (presumably Cornelia). She felt herself a 'Prisoner' to her husband's claims of 'Fondness and Jealousy'.[115] When John Manley confessed to her that his first wife was still alive, Manley describes herself as horror-stricken: 'my Surprize and Grief were beyond the ease of Words, beyond the benefit of Tears. Horror! Amazement! Sense of Honour lost! The World's Opinion! Ten thousand Distresses crowded my wounded Imagination!'.[116] After the birth of their son, she 'saw the future upbraiding him with this Father's Treachery, and his Mother's Misfortunes'. Not surprisingly, she seems to have fallen into a long post-partum melancholy. She explains, still in the persona of Delia, in this section of *The New Atalantis*, 'I wore aware three wretched Years, without either one Companion or Acquaintance'.[117]

Manley probably did spend the three years between 1691, after the birth of her son, and 1694, before becoming the temporary companion to the Duchess of Cleveland, in a certain amount of seclusion. Despite her melodramatic insistence on not having had any companion whatsoever, what she may mean, more precisely, is that she found herself cut off from respectable society. In the voice of Delia in *The New Atalantis*, Manley expresses regret not only for having been persuaded into an illegal union by her cousin, but also for her own poor management of her reputation. Writing in 1709 with the eye of a developing satirist, it is clear that Manley understood a person's reputation as a commodity that could be managed and repaired, although the timing of such spin-doctoring would have been critical. Thus her central regret almost two decades later is not only the fact of her husband's bigamy but that she did not denounce her spouse's villainy sooner: 'Oh that I had but then proclaim'd him through all the Streets of *Angela* [London]! For the betrayer of my Glory! The destroyer of an ancient, worthy Family! Which had never (in their Women) had a Stain! Then had I probably secur'd my self from the reproach of being a conscious Partner to my own undoing'.[118]

Despite her claim to having had no companions during the three years after the birth of her child, it is likely that her sister Cornelia was allowed to visit, since Manley describes the insistence with which she presses her 'Spouse' to allow her that companion: 'I was fixt to my point, and would have my Sister's Company' – although we do not know how often Cornelia was able to visit her older sister either before or after her own marriage to Markendale.[119] Whereas Delarivier Manley asserts in the preface to her first play, produced in 1696, that she had only attended the theatre twice 'in the six foregoing years' this claim seems somewhat implausible.[120] The fact that Manley was able to have two plays produced upon her return to London in 1696 demonstrates that she must have had some well-placed contacts in the theatre world. The plays themselves, moreover, demonstrate a certain knowledge of earlier stage productions. Manley's familiarity with the theatre might have been obtained merely by reading published plays, but it seems more likely that she did frequent the theatre when she was living in London, either with her husband or with other friends she eventually made, some of them the mistresses of other politicians.

Manley, not surprisingly, seems to have gravitated to the marginal society of mistresses of gentry and society figures. From her account in *Rivella*, it appears that she originally met the ageing Barbara Palmer, Duchess of Cleveland (once mistress of Charles II) through a neighbour identified in the key as Anne Ryder (or Rider), whose sister, Elizabeth Blount, was mistress to John, Baron Somers

(1651–1716), a powerful Whig politician, and whose daughter Anne Laurence was rumoured to have been the lover of several important society figures. Whatever companionship Manley may have subsequently found with other women similarly cut off from respectable society, during the years she spent with John Manley, she may have been obliged to spend many hours alone (or with the company only of a household servant). John Manley was presumably busy not only as legal advisor to John Grenville (1628–1701), first Earl of Bath, but, also, as Delia tells us in *The New Atalantis*, in 'those Excesses of Drinking and Play he could not abstain from'.[121] The only silver lining in this situation appears to have been that during these leisure hours Manley turned to reading – which she explains she had always 'lov'd' – to pass the time. Whatever education she might or might not have received at her father's house, this period of isolation might have helped her begin discovering the writers of her own day, such as Marie d'Aulnoy and Charles Gildon, whose style of writing and choice of genre seem to have provided inspiration for her early prose works.

However, having a small child, few resources and a reputation ruined by a bigamous marriage, Manley probably had not yet envisioned a career for herself as a writer. During the painful three years immediately following the birth of her son, she clearly felt trapped, with few options before her. As she explains in *The New Atalantis*, her 'Fortune' (i.e. the £200 and the share in houses in Wrexham that she had inherited from her father) was in her husband's hands, 'or worse, already lavish'd away' on gambling and drink. Moreover, as she explains, life in her father's household had accustomed her to 'a handsome manner' of living, and she had never been 'expos'd to any Hardships'. Delia presents her dilemma at that time to her sympathetic auditors in *The New Atalantis*:

> What cou'd I do? Forlorn! Distress'd! begarrd! To whom cou'd I run for Refuge, even from Want and Misery, but to the very Traitor that had undone me? I was acquainted with none that wou'd espouse my Cause, a *helpless, useless* load of Grief and Melancholly! with Child! Disgrac'd! my own Relations, either impotent of Power or Will to Relieve me![122]

It would appear that Manley began to extricate herself from this dire situation during a period, probably in 1693 to 1694, when John Manley was 'gone into the Country' for an important legal employment, and she declined to go with him. To judge by Manley's account, this does not appear to have been an irrevocable separation, but it seems to have marked the beginning of Manley's establishing herself as an autonomous agent, looking out as best she could, with help from a variety of different friends and contacts, for her own interest.

In *The New Atalantis* Manley indicates that her husband 'had lately got a considerable Employment; the Duties of it oblig'd him to go into the Country where his first Wife liv'd',[123] i.e. Truro, Cornwall. In fact, Manley had had a legal practice in Truro before being made legal advisor to the Earl of Bath in 1685, and so probably travelled regularly back and forth between Cornwall and London. However, in about 1694, he seems to have officially been appointed 'Steward of the Manor' for Lord Bath's landholdings in Cornwall.[124] Delarivier declined to go with him, presumably not wanting to establish herself too close to Ann Manley, or perhaps she simply preferred to remain in London; she might already have become a favourite of the Duchess of Cleveland and wanted to follow her fortunes in Cleveland's circle of friends. Manley suggests that her spouse 'took a tender farewell of me, and promis'd a due Care of my self and Child; said he would now endeavour to do me Justice in my Fortune, and save the greatest part of his new Income, to repair to Wasts that he had made'. However, Manley continues, 'When he was gone, he soon relaps'd into his former Extravagancies, and unworthily left me to Repine and Complain at his Neglect and Barbarity'.[125] What subsequent assistance John Manley offered for the child is unknown, nor do we know who raised the boy. From a request Delarivier Manley would make to Robert Harley in 1710 for his influence in helping a young man obtain a lieutenant's position, it is possible to imagine that this son pursued a naval career.[126] However, since Manley does not mention this son (or any other children) in her will, it is likely that he predeceased her.

It was at this point, or perhaps shortly before John Manley left London, that Manley apparently met Barbara Palmer, Duchess of Cleveland, through her neighbor, Anne Ryder, whom her narrator claims (somewhat implausibly) was the 'only Person that in three Years *Rivella* had convers'd with and that but since her Husband had gone into the Country'. Manley's narrator in *Rivella* explains that Cleveland (Hilaria), who was 'passionately fond of new Faces, of which Sex soever, us'd a thousand Arguments to dissuade her from wearing away her Bloom in Grief and Solitude'. She then discoursed on the 'Ill-nature of the World, that wou'd never restore a Woman's Reputation, how innocent soever she really were'. Cleveland also offered advice that Manley seems to have taken, judging from the trajectory of her future life and career: '*To make her self as happy as she could without valuing or regretting those, by whom it was impossible to be valu'd*'.[127] Manley apparently so charmed Cleveland that the latter asked her to take lodgings nearby so that she could be a convenient companion to her. The Duchess of Cleveland's invitation was probably offered in late 1693 or early 1694, since Manley left in June 1694 for Exeter, according to the dates given in her published trajectory of that journey in *Letters Written by Mrs. Manley*, and she claims in *Rivella* that she was companion to Cleveland for about six months.

In *Rivella*, Manley is merciless in her depiction of Cleveland as '*Querilous, Fierce, Loquacious*, excessively fond, or infamously rude'. Her narrator compliments Manley for having 'reign'd six Months in *Hilaria's* [Cleveland's] Favour' which was 'an Age to one of her inconstant Temper'.[128] According to this account, Manley was eventually turned from the house because Cleveland seems to have suspected her of having had designs both on Cleveland's 'Favourite', the former actor and highwayman Cardonell Goodman, and on Cleveland's own son, Charles Fitzroy (1662–1730), Duke of Southampton and Cleveland who had been widowed since 1680 and who would marry his second wife, Anne (1663–1746), the daughter of Sir William Pulteney, in 1694. Manley insists in *Rivella* that Goodman falsely accused her of having 'made Advances to him' in order to 'ruin *Rivella* for fear she should ruin him' by informing Cleveland of the other mistress he was keeping, presumably at Cleveland's expense. Manley also suggests that Cleveland herself set her up to appear guilty in attempting to seduce her son, by inviting him to visit frequently and leaving Manley and him 'alone together upon such plausible Pretences, as seem'd the Effect of Accident, not Design'.[129]

Cleveland subsequently accused Manley of having become intimate with this son and forced her to decamp. In *Rivella*, Manley insists on her innocence in this instance, using the excuse of having to rush to see her sister 'Maria' (Mary Elizabeth) since she had just heard the latter's 'Husband was fallen into great Distress', but does not entirely deny the charges. As her narrator points out, in describing the many occasions she and Cleveland's son were thrown together: 'What might have proceeded from so dangerous a Temptation, I dare not presume to determine, because *Hilaria* and *Rivella*'s Friendship immediately broke off'.[130] Although Manley may have been innocent on the particular evening in question (however implausible the alibi of the sister from whom her narrator claims she had long ago broken off relations), it is perfectly plausible that she might have been making a play for Fitzroy, either in advance of his engagement to his second wife, or with the express intention of trying to prevent the intended union. As someone who herself was not legally married, Manley was presumably free to enter into a marriage with anyone she could persuade to marry her. It is just conceivable that she might have had an idea of persuading Fitzroy, an illegitimate and mentally deficient son of Barbara Palmer and Charles II, into a match. As Manley explains, he was 'a Person tho' of weak Intellects, yet of great Consideration' who would be persuaded to marry Ann Pulteney, whom Manley describes as (not unlike herself) a 'young Lady of little or no Fortune'.[131]

As someone who would later attempt to mediate in the Bath-Albemarle lawsuit, Manley herself was perfectly capable of devising complex schemes for manipulating the rich and the famous if she felt there might be some reward in it for her. If Manley had made some scheme involving Charles Fitzroy, however, she seems to have been outmanoeuvred by Cleveland, who had, after all, had decades of practice manipulating courtiers and sovereigns. In her own account of things, Manley at least seems to have maintained her dignity during the scene following her false accusation by Cleveland. In the account in *Rivella*, to which the narrator Lovemore claims to have been an eyewitness, Manley asked Fitzroy to vouch for her innocence against Cleveland's insinuations, then 'went to take her Leave of' Cleveland 'with such an Air of Resentment, Innocence, yet good Manners, as quite confounded the haughty *Hilaria*'.[132]

Manley was probably justified in complaining about Cleveland's haughty and demanding nature and her skill at manipulating others. Such personality traits, along with her other charms, apparently allowed Cleveland to hold sway over Charles II for many years, and to guarantee fortune, income and status for herself and her children long after Charles's death. On the other hand, Manley herself did not lack charm or the ability to persuade others to do her bidding. Just as Cleveland strategically collaborated with the court painter John Lely, whose 'many and influential portraits of her' helped establish her 'as a great court beauty and the king's accepted mistress',[133] so Manley would strategically deploy her own pen to present herself to the world in the most sympathetic light possible. Manley, who was apparently eager to accept the invitation Cleveland offered her (even, as her own narrative indicates, at the cost of slighting the neighbour who originally introduced them), might then be accused of an inconstancy perhaps similar to that with which she charges Cleveland.

Manley, in fact, probably benefited substantially from her stay with Cleveland. If nothing else, much of the court gossip Cleveland no doubt shared with her presumably informs Manley's satirical secret histories. As her narrator explains in *Rivella*:

> from *Hilaria* she receiv'd the first ill Impressions of Count *Fortunatus* [John Churchill, first Duke of Marlborough], touching his Ingratitude, Immorality, and Avarice; being her self an Eye-Witness when he deny'd *Hilaria* (who had given him Thousands) the common Civility of lending her Twenty Guineas at *Basset*; which together with betraying his Master, and raising himself by his Sister's Dishonour, she had always esteem'd a just and flaming Subject for Satire.[134]

The gossip that Cleveland supplied about the Duke of Marlborough, a cousin and once a lover of hers, provided Manley with important ammunition for her satirical depictions of this important political figure, with whose policies Manley and other Tory propaganda writers would subsequently take issue. Whether or not Manley was actually a witness to the purported exchange between Marlborough and Cleveland over twenty guineas, her account of him would help etch for posterity Marlborough's purported lack of gratitude to the mistress whose financial generosity had helped launch his career.[135]

While in the company of Cleveland, Manley apparently made the acquaintance of other powerful court figures (and heard many stories about them), including, according to her account, 'Lord Crafty', i.e. Ralph Montagu (*c.* 1638–1709), first Duke of Montagu. He was a wealthy and influential Whig peer (and once lover of the Duchess of Cleveland) whose son's marriage in 1705 allied him to the Marlborough family. Manley's acquaintance with Montagu not only provided material for her depiction of him in *The New Atalantis*, it also allowed her to continue her satire of ambitious and 'crafty' Whigs, such as Montagu, in her fictional autobiography. Although those of us interested in teasing what we can of Manley's own life from *The Adventures of Rivella* tend to focus on the elements of the book that provide some clue about Manley's own life, in fact about one third (around 8,000 out of about 20,000 words) of the brief narrative of *Rivella* is an account of the Bath-Albemarle lawsuit, in which Manley and John Tilly were attempting to mediate. In other words, what is striking about *Rivella*, by comparison with more modern memoirs, is how little Manley really tells us about her own life. Eighteenth-century readers, however, might have been distracted from such omissions by the diverting accounts, highlighted in the initial advertisements for the work, of 'several Persons Cotemporary with the said Author'.[136]

'Two Years' in the West Country

After falling out with the Duchess of Cleveland, Manley apparently took the stagecoach to Exeter in June 1694, a journey that she describes in her first prose publication, *Letters Written by Mrs. Manley*, and stayed in the west of England for about eighteen months. After her ejection by Cleveland, she was quite likely short of funds (especially since John Manley seems not to have kept his promise of restocking her modest inheritance) and possibly lacking a place to stay.

We know almost nothing of Manley's eighteen months in the West Country. It may be that she took John Manley's original suggestion of following him into Cornwall, although from her accounts of her stagecoach journey, her original destination appears to have been Exeter (in Devon), rather than Truro, where her husband lived in Cornwall (which would have been further along the same route by stagecoach). Whether she settled in Devon or Cornwall, in a town or in the country, we simply do not know. Were she living in the town of Exeter, she would have been closer to where her cousin-husband was living than she was in London (and he might have been providing her means of support), but not so close that she would risk moving in the same spheres as his legitimate wife.

It is conceivable that Manley left London because she was pregnant (whether by John Manley or by someone else). There is no surviving record of her having given birth in Exeter in 1694. There is, however, a birth record for a Francis Manley, baptized in Truro on 9 August 1694 and listed as the son of John Manley and his wife Ann.[137] This couple had produced only one other child in the fifteen years of their marriage, so some scholars have speculated as to whether the child – possibly named after John and Delarivier's uncle Francis (d. 1684) or Delarivier's brother Francis (d. 1693) – might in fact have been born to Delarivier but acknowledged as son and heir by John and Ann. This child, whoever his mother was, died in December 1694.[138]

If Delarivier Manley had moved to the west of England simply to give birth, whether to the child recorded as the son of John and Ann or to another child for whom no record has been found, she might conceivably have returned shortly thereafter to London – either having left the child with her husband and his wife, or in the care of a wet nurse. It is conceivable, of course, that she wanted to live in the West Country to be near either this hypothetical second child or the son born in 1691, if he had been placed in the care of someone in the west at the time that John Manley returned to Truro and Delarivier joined the Duchess of Cleveland's circle. Manley, however, does not seem to have based her major life decisions around the needs of her children. It seems more likely that she simply found London too expensive and realized she could not live there without some sort of patron or benefactor. In *Rivella*, her narrator suggests that 'her Design was to waste most of her Time in *England* in Places where she was unknown'.[139] It would also appear that she spent some of her time in the west of England attempting to become a writer.

By the time Manley returned to London in the spring of 1696, she had written, or at least drafted, her first two plays and her first epistolary work, *Letters Writen by Mrs. Manley*. She seems to have decided that she would attempt to live by her pen, possibly trying to follow the model of Aphra Behn, who had been so successful in the theatre in the 1670s and early 1680s, or else following the example of Marie d'Aulnoy, to whose epistolary histories Manley's *Letters Writen* alludes. By the time Manley had returned to London, she had not only begun imitating the other writers of her day, but she had also already begun to define her own writing style as a poignant yet satirical mixture of the personal and the political. As we will see in the next chapter, Manley's first two plays, which satirically rework familiar dramatic conventions, have distinct political overtones. Her first prose work, while in some ways a witty personal travelogue, is framed, through an initial quotation from the poet George Granville, as an account of a political exile.

4 A 'FEMALE WIT': 1694-6

The dates in *Letters Writen by Mrs. Manley*, a short autobiographical epistolary narrative of a journey from London to Exeter, suggest that Manley took the stagecoach to Exeter in June 1694. At this time, she was probably short of money and may have had creditors to pay. She might possibly have been pregnant. She might also have been beginning to think of trying her hand at writing. She was probably back in London by late 1695, as *Letters Writen* was advertised in late February 1696.[1] Her first play, *The Lost Lover; or The Jealous Husband: A Comedy*, was produced by Skipwith and Rich's Drury Lane Theatre in about March 1696 and her second play, *The Royal Mischief: A Tragedy*, was produced by Betterton, Barry and Bracegirdle's rival theatre company at Lincoln's Inn Fields in about May of the same year.[2]

The narrator of *Rivella* suggests that following her journey to Exeter, Manley spent 'Two Years' away from London.[3] The stagecoach journey described in *Letters Writen* suggests that Manley headed originally to Exeter, but she could not have acquired her knowledge of the theatre from her time in Devon or Cornwall. After the closing of the theatres during the Civil Wars and the Interregnum, many of the major towns in the West Country, including Exeter, continued to feel the anti-theatre influence of religious dissenters into the 1680s. The West Country also suffered more than any other part of England from the Assizes following Monmouth's 1685 landing in Lyme Regis, Dorset. Although there may have been some informal theatrical productions staged in pubs and inns during the decades following the Restoration, no theatres reopened in the West Country until 1705, when one opened in Bath.[4] Manley's knowledge of the major works of Restoration comedy and tragedy and her familiarity with the acting styles of the major comedians and tragedians of her day, therefore, almost certainly came from her having frequented the theatre in London both before and after her stay in the West Country.

The Female Wits: or The Triumvirate of Poets at Rehearsal (1704), an anonymously authored dramatic comedy first produced in October 1696, satirized the female playwrights Manley, Catharine Trotter, subsequently Cockburn (*c.* 1674–1749), and Mary Pix (*c.* 1666–1709). In this production Manley is portrayed as someone well connected in the world of theatre, already close friends with Pix and Trotter, and followed by a retinue of flatterers and admirers. This comedy satirizes the exaggerated heroics of Manley's *The Royal Mischief*, following the model of Buckingham's *The Rehearsal* (1671) in its mockery of heroic drama. *The Female Wits* was probably written by a group of actors and actor-writers who clearly knew the personalities of their theatrical contemporaries. It was possibly spearheaded by the comedian, satirist and occasional playwright Joseph Haynes, who had played a small role in Manley's *The Lost Lover*. Moreover, from what is known of the other personalities involved, the depictions in *the Female Wits*, however 'outrageously exaggerated', seem to reveal a 'kernel of truth'.[5]

Marsilia (representing Manley) is unbearably arrogant, overly fond of flattery and a terrible snob. In this comic rendition, she leaves actors waiting for her at a morning rehearsal, having been detained, she explains, because 'two or three idle People of Quality, who thinking I had no more to do than themselves, stop'd my Chair and teaz'd me with a Thousand foolish Questions'.[6] Once at the rehearsal, Manley then offers advice that suggests that she had a less sophisticated understanding of classical and dramatic traditions than many of the actors had. We also learn, whether it is true or not, that Manley is impatient for her first glass of sherry in the morning and quick to take offence. In this depiction of her, Manley invariably slights those of lesser importance for those of more importance. After spending a scene or two disparaging in turn (in the other's presence) both Pix (Mrs Wellfed) and Trotter (Calista), then arrogantly correcting the actors in their delivery of their lines, Marsilia pronounces in dismay, 'I wonder my Lord Duke's not come, nor Sir *Thomas*'.[7] Sir Thomas is presumably Thomas Skipwith (*c.* 1652–1710), partner in the Drury Lane Theatre, which produced Manley's *Lost Lover*. The 'Duke' might possibly be William Cavendish (1641–1707), Duke of Devonshire, an influential patron of the theatre, to whom Manley dedicated *The Royal Mischief*. As we consider Manley's development both as a writer and as a political thinker, it is worth noting that both of these influential men from whom she probably sought patronage were Whig politicians. Skipwith, who served as MP for Malmesbury from 1696 to 1698, was not particularly active in his political role (there is no record of his having spoken in Parliament[8]); Devonshire, however, was a staunch Whig, who had actively participated in bringing William to England in 1688, and was a member of the Privy Council from 1689 until his death in 1707.

Manley was probably also in contact in the mid 1690s with the Tory-Jacobite playwright and politician George Granville, later Baron Lansdowne, nephew to John Grenville, Earl of Bath, for whom Manley's spouse, John Manley, was a legal advisor. In *Letters Writen*, Manley cites a then unpublished poem by Granville about his political exile after 1688 in describing her own 1694 retreat to the country. It is not surprising, given Manley's upbringing and the tropes of her father's narratives of exile, that she should instinctively frame her first published account of herself and a description of her own time outside London as a narrative of political exile. However, it also seems likely that Manley was necessarily flexible, as her father had been in his years seeking military employment in exile, about the persons from whom she sought patronage as she was beginning her career as a writer.

The overarching ideology of Manley's first tragedy is generally Tory, although the play would probably not have offended either Whigs or Tories in the audience. What is striking about Manley's first two dramatic works is not their expression of partisan politics per se but their manipulation of certain standard theatrical conventions: for example, Manley's unconventional depiction of the deserted mistress in *The Lost Lovers* and her re-gendering of the desiring gaze in *The Royal Mischief*. While such innovations certainly have political implications, it would be more accurate to describe Manley's first literary productions as experimental, both in the genres she chose, the literary conventions she revised, and in the persons from whom she sought patronage.

Manley's Possible Patrons

However it may have exaggerated Manley's personal foibles, *The Female Wits* may well provide an accurate sense of whom Manley knew in the theatre world at the time that her first plays made their debut on stage. It seems reasonable to accept, following *The Female Wits*, that by the spring of 1696 Manley was friendly with Pix and Trotter. It also seems reasonable to assume that she openly encouraged an entourage of men who would flatter her or offer some form of support or patronage. In *Rivella*, Manley's narrator suggests that during this period in the early 1690s when she was writing for the stage, 'Her Appartment was daily crouded' with 'Men of Vogue and Wit'.[9]

It is conceivable that Manley acquired her knowledge of the theatre simply by reading published plays, as is suggested by her claim in the preface to *The Lost Lover* that she had attended only two plays in the six previous years. However, it is difficult to imagine that Manley had not attended the theatre regularly while living with her cousin-husband in London, either in his company or in the company of some of her female acquaintances, such as Anne Ryder or Barbara Palmer, Duchess of Cleveland. Although the theatres were closed for four months in 1694, following the death of Queen Mary, Manley demonstrates familiarity with the theatre of 1693 and 1695. In *Letters Writen* she makes an allusion to a 'Lady-Sister', a somewhat unusual turn of phrase that probably derives from a line from Congreve's *The Double Dealer* (1693).[10] In the preface to *The Royal Mischief*, Manley refers to the 1695 production of Southerne's *Oroonoko*; she also refers to Dryden's *Aureng-Zebe* (1676), which was reprinted in 1694 and probably revived for the 1693–4 season. Moreover, Manley's first play, *The Lost Lover*, strongly echoes Etherege's *The Man of Mode; or, Sir Fopling Flutter* (1676), which was probably revived in 1693 when a new edition appeared in print. The main plot of *The Lost Lover* also bears some resemblance to the plot of Congreve's *Love for Love*, which played to enthusiastic audiences during an impressive thirteen-week run in early May 1695.

Further evidence that Manley had returned to London sooner and was more familiar with the world of theatre than her preface to *The Lost Lover* suggests is the fact that she wrote a dedicatory preface to Catharine Trotter's first play, which was published in January 1696 and so probably produced in December 1695. Manley might have sent a preface to Trotter from wherever she was living outside of London. However, it is difficult to see why she would have been perceived, at least by Trotter and her printer, as an aspiring writer herself unless she were already living in London and acquainted with Trotter by mid to late 1695. Manley's dedication to Trotter concludes:

> O! How I long in the Poetick Race,
> To loose the Reins, and give their Glory Chase;
> For thus Encourag'd, and thus led by you,
> Methinks we might more Crowns than theirs Subdue.[11]

Whoever invited, or permitted, Manley to present the dedicatory verses to Trotter was clearly comfortable with these lines serving as a prelude to Manley's own planned career as a writer and to the triumph of women's writing for the stage.

Given that Manley was already announcing her presence as a playwright through her dedicatory verses to Trotter's first play in December 1695, it seems likely that she actually returned to London relatively early in 1695, perhaps in time to see the production of Congreve's *Love for Love* in April. If Manley intentionally exaggerated the time she spent away from London between 1694 and 1696, there are several reasons why she might have done so. One possible explanation, consistent with her insistence in her preface to *The Lost Lover* that she had been to the theatre only twice in the previous six years, might have been to provide an excuse for the lacklustre performance of *The Lost Lover*, which ran only three nights. By suggesting that she had only recently returned from the country and was unfamiliar with the London stage, Manley offers an excuse for the fact that her first comedy did not have the flair or appeal of, for example, the successful 1690s comedies of the classically educated William Congreve (1670–1729) or those of Colly Cibber (1671–1757). Cibber was an experienced actor familiar with both Restoration and classical repertoire, who also had a good ear for the timing and pacing necessary for crowd-pleasing comedy.

Another possible reason for Manley to dissemble about her whereabouts in 1695 might be that she had returned to London incognito as mistress of someone, as yet unidentified, whose reputation she was trying to protect, along with her own. Her account of her stagecoach journey to Exeter in *Letters Writen* includes seven letters ostensibly written in June 1694, during the week of the journey. There is then a gap in the sequence, followed by one letter dated 15 March 1695, in which Manley refers to her eventual return to London, adding: 'when that will be, I have not the Pleasure so much as to imagine'.[12] Despite her seeming uncertainty in the spring of 1695 as to when she would be able to return to London, it would appear that Manley may well have returned shortly after this letter was sent (if in fact she actually sent such a letter to anyone).

Assuming Manley did return to London some time in 1695, under the protection or patronage of some unknown person, we still do not know whether she returned with complete drafts of two plays and her first epistolary prose work – which would indicate that the time she spent away from London may in fact have been a sabbatical dedicated to becoming a writer – or whether she was inspired to write after her return. As indicated by the speed with which Manley would produce *Memoirs of Europe*, the sequel to *The New Atalantis*, in the winter of 1710, she apparently could write quickly when necessary. This speed is also suggested in her preface to *The Lost Lover*, in which she describes this first comedy as 'the Follies of seven days', indicating that she drafted the play in about a week. She also indicates that, however quickly she wrote it, she was publishing it 'after two years reflection', giving the impression that she had written it two years earlier, or about the time that she left London in June 1694.[13] At the time that she left, therefore, she seems to have had the intention of living quietly in the country, reading and writing.

In the seventh letter in *Letters Writen*, dated 30 June 1694, Manley gives the impression that, having arrived in Exeter, she intended to devote herself to intellectual pursuits; she tells her correspondent that 'My Study has fallen upon Religion'.[14] From her references to the major religious controversies of the day in *The Unknown Lady's Pacquet* and from Richard Steele's grateful description of her as a 'Deist' (for her morally tolerant attitude towards his illegitimate child), moreoever, it would appear that she did take an open-minded interest in the study of religion, despite the High-Church Tory position she would support in her later political writings.[15]

The epistolary narrative *Letters Writen*, Manley's first prose publication, is a short sequence of letters ostensibly written to someone Manley was leaving behind when she left London in June 1694. If these letters really were copies of or recollections of letters Manley sent to a friend or lover, then they suggest that she maintained a correspondence with at least one intellectual and literary contact in London while she was away. It also suggests that she may well have left London in 1694 with the intention of becoming a writer and with the intention of returning to oversee the production and publication of her works. Moreover, it would appear from the first letter in *Letters Writen* that her correspondent had pleaded with her not to leave:

> The Resolutions I have taken of quitting *London* (which is as much as to say, the World) for ever, starts back, and asks my gayer Part if 't has well weigh'd the Sense of *Ever*? Nor does your Letter, which I receiv'd this Morning, (taking Coach) less influence me, than when I first form'd the Design. You shou'd have us'd but half these Arguments, and they had undoubtedly prevail'd.[16]

Whatever Manley's reasons for leaving London, they were clearly pressing enough to override this person's persuasions, but she may well have returned to his protection some time in 1695, or perhaps even late in 1694, with drafts of her first comedy and tragedy as well as copies of these letters, which she might have reworked for publication.

Manley's *Letters Writen* was ostensibly published without her consent, and introduced by a preface signed J. H., who claims to have been a friend of Manley's father. Various possible identifications have been offered – James Hargreaves, of the Middle Temple, or John Hughes, a friend of the theatre patron Bevil Higgons.[17] Another possibility is John Hervey (1665–1751), subsequently first Earl of Bristol, a friend and patron of the extended Manley family in Wales. There is some extant correspondence between Hervey and Delarivier Manley from 1717 and 1718 that suggests that he knew her much earlier. In a letter to Manley written in 1717, Hervey not only compliments her 'natural genius' but suggests that he had the 'pleasure & advantage of being early acquainted with' the 'fruitfulness' of it, suggesting that he may have known her earliest writings and could in fact have helped her to publish her first prose work.[18] If this identification of J. H. is correct, it would explain why he suggests in the preface to *Letters Writen* that he was a friend of Manley's father.

Of course, if J. H. helped Manley publish these letters, it does not mean that he would have been the recipient of them, although he may have been. John Hervey, if he was J. H., might have met up with Delarivier Manley in London after his first wife's death in 1693 and perhaps have engaged in a slightly flirtatious relationship with her, consistent with the tone of the published letters, before she left for Exeter in 1694 and before he married his second wife in July 1695. It is also possible that the letters (or ones very like them) were written to Sir Thomas Skipwith, who owned a half share interest – along with Christopher Rich (bap. 1647, d. 1714) – in the Drury Lane Theatre, and with whom Manley claims to have enjoyed a flirtatious correspondence. It is likewise possible that the letters were never actually sent to anyone, but were literary constructs, designed in imitation of d'Aulnoy's epistolary travelogues.

At some point, either before she left for the West Country or shortly after her return, Manley was apparently introduced to Sir Thomas Skipwith. As

Manley's narrator in *Rivella* explains, 'a certain Gentleman, who was a very great Scholar and master of abundance of Sense and Judgment, at her own Request, brought to her Acquaintance one *Sir Peter Vainlove*', i.e. Skipwith, according to the published key. Vainlove had 'then Interest enough to introduce upon one Stage whatever Pieces he pleas'd',[19] so it was probably through Skipwith's interest that Manley managed to have her first play produced at Drury Lane. It is also possible that the person to whom Manley was writing as she left London in June 1694 was the 'certain Gentleman' who introduced her to Skipwith. It has been suggested that this 'Gentleman' was George Granville,[20] but given that she refers to Granville as the author of the verses she cites in the first letter of *Letters Writen*, she was probably not writing to him. We cannot, therefore, determine for certain exactly when Manley returned to London, nor under whose protection (if anyone's), but it does appear that upon her return Manley was receiving encouragement, and some form of patronage, from Sir Thomas Skipwith.

The Lost Lover includes a song, 'O Dangerous Swain', which Manley claims in *Rivella* to have been based on verses she first wrote to Skipwith. The lines give the impression that Manley was, at the time she wrote them, attempting either to lure Skipwith away from another mistress, or at least flatter him into producing her first play through the ploy of romantic jealousy:

> *Ah Dangerous Swain, tell me no more,*
> *Thy Happy Nymph you Worship and Adore;*
> *When thy fill'd Eyes are sparkling at her Name,*
> *I raving wish that mine had caus'd the Flame.*[21]

The flattering tone of lines such as these might have been enough to persuade Skipwith to produce Manley's first play. It is not clear whether Manley's relationship with him extended beyond a flirtation, but it may have resulted in financial support from Skipwith, perhaps in the form of money advanced against the hope of future proceeds from an author's benefit for her plays. Such support would explain how Manley could maintain the apartment 'daily crouded' with men of wit and to maintain something of an elegant wardrobe, with which she is frequently fussing in the satirical depiction of her in *The Female Wits*.

Manley's depiction of Skipwith in *Rivella* suggests that they had something close to a romantic relationship: 'He wrote very pretty well-turned *Billet deuxs* [i.e. *billets doux*, love letters]; he was not at all sparing of his Letters when he met a Woman that had any Knack that Way: *Rivella* was much to his Taste, so that presently there grew the greatest Intimacy in the World between them'. Manley's narrative suggests that there were some limits on the actual nature of their physical relationship, however, limits possibly imposed by Skipwith's own past: 'Sir Peter was supposed to be towards Fifty when he became acquainted with Rivella, and his Constitution broken by those Excesses, of which in his Youth he had been guilty'. Manley describes herself as offering more than Skipwith could or would return:

> but because he found she was a Woman of Fire, more than perhaps he could answer, he was resolved to destroy any Hopes she might have of a nearer Correspondence than would conveniently suit with his present Circumstances, by telling her his Heart was already prepossess'd.[22]

The person with whom Skipwith was in love, Manley's narrator informs us, was not his wife, described in *Rivella* as 'a Lady of Worth and Honour who brought him a very large Joynture' and was tolerant of her husband's many flirtations with other women, but another mistress.[23]

In her depiction of Skipwith in *Rivella*, Manley does not devote much of the narrative to how he actually helped her career or what happened to rupture their relationship or cause her to have her second play produced by Betterton's rival theatre company. Instead of delving into this complex set of circumstances, which might not portray Manley herself in a flattering light, Manley's narrator recounts at some length the difficulties Skipwith apparently was having with his long-term mistress and related the gossip circulating about him at the time. As her narrator claims that Skipwith explained to her, and she subsequently to her narrator: 'It cost the Knight according to his own Report three Hundred Pounds a Year (besides two Thousand Pounds worth of Jewels presented at Times) to see her but once a Week, and give her a Supper'. Manley is quick to point out that 'Sir Peter was however exactly scrupulous in doing Justice to the Lady's Honour; protesting that himself had never had the Last Favour, tho' she Lov'd him to Distraction'.[24] Manley intimates that Skipwith possibly did not have 'the Last Favour' from this mistress because he was incapable of it. She relates of another young actress that 'he had pass'd three Days and Nights sucessively in Bed with her without any Consequence, he was thought rather dangerous to a Woman's Reputation than her Vertue'.[25]

Manley's own reputation was at one point at risk because the world assumed that she and Skipwith were lovers and that when he was obliged to enter a course of physic (for syphilis) she was the cause. Here she insists on her innocence by emphasizing his impotence and the false rumours he allowed to be spread about a disorder that was not in fact syphilis at all:

> For some Time poor *Rivella*'s Character suffer'd as the Person that had done him this Injury, till seeing him equally assiduous and fond of her in all publick Places, join'd to what the *Operator* discover'd of his pretended Disease; the World found out the Cheat, detesting his Vanity and *Rivella*'s Folly; that cou'd suffer the Conversation of a Wretch so insignificant to her Pleasures, and yet so dangerous to her Reputation.[26]

This depiction of a former confidant and patron, in Manley's politicized fictional autobiography penned in 1714, may reflect her desire to demonize a former (Whig) intimate. It also provides her the opportunity of defending her own reputation, and reinforcing her consistent depiction of herself in her own romanticized self-portrait as wronged (Tory) innocent. We should bear in mind, however, as we interpret Manley's satirical portrayal of Skipwith, who died four years before the publication of *Rivella*, that this style of mockery is typical of how she would depict many former friends who had once offered her assistance but with whom she subsequently fell out – including Barbara Palmer, Catherine Trotter and Richard Steele. This is not to suggest that any of these persons were entirely without blame in their relations with Manley. However, it is fair to note that there is a certain pattern in Manley's manner of denigrating those with whom she was once friends, even those who may have helped her launch her career as a writer or assisted her in other ways.

Manley clearly flattered Skipwith and charmed him with enough witty verbal talent to persuade him to produce her first comedy. At the time of its publication, she acknowledges in her preface: 'Sir *Thomas Skipwith*'s Civility, his Native Generosity, and Gallantry of Temper'. She also observes that Skipwith 'took care nothing on his part shou'd be wanting' to make her play 'pleasing'.[27] If this gallantry as a theatre director is as far as their relationship extended, it may not have been his financial assistance that set her up in London, paid for her lodgings, her wardrobe, her transportation in chairs in and around London, or the wine she is depicted as ordering while attending the rehearsal. In *The Female Wits* Manley is shown as encouraging a variety of fawning and flattering men simultaneously. She allows one Mr Awdwell to order a dinner to be prepared for her, which she never eats, leaving in a coach with Lord Whiffle and Mr Praiseall, referring confidently to 'my lord Duke', from whom she assumes she will be able to borrow the jewels necessary for one key scene. In other words, it would appear that Manley was not averse to accepting gifts or meals from various admirers, which could indicate that her maintenance at this time might not have been entirely secure.

It is of course conceivable that Manley was being supported in part at this point by her cousin-husband John Manley. Her stay in the West Country probably from about 1694 to 1695 may have been motivated by his connections to Cornwall; he might have found her a place to live, in Devon or Cornwall, and her proximity to his parliamentary constituency may have prompted him to pay her a regular maintenance.[28] Manley's casual references to 'my Lord Duke', whose attendance she anticipates at the rehearsal and from whom she appears confident she might borrow jewels, could be a reference to the Duke of Devonshire, who is rumoured to have had liaisons with a variety of women and a long-term liaison with the actress Anne Campion (*c.* 1687–1706). It is conceivable that Manley may also have engaged in some sort of intrigue with him, or he may have been otherwise amenable to helping her launch her career. In Manley's *The Remaining Part of the Unknown Lady's Pacquet of Letters* (1707), she includes two love letters, ostensibly written by 'the Late D— of D—', one of which makes a reference to the addressee (clearly a lover) 'going out of Town'. The writer pleads in this letter, 'If this cruel Journey cannot be put off, let me at least live in the hopes of seeing you in the Country'. In the next letter, he insists, 'Give me your Permission, and ... I will find a means to come down in some disguise'.[29] There is no way of knowing when or to whom these letters were written (or if they were in fact real letters), although if they were written to Manley, they might indicate a brief liaison with Devonshire, a powerful and wealthy Whig minister, whom she might have met either before she left London in 1694, possibly in the company of the Duchess of Cleveland.

Manley dedicates *The Royal Mischief* to Devonshire, and some scholars have speculated that he wrote the dedicatory verses 'sent by an unknown hand', and that he also helped Manley bring her first comedy to the stage.[30] However, another scholar has suggested that those verses might have been written by George Granville.[31] Moreover, the dedication to Devonshire might represent a wish to cultivate a potential patron rather than to reward an existing one. If Manley returned to London six to twelve months sooner than she suggests in *Rivella* (staying in the West Country only a year, rather than two) and lived under the protection of either Skipwith or Devonshire, or perhaps the unidentified J. H., before attempting to launch her career as a playwright, then her emphasis in *Rivella* on the amusing gossip about Skipwith and his wife and long-term mistress would serve to distract readers from the missing portions of her own story. Given that three centuries of scholars have accepted at face value Manley's own claims about the chronology of this period of her life, this strategy of distraction seems to have worked.

Another person to whom Manley seems to have been indebted in her attempt to establish herself as a playwright in the mid-1690s was the 'certain Gentleman' scholar who apparently introduced her to Skipwith. One possibility is that it was John Tidcomb, who might have known Skipwith through the military: they were both made captains in the Earl of Huntingdon's Regiment of Foot in June 1685.[32] Tidcomb, identified in the keys as the narrator Lovemore of *Rivella*, was something of a wit and subsequently a member of the Kit-Kat Club, and as narrator, might wryly be referring to himself as 'a Scholar'. It is also possible that the 'certain Gentleman' was George Granville, whose first play was staged, like Manley's, during the season of 1695–6. Granville, who had composed and presented verses to Mary of Modena, while still a student at Oxford, considered himself so loyal to the exiled Stuarts that he refused to serve actively in government during the reign of William and Mary. From about 1690 until 1702 he lived in retirement at the family estate Marr, near Doncaster in Yorkshire. However, Granville must have visited London regularly enough in the mid-1690s to oversee the production of his first two plays: *The She Gallants*, a comedy staged in early 1696, and *Heroick Love*, a tragedy produced in 1697. It has also been conjectured that Granville may have written the commendatory verses to Delia prefixed to Manley's *Royal Mischief*, and that he jokingly gave that name to the 'handmaiden to a sorceress' in *The British Enchanters, or No Magick Like Love* (1706) as a joke between old friends.[33] Manley's admiration for Granville would remain strong throughout her life; she would dedicate her last published work, *The Power of Love in Seven Novels*, to his wife. It would make sense then that Manley would refer to Granville as a 'Gentleman' and a 'Scholar'; it would also make sense that, out of respect to him, he would be given no fictional pseudonym and his name would not be listed in the published keys to any of her works, over which Manley presumably had some editorial control.[34]

Manley may have met Granville through her spouse, John Manley, before she left London in 1694 or even while she was in exile in the West Country, where Granville might conceivably have gone to visit his uncle. Granville's first comedy, *The She-Gallants*, was produced by Betterton's company at Lincoln's Inn Fields, in early January 1696 (or late December 1695).[35] Since Granville, a second son, seems to have been living as something of a dependent relation on other family members, he might not have had the financial resources necessary to support a mistress. However, he seems to have been a friend and a supporter of Manley's attempts at playwriting; he may be 'Mr Awdwell' in the retinue of her admirers in *The Female Wits*. Manley's consistently positive depictions of him give the impression that he was a friend and a perhaps a mentor, whose own writing and political positions she admired, but not someone from whom she expected financial patronage or romantic relations.

One preliminary conclusion we might draw about Manley's search for patronage upon her return to London in the mid-1690s is that she sought out the intellectual and political comradeship from politically purist Tory writers such as Granville, while simultaneously seeking the financial patronage of womanizing Whigs, such as Skipwith and Devonshire, who were well connected to the theatre and apparently ready to help a witty, flirtatious woman. John Hervey, the family friend who might have written the preface to *Letters Writen*, was also a staunch Whig. In other words, Manley seems to have been following the footsteps of her father, who, out of practical necessity, had written letters of intelligence to Cromwell's government during his years in exile, even though his post-Restoration correspondence and publications articulated a strongly royalist ideology. While Whig patrons might have helped Delarivier Manley produce her first plays, however, she clearly felt no obligation to follow the dramatic conventions of the Whig writers of her time.

Comic Conventions and *The Lost Lover*

In the London theatre season of 1695–6, it was relatively easy to get a new play produced but relatively difficult to attract an audience to sustain it beyond a few nights. After the actor Thomas Betterton (bap. 1635, d. 1710) broke away with Elizabeth Barry (*c.* 1656–1713) and Anne Bracegirdle (bap. 1671, d. 1748) from Skipwith and Rich's United Company and began producing plays at Lincoln's Inn Fields in April 1695, there were for the first time in twelve years two rival theatre companies in London. This renewal of competition increased the demand for new plays. At the same time, there was a relative scarcity of experienced playwrights in part because the theatrical slump of the mid-1680s had pushed many playwrights into other careers and had discouraged new talent from attempting to write for the stage.[36] By the end of 1692, the most experienced active playwrights were John Dryden and John Crowne (bap. 1641, d. 1712). Thomas D'Urfey (*c.* 1653–1723), Thomas Southerne (1660–1746) and William Congreve would soon launch their careers, but with the opening of the new playhouse, it is not surprising that new talent was sought nor that the plays of three witty literary women – Trotter, Manley and Pix – would be welcomed by theatre managers and actors. After all, the works of Aphra Behn had enjoyed great popularity on the stage during the 1670s and 1680s, and her works were still being performed regularly in the 1690s. At the same time, however, because of the opening of the second theatre, audiences now had more choice in what to see: each new play was in competition with a production at the other theatre.

Within this context, it makes sense that Manley's first comedy, a fascinating work, but one that could have benefited from revision, would run for only three days. If she returned to London in mid to late 1695 and grasped the opportunities suddenly open because of the new theatre (as well as the potential new freedom for playwrights following the expiration of the last licensing laws in May 1695), Manley may have allowed her first comedy be produced without seeking the advice of more experienced playwrights in revising it. She claims in her preface that the play was written in 'seven days' and that 'the better half was cut'.[37] The excised 'half' is probably the subplot about a 'Turkey' merchant who mistakenly believes he will be cuckolded by his young, beautiful and virtuous wife. This subplot would probably not be perceived by most critics, then or now, as the 'better half', but apparently Manley was not given any advice as to how to integrate the subplot effectively into the whole. By contrast, William Congreve drafted his first play, *The Old Batchelor*, in about 1690 but was able to spend a summer revising it, benefiting from John Dryden's suggestions and encouragement; it was produced to great acclaim only in 1693. Congreve subsequently helped to mentor and advise Catherine Trotter.[38]

Whether Delarivier Manley desired or sought advice from any more experienced playwright is not known. Trotter, a staunch Whig, may have been more comfortable asking advice from the Whig Congreve than Manley would have been, although Manley seems to have had no difficulty in seeking patronage from the Whig Duke of Devonshire. Manley may simply not have been given time to revise her first play once it went into production. On the other hand, it might have been difficult for a more experienced playwright to offer useful suggestions to a self-confident younger writer determined to challenge some of the familiar conventions of the stage; in other words, Manley's first play might have been destined not to run for more than three nights because it ruptured familiar social and dramatic conventions.

The Lost Lover shares much in common with the plots of other Restoration comedies; however, it does not fit neatly either the traditional category of Restoration 'comedy of manners' or the newer 1690s genre of 'sentimental comedy'. Although Manley includes two male characters with rakish tendencies, they are neither traditional Restoration rakes nor the reformed rakes of later sentimental comedy. The Restoration rake, a cunning master of manipulation, was best exemplified by Dorimant in Etheredge's classic comedy of manners *The Man of Mode; or Sir Fopling Flutter* (1676 and probably revived in 1693 when a new edition was issued). Dorimant views life as 'a game to be won by the clever' and 'loves not only the game, but the awareness of play'.[39] He may agree to marry at the end of the play, but he is not reformed: he takes for granted that he will continue to have mistresses once married and he will continue to view life as an amoral game. The reformed rake, however, could not triumph merely by manipulating others but was obliged to correct his behaviour, as did Loveless in Colley Cibber's sentimental comedy *Love's Last Shift; or The Fool in Fashion* (1696), which was first staged at the Drury Lane Theatre by Skipwith and Rich's company in January 1696, just two months before Manley's *The Lost Lover* would be staged by the same company. Loveless stands in sharp contrast to the amoral rake of Restoration comedy. Unlike Dorimant, whose immorality might have pleased audiences at the height of the rakish Charles II's reign, Loveless is a former rake and delinquent husband who returns from France destitute and miserable only to be ingeniously tricked into falling in love again with his own wife, who generously forgives his mistakes. His virtue, probably appealing to court and society under the morally circumspect reign of Mary II (1662–94) and her husband, the Calvinist William III, is rewarded by the discovery that his wife has inherited a separate fortune during his debauched exile.[40]

The hero of Manley's *Lost Lover*, in contrast to both Etherege's Dorimant and Cibber's Loveless, is neither charmingly amoral nor fully morally reformed. Manley's Wilmore is a not entirely likeable character who has seduced and jilted the virtuous Belira but who nevertheless wins the beautiful Marina away from his father. While Etherege's Dorimant is universally charming and witty, how-ever duplicitous and untrustworthy, Manley's Wilmore is sometimes simply unpleasant. Both Etherege's Bellinda and Manley's Belira accuse their jilting former suitors of breaking vows, and both rakes reply with similar speeches con-doning their own behaviour. However, Dorimant manages to keep his banter with his mistress witty even though he is simultaneously courting an heiress, while Wilmore is unable to maintain his charm to his former lover once he has begun courting someone else.

Both Etherege's and Manley's male protagonists are portrayed as vow-break-ers. Dorimant observes to Bellinda: 'Th'extravagant words they speak in love. 'Tis as unreasonable to expect we should perform all we promise then, as do all we threaten when we are angry.'[41] Wilmore echoes this line when he informs Belira: 'I lik'd you once, and still esteem you, but Vows that are made in Love, are writ in sand: It's impossible to recal a Lovers Heart, when once 'tis made a Present to another; shou'd it return, 'twou'd sooner Love a third.'[42] The strongly royalist Etherege, writing twelve years before his loyalty to the Stuarts would oblige him to join James II in exile in France, permits Bellinda to retort to the vow-breaking Dorimant's ever optimistic 'We must meet again', with a satisfy-ing, 'Never.'[43] Dorimant is surprised by Bellinda's reply but he never loses his calm or his wit. Manley, also of royalist stock, but writing eight years after James II was forced off the throne, when the issue of vow-breaking had particular reso-nance for loyal royalists, does not allow her vow-breaker to express himself quite so smoothly.

Manley's Wilmore is anything but charming as he ineffectively attempts to normalize relations with the woman he seduced then jilted, who herself has helped to arrange a marriage between his father and the young woman Wilmore loves. He demands, 'What have I done, that you shou'd wish to make me Wretch'd'. Belira retorts, 'What hast thou left undone to make me such?'. Wilmore, however, like earlier Restoration rakes, is not bothered about protect-ing a woman's virtue, but only the appearance of it: 'Your Reputation yet stands fair, and u[n]less your own Indiscretion betrays you the Secret shall be such, with me for ever'. Belira demands, 'But thy heart, Traytor, thy perjur'd Heart; tell me, how shall I get it back?' Wilmore replies simply, without wit or charm: 'Never this way, I assure you.'[44]

Manley refuses to make Wilmore as charming as the pre-1688 vow-breaking royalist Dorimant. At the same time she refuses to suggest that he will reform as fully as Colly Cibber's delinquent husband in *Love's Last Shift*. In other words, Manley eschews the misogynistic royalist optimism from the reign of Charles II even as she casts doubt on the mid-1690s Whiggish optimism of Colly Cib-ber's sentimental comedy, an optimism that assumes that vow-breakers (i.e. the Whigs who broke their vows to James II) could be forgiven and be trusted to act virtuously in the future. Wilmore's lack of charm is probably, for Manley, tied to his political ambivalence. His father, Sir Rustick Good-Heart, described in the list of characters as 'an ill-bred Country Gentleman', is also an MP who admits to the woman he is courting that he 'never came to *London* but in times of Parliament, which thank Heaven were not very frequent in our late Reigns'.[45] Here Sir Rustick represents a gentry more concerned with its own country pleasures than disturbed by the fact that Charles II and James II convened Parliament so infrequently; Rustick is clearly ill-disposed to the requirements of the Triennial Act (1604) that Parliament be convened at least once every three years.[46] It is not surprising that his son Wilmore demonstrates neither the loyal post-1688 Tory's respect for the sanctity of vows nor the earlier rakish Tory's skill at gallantry.

After Wilmore responds coldly and ungallantly to Belira, she arms herself with a sword to murder her rival Marina. At this point, Belira could become a tragic heroine, except that she is stopped from committing murder by the presence of Wildman, a rakish friend of Wilmore. Prevented from killing her rival, Belira also declines to take her own life, thereby refusing the silencing closure of suicide enforced on many a ruined heroine throughout literary history. Refusing the standard conventions of the ruined jilted lover, Manley has Belira simply call a chair and leave.[47] The ruin of an innocent woman, one of Manley's favourite motifs in her representation of her own life, is not prevented by a Tory hero in *The Lost Lover*, since there are none in her play. However, Belira is also interestingly not punished for having been ruined; she is potentially allowed a second chance, perhaps to emerge in a different part of the country and invent a different life for herself. Like Manley, who left for Exeter in 1694, only to return to London and make a name for herself in the theatre two years later, Belira is allowed the possibility of surviving the loss of her reputation. She might, like Manley, some day cite the line of Dionysius with which Manley concludes her preface: 'That *Plato* and Philosophy have taught me to bear so great Loss (even of Fame) with Patience'.[48]

Although she was clearly not focused on the plight of women as a matter of social and philosophical study – as, for example, was the Tory and proto-feminist philosopher Mary Astell (1666–1731), author of *A Serious Proposal to the Ladies* (1694) – Manley nevertheless frequently ruptured traditional representations of gender roles in her stage productions. Not only does she allow Belira to leave the scene without having to commit suicide, she also refuses some of the violence against women still standard in comedies of her time, as for example the gratuitous rape of the servant-woman in Colly Cibber's influential sentimental comedy *Love's Last Shift*.[49]

Manley's subplot about the 'Turkey' merchant, which was apparently excised in the performance by Skipworth and Rich's company, underscores Manley's sense of the dearth of heroes in the Whig era of William and Mary. Echoing some of Aphra Behn's comic depictions of Whig merchants in comedies such as *The Luckey Chance, or An Alderman's Bargain* (1686), Smyrna, who is married to the beautiful, chaste, virtuous Olivia, a model of loyal (and, presumably, for Manley, Tory) virtue, has convinced himself that she has cuckolded him. Olivia actually is attracted to the rake Wildman, but refuses his advances despite her confession that she finds her husband unsatisfying in bed. This Tory rake from an earlier literary era is rendered impotent through his inability to succeed at the 'game' of seducing women, while the Whiggish merchant is both impotent and paranoid. Manley's *Lost Lover* thus undercuts the optimism of Whig sentimental comedy yet refuses to return to the exuberant misogyny of earlier royalist comedies of manners. It probably fell flat because its style did not feel very humorous to 1690s London theatregoers accustomed to a different set of comic conventions. Manley's first play expresses remarkable cynicism, both about romance and about politics; it is not surprising that her next play was a tragedy.

Heroic Tragedy and *The Royal Mischief*

In the preface to *The Lost Lover* Manley asserts that she is 'now convinc'd Writing for the Stage is no way proper for a Woman, to whom all Advantages but meer Nature, are refused'.[50] In other words, some women have the natural talent to write; the difficulty is their lack of education. Nature may have given women such as herself 'a Genius to Poetry' and the charms to attract indulgent 'Flatterers'. These attributes of Nature, however, may well lead to the 'Ridicule' she experienced in the response to *The Lost Lover* unless combined with something beyond nature. Here we see Manley acknowledging the need for education, experience and disciplined revision in order to produce a polished dramatic work. *The Lost Lover*'s bold rejection of familiar dramatic conventions would have needed very skilful revision to have rendered it pleasing to audiences. Manley, however, allowed her first play to be printed as it was, without even excising the subplot that apparently was not included in the performance, and she used the preface to announce the appearance of her next play: 'Once more, my Offended Judges, I am to appear before you, once more in possibility of giving you the like Damning Satisfaction; there is a Tragedy of mine Rehearsing, which 'tis too late to recall'.[51]

Manley's second dramatic production demonstrates that she learned the lesson she gestured towards in the preface to *The Lost Lover*: that natural talent needed to be augmented by disciplined editing. Manley apparently had a falling out with the actors or managers of Rich and Skipwith's company during initial rehearsals for the production, as satirically documented in Manley's walking out of the theatre in the final scene of *The Female Wits*, and *The Royal Mischief* was promptly produced by Betterton , Barry and Bracegirdle's rival theatre company.

This may have been at the behest of the Duke of Devonshire, to whom it is dedicated, and whose 'Approbation' Manley suggests in the dedication was given 'in some sort ... before it came upon the Stage'.[52] Thomas Betterton and Elizabeth Barry, the leading practitioners of heroic tragedy, were particularly well suited to bringing Manley's tragic protagonists to life. If Manley had begun drafting the play while away from London in 1694, these are the actors she would probably have imagined in the leading roles. Despite the fact that the exaggerated heroics of the play would be easily mocked in the production of *The Female Wits* the following autumn, *The Royal Mischief* was a modest success, running for six nights.

Although the taste for heroic tragedy, popular in the 1670s, had declined by the mid-1690s, its best practitioners were the mainstays of Betterton's new company and Dryden's heroic drama was still frequently being revived. Manley's first tragedy, however, was and was not typical of earlier heroic models. On the one hand, her play exaggerated the conventions of heroic tragedy; at the same time it also revised and reworked standard gender roles for the genre. In writing a successful tragedy, Manley demonstrated her ability to discipline her natural literary talent into the unities that Restoration tragedians took more seriously than had their Elizabethan predecessors. The unities of Restoration tragedy had been adapted and described by its best-known practitioner, John Dryden, to suit the patriarchal royalist ideology that flourished during the first several decades of the Restoration. By virtue of its traditional focus on the plights of important men, of course, Restoration tragedy did not easily incorporate the proto-feminism of the female playwrights of Manley's era. The complaints about 'the excessive warmth' of Manley's *The Royal Mischief*, which may have prevented it from a longer run or a subsequent revival, may have stemmed from its reversal of conventional gender roles, especially as depicted in dramatic tragedy.

In his Preface to *Troilus and Cressida*, John Dryden outlines the traditional purpose of tragedy, which, it had long been understood, should concern men who are in a position of public responsibility. Following Aristotle's *Poetics*, Dryden insists that the tragic hero should be someone 'of the highest Quality ... so that when we see that the most virtuous, as well as the greatest, are not exempt from such misfortunes, that consideration moves pity in us'.[53] The Tory writer of Restoration dramatic tragedy also frequently conveyed a vision of patriarchal passive obedience that underscored the newly reinstated monarchical order. In *All For Love, or the World Well Lost* (1678), Dryden's uses the final speech to reinforce an ideal type of female devotion not emphasized in, for example, Shakespeare's *Antony and Cleopatra*. Shakespeare's final references to Cleopatra are devoted to Caesar's speculation about the method by which she took her life, thus emphasizing her agency in the matter. By contrast, the final speech by Serapion in Dryden's *All for Love* emphasizes Cleopatra's devotion to Antony:

'Th' impression of a smile left in her face, / Shows she dy'd pleas'd with him for whom she liv'd'.[54]

Aphra Behn, a royalist like Dryden and clearly a role model for Manley, wrote about fifteen dramatic comedies but only one tragedy and three tragicomedies for the stage; in other words, she seemed wary of a genre whose Restoration conventions demanded a patriarchalism that she avoided in her comedies, in which she routinely mocked the chivalry and masculinity of Roundheads and Whigs. When Behn turned to tragedy, she often chose the genre of the novel or the novella, where she was able to develop characters less bound by the conventions of patriarchalism and passive obedience. Her novel *Oroonoko: or The Royal Slave, A True History* (1688), for example, depicts a tragic royalist hero and martyr whose murder of his own pregnant wife (so their child will not be born into slavery) is emphasized in Behn's description of the stench of the rotting corpse. Thomas Southerne excised this troubling scene in his popular 1695 stage adaptation of Behn's novella, a production to which Manley alludes in her preface to *The Royal Mischief*. Southerne, a Tory dramatist with whose political views both Behn and Manley would probably have been sympathetic, simplifies Behn's novella so that the tragic royal protagonist simply requests his wife's suicide, which she quickly performs; he then stabs the governor, then himself, in quick succession. In Behn's novella the reader is uncertain how to view Oroonoko: the text evokes sympathy for his plight as exiled and enslaved monarch and yet horror at what he has done. Southerne's revision of Behn's novel into more conventional dramatic tragedy, marked by the swift double-suicide of the lovers, reminds us of the challenge that Behn's novelistic revision must have posed to male Restoration dramatists, Tory and Whig alike.[55] Southerne's *Oroonoko: A Tragedy*, which was performed in November 1695, also includes a misogynistic (ostensibly comic) subplot about two unmarried women so desperate to get married that they travel to Surinam and settle for ridiculously undesirable men.

Before we conclude that it was only men who were threatened by Behn's revision of dramatic conventions, it is important to note that the Whig Catharine Trotter also revised and made less troubling Behn's depiction of gender roles. In her dramatic adaptation of Behn's novella *Agnes de Castro: or, The Force of Generous Love* (1688), Trotter reinscribes some of the patriarchal conventions of the Restoration stage. Trotter makes Agnes a tragic heroine of irreproachable virtue, following the conventions of male Restoration tragedy, whereas Behn's novella implicitly suggests that the heroine may have harboured an adulterous desire for the hero even before his wife was murdered.[56] Given that Trotter contrasts her flawless heroine to the male characters who are, in her drama, never perfect, Trotter might be said to be expressing a more positive proto-feminism than Behn. Aphra Behn, however, seems to have been disinclined to depict women as not quite so pure; she instead asserts a 'truth' about female desire (that it is not always monogamous) that other Restoration dramatists were reluctant to ascribe to their virtuous heroines. Delarivier Manley followed Behn's lead in her depiction of female desire; she was also, therefore, like Behn, obliged to break the gender conventions of Restoration dramatic tragedy.

Whereas Aphra Behn circumvented the conventions of dramatic tragedy most often by telling tragic stories through the form of heroine-centred tragic novellas,[57] Delarivier Manley boldly departed from the conventions for tragic drama in her first dramatic tragedy. First of all, the central focus of Manley's tragedy is not a tragic hero, the conventional 'great man' that Dryden describes, but a tragic heroine, Queen Homais of Phasia, wife of the Prince of Libardian, whose downfall stems from her falling in love with her husband's nephew, Levan Dadian. The play reworks many traditional gender stereotypes, including the romantic trope of a man falling in love with a woman merely from seeing her picture. Here, Queen Homais conceives a desire for her husband's virtuous and recently married nephew after seeing his portrait.[58] Although the nephew subsequently is brought to desire Homais by a portrait of her being shown to him, the desiring male gaze is less central here to the tragedy than Homais's initial expression of desire, which is the engine of the plot that ends with Bassima, Dadian's innocent wife, falsely accused of adultery and poisoned; Bassima's admirer, Osman, caught and stuffed alive into a canon and shot off; Dadian himself brought to commit suicide after he feels guilty for storming his uncle's castle; and finally the unrepentant Homais being stabbed to death by her husband.

The final tragedy is summed up as a visual spectacle of horror narrated by the surviving Prince of Libardian:

> O horrour, horrour, horrour!
> What Mischief two fair Guilty Eyes have wrought;
> Let Lovers all look here, and shun the Dotage.
> To Heaven my dismal Thoughts shall straight be turn'd,
> And all these said Dissasters truly Mourn'd.[59]

As one critic has observed, everything about this play demonstrated excess, which might explain how readily it was mocked in *The Female Wits*:

> No woman had ever been so lustfully wicked as Homais (played by Elizabeth Barry), no heroine so pure as Bassima (Anne Bracegirdle), no hero so faithfully platonic (Thomas Betterton), no husband so duped as the Prince of Libardian (Edward Kynaston), no wife so weakly jealous as Selima (Elizabeth Bowman), no man so easily a prey to lust as Levan Dadian (John Bowman), so much a creature as Ismael (John Hodgon), so vile a tool as Acmat (John Freeman).[60]

Elizabeth Barry apparently had some reservations about playing the lustfully excessive Homais. However, she presumably overcame her scruples and, as Manley attests in *Rivella*, her performance was impressive. Having been given not the usual two but six opportunities for the tragic rant at which she excelled, Barry, as Manley acknowledges in *Rivella*, 'distinguish'd her self as much as in any Part that ever she play'd'.[61]

In her preface to the published play, Manley credits as her source John Chardin's *Travels into Persia*, in which there is an account of Homas and Dadian – who in real life did not suffer tragic consequences for their adultery but reigned together until they died natural deaths. However, as Ruth Herman has pointed out, it appears that Manley borrowed less from Chardin's text than from *The Rival Princesses: or, The Colchian Court: A Novel* (1689), an anonymous novel included in R. Bentley's twelve-volume collection, *Modern Novels*.[62] Some of the excesses of Manley's play ridiculed in *The Female Wits* are in fact drawn directly from this novelistic version of Chardin's story, even the detail about the power of Homais's gaze:

> A Princess more wicked, and more ambitious than any ever was: She is guilty of all
> the Passions a Lover's Breast can be capable of: for such are the regards of her pas-
> sionate, tender, and languishing Eyes, that she never looks but to command Love,
> and inspire Hope.[63]

Audiences apparently reacted strongly to this depiction of female power and lustful gaze; Manley indicates in her preface that the '*principal Objection made against this Tragedy is the warmth of it*'. She herself points out that some of the scenes in Dryden's *Aurege-Zebe* and in Southerne's *Oroonoko* '*have touches as full of natural fire as possible*'.[64] Manley, however, does not make female desire an object of ridicule as Southerne does in his comic subplot about women desperate to get married; rather, Homais's lust is of royal proportions, and she is unrepentant to the last. Instead of realizing her guilt of disloyalty, even treason, against her husband, at the moment that he stabs her, Homais instead begins a final rant, as she is dying, taunting her husband: 'Thou dotard, important in all but Mischief, / How could'st thou hope, at, such an Age, to keep / A Handsome Wife?'. She goes on to complain about the cowardice of her lovers: 'What an effeminate Troop have I to deal with?'. As the rant reaches its emotional climax, Homais embraces the afterlife that she believes awaits her: 'O! I shall Reign / A welcome Ghost; the Fiends will hugg my *Royal Mischief*'. Her final wish is that she had the strength, while dying, to strangle Levan, so that they could 'Thus die together'; unable to muster the strength to do this, in her last breath she puts 'a Curse on Fate and my exspiring strength'.[65] This ending, significantly, punishes the ambitious Homais, even though she was not punished either in real life or in the novel Manley used as her source. In *The Rival Princesses*, the narrator apologizes for the ending, since 'the end of all things ... ought to be a Punishment of Vice, and Reward of Vertue', but, in fact, Homais not only escaped punishment but eventually she had Levan poisoned for her crimes, 'to make room for the Coroation of her Son *Alexander*, and her own Regency'.[66]

Manley coyly suggests in the preface that the *'warmth'* that audiences complain of derives merely from *'the softest'* passion, i.e. love. She admits that she had intentionally stayed away from any stronger passion – such as *'Ambition'* which she realizes would have been *'too bold for the first flight'*.[67] However, here Manley certainly dissembles, for there is nothing delicate about the powerful lustful desire Homais expresses for her nephew. Furthermore, during the brief moment of Homais's triumph before she is slain, she has not only won over (although not yet enjoyed) the lover she desired, but she has also seen the army rise up against her own husband and declare 'Long life the Princess *Homais*'.[68] In fact, in many ways, Manley's Homais is the embodiment of ambition, almost always a negative trait for a Tory – and Manley's revision of the ending in *The Rival Princesses* clearly punishes Homais's ambition, reinforcing a royalist Tory ideology. This ideology is further upheld in Manley's version, since, unlike the real events in history or the version of the story in *The Rival Princesses*, the usurping nephew here realizes his wrongs and falls on his sword. Moreover, as Ros Ballaster points out, Manley reverses Mary Pix's Whig depiction of 'the polygamy and enslavement of the seraglio' in her *Ibrahim, the Thirteenth Emperour of the Turks* (1696), by 'presenting a Persian minister as a version of Oliver Cromwell [the Prince of Libardian] and satirizing Whig/Protestant figures as driven by hidden venal desires that led to the dangerous influence of lust-driven women'.[69] Nevertheless, the fact that the magnificently unrepentant Homais is clearly the strongest character on the stage undercuts the plot's tidy patriarchal Tory resolution.

The Royal Mischief is in some sense a Tory reworking of Elkannah Settle's Exclusionist (Whig) tragedy *The Female Prelate: Being the History of the Life and Death of Pope Joan* (1680), which demonizes the legendary Pope Joan as an ambitious, power-hungry and lustful politician in order to stir up fear of the then heir to the throne, the Catholic James, Duke of York. There is, however, nothing regal, nothing arresting, nothing commanding about Settle's monstrously demonized cross-dressing schemer. She is ruthless and pragmatic, expending more emotional energy on her schemes than on her passion. Of her scheme to seduce an unwitting nobleman, she observes to her co-conspirator: 'Oh, I could hug thee for this rare design / Never was a Night so pleasant, or a Plot / So artful, or so prosperous'.[70] By contrast, Manley's Homais is excessive, but also impressive in her lustful rants. Even though Manley allows her tragic protagonist to die at the end of *The Royal Mischief*, there clearly is no male character who can match Homais's presence on stage. Manley, like her royalist father before her, no doubt understood that raw ambition was an unattractive trait usually associated with ruthless Commonwealthmen or unscrupulous and self-serving Whigs. However, in *The Royal Mischief*, Homais's ambition is given heroic stature; the Prince of Libardian's own soldiers, after all, rally to Homais's cause.

Having Dadian die nobly on his own sword, an appropriate end for a traitor in a royalist universe, leaves the awkward question, however, of who will rule when Homais's ageing and impotent husband dies. In *The Rival Princesses*, the novel on which Manley is drawing, the Prince of Libardian is old but not impotent; rather than leaving Homais lie 'neglected by his side' as he does in Manley's version, he retains an 'amorous' soul in the 1689 novel and Homais bears him a son. The revisions Manley made to the plot of her novelistic source are significant, as Ruth Herman has shown.[71] In Manley's version, the prince himself clearly regrets his nephew's decision to expiate his crimes by suicide; he would have preferred that Dadian live and prove his worth by 'a more just and glorious Reign'.[72] In *The Royal Mischief*, as in *the Lost Lover*, Manley demonstrates the tragic consequences of an age when there are apparently no real heroes left to rule the country.

A question for once loyal supporters of James II loomed large after 1688: what did loyal royalism mean once James II had been replaced by William and Mary? One way of interpreting *The Royal Mischief* is as a critique of the problem for royalists of a weak (hence impotent) monarch, such as James II.[73] Manley herself acknowledges James II's weakness in her *The New Atalantis* (1709), when she renders him as the politically ineffectual Princess Ormia in her satirical retelling of his 1688 flight. Or, perhaps more tellingly, in 1696, under the reign of William III (since Mary II had died in 1694), we might read the impotent prince as William himself. It is not known whether or not William was impotent but Mary never bore him a child, and rumours about his possible homosexual preferences were familiar in opposition political writing. Manley herself would recycle such rumours in her depiction of William and his political favourites, Portland and Albemarle, in *The New Atalantis* (1709). Moreover, while William was an effective military commander, he failed to command the love of the English people, so he might have been seen as impotent in this sense as well.

For the cynical Manley – having been tricked into marriage with a cousin who had been born into the dissenting and Cromwellian branch of the family, but even after becoming Tory would never qualify as a chivalrous Tory hero – the age she inhabited probably seemed empty of true heroes. Manley's decision to end *The Royal Mischief* with no obvious heir to the prince also suggests that she saw no heroic saviour for her country either in the exiled James II or in his son, James Francis Edward Stuart (1688–1766). Rather than yet expressing staunchly partisan political opinions, Manley's second dramatic production demonstrates, more than anything else, stunning political cynicism.

Letters Writen

While her first play was probably being rehearsed for the stage, Manley brought out a brief epistolary account of the stagecoach journey she apparently took to Exeter in June 1694. The ostensible editor of Manley's *Letters Writen by Mrs. Manley*, the J. H. who claims that he was a friend and admirer of Manley's father (who might possibly have been John Hervey), indicates in the dedication 'to the Incomparably Excellent Mrs. Delarivier Manley', that he was publishing it without her permission:

> *whilst Sir* Thomas Skipwith *and Mr.* Betterton *are eagerly contending who shall first bring you upon the Stage, and which shall be most applauded, your Tragick or Comick Strain, I cou'd not refuse the Vanity (my Soul whisper'd to me) of stealing you from the expecting Rivals, and dexterously throw you first into the World, as one that honour'd me with your Friendship before you thought of theirs. Doubtless, you will speak me a vain-glorious Rascal, and unworthy of that Esteem I betray. Perhaps you may most justly object, These Letters which I expose, were not proper for the Publick; the Droppings of your Pen, fatigu'd with Thought and Travel. But let them who are of that Opinion imagine what Ease and Leisure cou'd produce, when they find themselves (as they necessarily must) so well entertain'd by these.*[74]

Although scholars have traditionally taken at face value this unidentified editor's claim that he brought out this publication without Manley's permission, it seems more likely that such a claim was intended as a sales pitch, to suggest that there was something more risqué than there actually was in this brief epistolary collection. At the same time, the suggestion that Manley did not herself sanction the publication also offers her a cloak of modesty, albeit one that is somewhat inconsistent with her confident self-presentation in the prefaces to her published plays.

Manley's first two plays were printed, according to the title pages, for several publishers including the bookseller R. Bentley of Covent Garden. The other publishers listed on these plays include the booksellers F. Saunders and J. Knapton, who, like Bentley, published many other works of drama (as well as a range of other writings); Bentley also published the multi-volume collection *Modern Novels*, which included *The Rival Princesses*, the novel on which Manley based her *Royal Mischief*. The title page of *Letters Writen* indicates that this work was printed for R. B., and it is listed in *The Term Catalogues* as having been printed for 'R. Buts' and having appeared between April and June 1696; however, this is probably incorrect.[75] *Letters Writen* was in fact probably the first of Manley's works to be published, since it was advertised in late February 1696, while her plays were advertised in April and in June.[76] A subsequent advertisement for the printed versions of *The Lost Lover* and *The Royal Mischief* also mentions *Letters Writen* as printed for 'R. Bently'.[77] Bentley, like Knapton and Saunders, who also had shares in her first two plays, was a bookseller who would purchase a work from an author outright (possibly jointly with others) rather than a 'trade publisher', who would help produce and distribute, for a percentage fee, a work still owned by an author or printer, who would share the risks and also the profits.[78]

Most of Manley's subsequent, and more politically risky, works would be published by the trade publisher John Morphew (sometimes jointly with John Woodward), but Manley seems to have sold her first epistolary prose work to Bentley, perhaps on the recommendation of the J. H. who wrote the preface. Since she subsequently also sold her first two plays to the same bookseller, it seems unlikely that Bentley had somehow purchased an unauthorized selection of her letters and brought them out without her permission. He may have chosen to list only his initials on the title page as part of the cloak of confidentiality the preface was designed to convey.

The prefatory suggestion that the letters were published without Manley's permission is not only somewhat implausible but may represent a literary allusion. The dedication to Manley's *Letters Writen* echoes the preface to Catharine Trotter's epistolary novella, *The Adventures of a Young Lady*, which first appeared anonymously as part of *Letters of Love and Gallantry and Several Other Subjects, All Written by Ladies* (1693), better known to later readers by the title under which it was republished in 1718: *Olinda's Adventures: or The Amours of a Young Lady*.[79] The ostensible recipient of some of Trotter's letters, her friend and confidant Cleander, insists in his introductory note to the reader that the letters were 'Writ Extempore, and without any design of Publishing'.[80] He acknowledges that his 'partial kindness for his Friend, made him admire all she said', and he suggests, somewhat implausibly, that the letters from the author were not originally directed to him but 'were sent me in unknown Hands, by the Penny Post'. He also suggests, tantalizingly, as her friend, that one of his reasons for publishing these letters is that he believes they will 'satisfie those who might have the Curiosity to know how she Writ to her Lover, since she Treats her Friend with so much Tenderness'.[81] Trotter, of course, was attempting to supplement otherwise meager family resources by her pen, and she may well have written Cleander's epistle to the reader herself.

In *Olinda's Adventures*, Trotter ruptures many conventions of the seventeenth-century heroic epistolary novel. As a Whig, she also breaks in particular with the tragic heroic style of the Tory Aphra Behn's epistolary *Love Letters Between a Nobleman and His Sister* (1684–7). Rather than a heroine who is innocent, vulnerable and tragically seduced by an ambitious, immoral and (in Behn's novel) Whig nobleman, Trotter makes her heroine a rational agent who mockingly describes a serious suitor whom she does not love and refuses to be seduced by the married aristocrat Coridon, even though she falls in love with him.

In her first prose publication, Manley seems to carry Trotter's revision of heroic epistolary fiction even further. Rather than giving her heroine agency within a courtship – or seduction – plot, Manley circumvents such a plot altogether. The editor's preface to Manley's *Letters Writen* suggests that her tale, like Trotter's, might represent the intercepted love letters of a young woman and her suitor, and Manley's first letter begins with the suggestion that she wished that the person she was leaving behind had tried sooner to persuade her to stay in London. However, the rest of the letters do not really develop the theme of long-distance love, but comprise a witty travel narrative, in which Manley satirically relates the awkward exigencies of stagecoach travel in the 1690s. She describes the coachman, who would 'not stay dressing a Dinner for the King', forcing them to stop and take unappetizing meals at unaccustomed times.[82] She recounts her encounter with a landlord who was 'a Master in the Trade of Foppery' and a boring but flirtatious travelling companion, whose interest she piques by refusing to show any interest in him; she explains, 'He perceiv'd by my Sullenness that I had a great deal of Wit; though I understood he had but little by his Remark'.[83]

Quite unlike the heroine of Trotter's *Adventures of Olinda*, Manley's narrator is not concerned with making a rational moral choice between suitors. She may miss her correspondent in London but his existence in the world will not prevent her from permitting the flirtations of her travelling companion, 'Beaux' (Manley's consistently plural misspelling of 'Beau'). While Manley's narrator may allow the flirtations of this baronet's son she never entertains the illusion that he is to be taken seriously. When, after a few days of travel, this baronet's son becomes less assiduous in his attentions, Manley's narrator is neither surprised nor alarmed, but satirically describes the change in his manner as a not-unlikely result of the rigours of their journey, for which they are roused every morning at 2 o'clock:

> The Fatigue, which he seems more sensible of than any of us, has tarnish'd the Lustre of his Eyes; and, instead of any further Oagling, drowns all his Amorous Pretensions in as profound Sleep as the uneasie Jolting of the Coach will permit.[84]

Manley remains a dutiful correspondent to the person she has left behind in London, although her letters are not filled with pining or love-sickness, but with humorous accounts of her own journey and diverting stories about her fellow travellers. As she explains at the end of Letter II: 'I cou'd not forbear, late as it was, sending you an Account: If you laugh in your Turn, I am paid for my Pains'. Manley continues in a strain that might be interpreted as heroic: "Tis now past Eleven, and they'll call us by Two: Good Night; I am going to try if I can drown in Sleep that which most sensibly affects me, the cruel Separation we have so lately suffer'd'.[85] Manley invokes such a heroic strain of tragic separation only occasionally, and she never sustains it long. However, there is nothing that we might describe as a tone of heroic tragedy in the separation that she and this cor-respondent apparently intended to endure. By the time Manley's narrator arrives in Exeter, she cuts her letter short, in order to read the one she has just received: 'Forgive me for leaving you thus abruptly, since 'tis more pleasingly to entertain my self with a Letter of yours just brought to me'. As she ends this letter, she lets her correspondent know that she will not entirely cut off contact with the flirtatious beau she acquired on the journey: 'I am now got safely, weary, into Exeter; and, I thank God, rid of the Impertinency of my Fellow-Travellers, Beaux excepted, who will see me safe home, tho' distant from his'.[86]

While Catharine Trotter ruptures some of the conventions of Tory tragic-heroic epistolary novels by creating a sensible and rational heroine who steadfastly refuses to be seduced by her married aristocratic suitor, Manley crafts an episto-lary narrator who does not appear to be inviolably in love her correspondent. Manley's narrator is obviously attached to her correspondent, but she will clearly attend to her own needs, allowing men to flirt with her so long as it amuses her (or perhaps proves to her material advantage), but pledging loyalty to no one and maintaining her own rational control over where she will live and how she will conduct herself.

Manley recounts her journey to Exeter in seven letters ostensibly written in June 1694; an eighth letter is included, dated March 1695, in which Manley encloses a letter she claims was written by one Colonel Pack, in the style of 'the Portugal-Nuns', i.e. imitating the popular tragic epistolary collection *Five Love-Letters from a Nun to a Cavalier* (1678).[87] Whether or not the enclosed letter was actually written by Pack, who has not been identified, or by Manley herself as an exercise in stylistic imitation, the overblown mode of heroic tragedy is an impressive rendering of the high heroic style of the original: every page trembles with the accusations of the ruined nun against the indifference of the French cavalier who seems to have seduced and abandoned her but who will never be forgotten by her. The inclusion of a letter in this style in Manley's collection serves to heighten the contrast between Manley's own narrator – who goes into self-imposed exile but never suggests that she is leaving because anyone misled or mistreated her – and heroines of more conventional late seventeenth-century heroic epistolary tragedy.

Catharine Trotter and Delarivier Manley both refute the tragically heroic conventions of works such as Behn's *Love Letters* and the anonymous *Five Love-Letters from a Nun to a Cavalier*. Trotter's particular innovation is in having her protagonist tell her story not through a direct correspondence with Cloridon but by describing her romantic struggles to her platonic friend, Cleander. She insists boldly in her final letter to him that the world is in 'Error' to assume 'that there can be no such intimacy betwixt two of different Sexes without the Passion of Love'.[88] Manley's *Letters Writen* carries this sort of stylistic innovation one step further by including a letter (ostensibly written by a colonel in the military) in the tragic romantic style she avoids in her other letters. We might liken Trotter's rational and moral (proto-feminist) Whig revision of the genre of tragic heroic epistolary love letters to Colley Cibber's reworking the genre of royalist Restoration comedy into Whiggish sentimental comedy. Manley, however, in *Letters Writen* as in her first two dramatic productions, refuses both the tragedy of ruined Tory innocence (even though it is a trope she will later invoke in her own fictional autobiography) as well as the (comic) resolution of rationally conventional Whig virtue.

Manley's *Letters Writen* is a brief and curious set of letters. It gives the impression of being something of a literary experiment, written by someone who was familiar with contemporary epistolary genres but not interested in limiting her literary experimentation to a single mode or style. Through her allusion to the Portuguese nun's *Five Love-Letters*, Manley gestures towards, but refuses, the conventions of standard epistolary courtship plots, either comic or tragic. At the same time, however, Manley makes an allusion to Marie d'Aulnoy's fictitious epistolary travel narrative, *Relation du Voyage d'Espagne* (1691), which first appeared in English translation in 1692 as *Ingenious and Diverting Letters of the Lady — Travels into Spain, or a Genuine Relation of the Religion, Laws, Commerces, Customs, and Manners of that Country*. In some sense Manley's first brief epistolary publication really is a travelogue, but not developed so as to represent a complete picture of an entire nation or culture. Manley in fact calls attention to her intention not to include the sort of lengthy architectural descriptions found in d'Aulnoy's narratives, when she explains to her correspondent:

> I need say nothing to you of *Salisbury*-Cathedral: If in a Foreign Country, as the Lady in her Letters of *Spain*, I cou'd entertain you with a noble Description but you have either seen, or may see it; and so I'll spare my Architecture.[89]

Manley refuses to describe every architectural marvel she passes, but her letters suggest that she nevertheless believed there was as much of interest in a week-long stagecoach journey from London to Exeter as there might be in a noblewoman's ostensible travels around an entire country.

Interestingly, while d'Aulnoy's popular travelogues were apparently generally received by her contemporaries as actual historical accounts, subsequent scholarship has shown that d'Aulnoy borrowed from historical and journalistic sources to describe the countries she claims to have toured.[90] Although Manley seems to have been working from her own experiences rather than from other journalistic sources, she follows d'Aulnoy in mixing the quotidian detail of travel with the serious observation about important political events. Just as d'Aulnoy mingles humorous anecdotes about having her watch swindled from her at an inn with observations on various important political events, such as the signing of the peace treaty of Nijmegen (1678), so Manley combines her witty observations about foppish innkeepers and flirtatious fellow travellers with some serious remarks about the death of General Thomas Tollemache (1651–94), whose body Manley claims was brought to Salisbury the evening the stagecoach Manley was taking passed through that town – i.e. Saturday, 24 June 1694. In fact, Tollemache's body probably did pass through Salisbury on about the day that Manley claims, since he died in Plymouth on 12 June and was buried in Helmingham, Suffolk on 30 June.[91]

Tollemache, who had served under Marlborough before replacing him as lieutenant general in 1692, was a popular hero among Whigs. Manley informs her correspondent of her 'Melancholy' in learning of the death of 'so great a Man',[92] and mentions that she will dine with his 'Secretary', with whom she claims to already have been acquainted, but she does not go into great detail about Tollemache's career or what made him a great man. Manley, however, is clearly not yet styling herself as an overtly partisan writer – and her reflections on Tollemache's death do not have an obviously Tory resonance. Rather, in *Letters Writen* she seems more generally to be establishing her credentials as someone knowledgeable about the political sphere.

Manley begins her first letter with a quotation from George Granville's then unpublished 'An Imitation of the Second Chorus in the Second Act of Seneca's Thyestes':

> *Place me, ye Gods, in some obscure Retreat:*
> *Oh! keep me innocent: Make others Great:*
> *In quiet Shades, content with Rural Sports,*
> *Give me a Life, remote from guilty Court:*
> *Where free from Hopes and Fears, at humble Ease,*
> *Unheard of, I may live and die in Peace.*[93]

The poem from which these lines are taken, which Manley must have known in manuscript form, describes a politician retreating to the country, as a response to 'Factions', 'Wars' and 'Crowns usurp'd'.[94] Granville's 'Imitation' eloquently articulates his own decision to stay out of politics while William and Mary, who 'usurp'd' James's throne, reigned. As a woman, of course, Manley was not at risk of being offered any political appointments (regardless of who was on the throne), and her retreat to the country was probably motivated by financial considerations rather than a more specific partisan political cause. However, her choice to narrate her departure from London in terms of someone else's political retreat reminds us that she saw herself, from a very early age, as an engaged observer of the political events of her day.

Manley not only frames her retreat in political terms but she also uses *Letters Writen* to demonstrate her wide reading in both classical and neoclassical literature. In these letters which she claims to be writing each day in coaching inns either waiting for a meal or before going to bed at night (i.e. presumably without benefit of a library of books), she cites from poems by John Donne (1572–1631) and John Cleveland (bap. 1613, d. 1658), as well as a line from *The Country Mouse* by Abraham Cowley (1618–67). She also makes an allusion to a line in a play by Congreve, refers to an anecdote about Themistocles, and retells the story of 'Amadorus the Helvetian Hero'. It is certainly possible that Manley was drawing these citations and allusions from memory. The lines from Granville correspond quite closely to the poem in its subsequently published form, but the lines from Cowley are slightly misquoted, as they might have been if Manley were working without the original source. It is also likely that Manley reworked drafts of these letters (if they were in fact once real letters sent to a real correspondent) for publication, adding and embroidering citations for literary effect.

Manley mentions in *Rivella* that her father provided her a 'Liberal Education',[95] presumably by allowing her access to his library and encouraging her to read. Apparently she continued this self-education while in London by reading widely and attending the theatre regularly. Through the frequent literary allusions in *Letters Writen*, Manley is clearly attempting to establish her credentials as a literary and political observer. She was also, like Trotter and Behn before her, attempting to make her living by the pen; she therefore needed to demonstrate that her ability to drop relevant political and literary citations was equal to that of most of the male wits and writers around her, even if she was not given the advantages of education that they were.

For all of these attempts at literary endeavours in 1696, Manley did not persist in attempting to produce any more epistolary miscellanies or productions for the stage until late 1706, when her tragedy *Almyna: or, The Arabian Vow* was produced; her second epistolary prose work, *The Unknown Lady's Pacquet of Letters*, appeared the following year. By 1697, however, Manley had at least temporarily ceased trying to make a living by her pen. It could be that she was put off writing for the stage by the criticism of her in *The Female Wits*, which apparently greatly pleased 'the Taste of the Town in General' in the autumn of 1704. However, its run seems to have been halted because it did not please 'some particular Persons', which would indicate that some of the patrons of Manley, Pix, or Trotter – perhaps Devonshire – brought its run to a premature close.[96] Both Catharine Trotter and Mary Pix, who had also been satirized in *The Female Wits* (although not so personally or so pointedly), persevered as playwrights, gaining experience and modest success during the next decade. Manley, however, despite the intervention of whichever patrons or sympathizers had halted the performance of *The Female Wits*, seemed to have been put off writing for the stage.

Although Manley's second play was more successful than her first, it was probably not obvious in the spring of 1696 that she would be able to make a living by writing for the stage. Even the successful comic dramatist Aphra Behn had frequently been short of money. Male dramatists also suffered from the hard fact of how difficult it was to earn much money writing for the theatre, but male writers often had political patrons and political appointments that offered them some form of regular income.[97] Dryden, of course, had enjoyed patronage from the Earls of Mulgrave and Dorset, as well as the posts of poet laureate and historiographer royal. William Congreve was appointed one of the commissions of the malt lottery in 1693, an appointment worth about £100 which was facilitated by his patron, the powerful Whig politician Charles Montagu (1661–1715), Earl of Halifax. Congreve also subsequently held the post (worth £48 per annum) of customs collector at Poole and later he became one of the commissioners for wine licenses, a position worth £200 per annum.[98]

Manley was probably frustrated at the difficulty of making a living by one's pen without the sort of political sinecures enjoyed by successful male writers. She might also have discovered that she was not interested in writing comedies or tragedies that would fulfill the expected conventions of her audiences. It is also likely that Manley was not careful enough in her treatment of the actors and managers of the two London theatrical companies to warrant their producing another of her plays: her next dramatic production, *Almyna*, was produced after a new manager had taken over the Haymarket Theatre.

By 1710, of course, Manley would have found her niche as a writer, in the genres of political secret history and partisan political pamphlets. In 1697, however, she seems not yet to have settled on a genre of writing to which she wanted to devote her energies, nor to have found a coterie of politicians or writers with whom she could join forces. She was clearly cynical about politics and about writing, as well as about the possibility of a woman making a living as a writer. It is not surprising, as is remarked in the preface to the published version of *The Female Wits*, that after the spring theatre season of 1696, Manley seems to have sought (and perhaps briefly found) 'some more profitable Employ'.[99]

5 'SOME MORE [AND LESS] PROFITABLE EMPLOY': 1697–1705

Having apparently lost interest in writing for the theatre and not having yet discovered a prose genre to which she wanted to devote her time, Delarivier Manley seems to have been amenable by late 1696 to other means of making a living. Manley does not tell us what she was doing after the spring theatre season of 1696 ended. By late 1696 or early 1697, however, Catharine Trotter apparently asked for Manley's help in influencing John Manley, who as an MP could interve to assist the incarcerated John Tilly. Tilly had been taken into the 'Custody of a *Sergeant at Arms*' for misdemeanours, presumably as part of the parliamentary inquiry into the management of the Fleet Prison, of which Tilly was warden.[1]

Manley claims that at the time that Trotter made this request, she was living 'in a pretty Retirement, some few Miles out of Town, where she diverted her self chiefly with walking and reading',[2] although she does not tell us how she was supporting herself at this time. We might guess that she was either living frugally on the amount she had earned from the author's benefit of *The Royal Mischief*, that she was receiving some maintenance stipend from John Manley, or that she was staying with a friend, or perhaps with her sister Cornelia.[3]

When Trotter asked for Manley's help, Manley, according to her account in *Rivella*, immediately asked if Trotter and Tilly were lovers. Manley claims not to believe Trotter's denial, although such gossip would not be mentioned in *The Female Wits*, a production that seems to have exposed every known foible of the three women writing for the stage in 1696. The narrator of *Rivella* tells us that because Trotter claimed not to be Tilly's lover, Manley felt she could not trust Trotter's account of her situation and insisted on meeting with Tilly herself before committing to trying to help his case. Whether this was the real reason for her wanting to meet Tilly, or whether she had other motives, Manley explains that she went to meet Tilly, apparently carrying with her a copy of la Rochefoucauld's *Moral Reflections* to read while she waited for her audience with him.[4] Her narrator describes the scene of their meeting as one in which Tilly inadvertently takes the book Manley was reading:

> *Cleander* [Tilly] came to Wait on her, tho' but for two or three Moments till he could
> dismiss his Company, praying her to be easy till he might have the Honour to return;
> during this short Compliment, *Rivella* had thrown her Book upon the Table, *Clean-*
> *der* whilst he was speaking took it up, as not heeding what he did, and departed the
> Room with the Book in his Hand ...[5]

Although in the opening sections of *Rivella* Manley's narrator describes Rivella's physical charms, in this part of the narration Manley clearly emphasizes that
the attraction between her and Tilly was a meeting of minds. Manley's narrator
observes of la Rochefoucauld's work:

> Who that has ever dipp'd into those Reflections, does not know that there is not a
> Line there, but what excites your Curiosity, and is worth being eternally admired and
> remembred? *Cleander* had never met with it before: He form'd an Idea from that
> Book of the Genius of the Lady, who chose it for her Entertainment, and tho' he had
> but an indifferent Opinion hitherto of Woman's Conversation, he believ'd *Rivella*
> must have a good Taste from the Company she kept. He found an Opportunity of
> confirming himself, before he parted, in *Rivella's* Sense, and Capacity for Business as
> well as Pleasure; which were agreeably mingled at Supper ... Behold the beginning of
> a Friendship which endured for several Years even to *Cleander's* Death.[6]

Following the example of Trotter's depiction of her friendship with Cleander
in *Olinda's Adventures*, Manley here also claims the privilege of friendship with
a man, a friendship based on a shared love of intellectual ideas and a shared
appreciation of good business sense. Although Manley and Tilly's subsequent
romance almost certainly involved a physical relationship, Manley's emphasis is
on a rapport that also involved a shared appreciation for philosophical ideas as
well as for creative business schemes.

Manley's narrator in *Rivella* describes Tilly as appealing for his physical
attractiveness as well as for his professional training: 'His Face was beautiful, so
was his Shape, till he grew a little burly. He was bred to Business, as being what
you call in France [following the conceit that the original narrative of *Rivella*
derived from a conversation in French between Manley's narrator and a French
diplomat], one of the long Robe',[7] i.e. trained as a lawyer. As has already been
noted, he was a member of the Inner Temple; in the records of one of the investi-
gations against him, he is described as 'a barrister of Hatton Gardens'.[8] In *Rivella*,
Manley also refers to Tilly's 'Genius for Business',[9] which her narrator claims that
Baron Meanwell (Lord Bath) acknowledged, and this phrase may provide the
most pertinent description of Tilly. He purchased the mortgage of Fleet Prison
in about 1693, following a 1692 act of Parliament authorizing its sale, an act
whose passage Tilly may have helped effect by bribing various members of the
House of Commons.[10] This purchase allowed Tilly to serve as warden of the
Fleet.

For over a decade Tilly managed to run the prison as a lucrative business. In 1708 the repeated lawsuits, petitions and challenges to his position, brought by Colonel Balwin Leighton over a twelve-year period, finally resulted in the wardenship passing to the crown and then being re-assigned to Tilly's challenger (who probably did not intend to govern with less profitable practices). Although Tilly's method of administering the governorship of the Fleet was clearly at best only one step ahead of the law, there may also have been politics involved in the eventual success of Leighton's persistent petitions against him. Leighton had fought for William of Orange in 1688, while Tilly had been accused in 1695, along with Matthew Goodyear, a prisoner in the Fleet, of sedition.[11] Tilly's possible opposition to William III's Whig government may also have made him attractive to someone of Manley's royalist-Tory background.

By modern institutional standards, Tilly would have been deemed a crook and a swindler, although his practice of charging prisoners for their days of liberty (at the rate of between ten and thirty guineas a day) was not unheard of in this era. As one deputy warden explained to a prisoner, as long as he 'could feed Mr Tilly with money, he would have liberty to go where he pleased'.[12] Tilly's innovative trick of putting prisoners in the custody of deputy wardens (some of them prisoners themselves) allowed him further legal deniability against charges brought for a prisoner's escape; moreover, his practice of remortgaging his own mortgage made it legally difficult for creditors to pursue their claims. However, Delarivier Manley's admiration for Tilly's 'Genius for Business' indicates that his schemes for making a quick profit might have struck her, at this point in her life, as a possibly quicker or more practical way of earning a living than by writing. During the five years that Manley was probably involved with Tilly, they seem to have pursued a variety of intriguing and somewhat risky ventures, not all of them legal, and not all of them successful, but Manley's admission of pleasure in Tilly's 'Genius for Business' suggests that she herself enjoyed the process of planning and executing these various 'get-rich-quick' schemes.

After Tilly left Manley to marry a wealthy widow in 1702, Manley continued to attempt to make money in ways clearly inspired by Tilly's own creative business practices. In 1705 she assisted with a fraudulent and eventually unsuccessful palimony suit, employing a criminal from the Fleet as a false witness. Apparently at risk of going hungry at some point after having been left by Tilly, Manley may have persuaded their cook to continue serving her meals; this cook may then have sued Tilly unsuccessfully for maintenance. In October 1705, Manley had reassigned to John Tilly a debt owed for the nursing of children, quite likely hers by Tilly. In December 1705, Manley was imprisoned in the Fleet herself because of her 'Disregard of Her baile' in a lawsuit about which no other details have been discovered.[13] Manley helped organize a collection of poems in recognition of the death of John Dryden, which was published in 1702, and she also cultivated a friendship with the writer Richard Steele during the years she spent with Tilly. However, between 1697 and 1705, Manley seems to have been busy with many things other than writing, and often occupied with schemes that resulted in entanglements with the legal profession.

Mediating for Potential Reward

As an MP who was also a qualified lawyer, John Manley was automatically a member of the parliamentary investigating committee, and his membership is confirmed by historical records.[14] According to Delarivier Manley's account in *Rivella*, he was in fact chair of the parliamentary committee bringing the investigation against the officers of the Fleet, although it has not been possible to confirm or deny this detail. Manley claims that she cleverly managed to surprise her cousin-husband in front of Westminster Hall on the very day when he should have been chairing the meeting to prosecute Tilly. Instead of chairing the meeting, John Manley apparently took her for a drive in a coach so that he would not be seen with her in public by his parliamentary colleagues; only afterwards did he realize that she had in fact tricked him into missing an important meeting:

> THUS was that important Affair neglected, they chose another Chairman for the Committee, which sat that Morning: Cleander was acquitted, with the usual Reprimand, and order'd to be set at Liberty, very much to the Regret of Oswald [John Manley] when he came coolly to consider how scandalously he had abandon'd an Affair of that Importance, and which Lord Meanwell [Lord Bath] had left wholly to his Management.[15]

Whether or not John Manley really was chair of this committee, and whether Delarivier Manley really played as decisive a role as she claims in disrupting the investigation of the abuses in the Fleet, John Tilly was in fact released from custody on 3 February 1697.[16] However, the parliamentary committee apparently found Tilly guilty of abusing his office, since he was released only after being reprimanded and fined. Moreover, the committee's recommendations resulted in 'An Act for the more Effectual Relief of Creditors, in Cases of Escapes, and for Preventing Abuses in Prisons', which was eventually passed in May 1697, albeit with some 'saving' clauses introduced that rendered it less effectual than it was originally intended to have been in preventing the sorts of abuses of which Tilly was apparently guilty.[17]

Manley's focus in *Rivella* is less on the investigation of Tilly (which would not take full effect until he was relieved of his office in 1708, six years after her affair with him ended), than on the scheme that resulted from it: that of John Manley, Delarivier Manley and John Tilly's scheme to become intermediaries in the famously protracted Bath-Albemarle lawsuit. According to Manley's account in *Rivella*, it was John Manley who first suggested that she might seek Tilly's aid in attempting to mediate in the long-running legal battle. He apparently advised her to leave her residence in the country (presumably on the outskirts of London) and take lodgings in London itself. This detail suggests that John Manley might still have been paying his cousin-wife's maintenance, despite the fact that Manley's narrator in *Rivella* claims that she had not seen him 'in some Years'[18] before she surprised him in front of Westminster Hall. It also suggests that despite Manley's subsequently unflattering depictions of her cousin-husband in *The New Atalantis* and *Rivella*, she still had at least some respect for his advice and suggestions at this point. As Manley's narrator explains in *Rivella*, Oswald (John Manley):

> bid her be sure to cultivate a Friendship with *Cleander* [Tilly], who would doubtless come to return his Thanks for the Service she had done him; recommending to her at the same Time, *First*, not to receive the Money which had been promised her, because there were better Views, and which would be of more Importance to her Fortune; and *Secondly*, to leave her House in the Country for some Time, to come and take Lodgings in *London*, where he would wait upon her to direct her in the Management of some great Affair.[19]

The 'great Affair' that John Manley had in mind was no less than using the influence he supposed Tilly had with Ralph, Earl of Montague, to reach some sort of settlement between Montagu, and John Grenville, Earl of Bath, Manley's employer.[20]

John Manley apparently felt that '*Cleander* [Tilly] was the Person that could do Miracles in Point of Accommodation between Lord *Crafty* [Ralph Montague] and Baron *Meanwell* [Lord Bath]'.[21] This gives the impression that, as a member of the parliamentary committee investigating Tilly's management of the Fleet, John Manley might have been impressed with Tilly's ability to manage things profitably and stay slightly ahead of the law. It also reminds us that Delarivier Manley, John Tilly and John Manley (who had no sooner married his first wife than he began mortgaging her property) were all strongly attracted to 'get-rich-quick' schemes. In *Rivella*, Manley's narrator suggests that one of the reasons that both she and John Manley were drawn to the plan to mediate in the lawsuit was it could enable them 'to redeem all the Mismanagement they had both been guilty of in respect of her Fortune'.[22]

Although Manley frequently indicates in her published works that she was an innocent victim of John Manley's schemes and that he was responsible for squandering her inheritance, this passage suggests that one of the reasons she was interested in the scheme, and intent on persuading Tilly to assist them, was that she may have felt some responsibility for mismanaging, or allowing her cousin to mismanage, her inheritance. She also clearly was concerned about providing for the son of their union. John Manley apparently convinced her that they could gain £8,000 (probably an overly optimistic estimate) from successfully mediating in the Bath-Albemarle lawsuit, of which £2,000 would be settled 'after her Death, upon a Son which had been the Product of their Marriage.'[23]

The lawsuit in which the Manley cousins and John Tilly chose to mediate involved the estate of Christopher Monck (1653–1688), second Duke of Albemarle, son of General George Monck (1608–1670), first Duke of Albemarle, whose military leadership made possible the Restoration of Charles II. John Grenville, Earl of Bath and a relation of Monck, had apparently helped persuade Monck to forsake Richard Cromwell for Charles II in 1659. George Monck's son and heir, Christopher, second Duke of Albemarle, was childless and in a will of 1675 he left his fortune and estates to Bath, who was one of the most powerful politicians in Cornwall (as well as the employer and patron of John Manley). The legal validity of this will was seemingly reinforced by a 1681 codicil, which made Bath heir to all of Monck's possessions and also made any further revision of the will more difficult, since it required any new will to be witnessed by six persons, three of whom had to be peers.

Nevertheless, another will was drawn up in 1685, apparently at the insistence of Albemarle's wife, Elizabeth (1654–1734), daughter of Henry Cavendish, second Duke of Newcastle. The Duchess wanted her husband's fortune to descend to Colonel Thomas Monck (d. 1688), elder brother of General George Monck, and his male heirs. There was pressure on Albemarle to appease his wife, who was apparently suffering from bouts of mental illness that her doctors insisted would worsen if she were not appeased. However, Albemarle, who was governor of Jamaica and residing there, seems to have attempted to protect Bath's interests by delaying signing this new will until 1687. When he finally signed it, however, he did so in the presence of only three witnesses, none of whom were peers, thus not meeting his own stipulated requirements for a legally binding revision to the will. Although the second will would seem not to have been valid, its very existence provoked years of lawsuits following Albemarle's death in 1688. Because the legatee of the second will, Colonel Thomas Monck, died in Holland shortly before Albemarle died in Jamaica in October 1688, the dispute concerned the claim of the fourteen-year Christopher Monck (a prisoner in the Fleet at the time of the events described in *Rivella*), eldest son of Colonel Thomas Monck.

Ralph, Earl and subsequently Duke of Montagu, married Albemarle's widow in 1692, apparently disguising himself as the emperor of China to satisfy her insistence (presumably a result of her mental illness) on marrying royalty. Montagu subsequently lost no time in pursuing his own interests through whatever claims he could make in her name to her father's or her deceased husband's estates. One of his legal lines of attack was to press to invalidate Albemarle's will of 1675, an effort that necessarily made him the antagonist of Lord Bath. However, in 1694, Bath and Montagu joined together to resist the attempts of other Monck cousins to challenge the legitimacy of Christopher Monck, eldest son of Thomas Monck and so heir under the 1685 will, but whose father may have been born to George and Anne Monck before they were legally married. The feud between Montagu and Bath eventually resumed, and was not resolved until 1699, when Bath reached separate settlements with Montagu and Monck. However, it would appear that some time between 1697 and 1699, the Manley cousins and John Tilly expended a certain amount of time, effort and money to bring about a settlement between the parties.

As steward of Bath's estates in Cornwall, John Manley was probably keenly aware of the 'vast summes of money' Bath was spending on lawsuits, as well as the substantial amount he was spending on restoring the family seat at Stowe.[24] John Manley knew that it was in Bath's interest to settle matters expeditiously with Montagu and was no doubt hoping to use Tilly's possible influence with Montagu to help reach a settlement. In fact, Tilly claimed not to have any influence with Montagu but he thought he might help Bath reach a settlement with Christopher Monck, since Monck was imprisoned in the Fleet and therefore under Tilly's control. According to the account in *Rivella*, John Manley promised to split the hoped-for £8,000 with his cousin-spouse, with the understanding that she would divide her share with Tilly: 'it was her Business, either to come in for half, or to make what Terms she could with *Cleander*'.[25] John Manley then asked Delarivier to help persuade Tilly to arrange matters with Christopher Monck.

Although Lord Bath apparently was glad of the offered assistance, he was willing to advance only a small sum of money towards Monck's maintenance when Monck was released from prison and persuaded to agree to a settlement. In the meantime, according to the account in *Rivella*, Tilly was obliged to advance credit to his own tailor to accoutre the dandified Monck, and Manley herself was obliged to entertain Monck with extravagant meals and wine at her own expense. However, Ralph Montagu's servants apparently caught wind of the scheme, prompting Montagu to meet privately with Delarivier Manley, whom (according to *Rivella*) he had first met a few years earlier when she was living with the Duchess of Cleveland. As the narrator of *Rivella* explains, Montagu offered her money to help persuade her to take his side of the negotiations and flattered her by telling her that of all the ladies he had known 'he had never found any of so great Ability as her self'.[26] The series of discussions Montagu had with Manley apparently resulted in Lord Bath losing confidence in his intermediaries. Bath then 'clapt up an hasty Agreement with Crafty, without any farther consulting Oswald in the Matter', and Tilly and Delarivier Manley were apparently cut out of the scheme without any reward. Although Manley subsequently felt guilty that she had persuaded Tilly to enter into expenses in a scheme about which he had had doubts from the beginning, she tells us in *Rivella*, that 'he lov'd *Rivella* too well to reproach her with it'.[27]

The story of Montagu, Bath and the expensively attired, hard-drinking Christopher Monck is amusing in Manley's narrative, but it takes up a surprising percentage of the overall work: almost a third of *Rivella* is devoted to this lawsuit. By contrast, only one sentence is allotted to the seven-year period after Manley's relationship with Tilly ended in 1702 and before *The New Atalantis* was published in 1709. Moreover, it is a sentence that tells us nothing: 'AFTER that Time, I know nothing memorable of *Rivella*'.[28] Manley seems to have visited her friend Sarah, née Fyge, subsequently Field, Egerton (1670–1723) in Huntingdonshire in 1704. According to no longer extant records in Doctors' Commons, some time in 1705 Manley apparently assisted in a fraudulent and unsuccessful palimony suit. In December 1705, as was already mentioned, Manley is known to have been held as a prisoner in the Fleet. In 1707 she claims in a begging letter to the Duke of Montagu that an 'execution' had seized all her goods.[29] Another item about which Manley's narrator remains silent is the fate of the children that may have been the result of Manley's liaison with Tilly.

In focusing more on the Bath-Albemarle lawsuit in *Rivella* than on a difficult period in her own life, Manley is able to depict the prominent Whig Ralph Montagu (to whom she had turned for financial assistance in 1707) as cunning, grasping and self-serving, thus continuing, in her 1714 autobiography, the partisan depiction of court Whigs so central to her political propaganda from 1709 to 1713. Manley's focus on the foibles of this Whig peer, of course, also deflects readers' attention away from some of the most difficult years in her own life, those that followed her five years with Tilly. Before turning our attention to this difficult period, however, we must first consider Manley's friendship with Richard Steele, which flourished during the years that Manley spent with Tilly. We shall also consider Manley's foray into formal verse elegies during this time.

'The Pleasure of Retirement' and Friendship with Steele

The five years Manley spent with John Tilly, during which she suggests that she 'tasted ... the Pleasure of Retirement, in the Conversation of the Person beloved',[30] seem to have been satisfying ones. It is significant that even though Tilly left Manley in 1702, after the death of his own wife, to marry the wealthy widow Margaret, née Reresby, Smith, Manley never depicts him in anything but complimentary terms. She seems to have not only enjoyed his company, but also enjoyed their schemes to turn a profit. She, Tilly and Richard Steele at one point apparently joined forces in the elusive quest to turn ordinary metals into gold (apparently paying a scheming alchemist for his efforts and materials), an attempt that was no more successful than their mediation in the Bath-Albemarle lawsuit. The friendship with Steele, however, turned sour apparently shortly after Manley's break with Tilly.

It is not known when Manley first met Richard Steele, but she suggests in *The New Atalantis* that she remembered him from when he was 'but a wretched common Trooper' who 'had the luck to write a small Poem, and dedicates it to a Person whom he never saw' – i.e. John, Baron Cutts (1661–1707), to whom he dedicated 'The Procession' in 1695, and who would become his patron.[31] In her second epistolary publication, which appeared in two parts – *The Unknown Lady's Pacquet of Letters* and *The Remaining Part of the Unknown Lady's Pacquet of Letters*[32] – Manley includes sixteen letters (numbers XII to XXIII in the first part and numbers VII to X in the second part) that appear to be actual letters from Steele, or else close approximations of letters he seems to have sent her between 1697 and 1702. During this period, Manley was Tilly's mistress and Steele was ensign (with the brevet rank of 'captain') of the 2nd footguard, the Coldstream regiment, and busy writing his first plays and pamphlets.[33] Manley seems to have shared with Steele an interest in alchemy as well as literature, and a friendly concern for his romantic intrigues which extended, apparently, to her helping him find a midwife to assist with the birth of an illegitimate child he fathered.

The first letters in this group concern what appear to be Manley, Tilly and Steele's ventures in alchemy, although in Letter XII in *The Unknown Lady's Pacquet* Steele refers to Manley as a 'Muse' and is keen for her to spend Friday evening with him to 'inspire me with your Presence'. He continues: 'you are not only Author of all the elegant things you yourself speak, but of all that others say to you'.[34] In Letter XV, he thanks her for her 'Tenderness in answering my Impertinence with so much Civility' and conveying the news of 'Mrs. *Temperance*'s' (his natural daughter's) decease,[35] which gives the impression that Manley served as his liaison to the midwife who may have placed his natural daughter with a wet nurse. Steele gives the impression that he and Manley had discussed religion when he refers to her as 'so much a meer Deist' for not inquiring whether the child 'that came into the world guiltily, can go out innocently'. In the same letter he also refers to their separate losses in alchemy: 'I believe your Fireman as well as mine is turn'd into Ashes'.[36]

According to Manley's account in *The New Atalantis*, during the period when she and Tilly knew Steele, 'she was mightily taken with *Monsieur*'s Conversation' and gave him credit to her Midwife, for assistance to one of his Damsels, that had sworn an unborn Child to him'. Manley then goes on to explain:

> the Woman was maintain'd till her lying-in was over, and the Infant taken off his Hands, par *la sage Femme* [midwife], for such and such Considerations upon Paper; he had no Money to give, that was before-hand evaporated into Smoke: Still the Furnace burnt on, his Credit was stretch'd to the utmost; Demands came quick upon him, and became clamorous; he had neglected his Lord's Business, and even left his House, to give himself up to the vain Pursuits of Chymistry.

Here Manley emphasizes her kindness to Steele in her attempt to inform him that he was being cheated by the alchemist, despite Tilly's recommendation that it would be better not to tell him of the 'Cheat'.[37]

By the time that Manley was writing *The New Atalantis*, of course, she had long since fallen out with Steele, and her description of the scene in which she takes him aside to advise him to extricate himself from the money-draining alchemical operations is highly mocking, placing him at the level of a female gossip present at her lying-in:

> the Lady was then in Childbed, among a merry up-sitting of the Gossips, *Monsieur* made one his Genius sparkled amongst the Ladies, he made Love to 'em all in their turn, whisper'd soft things to this, ogled t'other, kiss'd the Hand of that, went upon his Knees to a fourth, and so infinitely pleas'd 'em, that they all cry'd he was the Life of the Company; the sick Lady was gone to repose her self upon her Bed, and sent for *Monsieur* to come to her alone, for she had something to say to him ...[38]

Manley continues this description by suggesting that Steele thought she was in love with him:

> vain of his Merit, he did not doubt but she was going to make him a passionate: Declaration of Love, and how sensible she was of his Charms; he even fancy'd she withdrew, because possibly she was uneasie at those Professions of Gallantry he had been making to others; he approach'd the Bed-side with all the Softness and Submission in his Air, and Eyes, all the Tenderness he well knew how to assume; the Lady desir'd him to take a Chair, and afford her an uninterrupted audience in what she was going to say; this confirmed him in his Opinion, and he was even weighing with himself, whether he should be kind or cruel, for the Lady was no Beauty, but lay all languishing in the becoming Dress of a Woman in her Circumstances. She entertain'd him very differently from what he expected; in short, she discover'd the Cheat, and advis'd him to take care of himself, and to withdraw from that Labyrinth he was involv'd in, as well as he could; he was undone if he sold his Commission.[39]

The gist of Manley's complaint against Steele, whom she represents as 'Monsieur Le Ingrate' (Mr Ungrateful) in *The New Atalantis*, is that he was never adequately appreciative of her kindness in extending credit with her midwife or warning him against the alchemist whom Tilly had discovered was a fraud. She points out also that 'she prevented him several times from being persecuted by the implacable midwife; he us'd to term her his *Guardian-Angel*, and every thing that was Generous and Human'.[40]

Manley's subsequent public venom towards Steele is difficult to explain by the cause she alleges – that he once refused to loan her a small sum of money to leave London (some time after Tilly had married Smith). This is Manley's version of the incident in *The New Atalantis*:

The Lady [Manley] who had serv'd him, lost her Husband [Tilly, when he married someone else], and fell into a great deal of Trouble; after she had long suffer'd, she attempted his Gratitude by the demand of a small Favour, which he gave her assurances of serving her in; the demand was not above ten Pieces, to carry her from all her Troubles to a safe Sanctuary, to her Friends, a considerable distance in the Country; they were willing to receive her if she came, but not to furnish her with Mony for the Journy: He kept her a long time (more than a Year) in suspense, and then refus'd her in two Lines, by pretence of incapacity; nay, refus'd a second time to oblige her with but two Pieces upon an extraordinary Exigency, to help her out of some new Trouble she was involv'd with.[41]

We do not know when Manley asked these favours of Steele, but presumably some time during her troubled years between 1702 and 1708, nor do we know where she was headed in the country. She might have asked Steele for money to travel to visit the Egertons, whom she probably visited in the summer of 1704; she might otherwise have asked Steele for money for the trip to Bristol, which she probably took some time between 1702 and 1707. In a letter to Manley written in September 1709, in response to a letter she wrote to him responding to his unflattering comments in the previous issue of the *Tatler* about the 'artificial Poisons convey'd by Smells' by the author of *The New Atalantis*, Steele insists that 'I had not money when you did me the favour to ask a loan of a trifling sum of me'; moreover, he asserts that he was in fact grateful 'for the Kind Notice you gave me when I was going on to my Ruin'.[42]

As attached as Manley apparently was to Tilly, her friendship with Steele seems to have developed into something of an intensely romantic flirtation: they shared a love of poetry, wit and writing, as well as a love for intellectual discussion and romantic gossip. Manley admits to giving advice to Steele that Tilly would have preferred she did not give him. Furthermore, Steele, during this era, wrote several verses with romantic references to Manley, including 'Anacreontique *to* Delia *on New-years-day*' in which he wishes 'Dear Time into her Breast inspire / Tender Grief and soft Desire'.[43] In 'On his Mistress: By a parson', a poem probably written some time between January and May 1702, Steele compares Delia to the other women he admires and concludes

> But in my *Delia* all Perfections meet,
> All that is Just, Agreeable, and Sweet,
> All that can Praise and Admiration move,
> All that the Bravest and the Wisest love.[44]

As Dolores Duff has suggested, Manley may have hoped for a romantic involvement with Steele, following Tilly's marriage to Smith. Duff speculates that the intensifying friendship between Manley and Steele might explain Manley's apparent 'indifference to the selfish shifts of Tilly'.[45]

Steele's flirtatious poems and letters to Manley suggest that he may have sought her as a mistress. However, since their friendship is believed to have ended soon after Tilly left Manley, it could have been that Steele was interested in a flirtation with Manley only while she was otherwise being provided for as the mistress of another. Steele's published comment, years later, in an issue of the *Guardian*, in response to an attack on him by the *Examiner* (a periodical written sometimes by Jonathan Swift and sometimes by others, including Manley), suggests that there may once have been the possibility of a romantic intrigue between them: 'it is nothing to me whether the *Examiner* writes against me in the character of an estranged Friend [Swift], or an exasperated Mistress [Manley]'.[46] However, to the original insult of suggesting that Manley had once been his mistress, Steele adds further insult in a subsequent issue: 'I declare then it was a false report, which was spread concerning me and a lady, sometimes reputed the Author of the Examiner; and I can now make her no Reparations, but in begging her Pardon, that I never lay with her'.[47]

Here we see the Whig *Guardian* and the Tory *Examiner* exchanging barbs as part of a strongly partisan pamphlet war. In other words, we should remember that the venomous exchanges between Manley and Steele often had a partisan edge, if not an entirely partisan origin. Moreover, as familiar as Manley was with such men as the womanizing Skipwith and Devonshire (not to mention her own bigamous cousin-husband), it seems improbable that she really would have expected much from the flirtatious Steele, especially since she was aware of Steele's inconstancy and frequent insolvency. It could not have come as a surprise to her that Steele, like Tilly, would marry for money – which he did in 1705, when he married his first wife, the wealthy widow Margaret, née Ford, Stretch (d. 1706) who owned valuable estates in the Barbados.

It is important to remember that the public feud between Manley and Steele did not begin until 1709, when both were political writers, committed to opposite parties. Manley's decision to publish the letters she intimates that Steele sent her (possibly either from copies of them she retained – edited as she saw fit – or recreated from memory) in her *Unknown Lady's Pacquet* in 1707 was probably motivated by the thought of pressing creditors and by the recognition that collections of 'found manuscripts' of letters were popular and therefore of interest to booksellers. Merely by including his rather charming letters to her in this collection (none of which were identified as having been written by 'St—le' until the second instalment, *The Remaining Part of the Unknown Lady's Pacquet*) does not in itself yet suggest a feud. We should also remember that no matter how insulting Manley and Steele may have been to each other publicly, Manley certainly still considered Steele a reliable enough friend to request his assistance when she was apprehended for libel in 1709.[48] However, long before Manley would turn to partisan propaganda, she tried her hand at a more traditional literary genre, while she was still involved with Tilly – a collection of elegiac poems in honour of one of the most recognized Tory writers of his era, John Dryden.

The Nine Muses

Between 1697 and 1702, while busy attempting to mediate in lawsuits and dabbling in alchemy, Manley also apparently maintained some contact with the world of literary publishing. There is evidence to suggest that she helped organize *The Nine Muses*, which was published in October 1700, a collection of poems on the death of John Dryden (who died in May) with poems attributed to Manley, Catharine Trotter, Mary Pix, Sarah Field (subsequently Egerton), Susanna Centlivre (bap. *c.* 1669, d. 1723), and Lady Sarah Piers or Pierce (fl. 1697–1714), among others. The elegy by 'Melpomene: The Tragick Muse' and the elegiac pastoral dialogue by 'Thalia: The Comick Muse' are both attributed to 'Mrs. M-----', presumably Manley. Catharine Trotter's contribution appears under the pseudonym 'Calliope: The Heroic Muse'; Pix ('Mrs. M. P.') contributes as 'Clio: The Historick Muse', Field (Mrs. S. F.) as 'Erato: The Amorous Muse', Lady P----- (i.e. Piers) as 'Urania: The Divine Muse'.[49] As is suggested by these pseudonyms, the various elegiac styles included in this collection are all replete with classical and mythical allusions, suggesting that the women involved were keen to demonstrate their education and their ability to follow the poetical models of their era.

The allusive style evident in Manley's contributions to *The Nine Muses* represents a natural continuation of her development as a writer following her *Letters Writen*, which is embroidered with citations of poetry and allusions to other works of literature. Writing in the voice of Melpomene, the tragic muse, in the first poem included in the collection, Manley asks her sister muses to comfort each other as 'Each weep her Fav'rite's loss with Tears Divine'. Melpomene then alludes to Dryden's own elegies, for John Oldham, Anne Killigrew, the Earl of Abington and Charles II, not neglecting to give *herself* credit, as his tragic muse:

> Who sang fair *Killigrew*'s untimely fall,
> And more than *Roman* made her Funeral.
> Inspired *by Me*, for me, he cou'd Command,
> Bright *Abington*'s rich Monument shall stand
> For evermore, the Wonder of the Land.
> *Oldham* he snatch'd from an ignoble Fate,
> Chang'd his cross Star for a more fortunate

> The Monarch *CHARLES* he has divinely Sung
> Well I remember, when my Graces hung
> On each inchanting Accent of his Tongue.[50]

Manley goes on to sing Dryden's praises in hyperbolic couplets typical of neoclassical elegies: 'Fixt, like the Sun, Superiour and alone, / His Glories o're inferiour Beings shone'.[51]

This elegy in the voice of Melpomene demonstrates that Manley could discipline her verse to the conventions of a neoclassical genre, and it reminds us that, although her political secret histories move far beyond the conventions of neoclassical dramatic or lyric poetry, she was capable of adhering to standard formal conventions of a genre when she chose. In her comedy *The Lost Lover*, Manley mocks a character named 'Orinda, an Affected Poetess', clearly intended as a caricature of Catharine Trotter, for her classical erudition. However, at some level Manley no doubt admired such erudition and might have been glad to have had the classical training to have emulated it. Moreover, Manley's two poems in *The Nine Muses* demonstrate at least as much talent and diligence in preparation as Trotter's contribution to the same collection. Manley's verse also adds a predictable touch – familiar from her father's moments of epistolary braggadocio – of repeatedly giving herself credit, as Melpomene, for Dryden's own skill as an elegist.

In her pastoral 'On the Death of John Dryden' written in her guise as Thalia, the comic muse, Manley demonstrates her ability to imitate the conventions of pastoral elegy. She stages a dialogue between traditional characters in pastoral poetry – Alexis, Daphne, Aminta and Thalia – that echoes the structure of Dryden's own 'On the Death of Amyntas: A Pastoral Elegy', which is written as dialogue between Damon and Menalcas. In Manley's poem, Alexis asks Daphne to explain why she mourns, and Daphne explains 'Our Bard is lost, our great *Apollo*'s Dead'. Deploying the traditional heroic couplets that Dryden himself used in his elegies, Thalia sings Dryden's praises: 'What Strength, what Wit, what Learning in each part, / Here to the Soul he speaks, there to the Heart'.[52]

The Nine Muses was dedicated to Charles Montagu, Earl of Halifax, Lord of Treasury from 1697 to 1699 and a member of the powerful Whig Junto in the late 1690s, as well as a writer and patron of the arts. The dedication might seem an odd choice for Manley, who would mock Montagu in *The New Atalantis* as 'the *Mecenas* [Maecenas] of the Age', dismissing his reputation for patronage as 'an honour acquir'd with little Expence, where few or none are found to contest it with him'.[53] Of course, the dedication to Halifax was not written by Manley, but by the bookseller of *The Nine Muses*, Richard Bassett, a regular publisher of poems and plays who apparently hoped to profit from Halifax's respect for Dryden, which Basset approvingly observes that he had demonstrated by 'contributing so largely towards His Burial'.[54] In other words, the commercial reality behind Manley's point – that patronage for poetry was less available in the competitive era of booksellers and print publications than it had been in earlier eras of court patronage – probably underlay Bassett's decision to dedicate the book to Halifax. Whether or not Bassett or any of the contributors to this edition received any monetary recognition for the dedication is not known; however, it seems somewhat unlikely that Manley received anything from Halifax, given her subsequent mockery of him in *The New Atalantis*. In fact, Halifax had seen his income reduced by £1,500 per year following his wife's death in 1698 and so had fewer resources for patronage than in previous years.[55]

Although Dryden was strongly Tory, his skill as a poet and position as poet laureate probably persuaded the staunchly Whig Halifax to offer support for his funeral, which apparently prompted the dedication to him by Manley's bookseller. *The Nine Muses*, however, did not mark the last time that Manley (or her publisher) would ever seek patronage from a Whig. In 1707, she would dedicate her tragedy *Almyna: or, The Arabian Vow* to Elizabeth Montagu (1674–1757), Countess of Sandwich, and Manley would also seek financial support from Ralph, Duke of Montagu, a powerful Whig peer, for the same play.

When Manley turned to more pointed political publications, of course, she would seek the patronage of Tories: she dedicated both volumes of *The New Atalantis* to Henry Somerset, second Duke of Beaufort, a staunch Tory and a Jacobite sympathizer. While the first volume of *Memoirs of Europe* would be mockingly dedicated to her former friend the Whig journalist Richard Steele, the second volume was dedicated to the strongly Tory courtier Abigail, née Hill, Lady Masham (*c.* 1670–1734), an attendant to Queen Anne who had, by 1709, replaced the Whig Sarah Churchill as Queen Anne's closest female confidant and advisor. Manley's final work, *The Power of Love in Seven Novels*, would be dedicated to Lady Mary, née Villiers, Lansdowne (d. 1735), wife of George Granville, by then Baron Lansdowne, whom Manley had long admired for his Tory politics as well as his skill as a poet and dramatist. However, before Manley would find her niche as a Tory propaganda writer, and seek the patronage of prominent Tory politicians, she suffered setbacks in her personal life after her relationship with John Tilly ended. About this period, however, she herself offers us, in her published writings, only carefully selected tidbits of information.

Carefully Selected Information

In the anonymous and undated letters (either real or written to look real) that comprise Manley's second epistolary publication, *The Unknown Lady's Pacquet of Letters*, one correspondent describes circumstances very similar to Manley's own experience when her lover John Tilly married a wealthy widow in order to pay his debts. This anonymous correspondent tells us that she first tried to lose herself in 'Diversions of the World', but then fell seriously ill and left London to recover in the country, returning two years after her lover's marriage (presumably about 1704), only to discover herself still attracted to her apparently unhappily married ex-lover, whom she describes as 'too dangerous for my Conversation'.[56] According to this account, she eventually left London again (no date is given) to stay in Bristol, lodging with a gentleman's family that had been recommended to her. She humorously recounts in several letters in *The Unknown Lady's Pacquet* her mocking satire of Mrs Wouldbe, her landlady, and her flirtations with the landlady's brother.

As in *Rivella*, however, in *The Unknown Lady's Pacquet* Manley recounts certain amusing anecdotes about events in her life, but, not surprisingly, avoids mention of certain other probable events and circumstances. Although scholars have assumed that Manley went to Bristol in 1704, shortly after her return to London, and two years after her breakup with Tilly, we do not know exactly when she went or with whom she lodged when she was there.[57] The date of 1704 suggested for the trip to Bristol is not given in the letter cited above and seems to derive from Manley's own reference to her return to London two years after having originally left it (presumably in 1702, following Tilly's marriage to Smith). It seems likely that she would have fled to Bristol in late 1705 or early 1706, whenever she was released from the Fleet (where she was imprisoned in December 1705), following a difficult year in which she had apparently quarrelled with her friend Sarah Egerton (one of the contributors to *The Nine Muses*) and had been unsuccessful in assisting another friend in a false palimony suit. Why Manley would have chosen to flee to Bristol remains something of a mystery.

John Tidcomb, who is identified in the key as Lovemore, the narrator of Manley's *Rivella*, had an estate in Calne, Wiltshire, which is about thirty miles from Bristol. In *Rivella*, Lovemore claims that he offered Manley asylum at his country estate when she was dismissed as the companion of the Duchess of Cleveland in 1694. Although we do not know whether Manley knew Tidcomb in 1694 (or, in fact, whether she knew him at all), if the alleged offer of asylum at Calne had been made not in 1694 but in 1704 or 1706, Manley might have perhaps refused the invitation but accepted Tidcomb's recommendation of affordable lodging in nearby Bristol. It may have been at this point that Richard Steele would or could not to lend her money for travel fare. Bristol, of course, is also not far from Badminton, the estate of the Dukes of Beaufort, but it seems unlikely that Manley would have had any acquaintance with Beaufort before her dedication to him in 1709, if she ever did afterward. Between 1702 and 1708, however, because Manley had not yet established herself as a Tory party writer, if she did receive assistance from someone with an estate near Bristol, it seems more likely that this would have come from a womanizing Whig army officer such as Tidcomb than from a Jacobite-Tory peer. Her trip to Bristol probably was not connected to her acquaintance with John Hervey, who was not made Earl of Bristol until 1714, and whose estates were mostly in Suffolk, nowhere near Bristol.

We may not know exactly when Manley went to Bristol, but letters V to IX in *The Unknown Lady's Pacquet of Letters* suggest that Manley spent the winter and early spring of 1704 in London, living with someone she refers to as her 'Spouse', and that she went to visit the poet Sarah Egerton in Buckinghamshire in the spring of 1704. Although these letters are neither dated nor signed (nor are they specifically addressed to Egerton, although the reference of visiting her in the country accords with the mention of Manley's visit to the Egerton in *The New Atalantis*), their author (presumably Manley) refers to plays that were being produced and printed in London. These include Joseph Trapp's *Abra-Mule: or, Love and Empire*, which was performed in mid-January 1704 and published at the end of the month, and John Dennis's *Liberty Asserted*, which was produced in late February 1704, and whose first performance Manley anticipates in Letter VI, although she is not certain that she will be able to attend it.[58]

Manley indicates in these letters that she has been confined at home for the last month because of 'Mr — —'s illness'; she refers in the same letter to 'my Spouse's illness' and to the 'ever charming —', an acquaintance 'whose Conversation will recompence the greatest Fatigue'.[59] We do not know who this ill 'Spouse' might have been. It is possible that Manley was looking after her cousin John Manley, with whom she had probably not cohabited in ten years. The choice of the term 'Spouse' (the term she uses in *Rivella* for her cousin-husband) and the reluctance she expresses for being confined to playing card games with the invalid, rather than attending the theatre, might indicate that she went to John Manley's house when she returned to London in 1704, because she simply had no other place to go. It is also possible that John Manley had stepped in to assist her when she fell ill following Tilly's marriage and might have helped her find a place to recuperate 'in the Country'[60] before her return to London. The 'ever charming —' might be Tilly, whose conversation she seems to have found 'dangerous' on her return to London in 1704. If the 'Spouse' in these letters is not John Manley, it could conceivably refer to some other lover about whom we have no other information. In either case, according to the exchange of letters, Manley was busily making arrangements to leave this 'Spouse' for a two-month visit to stay with her correspondent, presumably Sarah Egerton, in the country.

Although, according to the letters recorded in *The Unknown Lady's Pacquet*, both Manley and Egerton were looking forward to the visit, it would appear that it did not turn out to the satisfaction of either. In *The New Atalantis*, Manley mocks the Egertons for their frequent arguments, recounting (or inventing) a scene in which Sarah Egerton threw a hot apple pie at her husband.[61] She also suggests in this account that she and Sarah Egerton quarrelled. Something Manley said to her friend was apparently so ill received that Egerton offered 'voluntary Evidence in a Law-Suit against her, of all the Discourse they had had together in freedom, and by adding a great deal of false to the true, made her lose her Cause'.[62] Scholars have assumed that Egerton foiled Manley's attempt to assist Mary Thompson in a palimony suit brought to Doctors' Commons. Although this is certainly possible, it is also conceivable that Egerton could have interfered in another lawsuit in the Court of Chancery, about which there is even less information, as will be discussed in the next section.

We do not have precise evidence of how Egerton intervened in Manley's concerns at law. However, there is evidence that Manley conspired with a Mary Thompson, formerly mistress to the recently deceased Mr Pheasant, of Upwood, Huntingdonshire, to bring a suit in Doctors' Commons demonstrating a marriage between Thompson and Pheasant so that Thompson could establish a right of dower out of Mr Pheasant's estates. Manley apparently would have secured an annuity of £100 per annum for her assistance with the lawsuit. According to records for Doctors' Commons that no longer survive but are cited in a footnote to a late eighteenth-century edition of Steele's correspondence, Manley and Thompson's scheme, quite possibly hatched with assistance from John Tilly, was to have Edmund Smith, then a prisoner in the Fleet, forge a marriage entry for Thompson and Pheasant's alleged marriage and appear as witness in the case, claiming to have been a witness to their wedding, which they claimed was performed by Dr Clever, a clergyman known to perform 'Fleet weddings' (i.e. ones taking place outside the jurisdiction of the established church and parish, many of which were performed on the grounds of Fleet Prison). Evidence from the 1705 suit brought to Doctors' Commons indicates that the suit was not successful, because of the reputations of the persons involved and because Smith did a poor job in forging Pheasant's signature.[63] Once this scheme had failed, Manley apparently fell into further difficulties, although none of these are mentioned in *Rivella* or in the autobiographical sections of any of her other writings.

Not Mentioned in Her Published Works

According to a preface to the fourth edition of *Rivella*, published shortly after Manley's death in 1724 as *Mrs. Manley's History of her Own Life and Times*, the bookseller Edmund Curll describes the circumstances that ostensibly first led Manley to write an account of her life. Although we do not know if this preface represents what actually happened, the narrative he outlines is certainly plausible.[64] He explains:

> In the year 1714 Mr. Gildon, upon a Pique, the Cause of which I cannot assign, wrote some Account of Mrs. Manley's Life, under the Title of, The History of Rivella. Author of the Atalantis. Of this Piece, Two Sheets only were printed, when Mrs. Manley hearing it was in the Press, and suspecting it to be, what is really was, A severe Invective upon some Part of her Conduct, she sent me the following Letter ...

Curll goes on to explain that Manley wrote asking to meet with him to discuss this publication; following this, they arranged to meet with Gildon and, as Curll explains, 'all Resentments between them were thoroughly reconciled'; Gildon agreed to 'a Total Suppression of all his Papers; and Mrs. Manley, as generously resolved to write The History of her own Life, and Times, under the same Title which Mr. Gildon had made Choice of'.[65]

In this explanation of the ostensible provenance of Manley's autobiography (in which he does not mention that it would have been greatly to his own advantage to publish something written by the best-selling Mrs Manley), Curll sounds a note of innocence, claiming not to know what might have inspired Gildon to write or himself to publish what presumably would have been a narrative damaging to Manley's reputation. In his explanation, Curll disingenuously ascribes Gildon's intent to some presumably personal 'fit of Pique', thus leaving out the most obvious explanation for Gildon's planned attack on Manley – her role as Tory satirist. Charles Gildon was a not only a Whig, but his patron was Arthur Maynwaring, who served as political secretary to the Duchess of Marlborough – mother-in-law of Secretary of State Charles Spencer (1675–1722), third Earl of Sunderland, at whose request Manley was apprehended and questioned for writing The New Atalantis.[66]

Manley had, to some extent, insulated herself from a direct attack on her irregular marriage to her first cousin by having told a version of that part of her life in her New Atalantis, in which she portrays herself as a naive and innocent victim of an older cousin who had masqueraded as a widower in order to seduce her. She had also referred openly in that work to her 'wretched Son ... the errors [of whose] birth glared full upon [her] Imagination'.[67] In Rivella Manley had likewise referred to 'a Son which had been the Product of that Marriage'.[68] Gildon almost certainly would have mentioned her relationship with John Tilly, but this relationship was already well known, and in any case Manley had already alluded to it in The New Atalantis when she referred to herself as the 'airy wife' of a character easily identifiable as Tilly.[69] Taking over the task of writing her biography from Gildon, Manley, in Rivella, simply acknowledges the scandal and the gossip that spread about it. Referring to herself (through the voice of an adoring male narrator) she explains that 'she was made the Town Talk by her scandalous Intriegue with Cleander'.[70] If Manley had already acknowledged in print two irregular relationships and one illegitimate child, we might well wonder what else there was in her personal life or her 'Conduct' that Charles Gildon might have felt warranted such 'severe Invective' as alluded to in the version of her story that he and Curll had promised the public? In other words, if Manley had already been so open and forthcoming about her experiences in her own satirical writing, would there have been anything else she might not have wanted to reveal?

Certain early eighteenth-century gossip may give some indication of the nature of the attack that Gildon may have been planning. A note in Mary, Lady Cowper's papers in the Hertfordshire Archives recounts gossip about Manley which Mary, née Clavering, Cowper, the second wife of William, Lord Cowper, a staunch Whig and Lord High Chancellor of Great Britain from 1707 until 1710, apparently considered important enough to jot down neatly on a sheet of paper and preserve for posterity. The note, not addressed to anyone, but simply dated 14 February (in a file of documents classed by archivists as dating from 1714 to 1718), Mary Cowper relates what she had heard about Manley, by way of explaining Manley's motives for having maligned the Cowpers so mercilessly in her *New Atalantis*:

> A Clergy man told me this
> De la Riviere Manley Authoress of ye Atalantis was the Daughter of an apple woman in St. Andrews Holbourn[.] She gave herself ye name for the beauty. Shee married John Manley Esq, at ye time his first wife was alive in Cornwall (tho the first was an old woman). She had a son by him.[71]

The information about the previous wife and the son, of course, Manley had already conveyed in *The New Atalantis*. Manley also had already referred to her relationship with 'Tilly of ye fleet' (as he is described in Lady Cowper's paper). Nowhere does Delarivier Manley suggest that her husband was jealous of Tilly, but Lady Cowper's source suggests that '[John] Manley would have hanged Tilly but that Tilly having taken her for his mistress by her kept Manley in awe, for by her means he could have hanged him for having 2 wives'. Bigamy, which had previously been an ecclesiastical offence, was made a felony in England during the reign of James I and was punishable by hanging – although the literate generally pleaded 'benefit of clergy' and so avoided hanging and also often avoided the lesser penalty of being burnt in the hand.[72] Of course, if John and Delarivier Manley had been wed in a non-standard ceremony, itself of dubious legal validity, then bigamy might have been difficult to prove.

Lady Cowper's source also adds another detail which Delarivier Manley herself never mentions, but which is not entirely implausible:

> She had 3 bastards by Tilly wch he put out to Nurse to a Fellow that had outlived all his Creditors & got out of ye fleet & they now are all 3 alive in a Cellar in fetter lane, they are 3 red haird boys & ye man begs wth y^m. After Tilly she was kept by the Cook y^t Tilly had given her credit upon for when[?] she wanted to eat. The Cook sued Tilly in the Ct of Ch: for her board after he had left her & had forbid the Cook to trust her. Mr Frances Cowper was Tillys Council & the Cook and Mrs. Manley were cast. W^{ch} ws the reason of her spight to the family of the Cowpers.[73]

Lady Cowper's papers reprsent an undeniably biased source, for in *The New Atalantis* Manley had recounted at length scandalous gossip about both the murder trial of Spencer Cowper for the drowning of a Quaker girl believed to have been his mistress and an alleged extramarital affair by his brother William, Lord Cowper. The brothers, in Manley's narrative Mosco and Hernando Volpone (or, the fox, a derogatory name familiar from much political satire of the period), are depicted as vicious and amoral rakes, perfectly capable of seducing innocent girls and either abandoning or, if necessary, drowning them when they began to seem troublesome. From Manley's point of view, the cunning and immorality indicated by the personal lives of the Cowper brothers would have helped tarnish the reputation of an extremely powerful Whig family, one in a long list of powerful political families whose reputation she tarnishes in *The New Atalantis*.

The clergyman who related the denigrating account of Manley to the second Lady Cowper (who would have been very young herself during the years when the Cowper brothers' scandals occurred and who had not yet married William Cowper at the time that Manley was living with Tilly), was presumably a loyal friend of the Cowpers. This unnamed cleric was clearly assisting the family in denigrating the person who had attacked them.[74] In fact, there is a certain symmetry in the clergyman's account of Manley's family and Manley's account of the Cowper family: each begins by casting aspersions on the parentage (or the parental morals) of the person in question and ends with an account of that person's illegitimate children. It would be tempting to assume that the clergyman recounting Manley's story to Lady Cowper is as wrong about Manley's progeny as about Manley's ancestry. Manley was certainly not the daughter of an 'apple woman'. However, while the unidentified clergyman's account of her parentage is entirely erroneous, the gossip the clergyman relates about Manley's children by Tilly may not necessarily be so far-fetched.

Another piece of archival evidence also points to children by this relationship. A torn and somewhat illegible document in the London Metropolitan Archives, from the Middlesex Sessions of the Peace for 1705, acknowledges that 'Dela Riviere Manley stands [missing words?] indebted to Mr. George Haynes in ye sum of thirty pounds for Nursing her Children'. The precise intent of the note, which is dated 4 October and signed by Manley, is difficult to follow, because of missing portions of the paper. However, the document indicates that Manley acknowledges that 'John Tilly has [had?] given out [missing words] for the said thirty pounds of Debt'. Too many words are missing to be certain; however, this presumably refers to security that Tilly promised. Manley also asserts that she 'does promise to give [missing words] to Mr. Tilly any share[?] [illegible and missing words] for that [illegible word] Enbaling him to obtain ye same fr[om?] [missing words] the sd. Mrs. Manley ...'.[75] While the details of the financial agreement are somewhat obscure, the fact that Tilly apparently took at least some responsibility for this debt provides some circumstantial evidence of his paternity of the children being raised by Haynes.

That 'children' are mentioned in the plural in the account in Lady Cowper's papers is consistent with the note Manley herself signed, as is the detail about their nurse being male. Manley's being 'cast' at law by Tilly may seem somewhat inconsistent with her generally positive depictions of him in *Rivella*. However, another document in the London Metropolitan Archives indicates that in December of 1705 Manley was 'A Prisoner in the Fleet'. The note is short on legible details, but it refers to her having done something in November 'in Disregard of Her baile at the suit of our [illegible word].'[76] The 1705 imprisonment conceivably might be related to the trial to which Lady Cowper's source is referring.

Whether or not Manley was cast at law by Tilly, it does seem reasonable to assume that she probably did bear him several children during their four- to five-year liaison. We do not know their living arrangements at this time, but it is possible that Manley lived with Tilly in the governor's residence in the Fleet. There is no evidence of the births of such children in the extant parish records for the churches in the vicinity of Fleet Prison. However, since the Fleet was considered to be out of the bounds of ecclesiastical jurisdiction (hence the term 'Fleet marriage'), births within the confines of the Fleet would presumably have been outside of normal church record-keeping.

It is likely that Charles Gildon would have mentioned something about these children, possibly in a form similar to the gossip related to Lady Cowper, in the biography he and Curll had planned in 1714. However, in whatever other ways she was honest and forthright about her own life and relationships and her child by John Manley, Manley chose to omit any mention of these other children in her account of her own life. On the other hand, it is significant, as has already been noted, that Manley never refers to Tilly in an unflattering way in any of her published works – as she does to many other former friends or lovers – which makes us wonder whether Lady Cowper's source was entirely correct about Manley's legal tangles with Tilly. Since no information about the Chancery suit referred to in Lady Cowper's papers has been found, we can only speculate as to the exact relationship between Manley and her former lover.

Manley suggests in *Rivella* that she encouraged Tilly to marry the wealthy Smith as a way out of his financial troubles. Her narrator indicates that Tilly would have married her but for the debt burden he was suffering under as a result of lawsuits brought against him and the costs incurred in the Bath-Albemarle mediation: 'she ask'd him if he would marry her; he immediately answer'd he would, tho' he were ruin'd by it'. Manley, however, insists that she did not want him to marry her and suffer a life of poverty; she would rather lose him 'than to see him Poor and Miserable, an Object of perpetual Reproach to her Heart and Eyes; for having preferr'd the Reparation of her own Honour, to the Preservation of his'.[77] The mean-spirited gossip in Lady Cowper's papers, however, offers another interpretation of their parting. If by the time he left Manley Tilly actually warned their former cook against trusting her (or presumably against cooking meals for which she could not pay), it would appear that Tilly was aware of her ability to persuade others to take her part and did not necessarily feel that he owed her subsequent financial support, especially if he had taken over financial responsibility for their children's maintenance. Manley, however, was not only frequently capable of persuading others to take up her cause, but quite capable of representing the facts of her life in a way that best suited her own purposes, whether personal or political.

Gossip and Satire

One important meaning of the word 'gossip' in Manley's time was a close friend, especially, 'applied to a woman's female friends invited to be present at a birth'.[78] Gossip becomes then the private, even intimate, domain of women, rather than the supposedly more public world of men and politics. Manley is treated as a gossip, rather than a satirist every time it is suggested that she is making a person-ally motivated rather than a politically motivated attack. Lady Cowper dismisses Manley as a gossip about whom she herself feels free to gossip when she ascribes Manley's motivation for writing political satire to the outcome of a personal lawsuit, rather than to a broader-reaching satirical schema designed generally to tarnish the reputation of politically powerful Whigs such as the Cowpers.

Manley herself interestingly offers us a clue as to how she might have spun her own narrative about her children by Tilly should she have deemed it nec-essary or prudent to relate it herself. When Edmund Curll ascribes Charles Gildon's motivation for his original plan to write a severe Invective against some part of Manley's behaviour to a 'fit of Pique', he turns Gildon's schemes as a Whig political hack (yet another marginalizing literary category – although one that may be considered perhaps a rung higher than that of a gossip) into a personal vendetta between Manley and Gildon about which we might gossip. In dimin-ishing Manley's political influence by ascribing the relationship between her and Gildon in terms of personal resentment, Curll's preface also turns Gildon into more of a gossip than political hack and (probably inadvertently) transforms Curll himself – as publisher and purveyor of Gildon's narratives – into a gossip-ing bookseller.

Manley of course understood that however much she insisted that she was writing satire, it would be perceived as gossip. Part of her strategy, however, was to acknowledge the overlap between the two categories and publicly to trans-form her Whig combatants, such as Steele, into gossips themselves. Having framed the narrative of *The New Atalantis* as an account of anecdotes of court and society figures related by the allegorical Princess Fame, Manley presents her best-selling *Secret Memoirs ... from The New Atalantis* as simultaneously both gossip and satire. Moreover, in the passage in *The New Atalantis* in which she denigrates her quondam friend Richard Steele, Manley describes him as present (presumably as one of the gossips) at her lying 'in Childbed'.[79] The relationship between Manley and Steele – which evolved from flirtatious friendship to public vendetta, has often been understood in terms either of a lovers' quarrel or some other personal misunderstanding. As I have already suggested, it is probably more accurate to understand it as a political feud between the officially sanctioned and handsomely paid Whig Gazetteer (a position Steele was offered through the interventions of Lord Sunderland, the official responsible for Manley's apprehension for *The New Atalantis*) and Manley, a never officially sanctioned and only irregularly remunerated Tory satirist.

Until now scholars have only speculated – in part because of this scene in *The New Atalantis* – that Manley's liaison with Tilly might have produced children. We now see that this scene seems to refer to the birth of one of the three children that Tilly probably fathered. Moreover, we can now see that Manley herself had made reference to the imminent birth of one of these offspring in this work published in 1709, but had referred to it in such a way as to translate whatever shame she might have felt for giving birth out of wedlock into embarrassment for Steele, who is transformed from serious journalist into just another gossip at this lying-in. Before we turn to Manley's years as a Tory satirist, trusted by Jonathan Swift and Robert Harley, however, we must first examine the period between 1705 and 1708 when she was not, despite frequent scholarly assumptions to the contrary, yet writing for the Tories.

6 NOT YET A PROPAGANDA WRITER: 1705–8

The standard twentieth-century scholarly assumption that Delarivier Manley wrote *Queen Zarah and the Zarazians* (1705) has led most Manley scholars to presume that Manley had already become a Tory propaganda writer by 1705 and that she already knew John Barber at this time. J. A. Downie's critical reassessment of the authorship of *Queen Zarah* changes the way we view what Manley was doing and writing, and from whom she was seeking patronage, not only in 1705 but also during the subsequent three to four years before she wrote *The New Atalantis* (which she might have begun some time in 1708 or else in early 1709).

Once we acknowledge that Manley probably did not write *Queen Zarah*, then we see that it was in 1706, rather than 1705, that Manley recommenced the writing career she had essentially suspended in 1696, having published only the two poems in *The Nine Muses* in the intervening years. Her return to writing did not begin with a secret history but with a tragedy for the stage, *Almyna: or, The Arabian Vow*. The next year, she brought out her second epistolary prose work, *The Unknown Lady's Pacquet of Letters*, a work that resembles her subsequent secret histories *The New Atalantis* and *Memoirs of Europe* in its incorporation of anecdotes about well-known public figures. Careful analysis of *The Unknown Lady's Pacquet* helps us to delineate a continuum between Manley's early autobiographical epistolary writing and her subsequent politically charged secret histories, offering a more plausible trajectory of Manley's career as a writer and a political satirist than is possible if we assume that she wrote *Queen Zarah*.

Queen Zarah and the Zarazians

The personal difficulties that Manley was experiencing in 1704 and 1705 – the failed palimony case, the problems with paying the debt for the care of her children, and her December 1705 imprisonment – suggest that she would have had many concerns more pressing to her than the details of the May 1705 parliamentary elections, the partisan furor surrounding Occasional Conformity legislation, or Tory complaints against 'moderation'. Manley's personal circumstances in 1704 and 1705 probably meant that she did not have the time to follow the behind-the-scenes partisan infighting that *Queen Zarah* addresses.

Moreover, the style of writing itself bears little resemblance to that of Manley's other prose works.[1]

The text of *The Secret History of Queen Zarah and the Zarazians Being a Looking-Glass for ------ --------------- in the Kingdom of Albigion* offers a crude allegory of Sarah Churchill, Duchess of Marlborough, a close friend of Queen Anne and wife of the powerful military commander John Churchill, Duke of Marlborough, one of Anne's most trusted political advisors. *Queen Zarah* predictably satirizes Marlborough's political influence by suggesting, following the pattern of other anti-Whig pamphlets, that she was the lover of various powerful ministers, including not only Sidney Godolphin (1645–1712), first Earl of Godolphin, Lord Treasurer and the Marlboroughs' closest political ally, and Charles Talbot (1660–1718), Duke of Shrewsbury, one of the seven signatories to the 1688 invitation to William of Orange, but also John Sheffield (1648–1721), third Earl of Mulgrave, whom Marlborough and Godolphin were attempting to force out of the ministry in 1705. Generally speaking, the gossip recounted in *Queen Zarah* was not based on real-life rumours about the persons involved. Outside of the realm of such anti-Whig propaganda, it was not usual for anyone to assume that the Duchess of Marlborough was having an affair with any of these court figures, and certainly not juggling liaisons with several of them simultaneously. *Queen Zarah* also follows other anti-Marlborough propaganda in its misogynistic depiction of Sarah Churchill's mother, depictions that bore little resemblance to what is known of her.[2]

By contrast, many of the anecdotes Manley would recycle for partisan purposes in *The New Atalantis* were already well known as gossip; some were recorded separately in Narcissus Luttrell's then private chronicles of London life. Manley would probably invent some stories for partisan effect or personal vendetta (the story about Sarah Egerton throwing a hot apple pie at her husband, for example). She would also recycle certain tropes familiar from partisan propaganda and not based in real gossip, including a few used in *Queen Zarah*, such as the Duchess of Marlborough's putative romantic intrigue with Sidney Godolphin. However, in *The New Atalantis*, Manley more typically relates anecdotes already known to her readers from sources other than partisan political propaganda. For example, she recounts a story about someone easily identifiable as William Lord Cowper who bigamously marries a second wife (Elizabeth Cullen) by whom he has two children. This well-known rumour about the Whig Lord Chancellor, a close friend and political supporter of the Marlboroughs, was probably true, since in his will Cowper would leave £2,000 to Cullen's natural daughter, Mary (Cullen's son, rumoured to be Cowper's, would predecease him).[3]

Moreover, Manley's satirical portrait of the Marlboroughs in *The New Atalantis* is a much more nuanced critique of the Duke of Marlborough's real political skill and charm than the misogynistic caricatures of Marlborough's wife and mother found in *Queen Zarah*. For example, in *Queen Zarah*, Jenisa (Frances Jenyns) is portrayed as aggressively manipulating Hippolito (John Churchill) into marrying her daughter Zarah (Sarah Jenyns). Although in reality John Churchill fell in love with Sarah Jenyns and married her rather than the wealthier heiress his parents had chosen for him, in *Queen Zarah*, Sarah's mother tricks Churchill into a rendezvous that appears to compromise her daughter's honour. He responds, 'Let me but know what you desire of me, and what it is you'd have me do'. Her reply is brief and to the point: 'I wou'd have you resolve … instantly to Marry Zarah; I have a Priest attends without ready to perform the Ceremony'.[4]

The author of *Queen Zarah* then describes a passionate embrace between Zarah and Hippolito, only to conclude the anecdote with a scene of violent slapstick in which Clelia (the Duchess of Cleveland, John Churchill's cousin and his lover as well as mistress to Charles II) attempts to revenge herself on Churchill for his marriage. In fact, Cleveland, who gave Churchill a present of £5,000 – a sum crucial to his future advancement – may well have been angry with Churchill for marrying Jenyns. However, this depiction of her in *Queen Zarah* is not particularly nuanced satire:

> *Clelia*, in a desperate Frenzy, occasion'd by what had happen'd that Night, enter'd the Room, where these two Lovers seem'd so happy; but hearing of a Voice she knew, and *Hippolito's* Name, she had not Conduct enough to stay and observe them, but hasten'd forward, and rush'd upon them, when she was too well satisfy'd 'twas *Zarah* and *Hippolito* she saw. *Ah, Traytor*, cry'd she, *is it possible you shou'd be thus ungrateful?*

When Churchill tries to defend himself and his new wife, Cleveland continues:

> *Good Heavens!* said she, *to what will this Impudence arise?* At that she seiz'd the Sword he had on, not knowing which of the two to begin with first, being both equally perfidious; she thought at last *Zarah*, as most criminal, was first to be sacrificed to her Revenge; and just as she was going to stab her, *Hippolito* interposed, and receiv'd a slight Wound upon himself by staying of her Hand, when she threw her self upon him, *Traytor*, said she, *this Blow was not reserv'd for thee, thou shalt not have the Power of being first reveng'd.*[5]

Delarivier Manley is unlikely to have offered such a depiction of the Duchess of Cleveland. Having spent six months in Cleveland's household in 1694, Manley had a more subtle appreciation of Cleveland's skills as a courtier than this scene demonstrates. Describing Cleveland's probable anger in response to John Churchill's marrying Sarah Jenyns, in a parallel scene in *The New Atalantis*, Manley emphasizes John Churchill's political skills in handling the situation so as to avoid an angry outburst from the tempestuous and fickle Cleveland:

> he got his Master's [Charles II's] Consent for Marrying the young *Jeanitin* [Sarah Jenyns], and the promise of his Protection against the Dutchess [Cleveland]; who when she heard she was going to lose her *dear Count*, or at best, divide him with a Wife of *Inclination*, her haughty Soul, conscious of Beauty and superior Charms, resolv'd to revenge the neglect of 'em ...[6]

In Manley's version, Churchill manages the situation by charm and flattery, as he managed most political situations, outwitting Cleveland's own well-known skills as a manipulator of courtiers and sovereigns:

> but what could he do? He had never lov'd her, cover'd with Charms as she was, 'tis only to be suppos'd that he well dissembled it, and in that point the *false* Lover, has a thousand Advantages over the true, they can personate all that's *necessary*, and are in no danger of the *Superfluous*; can imitate the *Transports*, and avoid the *Digustive* part; *Jealousy, Disquiets, Upbraidings*, are very well exchang'd, for perpetual *Applause, Flattery, Raptures,* pleasing *Sighs*, and never-ceasing *Joys*; the Dutchess was a Mistress in the Art of Distinction, as to the Merit of a Lover, and 'tis to be thought, that if the *Count* had not been a Masterpiece, he could not have tallied her Excellence.[7]

This comparison of Cleveland's and Churchill's ability to be disingenuously charming offers an effective satire of John Churchill's well-known political smoothness and of his skill at saying what others wanted to hear in order to achieve his own political goals. In other words, *The New Atalantis*, which is known to have been written by Manley, often offers a subtlety of characterization never evident in the crude caricatures in *Queen Zarah*, which is in many ways little more than an extended political pamphlet.

As J. A. Downie has pointed out, *Queen Zarah* was clearly written in response to other partisan pamphlets from 1705. It puts forth a Tory critique of political 'moderation' (or too much cooperation with the Whigs), following the model of *The Memorial of the Church of England*, for example, which appeared in early July 1705. *Queen Zarah* also appears to respond to several works of propaganda written by Daniel Defoe to influence the 1705 elections.[8] Although Delarivier Manley certainly became an adept political pamphleteer and sparred effectively in partisan pamphlet wars from 1710 to 1713, *Queen Zarah* bears even less stylistic resemblance to Manley's later pamphlets than it does to her *New Atalantis*.

Most twentieth-century Manley scholars, who largely focused on Manley's political secret histories (or 'novels' as they saw them) outside the context of the rest of Manley's works, assumed the difference in structure and style between *Queen Zarah* and *The New Atalantis* could be explained by simple chronology. If they addressed Manley's prose structure at all, most twentieth-century critics presumed that it simply became more sophisticated between 1705 and 1709.[9] This might seem a reasonable conjecture if one had never read *Letters Writen*, published almost a decade before *Queen Zarah*, or *The Lady's Pacquet of Letters*, which appeared two years after *Queen Zarah*. As I have already indicated, *Letters Writen*, like *The Lady's Pacquet*, which will be discussed later in this chapter, incorporates references to many contemporary and classical authors, indicating Manley's desire to be taken seriously as a liberally educated writer and conversationalist. Similarly, in *The New Atalantis*, Manley includes frequent citations from other literary works (some of which she clearly borrowed from *Politeuphuia*, *Wits Common-Wealth*), an effort to demonstrate a cultivated mind not made by the author of *Queen Zarah*.[10]

Queen Zarah and the Zarazians was first published anonymously, with no printer or bookseller listed on the title page, probably in the summer of 1705. A second part, mentioned in the Term Catalogues for Michaelmas Term, appeared in autumn of the same year.[11] Although the work seems to have been popular in French, appearing in five different editions between 1708 and 1713,[12] the original English edition does not seem to have sold particularly well. J. A. Downie has pointed out that the 1711 English edition, the first edition to suggest a connection to Manley, appears to be a reissue of some of the original unsold sheets from the 1705 edition.[13] A new title page was added, which included the words, 'By Way of Appendix to the New *Atlantis* [sic]'. This tag, clearly intended to increase sales by associating *Zarah* with the best-selling *New Atalantis*, represents the first time that the work was linked to another work by Manley. The printer or bookseller responsible for this title page, however, does not actually claim that the work was written by the author of *The New Atalantis*. Nor does Manley herself mention *Queen Zarah* in *The Adventures of Rivella*, in which she does mention her authorship of and prosecution for having written *The New Atalantis*.

In *Rivella*, Manley's narrator refers to her courage in writing *The New Atalantis* as 'thowing the first Stone', suggesting that this text, rather than *Queen Zarah*, was Manley's first foray into opposition political propaganda.[14] The first eighteenth-century publication to assert Manley's authorship of *Queen Zarah* was the 1741 *An Impartial History of the Character, Amours, Travels, and Transactions of Mr. John Barber ... Written by Several Hands*, which was printed for Edmund Curll and which did not appear until seventeen years after Manley's death. In one of the two biographical sketches of Manley in what appears to be a hastily assembled biography of Barber compiled for a bookseller known for bringing out unauthorized biographies of public figures within a very short time after their deaths, *Queen Zarah* is listed as one of her publications.[15] However, in Giles Jacob's entry on Manley ('the *Atalantic* Lady') in *The Poetical Register*, published a year before Manley died, *Queen Zarah* is not mentioned.[16]

Ruth Herman has pointed out that Manley did not explicitly renounce the association with her suggested by the 1711 title page of *Queen Zarah*, whereas she did object in a 1711 issue of the *Examiner* against a pirated edition of *The Unknown Lady's Pacquet of Letters*, 'very uncorrectly Reprinted ... without the

Consent or Knowledge of the Author of the Atalantis'. In 1714, in another issue of the *Examiner*, Manley further disclaims authorship of *The New Atalantis for the Year 1713*.[17] Of course, the fact that Manley seems not to have publicly protested against the 1711 title page of *Queen Zarah* could mean that she simply did not notice the work's appearance. Or perhaps she was not troubled by someone else's attempt to capitalize on her success by offering his work as an 'Appendix' to hers. A very topical work about issues of particular political concern in 1705, *Queen Zarah* does not seem to have held much interest for the public after its initial appearance, except among Francophone readers, who may have found its introductory material a useful guide to early eighteenth-century party politics in England.[18] It is not known whether with the new 1711 title page, the bookseller even managed to sell all of the sheets remaining from the 1705 printing.[19]

Queen Zarah did not reappear again in a stand-alone English edition until 1743, and that edition – whose publication was probably prompted by the 1742 publication of *An Account of the Conduct of the Dowager Duchess of Marlborough* (a defence of the Duchess so vehemently satirized in *Queen Zarah*) – followed the 1741 *Impartial History ... of John Barber* in its assertion of Manley's authorship on the title page: 'By the late Ingenious Mrs. Manley'.[20] *Queen Zarah* also appeared, without the original preface, in the first volume of a collection entitled, *State Tracts: Containing many necessary Observations and Reflections on the State of Our Affairs at Home and Abroad ... By the Author of the Examiner*,[21] under the title of *A Secret History Faithfully Handed Down From a Committee of Safety to a Committee of Secrecy* (1715). Although scholars originally believed that *State Tracts* may have included works by more than one author, David Foxon and J. A. Downie have reassessed that assumption. Foxon now believes that *State Tracts* was intended as 'a collection of Browne's works'.[22] Downie concurs with Foxon and also explains that, although Manley had authored some issues of the *Examiner* in 1710 and 1711, Joseph Browne was in fact its author in the spring of 1715, when *State Tracts* appeared.[23]

There are obviously some superficial similarities between *Queen Zarah* and *The New Atalantis*: both texts satirize Whig political figures by inventing or recounting salacious gossip, and both use the coded style of a *roman-à-clef*, giving real persons recognizable pseudonyms. In *Queen Zarah*, for example, the eponymous protagonist represents Sarah Churchill, Duchess of Marlborough; 'Princess Albania' is Princess, later Queen Anne; Mulgarvius is John Sheffield, third Earl of Mulgrave, and Solano is Robert Spencer (1641–1702), second Earl of Sunderland. In *The New Atalantis* many of the same figures appear under different pseudonyms. Both works also fit into the broad category of secret history, an important late seventeenth-century political genre. However, as has already been suggested, the prose style and narrative structure of *Queen Zarah* do not resemble those of Manley's other published prose works.

Despite the lack of evidence of Manley's authorship of *Queen Zarah* from her own lifetime, twentieth-century scholars have generally taken for granted Dolores Duff's unsubstantiated assertion that the 1705 appearance of Manley's

> first novel, *The Secret History of Queen Zarah* ... ushered in Mrs. Manley's period of commitment as a Tory propagandist and moreover contained in its preface a statement of Mrs. Manley's literary theory. The novel's publication also marked the beginning of her liaison with John Barber.[24]

J. A. Downie pointedly observes, 'There is no evidence to support any of these assertions'.[25] Not only is there no convincing evidence from Manley's own lifetime that demonstrates her authorship of *Queen Zarah*, but, the 'preface' to which Duff refers turns out to have been translated, more or less intact, from Jean Baptiste Morvan de Bellegarde's *Lettres curieuses de literature et de morale* (1702). Bellegarde's essay summarizes the ideas of du Plaisir's *Sentiments sur les lettres, et sur l'histoire, avec des scrupules sur le stile* (1683),[26] and so has less to do with the history of the English 'novel' (regardless of whether we consider *Queen Zarah* to be a 'novel' or not), than with the development of seventeenth-century French prose fiction.

As Downie has also reminded scholars, since the printer of *Queen Zarah* was unknown, we have no reason to assume that it was John Barber; moreover, although Manley and Barber may have known each other, and perhaps even lived together, before she wrote *The New Atalantis*, there is no tangible evidence demonstrating that Manley and Barber were living together until 1711, when Swift, in his *Journal to Stella*, mentions having dined with them.[27] In fact, a newly discovered warrant for the arrest of Manley and Barber suggests that Barber probably was the printer for *The New Atalantis*. Manley thus almost certainly knew him at the time that *The New Atalantis* went to press, if not earlier, and she may have been living with him as early as 1709.[28] However, there is no evidence to suggest that she knew him in 1705.

As several scholars have already observed, *Queen Zarah* also borrows extensively from a 1680 French novelistic source, *Hattigé: ou les Amours du Roy de Tamaran, Nouvelle* (1676), a political secret history designed to cast aspersions on Charles II by describing the power and influence of his lover, Barbara, Duchess of Cleveland.[29] Moreover, as well as borrowing a preface from Bellegarde's *Lettres curieuses*, the author of *Queen Zarah* inserts towards the end of the second part of that work, as a lengthy and somewhat inexplicable digression, a second long passage from an essay on 'good taste' in the same work by Bellegarde.[30] The impression is given, especially in the second part, of a work cobbled together with ever increasing haste. Bellegarde's essay on 'good taste' and the character of an 'honest man' (which the author of *Queen Zarah* adjusts to 'honest politician') stands out stylistically as a strange interruption in an otherwise coherent, if predictable, storyline. This second discovery of borrowing from Bellegarde – and in this latter case, the borrowing is definitely from the French edition, rather than from the available English translation, as in the case of the borrowings from *Hattigé* – adds further doubt to Manley's authorship of *Queen Zarah*. Manley's claim to having spent four months in her youth studying French at the home of a Huguenot minister in no way demonstrates that she was fluent enough in French to translate French moral-philosophical essays into English.

One scholar applauds 'Manley's ability to recognize and recycle appropriate material'.[31] I agree that a work such as *The New Atalantis* demonstrates Manley's ability to allude to and revise a range of contemporary, classical and mythological sources and genres in order to make her political points. However, the allusions and literary revisions in Manley's dystopian *New Atalantis* – a work whose very title signals that it is a revision of Francis Bacon's utopian *The New Atlantis* (1626) – often represent subtle literary manoeuvres. In *Queen Zarah* the effect is really that of what a modern reader would describe as awkwardly incorporated instances of plagiarism.

Even the stylistic structure of the coded secret history deteriorates markedly in the second part of *Queen Zarah*. Whereas in the first part, the author had relied on pseudonyms to refer to well-known political figures, in the second part, extensive use is made of blanks, probably unnecessary from a legal point of view. It was standard practice in the early eighteenth century to use blanks to identify someone but avoid prosecution for libel (such as 'R— St—le' to refer to Richard Steele); such practice also of course generated interest in readers, since the omissions suggested that the author was saying something that might be deemed scandalous. In the second part of *Queen Zarah*, however, blanks are inserted with abandon, being used for ordinary words – such as C—t (for Court) or L—ds—p (for Lordship). The author of *Queen Zarah* gives the impression, in other words, of writing in haste and to generate the appearance of more scandal than the work in fact seems to have generated. In *The New Atalantis* and *Memoirs of Europe*, by contrast, Manly relies consistently on pseudonyms rather than blanks or ellipses.

The Secret History of Queen Zarah and the Zarazians was probably not written by Manley. As J. A. Downie has so aptly observed, scholarly insistence on Manley's authorship of 'a crude political allegory that Manley never owned' does a 'disservice' to Manley as author of 'the *New Atalantis*, the *Memoirs of Europe*, her *Examiner* essays, and her political pamphlets on behalf of the Oxford ministry'.[32] *Queen Zarah*, however, does fit into a well-known literary-political genre that Manley herself would deploy in her later political scandal chronicles – the genre of the political secret history. This classical genre became familiar to seventeenth-century European and English readers through translations of the *Anecdota* of Procopius (*c.* AD 550), a work whose title means 'unpublished things'. The preface to the English translation of 1674 emphasizes the difference between the writer of official histories and the writer of secret histories. The first 'considers almost ever Men in Publick', whereas the 'Anecdoto-grapher', or writer of secret histories, 'only examines 'em in private'.[33]

The idea that anecdotes about the private life of public figures were deployed as serious political interventions may seem unexpected to modern readers, one of whom has dismissed Manley's secret histories as 'formally nothing more than a series of anecdotes, some swollen to novella length and complexity'.[34] However, as one modern historian has suggested, anecdotal secret history (also sometimes described as *la petite histoire* or 'little history') sometimes functioned as a counter-narrative to standard official histories because it was 'loosely structured', rather than tightly structured or exemplary.[35] Manley's *New Atalantis* might best be understood within this category of loosely structured secret history, as will be discussed further in the next chapter, whereas *Queen Zarah* offered a more tightly structured Tory revision to Whig secret histories of the 1670s and 1680s, as well as a pointed riposte to Defoe and others in the pamphlet wars of 1705.

The protagonist of the tightly organized *Queen Zarah* represents not merely Sarah Churchill, Duchess of Marlborough, but, as Ruth Herman has astutely pointed out, 'the symbol of the Whig Junto'.[36] In *Queen Zarah* the ambitious and lustful Zarah functions as an allegory of everything the author feels is wrong with the Whigs. By contrast, in *The New Atalantis*, Manley deploys a very loose overarching allegorical travel narrative (Astrea, the Goddess of Justice, tours Earth with her mother, Virtue, and Lady Intelligence) that allows her to recount well-known, but often unconnected, items of gossip – some about John Churchill and the Duchess of Cleveland, some about the Whig pamphleteer Richard Steele, some about herself and her bigamous husband, some the royal family, and many about prominent court Whigs (and a few Tories). Given that Manley's approach in *The New Atalantis* was to begin with largely unrelated anecdotes rather than starting with a coherent overall story, it is not surprising that in many ways her *Unknown Lady's Pacquet of Letters*, a loosely structured epistolary recounting of various items of society gossip, bears a closer stylistic resemblance to *The New Atalantis* than does *Queen Zarah*. Before turning to the genre of the ostensibly private packet of letters made public in 1707, however, Manley recommended her literary career in 1706 with the production of her second dramatic tragedy, *Almyna: or, The Arabian Vow*.

Almyna: or, The Arabian Vow

We do not know when Manley was released from prison, following her December 1705 arrest, nor do we know how she supported herself during or after her imprisonment. However, it would appear that by 1706 Manley had given up on other methods of earning income – such as intervening, whether legally or fraudulently, in law suits – and turned again to the literary sphere as a means of attempting to make a living. Her tragedy *Almyna* was produced in mid-December 1706.[37]

Given the difficulties Manley experienced in making money through other means, we can understand why she would have wanted to try her hand again at writing for the stage even though most playwrights of her era were not able to earn a living solely from their dramatic works.[38] Her earlier experiences with Skipwith and Rich's company, however, would have meant that she would have been unlikely to have had a play produced again at the Drury Lane Theatre. Moreover, it would appear from the satirical depictions of the rehearsals of *The Royal Mischief* in *The Female Wit* that Manley's tone in dealing with the actors in Betterton's company might not have made them enthusiastic about producing another of her tragedies. However, Manley seems to have been successful in persuading the new manager of the Queen's Theatre, Haymarket, the Irish impresario Owen Swiney (1676–1754) – who began managing the theatre in October 1706, having leased it from the playwright John Vanbrugh (1664–1726) – to make her second tragedy one of his first productions. Vanbrugh had already persuaded Betterton, Barry and Bracegirdle to bring their acting company to the Haymarket Theatre, so Manley, once again, was able to benefit from having her work performed by the most experienced actors in London.

In her published preface, Manley claims not to have been present at the production of her own work, having been 'at a great distance from the *HOUSE* at the time of Representation'.[39] We do not know where Manley was at this time, nor why she was away from London. The most plausible explanation, given the financial distress she had apparently been experiencing for the past several years, was that she had left London either to elude creditors or to live at the least possible expense. Despite having not seen the production, however, Manley graciously thanks both Betterton and Swiney in the preface to the play. She reports: 'All agree that *Almyna* was admirably Acted and advantageously Dress'd'. Manley acknowledges Swiney in particular for 'venturing upon the good Opinion of the Play', to 'make so great an Expence', presumably a reference to the cost of the costumes.[40]

Unfortunately for Manley, Swiney and the others hoping to profit from the production, the play was staged during the week before Christmas and was in competition with the opera *Camilla* playing at the Drury Lane, which Manley claims, in her preface, was attracting interest because of the performances of the 'Eunuch'.[41] *Almyna* only ran for three nights, although, according to Manley's preface, it was revised and a revival was planned, which never took place because of 'Mrs. *Bracegirdle's* quitting the *House*, three days before it was to have been play'd again'.[42] In fact, the planned revival would have made sense, if Swiney hoped to recoup his costs on costumes; moreover, Anne Bracegirdle did retire abruptly from the theatre on 18 February 1707, possibly out of frustration with the competition between her and Ann Oldfield (1683–1730).[43]

It would appear that neither the receipts from the December 1706 production of *Almyna* nor the patronage Manley must have hoped for from her dedication to Elizabeth Montagu, Countess of Sandwich, nor the proceeds from the publication of *Almyna* in May 1707, put Manley on a secure financial footing. She wrote to the Whig peer Ralph, Duke of Montagu (a relation of the Countess of Sandwich), shortly after the play's publication, sending him a copy of the play and asking for financial assistance to prevent the seizure of 'all her goods'.[44] In other words, although *Almyna* has certain Tory (and possibly occasional Jacobite) overtones, Manley's request for assistance from Montagu, a staunchly Whig peer, suggests that she had not yet in 1707 become the professional Tory pamphleteer that those scholars who credit her with the authorship of *Queen Zarah* have generally assumed she had.

Almyna reworks of one of the stories in *The Arabian Nights Entertainments*, which was available in a popular English translation in 1706.[45] Manley also claims, in her preface, that she draws from 'the Life of that great Monarch, *Caliph Valid Almanzor*'. In other words, her drama is ostensibly set in the Umayyad caliphate, established in Spain in the eighth century, although we do not know the exact literary or historical source she drew upon for the story.[46] The play is in part about the problem of political succession, in a situation when a monarch cannot provide a direct heir. In Manley's play, the Sultan Almanzor solves this problem by naming his brother as heir; here, Manley may be making an allusion to James II having succeeded his brother Charles II (who did not father any legitimate male progeny). However, Manley's play seems less focused on who will succeed the Sultan than on how he will treat his wives.

Angry at having once been cuckolded, the Sultan beheads the offending wife and, following the familiar plot of *The Arabian Nights*, decides to avoiding being cuckolded again by beheading every subsequent wife on the morning after their wedding night, following the logic that such murder is morally acceptable because women do not have souls. Manley's rational and morally upright heroine, Almyna, vows not only to marry the Sultan but to teach him that women do have souls, by demonstrating such dignity in meeting her death that he will change his mind about having her beheaded. Her success in this endeavour provides the play with a strongly proto-feminist resonance. As several modern scholars have already pointed out, Almyna offers almost an anagram of Manley's own name, suggesting that the author might well have identified with her educated, independent heroine.[47]

Almyna is in many ways much more conventional than *The Royal Mischief*, Manley's first tragedy. Whereas Homais, the protagonist of *The Royal Mischief*, was so monstrously evil that she pushed the bounds of dramatic conventions, expressing her amoral lust and desire in more heroic rants than had previously been witnessed on the Restoration stage, in *Almyna* Manley follows more traditional Restoration conventions by depicting a chaste tragic heroine whose virtue is beyond question. Moreover, female virtue is demonstrated, as in much Restoration tragedy, as ensuring its own reward: the heroine's virtue and dignity are tested; when they are proven, she triumphs. Manley's proto-feminism here follows the more conventional lead of Catharine Trotter, demonstrating women's worth through their virtue, rather than articulating, as she did in *The Royal Mischief*, women's capacity for lust and political ambition.

Manley's second tragedy, her third play to be produced, also shows her developing editorial skills. Unlike her first play, *The Lost Lover*, which gives the impression of having been hastily written and scarcely revised, *Almyna* shows evidence of careful plotting and revision.[48] There are no extraneous scenes or characters; individual characters are internally consistent. As in the two elegies she included in *The Nine Muses*, Manley demonstrates in *Almyna* that, when she chose to, she was perfectly capable of working within the confines and conventions of an established literary genre. The play also offers a politically resonant and proto-feminist reworking of an Oriental tale and so may be read in contrast to Mary Pix's *Ibrahim, the Thirteenth Emperor of the Turks* (1696), a Whig and proto-feminist depiction of the power-struggle between a sultan and a seraglian woman.[49]

In *Ibrahim*, Pix adapts, for obvious political ends, the story of the historical Ibrahim, who was emperor of the Turks from 1640 to 1648 and was killed by janissaries.[50] In 'The Present State of the Ottoman Empire', included in *The Turkish History*, Paul Rycaut suggests an analogy between the murder of Ibrahim and the execution of Charles I in the same year.[51] As Ros Ballaster explains, Mary Pix invents the character of Amurat, ostensibly the son of the janissaries' commander, who, like William III, peacefully deposes his father-in-law. Ballaster concludes: 'Pix replays the Glorious Revolution as a tragic oriental drama, placing at its centre a passively loving westernized couple, Amurat and his beloved Morena'.[52]

In *Almyna* Manley also westernizes her Oriental heroine, but her version of virtuous proto-feminism offers a very different echo to the monarchical succession of 1689. Some of Almyna's discourse, as Ballaster points out, echoes early seventeenth-century proto-feminist Christian discourse, although it is stripped of its radical religious overtones.[53] However, Manley's text also takes up the highly political issue of oath-taking. Ever since 1689, when William and Mary took the throne, oath-breaking had been a touchy political topic. Obviously many government officials and clergymen simply took an oath of loyalty to William and Mary, but others would not break their prior oath of loyalty to the alive but exiled James II by swearing allegiance to William. For Tory writers of an earlier era, such as John Dryden and Aphra Behn, vow-breaking in love or marriage had obvious political resonance, especially in their literary works written during the Exclusion crises of the early 1680s and during the years surrounding the Revolution of 1688–9.[54]

The topic of oath-taking became even more heated during Anne's reign as Tories attempted to push through Parliament a variety of bills limiting the right of Occasional Conformity (a right by which dissenting office-holders – usually Whig – held government office merely by taking communion once per year in the Church of England). In response to High-Tory propaganda, several Whig and anti-Jacobite pamphlets suggested that the refusal of High-Church nonjuring clergy to swear an oath to Queen Anne implied that these non-jurors would rather swear allegiance to the pope than to a woman:

> nothing can be more inconsistent then the Supremacy they claim by Divine Right over the Queen ... And can we think that such Men as these wou'd ever scruple, when they found their interests to prefer to the Supremacy of a Woman, that of the Pope, as Patriarch of the West.[55]

Here the matter of taking an oath of loyalty to Queen Anne supports an early eighteenth-century Whig proto-feminism, but in *Almyna* Manley appears to reassert not only a Tory proto-feminism, as articulated by her virtuous heroine, but also a Tory version of allegiance.

In a scene in Act I that alludes to the 1701 Act of Settlement – which specified a Protestant and Hanoverian succession, should both William III and the prospective Queen Anne die without a surviving issue – Manley has the courtiers in her play swear by 'this holy *Alcoran*' that upon the death of Almanzor, they will acknowledge Abdalla, brother of Almanzor, as 'King, and Lord, / Of all these Realms, as Lawful Successor, / To his great Brother, *Caliph Almanzor*'. Abdalla, the prospective successor, himself then swears:

> T'administer to all your People Justice,
> Maintain, and keep em in those Privileges:
> Your Predecessor Kings, in General,
> Or, in particular, have granted.[56]

The wording of this vow is politically fraught, however, as Ruth Herman has pointed out. Abdalla's oath, of course, not only alludes to the Act of Settlement but also echoes the oath taken by William and Mary in 1689 and subsequent monarchs upon their accession to the English throne; however, Abdalla's oath is closer to the language in James II's oath of office than to what William and Mary swore. As Herman explains, the oath taken by James II was to follow in the footsteps of his 'lawfull and Religious predecessors', whereas William and

Mary, interrupting the reign of the Catholic James II, swore an oath without any reference to their 'Predecessors'.[57] Anne took the same coronation oath as William and Mary, but in her first speech to Parliament she echoed her father's speech on his accession in 1685 by assuring her listeners that her own heart 'was entirely *English*'.[58] Moreover, less than a month later, she insisted in another speech to Parliament: 'My own Principles must always keep Me entirely from the Interests and Religion of the Church of *England*'.[59] Although Anne promised to uphold the Act of Toleration, in stating her plan to 'countenance those who have the truest Zeal to support' the Church of England, she gave hope to Jacobite sympathizers that her support for the Established Church (and, implicitly, for hereditary succession, passive obedience and non-resistance) might make possible a Jacobite restoration upon her death.[60]

This scene of oath-taking in *Almyna* takes on particular significance because the play's subtitle, *The Arabian Vow*, makes a direct reference to a vow or oath. Manley's appreciation of Queen Anne's strong support for the 'Established Church' might have encouraged her to include a scene of oath-taking echoing James II's coronation reference to 'predecessors'. Yet Manley is careful not to make a parallel too close to the current political situation: her scene of oath-taking concerns not the actual Sultan himself, but his heir-apparent brother, who is killed when he storms the castle in order to free his brother's bride Almyna (whom Abdalla also loves). In other words, the echo of James II's oath of office is delivered by a potential traitor who raises an army against the Sultan. Meanwhile, the Sultan Almanzor, who is presented at the start of the play as a tyrannical despot, succeeds in facing down the uprising his brother leads against him because he learns from his new bride the value of renouncing what she terms his 'Impious Vow'[61] to slay her on the morning after their wedding night. The play cannot therefore be interpreted as supporting a divine-right, or Jacobite, version of monarchical right or power, even though its scene of oath-taking was so provocative that it apparently disturbed the Countess of Sandwich, to whom Manley dedicated the play.

Ruth Herman concludes that *Almyna* expresses 'the essence of the dilemma in which good Tory subjects found themselves, wishing they could support the "rightful" heir to the throne but finding it impossible'.[62] On the other hand, this interpretation is based in part on the assumption that Manley had already begun her work as a Tory propaganda writer in 1705, with the publication of *Queen Zarah*, and also based on a misidentification of the play's dedicatee.[63] When Manley's professional chronology is revised and the dedication to the Countess of Sandwich clarified, it is possible to recognize multiple and conflicting political ideologies within the play. The play's challenge to the sanctity of prior vows (through the Sultan's revocation of his irrational and despotic vow to murder his brides) might then be seen as expressing a view that is less ideologically Tory than simply pragmatic. It is important to remember that during this period, with only two patent theatres staging plays, theatre managers would have been careful not to have staged overly partisan productions, since they would not have wanted to risk losing a significant portion of their audiences for reasons of political ideology, nor would a playwright badly in need of money want to do so. The political pragmatism evident in *Almyna* might thus have a commercial as well as a political motive.

Since the advice that persuades Almanzor to revoke his irrational vow is given by a woman, we might also see the play as expressing an almost Whiggish challenge to divine-right authority, since many Whig pamphlets following the Revolution of 1688–9 refuted the divine-right of monarchical inheritance by observing that, in Genesis, God granted dominion of the Earth to Adam and Eve jointly rather than wholly and singly to Adam.[64] On the other hand, the play could equally well be seen as giving advice to James Francis Edward Stuart, later known as the Old Pretender, who at the age of nineteen, in 1707, had not yet chosen a wife. Should he choose someone as rational and persuasive as Almyna – and someone who was also Protestant and could therefore rationally persuade James to convert to Protestantism, as others would unsuccessfully attempt to do – he might learn to break a vow (of Catholicism) whose rupture could change his monarchical prospects. Here Manley may be coyly including a nod to a very cautious form of (Protestant) Jacobitism.

Should James Edward Stuart allow himself to be persuaded into Protestantism, he might even, like the Sultan in *Almyna*, defeat the forces that would certainly be raised against him, should he attempt to retake the throne.[65] Such pragmatic political advice, and the play's positive ending (only the deaths of the heir apparent Abdalla and Almyna's sister, Zoraida, make the play tragic), renders this play less cynical than Manley's two earlier plays, which expressed remarkable political cynicism and offered no vision of a positive future world. *Almyna*, however, ends on a positive, politically uplifting note, one that seems to derive from its politically flexible stance.

Our understanding of the play is further illuminated by Manley's decision to dedicate it to Elizabeth, née Wilmot, Montagu, Countess of Sandwich, younger daughter of the poet and royalist John Wilmot (1647–80), second Earl of Rochester. Elizabeth Wilmot had married into the Whiggish Montagu family (whose relations included the Dukes of Montagu and Manchester as well as the Earls of Sandwich). Edward Montagu (1625–72), first Earl of Sandwich (and grandfather of Elizabeth Montagu's husband, third Earl of Sandwich) had demonstrated much more pragmatism than idealism in his political and military career. Having fought for Oliver and Richard Cromwell, he was persuaded, after the latter's fall, to support Charles II, in a 'pragmatic rather than an idealistic way'.[66] Montagu, whom Charles rewarded with the earldom of Sandwich, then continued his successful military and diplomatic career after the Restoration. The Earl of Sandwich's family history, in other words, demonstrates a pragmatism that we might not expect Manley to admire, if we judge from the pride she expresses in her own father's ostensibly unwavering royalism in *Rivella*. However, as I have already observed, *Rivella* was written only after Delarivier Manley had established herself as a Tory propaganda writer, and her presentation of her father's pragmatic political manoeuvring as unwavering royalism must be understood within her own political situation in 1714, when she was writing her fictional autobiography.

By 1707, Manley had not yet established herself as a Tory propaganda writer, and *Almyna* seems to express a political vision more pragmatic than rigidly partisan. Elizabeth Montagu, the dedicatee of the play, was, not surprisingly, offended by the provocative scene of oath-taking. Responding to Sandwich's concerns, Manley, however, demonstrated her political pragmatism in the published preface, by her promise to omit the 'Ceremony in the first Act' from any future performances, following Sandwich's expressed 'dislike' of it.[67] Moreover, the minor bookseller William Turner, for whom the play was printed, is not known to have been a strongly partisan publisher; however, his publications, including a play by Colley Cibber and a poem on Marlborough's victories, seem to have had a more Whig than Tory bent. Furthermore, once the play was printed, Manley included a copy of it when asking for pecuniary assistance from the politically powerful Ralph, Duke of Montagu, which suggests that she did not view the play as something that would offend a Whig peer whose son had married into the Marlborough family.

Once we understand *Almyna* as politically pragmatic rather than rigidly partisan, it becomes easier to make sense of Manley's second epistolary work, *The Unknown Lady's Pacquet of Letters*, which may be seen as a subtly disruptive, but not overtly political, secret history.

The Unknown Lady's Pacquet of Letters

Manley's *The Unknown Lady's Pacquet of Letters* and its continuation, *The Remaining Part of the Unknown Lady's Pacquet of Letters*, offers a collection of letters recounting various bits of contemporary gossip – some about well-known society figures, some about Manley herself. It follows the lead of Charles Gildon's *The Post-Boy Robb'd of his Mail: or, The Pacquet Broke Open, Consisting of Letters of Love and Gallantry, and all Miscellaneous Subjects* (1692), a fictional collection of ostensibly private letters, some of which were translated from Ferrante Pallavicinio's *Il Corriere Svaligiato* (1643).[68] The running-heads, 'The Lady's Pacquet broke open', to both *The Unknown Lady's Pacquet* and *The Remaining Part* underscore the connection to Gildon. *The Unknown Lady's Pacquet* also echoes the structure of the popular epistolary collection by Vincent de Voiture, *Familiar and Courtly Letters to Persons of Honour and Quality* (1700). As Michael McKeon points out, the genre of 'private' letters made public also alluded to the well-known example *The Kings Cabinet Opened* (1645), a collection of fictional letters ostensibly written by Charles I himself, which McKeon describes as 'One of the most spectacular secret histories of the seventeenth century'.[69]

Contrary to previous critical consensus, therefore, Manley's first foray into the genre of the secret history was not in 1705 with *Queen Zarah*, but in 1707 with *The Unknown Lady's Pacquet of Letters*, a work that has typically been mined for 'facts' about Manley's own life rather than interpreted within the logic of its own genre. To be fair, *The Unknown Lady's Pacquet* does offer suggestive clues about Manley's life: in it she describes her trip to Bristol apparently taken at some point after her liaison with John Tilly ended in 1702; she also includes letters (either real, reconstructed or fictionalized) ostensibly from her former friend Richard Steele and several assumed to have been written by another former friend, Sarah Egerton. However, Manley also recycles gossip about well-known society figures: one anonymous letter recounts the stories surrounding the mysterious death of Beau Wilson; another alludes to the trial following the marriage of the Duchess of Cleveland to the bigamous Beau Feilding (1650/1–1712); several letters tell stories of mysterious mistresses to former monarchs; some concern the visit of a Hessian prince whom Manley claims to have met during his visit to London. The first part of *The Unknown Lady's Pacquet* was issued in early January 1707, and the *Remaining Part* in September of the same year.[70]

While there is no overtly partisan message evident in this collection of letters – unlike the staunchly High-Church ideology that permeates *Queen Zarah* – their overall effect is very much that of a secret history in the mode of a loosely structured collection of anecdotes. As Lionel Gossman explains, such loosely structured collections

> worked to undermine established views and stimulate new ones, either by presenting material known to few and excluded from officially authorized histories, or by reporting 'odd' occurrences for which the established views of history, the world, and human nature do not easily account.[71]

However, we might well wonder what, in 1707, the standard 'official' storylines were that Manley was disrupting. She does not, as she later would in *The New Atalantis*, retell the story of the Revolution of 1688–9 from a Tory perspective. Nor does she offer a critical counter-narrative of British military policy in the War of Spanish Succession, as she would again in *The New Atalantis*, despite the provocative claim on the title page that the letters were '*Taken from her* [the Unknown Lady] *by a* French *Privateer in her Passage to* Holland' and '*Brought over from St.* Malo's *by an* English *Officer at the last Exchange of Prioners*'.[72]

Instead, Manley presents or recycles gossipy anecdotes about somewhat marginal or elusive political figures. Some of the letters, such as the one about Beau Wilson, and the ones about the Duchess of Cleveland, have the general effect of tarnishing the court figures or governmental administrations of earlier eras. The overall effect, however, especially in the first published portion of the work, does not convey a message of political opposition so much as a sense that beneath the public surface, things are not always as they seem.

The initial portion of *The Lady's Pacquet*, which appeared in early January 1707, was published as an addendum to a translation of Marie d'Aulnoy's *Memoirs of the Court of England*, a fictional account of six days of amorous adventures, involving the Dukes of Buckingham, Monmouth, Arran and other noblemen.[73] Unlike a novel such as *Hattigé*, in which an actual love affair (between Charles II and the Duchess of Cleveland) is used to criticize Charles politically for being too swayed by a domineering mistress, d'Aulnoy's *Memoirs of the Court of England* would appear to be amorous sentimental fiction without obvious political overtones. D'Aulnoy had never lived in England, nor does her work appear to be based on other journalistic or historical sources, as was her *Travels in Spain*.[74] Nor do we know at whose behest, or for whose profit, this work was published. The publisher listed on the title page of *The Memoirs of the Court of England*, B. Bragg, was a 'trade publisher', or someone who published for a fee or a percentage a work for which someone else was sharing in the risks and the profits. A trade publisher might have been employed when the work was deemed politically risky, or when an author could not find another publisher, or hoped to make more money than he or she would likely make by selling the book outright to a conventional bookseller (generally someone who had more available capital than a 'trade publisher'). D'Aulnoy's *Memoirs* might have given the perception of being politically risky, but since it was largely fictitious, risk might not have been the overriding reason that it was published with a trade publisher. D'Aulnoy herself or together with her translator may have decided that because her *Travels in Spain* had been so successful, she and her translator might maximize their profits by publishing with Bragg. Manley may have had a separate arrangement with Bragg, although whether or not she was obliged (or able) to fund some percentage of the printing cost at the outset is not known.[75]

The first part of *The Lady's Pacquet* does not give any clues about the identity of either the writer or recipient of any of the letters, nor was a key ever published, so its political effect would have been less obvious than would that of Manley's subsequent political secret histories. Although there are twelve letters that may have been written by Richard Steele included in this first portion of the *Pacquet*, Manley does not identify their author, so their political effect was not what it would be when she recounted similar gossip in *The New Atalantis*, for which separately published keys identified most characters, including Steele. In that subsequent work, by printing unflattering gossip about the Whig author of the governmental mouthpiece, the *Gazette*, Manley is clearly engaging in mudsling-ing for the Tories by publicly airing a private complaint. The inclusion of much of the same information in unidentified letters in the first part of *The Lady's Pacquet* would have had a less pointed political effect.

The first letter in the first part of *The Unknown Lady's Pacquet* recounts the story of one 'Mr. *W—l—*', probably Edward ('Beau') Wilson (d. 1694), who baf-fled court and society in the early to mid-1690s by his sudden and unexplained increase in wealth and by his subsequent death at the hands of John Law (1671–1729).[76] Manley offers an explanation to this decade-old piece of gossip by suggesting that Wilson was the lover of William III's female favourite, Elizabeth Villiers (*c.* 1657–1733). While this gossip generally tarnishes the reign of an earlier monarch with Whiggish sympathies, Manley's inclusion of it here would not damage William's posthumous reputation nearly to the extent as would her recounting in *The New Atalantis* suggestively homoerotic incidents between William III and his closest male advisors, William Bentinck, Earl of Portland, and Arnold Joost van Keppel (1669/70–1718), first Earl of Albemarle.[77]

The *Remaining Part of the Lady's Pacquet* was published nine months later, not by Bragg, but 'printed and sold by' John Morphew and John Woodward, the publishers listed on the title page of *The New Atalantis* who would be arrested in late October 1709 for publishing that work.[78] The *Remaining Part of the Lady's Pacquet*, like the earlier part of Manley's epistolary collection, was also appended to a translation of a work by d'Aulnoy, *The History of the Earl of Warwick, Sirnam'd the King-Maker: Containing his Amours, And other Memorable Trans-actions*. We do not know the reason for the change in bookseller. Morphew and Woodward were trade publishers, like Bragg, but their yearly output (especially Morphew's) was greater than Bragg's. Also, Morphew's shop, near Stationers' Hall, might have offered a better distribution point for sales. It might have been that d'Aulnoy or her translator decided to choose a publisher with more titles on his publishing list, or it might have been that Bragg (who collaborated on vari-ous projects with Morphew and other Tory publishers) had referred this work to Morphew and Woodward.

It is probable that Manley was not involved in the decision to change from Bragg to Morphew and Woodward. However, this change in publisher might have resulted in Manley's meeting John Barber, who printed many works with Morphew and Woodward's imprint, and who would be arrested two years later, along with Manley, for *The New Atalantis*.[79] Barber cultivated friendships with powerful Tories – including Bolingbroke and Swift – and would become involved in many Tory printing projects. By 1714, John Morphew observed, when interrogated in the House of Lords about the publication of *The Public Spirit of the Whigs* (for which he and Barber were apprehended for seditious libel), that 'he looked upon himself to be publisher to Mr. Barber'.[80] It is certainly possible that if Barber printed *The Remaining Part of the Unknown Lady's Pacquet*, he might have made Manley's acquaintance and discussed with her the possibility of a longer, more overtly political secret history.

Interestingly, unlike the first part, the *Remaining Part of the Unknown Lady's Pacquet* contains not only proper names of several of the writers or recipients of letters (either in full or in easily identifiable ellipses, such as R— St—le) but also a table of contents, which includes these names. Readers, therefore, were alerted to letters, for example, '*to the Prince of* Hesse Darmstadt' or '*by the late D. of D—*' or about '*the salacious Amours of Madam* Montespan, *one of the French King's Mistresses*'.[81] It is conceivable that either Morphew and Woodward, or possibly Barber as printer (if he were the printer), might have made the suggestion about the table of contents, a standard textual apparatus to help market a work. By naming in this table of contents the public figures not named in the first part of *The Lady's Pacquet*, the publisher or printer also calls attention to the work's status as secret history.

The letter ostensibly about Madame de Montespan in *The Remaining Part of the Unknown Lady's Pacquet* is particularly intriguing since in this case the details of an ageing royal mistress marrying a younger (and already married) opportunist do not correspond to the particular details of Montespan's life, but clearly allude to the 1705 marriage of Charles II's former mistress, Barbara Palmer, Duchess of Cleveland (for whom Manley briefly served as a companion in 1694), to the bigamous Robert or 'Beau' Feilding, who himself was already married to Mary Wadsworth. Manley also alludes in this letter ostensibly about 'Montespan' to Feilding's 'very diverting' trial for adultery 'before the council of State'. Thus, while the text of the letter and the table of contents identifies the person discussed as Montespan, this name is really a code or a pseudonym for Cleveland. In other words, this particular letter might be said to represent, in miniature, Manley's first coded secret history in which pseudonyms serve to camouflage but not entirely disguise the real identities of the persons being satirized.[82]

Rehashing this curious incident in the life of a former mistress of Charles II would not have had the same effect of political opposition as earlier secret histories about the Duchess of Cleveland, published during Charles II's lifetime. *Hattigé: ou les Amours du Roy de Tamaran*, for example, the secret history about Cleveland's immense power over Charles II, raised questions about his independence as a monarch – questions not insignificant for an English ruler who had negotiated secret treaties with France. When portions of the translation of *Hattigé* were incorporated almost verbatim into *Queen Zarah*, the effect was to tarnish a subsequent regime for its cooperation with the Whigs. By 1707, the effect of reminding readers of Cleveland's recent nuptial embarrassment would have been very different.

The 1705 incident of bigamy suggests not only that Cleveland no longer held sway over a sitting monarch, but that she herself had been manipulated and was being subjected to ridicule by an opportunistic swindler. Rather than tarnishing Anne's government, or her Whig ministry in 1707, the incident would have reminded readers that a society figure who had mingled with and been acknowledged by the powerful and the well-connected (and who had had love affairs with both John Churchill, Duke of Marlborough, and Ralph, Duke of Montague, among others) during the reigns of four monarchs was now an object of ridicule. What did this say about the wisdom of those current members of court and society who had once frequented her circle? The effect of alluding to this anecdote about Cleveland would not undermine any specific Whig policies, but it certainly would remind readers of the dark underside of contemporary court and society.

The letters in *The Unknown Lady's Pacquet* reference some recognizable society figures – including the Duchess of Cleveland, Richard Steele, the Duke of Ormond, the Earl of Peterborough, the Prince of Hesse-Darmstadt, Lady Wharton, wife of the Whig Thomas Wharton, and Sarah, Duchess of Marlborough – many of whom Manley would depict (under pseudonyms) in more developed satirical anecdotes in *The New Atalantis* and *Memoirs of Europe*. The anecdotes in *The Unknown Lady's Pacquet* are mostly brief, and no particularly denigrating items of gossip are related. Manley's allusions to these persons does not yet have the effect of focused or obviously partisan satire; rather, she is simply informing her readers that she was keeping track of the comings and goings of a large number of society figures.

Manley also establishes in *The Unknown Lady's Pacquet* her wide reading in contemporary literature and theology. She mentions or cites a range of current drama and poetry, including plays by Joseph Trapp (1679–1747), John Dennis (1658–1734) and John Crowne (bap. 1641, d. 1712); she alludes to Charles Gildon's recent translation of Apuleius's *Metamorphosis*, to unpublished poems by Anne Finch (1661–1720), and to Samuel Garth's popular long poem *The Dispensary* (1699). Manley also refers to Samuel Butler's *Hudibras*, a classical satirical poem once cited in a letter by her father, and to la Calprenède's long romance *Cassandra* (English translation 1667).[83] She touches on the contemporary religious controversies about the nature of the soul, including a sequence of treatises and pamphlets by William Coward; she also acknowledges Erasmus's colloquia.

The overall effect of *The Unknown Lady's Pacquet* is of an author or compiler who is not only conversant with the world of contemporary literature and ideas but aware of the comings and goings of many persons in contemporary court and society. The two parts of *The Unknown Lady's Pacquet* appeared anonymously, as would *The New Atalantis* about two years later. However, that subsequent work would sound enough alarm bells that Secretary of State Sunderland would seek out the author and investigate 'the noble and worthy Persons' whom she 'corresponds with'.[84] Already in *The Remaining Part of the Lady's Pacquet*, Manley (possibly with the assistance of her trade publishers and their printer) was establishing her authorial persona as someone who just might know a little more about most public figures than they would like her to.

7 '[T]HROWING THE FIRST STONE': 1709

In a letter written in the summer of 1714 to Robert Harley, Earl of Oxford, Manley 'most humbly' asks Harley's opinion of a plan she has for a pamphlet offering 'a true account of the Changes made just Before the Death of the Queen'.[1] These 'Changes' would have included Oxford's own dismissal from office two weeks before Anne's death. Having served since 1710 as Chancellor of the Exchequer and since 1711 as Lord Treasurer, Oxford had been Queen Anne's chief (or de facto 'prime') minister for four years. Moreover, by recruiting 'some of the most prominent and most effective pamphleteers of his age', he had over the previous decade helped create what J. A. Downie has described as a ministerial 'propaganda machine'.[2] Manley herself had been part of that propaganda machine since the spring of 1711, when she was asked by Jonathan Swift to write pamphlets on various topics of interest to the Oxford ministry (including one about the 1711 assassination attempt against Harley) and when she was subsequently asked to take over the *Examiner*, which Swift had previously authored.

As is evident from her August 1714 letter to Oxford, however, Manley considered herself more than a mere subcontractor to her friend Swift, 'cook[ing] ... in her own style' six-penny pamphlets he either 'had not time to do himself' or else was not willing to write in such a way as would satisfy Oxford.[3] In her August 1714 letter, Manley suggests, as an organizing analogy for her proposed pamphlet, a scene from Dampier about 'the Queen of Achins Court & Country' which she believes would help 'sett those men right [about Oxford] who only condemn for want of information'.[4] In other words, by the summer of 1714 Manley was obviously confident enough in her own skill at designing political propaganda to make a suggestion directly to Oxford, on whom she had waited in late May 1714 while he was still in office.[5]

Manley, of course, had some reason to be confident. Before writing pamphlets in support of Oxford's ministry, she had already made a name for herself as a Tory writer through her two best-selling political secret histories: *The New Atalantis* and *Memoirs of Europe*. She seems to have begun writing pamphlets for the Oxford ministry through her connection to Jonathan Swift (whom she appears to have met in early 1711), but she had previously written to Harley, whose 'acquaintance' she says she could 'only covet never hope', in the spring of 1710.[6] In one of her first extant letter to Harley, written in April (or July) 1710, she not only mentions that 'many Great and good' think she deserves 'some Regard' but she also requests Harley's recommendation for a lieutenant's position for the young man delivering the letter (quite possibly her son John Manley, who would have been of an age to have passed the lieutenant's exam she refers to in her letter). With her next letter, written about a month later, she encloses a copy of her *Memoirs of Europe*, which she describes as 'some imperfect pieces of painting of the heads of That [Whig] party that have mislead Thousands'. She offers to explain to Harley 'any thing' in the book that stirs his 'Curiosity'.[7] Clearly still hoping for some reward or recognition, she calls attention to her achievement in portraying the falseness of the Whigs.

In a subsequent letter to Harley (by then Earl of Oxford) written the following year, she refers to 'a Note from your Lordship, to command my Attendance, which I endeavoured in vain'.[8] In a letter written 3 June 1714, she describes this note as 'writt in your Lordshipps hand some months after my sufferings and imprisonment' – presumably in the spring of 1710 (some time after the charges against her for *The New Atalantis* were dropped in February 1710 and sometime before her May 1710 letter to him, enclosing *Memoirs of Europe*).[9] Although the desired meeting seems not to have taken place in 1710 (Manley explains in the letter of 3 June 1714 that she was 'in the Country to recover my Health' at the time Harley wrote), it would appear that even before she met Jonathan Swift, Manley had made an effective enough name for herself as a political writer that during the spring of 1710 Harley sought to meet with her. At this point, Harley himself was still out of the ministry but in contact with Queen Anne and urging the dismissals of Sunderland (which occurred in June) and Godolphin (which occurred in August) as well as his own appointment to Godolphin's position.

Four years later, in June 1714, when Oxford was anticipating his own dismissal from office, he sent Manley a 'Bill of fifty pounds' commanding her to 'Secrecy'.[10] This payment was sent shortly after the publication of *The Adventures of Rivella*, in which Manley remarks that the Whigs rewarded their writers more generously than the Tories.[11] However, the payment was probably prompted not by the publication of *Rivella* but by a letter Manley sent Harley on 3 June 1714, reminding him of the 'Fears and the Hardships' she suffered (because of her arrest for *The New Atalantis*) and informing him that 'Lord Masham and Sr. William Windham' had been 'commissioned' by 'The Society for Rewarding of merit' to request 'that your Lordship would send me an hundred pound'.[12] It appears from the wording of this request that Oxford had not yet sent Manley any financial remuneration.

The timing of Manley's request and directness of her demand for 'an hundred pound' may have been prompted by the anticipation of Oxford's dismissal, following his deteriorating relations with Queen Anne in the spring of 1714.[13] The payment Oxford sent Manley six weeks before he himself was dismissed from office acknowledges the value that his ministry placed on the sort of political propaganda she wrote. Although £50 may not seem like much money, it was the same amount Oxford once offered Swift (an offer Swift, of course, refused as a gentleman who did not write for payment, although he certainly hoped for a reward of preferment).[14] Moreover, £50 was not insignificant compared to Manley's total wealth at the time of her death in 1724, which, according to her will, consisted largely of some South Sea Stock worth about £350.

Before she met Swift, however, or was recognized by Oxford, Manley began her work as a writer of political satire on her own. She chose the genre of the political secret history, a favourite form of Whigs who recounted various intrigues in the reigns of Charles II and James II that helped justify the Revolution of 1688–9. Manley's first political secret history, *The New Atalantis*, written following the Whig ministerial coup of 1708, in which Robert Harley and Henry St John were forced from office at the insistence of Marlborough and Godolphin, retold the events of 1688–9 from a Tory perspective. This retelling was clearly designed to diminish the reputations of the nominal Tories Marlborough and Godolphin, who had not only abandoned James II in 1688 but, by 1708, had capitulated to many of the demands of the Whig Junto – the powerful Whig peers Somers, Halifax, Orford, Sunderland and Wharton – in order to gain their cooperation to continue funding the War of Spanish Succession.

When Marlborough's son-in-law, third Earl of Sunderland (the youngest member of the Whig Junto and a secretary of state), arrested Manley for libel in October 1709, his main concern was that the 'Intelligence' she had about court and ministry intrigues was beyond what a woman in her position was likely to know. Manley, however, may well have written the first volume of *The New Atalantis* without outside advice or encouragement; she may have had an inside source of court information for the second volume, although we cannot be certain of this. As Manley suggests in *Rivella*, she had the courage to throw 'the first Stone', that is, to write opposition satire during a period when the Whigs were very much in control of the government (and in charge of prosecuting the press). Her subsequent political writing – *Memoirs of Europe*, the *Examiner* and her pamphlets for the Oxford ministry – would be published when the Tories were regaining control of the government; she would, therefore, no longer be at risk of prosecution. However, in 1709 at a moment when the Whig Junto was in control of Queen Anne's ministry, Manley seems to have taken on the Whigs by herself, acting for herself, although with the possible financial backing of the Tory printer John Barber.

'An Authoress and a Printer': Collaboration with Barber

The publishers listed on the title page for Manley's *The New Atalantis*, the first volume of which was advertised in late May 1709, were John Morphew and John Woodward.[15] As I have already explained, however, Morphew and Woodward were trade publishers, who served as a front for the person who owned the work and financed its publication. It has long been assumed, without tangible evidence, that Barber was the printer for *The New Atalantis*. In fact, the warrant for the arrest of '— Manley & John Barber Printer' (before Manley's name, sex or profession was identified) has recently been discovered in the warrant book for Sunderland's years as secretary of state. In the warrant book, this item directly follows the warrant dated 28 October 1709 for arresting Morphew and Woodward for their role in publishing the same book.[16] Whether or not Morphew and Woodward revealed Barber's and Manley's names to Sunderland in a preliminary interrogation, or whether Sunderland found their names out by other means, the second warrant (which was undated but may have been issued on the same day as the warrant for Morphew and Woodward), which puts Barber and Manley together on the same order to arrest, suggests their joint participation in the work.

As has already been explained, when employing a trade publisher for a lengthy work, the person who 'owned' the work was expected to contribute 'progress payments in respect of both paper and print'.[17] Given that following the May 1707 publication of her tragedy *Almyna*, Manley had written a begging letter to Ralph, Duke of Montagu, suggesting that all of her possessions were about to be seized,[18] it would seem unlikely that she would have had many resources of her own a year and a half later to underwrite the publication of a lengthy and risky political secret history. It is possible that she had made some modest profit from the September publication of the *Remaining Part of the Unknown Lady's Pacquet*, but it seems unlikely that whatever sum was generated from the sale of this short epistolary work, appended to a translation of d'Aulnoy, would have been adequate to pay her debts, support her for the next year and a half, and also finance the publication costs for this new publication.

It appears from the wording of the arrest warrant for Manley and Barber that John Barber was the printer for *The New Atalantis*. As I have already suggested, it is possible that Barber was the printer for the *Remaining Part of the Unknown Lady's Pacquet*, for which Morphew and Woodward were the trade publishers. If he were the printer for this work, then it is possible that Barber met Manley through the process of printing this edition, which appeared in September 1707. Whether or not he met her as early as 1707, Barber almost certainly knew Manley by 1709, when he printed *The New Atalantis*. Early in 1709 their collaboration as author and printer was probably still in its early stages, since there is no evidence that Barber was involved in printing or publishing the poem Manley may have written about the military hero Major-General Webb, *An Heroick Essay Upon the Unequale'd Victory Obtain'd by Major-General Webb*, which appeared in February 1709 and was sold by the trade publisher and bookseller Abigail Baldwin (who may also have been the printer).[19]

The profits from the *Heroick Essay*, if Manley was the author, might have helped her to pay the trade publishers Woodward and Morphew the initial costs for publishing *The New Atalantis*. However, it is also possible, given Manley's precarious financial circumstances at this time, that John Barber might have financed the publication of *The New Atalantis* (and possibly even supported Manley while she was writing the work), and then saw most of the profits from it. As I have already explained, by 1714 John Morphew would testify in the House of Lords that he considered himself 'publisher to Mr. Barber'.[20] Although Morphew may not have considered himself to be such as early as 1709, *The New Atalantis* may have been one of the projects that would give Morphew reason to consider himself in this light. Moreover, in a posthumous biography of Barber, printed for Edmund Curll and supposedly 'written by several hands', the authors refer to the 'large Sums he [Barber] acquired' from Manley's 'writings'.[21] The unauthorized posthumous biographies printed and sold by Curll should not necessarily be trusted as reliable sources of fact. However, as a bookseller himself – and one who deployed the trade publisher J. Roberts in publishing Manley's *Adventures of Rivella* – Curll certainly understood the financial structure of the publishing trade and there is probably some truth in the assertion that Barber profited from Manley's work.

By the time of his death in 1741, Barber was wealthy enough to specify over £5,000 in legacies to his friends and relations, in addition to the bulk of his estate, which he left to Sarah Duffkin, presumed to be his common-law wife (apparently a former servant to Manley). Barber's fortune was accrued by years of hard work and savvy negotiations in the world of printing and publishing, including his acquisition of a range of profitable government printing contracts. His wealth also reflected either the good sense – or good inside information as printer to the South Sea Company – to have sold or converted into real estate some of his South Sea stock before the bubble burst, a move that was said to have netted him £30,000.[22] Part of his wealth (exactly what portion cannot be determined) certainly must have derived from profits for publishing Manley's best-selling works. The biography of Barber published by Curll suggests in an annotation to Barber's will (reprinted in the unauthorized biography) that Barber earned '*many Thousand Pounds*' from Manley's writings.[23]

Manley's own wealth at death (including £500 of South Sea stock purchased in 1721 but valued at only £352 when she wrote her will in 1723) does not suggest that she accrued particularly large sums from her writings or did as well from her South Sea investments as Barber. Curll's biography of Barber plays up his putatively tyrannical treatment of 'his best Friend Mrs. *Manley*' by insisting that Barber had profited from her writings and then forsook Manley as his mistress for 'a common House Maid' whom he had 'hired in the Country, and brought up to Town to attend' Manley.[24] However, in her own will, Manley does not mention any other money or profits owed to her by Barber for her published works. In fact, she refers to having 'received so many favours' from 'Alderman Barber' that she would not make 'any Claims from him' stemming from future profits of a printer's patent shared by Barber and the bookseller Benjamin Tooke (from which she was supposed to have been paid £50 per annum once the patent started turning a profit). She does, however, request the help of her 'much honoured friend the Dean of St. Patrick Dr. Swift' in securing for her legatees the profits owed her by Tooke's heirs.[25]

With the rise of Oxford and the Tory ministry in 1711, Barber became printer for the *Examiner* and then, jointly with the bookseller Benjamin Tooke, for the *London Gazette*. He was also elected that year to the Common Council of the City of London as a member for the Ward of Queenhithe.[26] Later in life, he would become Mayor of London. Even before he had achieved this advancement, however, Barber had already established himself as a flourishing printer. He was described by a second eighteenth-century biographer, clearly a Tory, as being, by 1705

> well known, and not better known than beloved ... His Name was up among the Booksellers and Authors in general; and if we may be allowed the Expression, he was become the Idol of a Set of Persons of Distinction, whose Wit and Sense will never be disputed, but by those who have no Pretensions to either.[27]

This biographer also suggests that Barber soon made the acquaintance of Manley and Henry St John (1678–1751), subsequently Viscount Bolingbroke. We in fact do not know exactly when Barber met Manley (although certainly by 1709) or St John. Barber appears to have made the acquaintance of Jonathan Swift in late December 1710, and this biographer suggests that St John introduced him to both Harley and Swift. As early as 1707 or 1708, Barber might have met the Tory military physician and writer Dr John Freind (1675–1728), whose *Account of the Earl of Peterborow's Conduct in Spain* he printed for John Boyer.[28]

While Barber seems to have published for both Whigs and Tories until about 1705, his subsequent business success and the new friendships he made resulted, according to his Tory biographer, in his avowing 'his Principles, which he had hitherto carefully concealed, and [he] openly declared for CHURCH and Monarchy; a Declaration he never deviated from'.[29] By the time he met Delarivier Manley, probably some time between 1707 and 1709, Barber was a successful printer who had already made some well-placed contacts with powerful Tories, but he did not yet know Swift and might not yet have met St John or Harley (whom he may not have known personally). Barber was a sensible enough businessman to appreciate the value of a high-risk but potentially popular publication. He probably also had the resources to finance the publication of Manley's lengthy first political secret history, *The New Atalantis*, and to support her while she was writing it. He might have helped pay the legal costs attendant on its publication and his and Manley's arrest for libel.

Part of the complexity in making sense of Manley and Barber's working relationship is the presumption that they were lovers as well as collaborators. In fact, they may well have been lovers, although if so there was certainly for each of them a practical advantage to their partnership. Aside from any romantic link between them, Barber certainly printed and quite possibly financed Manley's *New Atalantis*; he had 'an Apartment fitted up for her' in his house in Lambeth Hill, as Barber's Tory biographer explains with a certain sardonic emphasis, 'for the Sake, *only*, of being near the Press and more at hand, to se her own Work done *correctly*, and better attended to than it had been'.[30] This same biographer, writing in 1741 after Barber's death, attempts to describe the developing relationship between Manley and Barber, although he is able to provide few dates or specifics about the beginnings of a relationship that probably commenced over three decades earlier:

> The Transition from Friendship to Affection, is very easy, and often made, when the most amiable Part of the Species is concerned. Mrs *Manley* had not conversed many Months with Mr BARBER, but she began to view him in a different Light from the Rest; she found, that what had pleased her Ear, had touched her Heart; and she soon found, that his Person, good Sense, and Address, had made a Captive of her ...[31]

Again, without providing any specifics about how Manley and Barber met, this biographer describes their courtship in military terms, suggesting that Barber was 'an experienced General in this Part of the Art Military' who 'continued his Attack, and gained Ground every Day'. The writer concludes, again providing very little real information: 'at length a Capitulation was agreed to, and signed upon honourable Terms by both Sides; and the Conqueror remained in Possession of the Fort for several Years'.[32]

Leaving aside the trope of military siege, the contractual language used to describe a relationship apparently 'signed upon honourable Terms by both Sides' might aptly characterize Manley and Barber's partnership. In 1707, the year that Manley's *Unknown Lady's Pacquet of Letters* and her third play, *Almyna*, were published, she was apparently struggling to ward off creditors, if we take at face value her begging letter to the Duke of Montagu. In the previous winter, at the time of *Almnya*'s production, Manley appears not even to have been living in London – quite possibly because she could not afford to. She had also been obliged to leave London on numerous occasions in the previous decade and a half – in 1694, 1704 and possibly 1705 and 1706 – apparently because she did not have adequate resources to stay. Barber, a strikingly ambitious and successful printer, from a completely different social class than Manley, had aspirations to the social level into which Manley had been born (he would purchase a coat of arms with his South Sea profits) and was happy to publish works with enough references to the *beau monde* to guarantee large sales. Barber's Tory biographer suggests that it was Barber who made a conquest of Manley, but Manley was certainly capable of cultivating an intimacy with a successful Tory printer whose patronage might be to her benefit.

The agreement that Manley and Barber came to seems to have met the needs of both of them, at least for some years. Manley presumably wanted a secure place to live in London, good meals, enlivening companionship, and a room of her own (either literally or figuratively) in which to write. Barber seems to have met her material needs, although we have no way of knowing whether she ever paid him for her lodging or whether he believed that publishing her (best-selling) works was payment enough. Her witty conversation, which had once charmed the Duchess of Cleveland, Sir Thomas Skipwith and possibly the Dukes of Devonshire and Montagu, among others, would have added a certain cachet to Barber's dining table; her appreciation of her 'Ancient' family and the royalist lineage she asserts so confidently in her published works would have complemented Barber's Tory social circle.

Barber's Tory biographer suggests that Barber owed to Manley his 'Acquaintance with the Gay and the Great'.[33] It is in fact possible that Manley maintained her friendship with George Granville – whom she seems to have known when both were writing for the theatre in the mid-1690s – and it is possible that Manley introduced Barber to Granville and other aspiring Tory literati. It is also possible that as a Tory printer of increasing prominence, Barber made many of his own contacts with the Tory gentry. When Jonathan Swift first wrote to Stella of dining with Barber, he described himself as dining 'with no less a man than the city printer', suggesting that his acquaintance was first with Barber and secondly with Manley, whom he describes as an 'authoress' on his second mention of dining with Barber.[34]

Even if Barber was not of the right social class to have been part of the Honorable Board of Loyal Brotherhood, the drinking club organized in 1709 by the Duke of Beaufort for disaffected Tories frustrated with the Whig Junto, he may have known some wits and writers who knew some of its members, and may well have heard second or third hand some of the gossip from its meetings. In later years, after he became friends with Jonathan Swift, Barber would be invited to report to the meetings of another Tory 'Society' or 'Club' formed in 1711 for 'conversation and friendship, and to reward deserving persons with our interest and recommendation' (as Swift described it),[35] to which Manley refers in her June 1714 letter to Harley.

Manley and Barber may well have been lovers during some of the years they lived together. According to the *Journal to Stella* Jonathan Swift dined with them regularly between 1711 and 1714. However, Manley and Barber obviously kept separate investment accounts and to some extent separate lives. Manley visited her sister Cornelia in Finchley regularly during the first years that she lived with Barber (in later years Cornelia also seems to have taken up residence at Barber's house). Manley took her own house in Beckley, Oxfordshire, possibly in about 1717. Barber obviously was attentive enough to Manley that when Harley sent the 'bill of fifty pounds' to her in June 1714, Barber apparently rode from London to Finchley to bring her the monetary reward – a mark of political triumph for the works she had written and he had published, which he probably wanted to celebrate with her.[36]

By 1720, after about a decade of being friends, collaborators and probably lovers (for at least some of that period), Barber purchased (with his profits from South Sea stock) an estate in East Sheen and a coat of arms as well as a town house in Queen Square. Manley seems to have continued to reside at Barber's printing house on Lambeth Hill, whenever she was in London. The biography printed for Curll suggests that she died there.[37] According to this same account, Manley's sister Cornelia Markendale continued living in Barber's house after this time.[38] Barber himself was in exile on the Continent when Manley died, having left England in 1722 purportedly carrying £50,000 in bills of exchange from English Jacobites to support the Old Pretender. Barber was unable to return to England until August 1724, a month after Manley's death. Whether Barber's purported mistress at this time, Manley's former servant Sarah Duffkin, was living in the same house as Manley during Barber's exile on the Continent is not known; it is possible that Duffkin was living in the town house in Queen Square, where she apparently lived after Manley's death as 'Mistress of [Barber's] House ... in a handsome sumptuous Manner, suitable to his Opulent Fortune'.[39]

As I have suggested, John Barber might have begun supporting Manley at the time when she began writing her first political secret history, *The New Atalantis*. Moreover, from 1709 until 1713, the years when she wrote her most significant political works, Manley and Barber seemed to have been collaborators in all of her publishing ventures. With the exception of *Rivella*, published for Edmund Curll (for reasons already discussed), Barber remained Manley's publisher until the end of her life, bringing out her fourth play, *Lucius, the First Christian King of Britain* and her collection of novellas, *The Power of Love*. Although he probably did see significant profits from Manley's works, as Edmund Curll's biography of him suggests, at the time when Barber appears to have begun his collaboration with Manley, he was certainly taking a political risk. Despite Anne's reliance on

her Tory attendant Abigail Masham and her ongoing correspondence with Robert Harley, the Whigs, along with Marlborough and Godolphin, were in control
of Queen Anne's ministry, and Sunderland, without consulting the rest of the
Whig Junto, was actively harassing opposition writers.

'[T]hrowing the first Stone': *The New Atalantis*

As I have already suggested, the style and structure of Manley's *Secret Memoirs
and Manners of Several Persons of Quality, of Both Sexes, from The New Atalantis* is probably best explained through its similarity to her earlier epistolary
work *The Unknown Lady's Pacquet of Letters*. That shorter work offered a series
of anecdotes in epistolary form, some of which describe recognizable events in
the lives of public figures (such as Feilding's trial for bigamy following his marriage to the Duchess of Cleveland), some events in the lives of other writers and
quasi-public figures, such as Richard Steele, and some events in Manley's own
life that probably would not otherwise have been known to the public. The first
volume of *The New Atalantis*, which appeared in May 1709, includes a similar
mix of anecdote and gossip about both well-known public figures and lesser-
known acquaintances or former friends of Manley. However, in addition to and
interwoven between these gossipy anecdotes are mini-narratives of well-known
historical events, such as the Duke of Monmouth's Rebellion in 1685 and the
accession of William and Mary in 1688. Moreover, each of the volumes of *The
New Atalantis* is dedicated to Henry Somerset, second Duke of Beaufort, a well-
known Jacobite.

In *The Adventures of Rivella*, Manley describes her courage in 'throwing the
first Stone', that is, in calling public attention to the greed and hypocrisy of public figures currently in power. Her narrator explains,

> she was proud of having more Courage than had any of our Sex, and of throwing the
> first Stone, which might give a Hint for other Persons of more Capacity to examine
> the Defects, and Vices of some Men who took a Delight to impose upon the World,
> by the Pretence of publick Good, whilst their true Design was only to gratify and
> advance themselves.[40]

Although *The New Atalantis* does revise Whig secret histories popular after the
Revolution of 1688–9 through a Tory prism, the work also put on display the
hypocrisy and greed of public officials in both parties.

Deploying the genre of a dystopian travelogue, in a dark echo of Francis
Bacon's utopian *The New Atlantis* (1626), Manley creates in *The New Atalantis* a
loose structure that allows her to link together often unrelated anecdotes about
a range of public figures. As in *The Unknown Lady's Pacquet of Letters*, Manley
lays open a miscellaneous bundle of different items of gossip. Her unifying
structure is a visit to Angela (London) by Astrea and her mother, Virtue. Astrea

('starry maiden') was one of the deities who lived on earth with mortals during the 'Golden Age' until she finally withdrew to take her place among the stars (as Virgo). A celestial being associated with Elizabeth I in English iconography (as a virgin wielding a sword of justice), Astrea has apparently been asked to return to earth to oversee the 'Royal Education' of the 'young Prince' who is heir to the throne, following the death of his mother, the 'beautifullest' daughter (probably Sophia (1630–1714), Electress of Hanover) of an earlier princess (whose story corresponds to that of Elizabeth Stuart (1596–1662), Sophia's mother). Astrea's task is to be the 'Guide', 'Leader', and 'Guard' of this young heir to the throne, who has suffered 'under the greatest of Misfortunes, the want of Royal Education'.[41]

In other words, Manley begins her tableau of gossip and vice in London through the conceit of a future succession – represented not as a crisis of succession but as a crisis of education. Although most of the rest of the text will not concern this prince, except to describe the world of vice he needs to be taught to negotiate, it is significant that Manley makes the issue of royal succession central to a work that might otherwise be dismissed as merely a tableau of society gossip. As in *Almyna*, Manley makes the question of the monarchical succession a structuring theme of her narrative. Twentieth-century critics, taking Manley to be an anti-Jacobite Tory, generally believed that the 'young Prince' represented the future George II of England (1683–1760), although Ruth Herman has pointed out that this would mean she was insulting the highly literate Electress Sophia, who had supervised the education of George II. Herman suggests, plausibly enough, that the prince represents instead 'the future Hanoverian dynasty, unschooled in the ways of the British monarchy'.[42]

Despite her necessary nod to the ruling house of Hanover, however, it is also likely that Manley intentionally left the identity of this prince ambiguous. Given the dedication of the work to a known Jacobite and given that George II was already a grown man when *The New Atalantis* appeared, Jacobite readers might have identified Manley's 'young Prince' with a younger and more vulnerable claimant to the throne – i.e. James Edward Stuart. This young man, known in later years as the Old Pretender, arguably might have been more in need of guidance (as well as of Astrea's offer of military aid should he attempt to invade England after Anne's death) than would the heir apparent after Sophia (who was still alive at the time Manley was writing), the future George I (1660–1727). This Jacobite resonance is made more explicit by the fact that, according to Murray Pittock, 'Chief among the monarchical images of Jacobite high culture was Astraea, the embodiment of justice [and] ... an icon of a renewing and ascendant monarchy'.[43]

Moreover, since James Edward Stuart's education had been supervised by exiled Scottish Catholics, he might be described by Protestant Jacobites (possibly including the Duke of Beaufort), who supported the Jacobite cause on the condition that a Stuart claimant to the throne convert to Anglicanism, as truly 'in want of' a proper Protestant, 'royal Education'. Although passages such as this are clearly designed neither to offend Queen Anne nor overtly to challenge the Hanoverian succession, they also seem to have resonated with the work's dedicatee, an extremely wealthy Jacobite peer, to whom Manley effusively dedicated the second volume with the suggestion that she had received recognition (and presumably financial reward) for the first volume. Moreover, a letter in the Beaufort family archive also suggests that 'the Duke of Beaufort, Dr. Henry Yalden [Beaufort's chaplain], and Several Loyal Jacobites admired the Famous De la Riviere Mrs. Manley'.[44]

Manley was clearly appreciative of the reward from a wealthy Jacobite peer and depicts the Somerset family, as well as Beaufort's chaplain (who apparently was particularly supportive of Manley), in glowing terms in the second volume.[45] Moreover, Manley's own royalist background (despite her father's politically fraught years in exile) would have made her interested in the accession of a Protestant Stuart (if such were possible), who would support a Tory government. She would presumably have preferred this to the Whig government that the future heir apparent, George of Hanover, was expected to (and would) bring in. However, this somewhat intellectual or theoretical sympathy for the Jacobite cause did not mean that Manley was so enamoured of the Old Pretender that she necessarily would have been willing, for example, to travel to Rome with bills of exchange from English Jacobites for James Edward Stuart, as John Barber would later be prepared to do. Like her royalist father before her (as well as many of the Tories at court who remained in occasional correspondence with the exiled court at St Germain), the Tory Delarivier Manley seems to have seen the need to be both practical and flexible in acknowledging the (limited) possibility of a second Stuart restoration.

After introducing the problem of succession and the need to educate the unidentified young prince who was heir to the throne of the country, Manley then moves from her narrative frame to the tableau of vice her visiting deities have been brought to witness. The deities catch a glimpse of various naval officers from William's reign known for having been court-martialed or for having made tactical errors. Astrea and Virtue are also shown the current Admiral of the Fleet, identified as the Whig James Dursley (1680–1736), third Earl of Berkeley, who is dallying with an opera singer, presumably Susanna Mountfort (1690–1720). The goddesses are critical of the naval officers for their lax morality but are hopeful that this corruption will improve now that 'some great good Man' is 'at their Head'.[46] Here a nod is given to Thomas Herbert (1656–1733), eighth Earl of Pembroke, a moderate Tory who had been Lord High Admiral under William and was made so again after the death of Queen Anne's husband, who had served in that position. Manley's compliment to Pembroke would also remind politically alert readers that the well-respected naval leader finally given the command less than a year earlier was already at risk of being removed from his position. After pressure from the Whigs who had gained control of Anne's ministry in 1708, Pembroke would be removed from office in November 1709.

Passages such as the one described above point to Manley's specific critique of the ministers in charge of Anne's government, particularly Godolphin, whose power struggle with Harley had resulted in Harley being asked to resign in February 1708 and St John resigning out of solidarity with him (they would take office again only after Godolphin's dismissal in August 1710).[47] After this, the Whig Junto, with the support of Godolphin and Marlborough, demanded control of the ministry, rather than the previous arrangement of power-sharing. *The New Atalantis*, although it was apparently not written with any direct input by Robert Harley, nevertheless reflects the anger of those Tories forced out of office in 1708.

The first scene of naval corruption suggests a Tory critique of the corruption in a navy until recently under Whig control. The critique here is sharpened upon consideration of the probable reason that Harley and St John had been dismissed from office in 1708: Godolphin and Marlborough needed to satisfy the Whigs whose support was necessary to continue financing the War of Spanish Succession, for which Marlborough was captain general. This Continental war against French (Catholic) aggression had been popular enough in 1705 when Marlborough won the impressive battle of Blenheim. By 1708, though, it was seen as draining the country's resources for struggles over European territory that had little to do with the concerns of ordinary Britons. The Tories were also concerned that the British navy (the nation's pride since the Armada) was at risk because many resources had been poured into the army at Marlborough's command. Manley's overall critique of naval affairs, suggested in her initial scenes of naval commanders relaxing with their mistresses, is therefore very much in keeping with Tory concerns about the royal navy.

Manley's visiting deities are joined in London by 'Intelligence', described as 'First Lady of the *Bedchamber* to the Princess *Fame*',[48] who is able to recount scandals about almost everyone they see strolling in the parks and malls of London. The figure of Intelligence, of course, is a 'gossip' – a term traditionally associated with someone who keeps company with a woman lying in childbed. As I have already explained, Manley actually literalizes this allegory of gossip in the scene in which she describes Richard Steele as part of the 'merry up-sitting of the Gossips' at one of her own lyings-in.[49] She gossips, through the voice of her reporting deities in *The New Atalantis*, to the reader about Steele's illegitimate children and his speculations in alchemy even as she renders him a 'gossip' for his presence at the lying-in.

Steele was at this point establishing himself as a serious journalist: he had since 1707, through the influence of Secretary of State Sunderland (who would subsequently arrest Manley, Barber and their trade publishers for *The New Atalantis*), been the editor of the *Gazette*, the official government news medium (a Whig endeavour) and he was also making a name for himself through his *Lucubrations of Isaac Bickerstaff* (subsequently the *Tatler*). Manley, of course, reminds us through this scene of the overlap between gossip and 'serious' journalism, even as the first volume of *The New Atalantis* itself suggests the important connections between political satire and gossip. However, the account she provides of Steele sitting up with her and the female gossips at her lying-in would not prevent her from making use of Steele's Whig political connections following her arrest for libel. In a letter to Thomas Hopkins, under Secretary of State to Sunderland, in which Manley 'humbly' requests 'a speedy Examination', she mentions that she has already 'begged Mr Steels interest' for the same request.[50]

In the preface to the second volume, Manley would claim she was writing 'Varonian Satyr',[51] citing Dryden's discussion of satire in his dedication to his translation of Juvenal. In the first volume, however, rather than announcing herself publicly as a satirist, she intermixes techniques of dystopian satire and just plain gossip, thus signalling to readers that these different modes of discourse (the former of which is usually seen as more serious than the latter) have much more in common than critics usually assume. In fact, gossip may be the most insidious form of satire, since it in essence resists closure; as Jan Gordon has observed, it 'depends for its efficacy upon the circulation and speculation ... of that which cannot be verified'.[52]

In the first volume of *The New Atalantis*, Manley mocks a range of public and not so public figures. As I have already mentioned, she makes fun of her former friend, the poet Sarah Egerton, Catharine Trotter (who may have snubbed Manley following her marriage to Reverend Cockburn) and Mary Pix (in whose name Manley seems to have authored a funeral elegy for which she was never reimbursed). Trotter and Pix were Whig writers, but Manley had been friendly with both in the mid-1690s when all three were writing for the stage; Manley's reasons for mocking them were probably both personal and political.

In *The New Atalantis* Manley also satirizes various Tories, including her husband John Manley – 'this old Stallion of the Senate-House'[53] – and the Welsh tin magnate Sir Humphrey Mackworth (1657–1727) – a High-Church Tory MP and pamphleteer who would be prosecuted by Parliament for fraud and corruption. It is easy to see why she makes fun of her bigamous, adulterous husband and the corrupt Mackworth. It is harder to understand why she mocks the wealthy Tory Coke family in a section echoing the plot of Madame de La Fayette's *La Princesse de Clèves* (1678), suggesting that the recently deceased wife of the recently deceased Edward Coke (1676–1707) had been secretly in love with her husband's best friend, a gossipy assertion for which no other evidence has been found in biographies or diaries of contemporary events. It is also unclear why Manley mocks the Tory Haversham family with a story of incest that again seems to have no origin in real-life scandal. One scholar has speculated that Manley was suspicious of John Thompson (1648–1710), Baron Haversham, because he was a former Whig turned overzealous High Tory,[54] which may be the case, although the Duke of Beaufort, to whom the work is dedicated, could hardly be described as a moderate Tory. It certainly may be that Haversham was involved in some contemporary political manoeuvring or some particular act of political ingratitude (the vice for which Manley satirizes so many in *The New Atalantis*) that has been lost to history.

It is also possible that some of the stories in *The New Atalantis* are simply invention, which would be consistent with Manley's own defence of the work, in which she claims, in her account of her apprehension and interrogation in *Rivella*, that the work was a result of '*Inspiration*'.[55] Presumably Manley and John Barber anticipated the legal risks they were undertaking, which is why they chose to publish the work with trade publishers. They may also have anticipated a possible charge of libel and Manley may have intentionally included pure fiction along with the satire she based on real-life stories. It is also conceivable that some of the stories were incorrectly associated with certain real persons by keys for which Manley might not have been entirely responsible. No key was published with the first edition of either volume (a standard precaution to avoid prosecution for libel), although one was printed separately and handed about London, probably produced with Manley's assistance.

With the appearance of the second volume, more keys appeared (still published separately from the work itself). There are differences among the published keys, and the keys themselves do not identify persons by their pseudonyms but by the page in the text on which those persons appear. Mistaken identifications are therefore not only possible but likely. Keys are included at the back of some later extant editions, although these may have been produced separately and bound together subsequently. Advertisements for the posthumous 1735 and 1740 editions boast that the identifications are placed 'at the Bottom of each Page', not 'printed ... separate' as in 'all former Editions'.[56] The most central figures Manley satirizes, however, are unmistakably identifiable even without the use of keys: Godolphin, the Marlboroughs and the Cowper family. Moreover, the anecdotes most central to her Tory secret history concern the well-known story of the Revolution of 1688–9, or, for Whig historiographers telling a very different story than Manley, the 'Glorious Revolution'.

Tory Secret History

The most public figures Manley takes on in the first volume of *The New Atalantis* are the Duke and Duchess of Marlborough, who are mocked for their opportunism and their greed; their closest political ally, Sidney Earl Godolphin, Lord Treasurer; and William Earl Cowper, Lord Chancellor of Great Britain. I have already discussed Manley's mockery of John Churchill, Duke of Marlborough, for the smoothness and political skill with which he overcame the probable objections of his cousin and former lover, the royal mistress Barbara, Duchess of Cleveland, to his marrying Sarah Jenyns.[57] By using the pseudonym Count Fortunatus to refer to Marlborough, Manley also mocks the Churchill family motto *Fidelis sed infortunatus* (faithful but unfortunate), by describing Marlborough as much more fortunate – in royal bounty and reward from James II, William, and especially Anne – than he was grateful or loyal.

Marlborough's 'faithfulness' to James II was open to mockery, of course, since he had defected from James II's army in a carefully timed manoeuvre that coincided with his wife simultaneously fleeing St James's palace with James II's daughter, Princess (subsequently Queen) Anne. For Manley, of course, Churchill's infidelity and ingratitude to Cleveland – his patroness (who had helped launch his career with a gift of £5,000) foreshadows his subsequent abandonment of James II, who had placed so much confidence in him. As Count Fortunatus takes his final leave of the Dutchess de L'Inconstant (Cleveland), the latter remarks, 'Ah, the *Traitor!*'[58] Whereas in modern times a sexual scandal in and of itself will topple a politician's career, in Manley's era, the political scandal to which the sexual scandal alluded was probably more significant.[59]

Manley takes many more pages to describe Marlborough's jilting of Cleveland than his defection from James II, but readers would have immediately recognized the parallels between the two situations and the significance of 'his Ingratitude,'[60] a trait as unattractive in personal as in political relationships. Interestingly, Manley tells two different stories of Churchill's defection from James II. In a long paragraph in the first volume, she condenses the events of Monmouth's 1685 rebellion and William's 1687 invasion of England. She acknowledges that the Prince of Tameran (James II) was 'a Bigotted Christian' (i.e. a Catholic) and that he 'had not the Hearts of his Subjects'. She also suggests that Churchill felt that young Caesario (Monmouth) was 'a Prince of little depth, entirely in the Hands and Interests of a Factious Party', an opinion that echoes her father's description of Monmouth's character in his *History of the Rebellion*.[61]

In the single paragraph summarizing the events of 1685–8 – a paragraph which functions as a secret history in miniature within her longer *New Atalantis* – Manley mocks not only Count Fortunatus (Marlborough) but also (as would befit the Tory daughter of a royalist) Monmouth, as well as the 'Bigotted' James

II. Although it might seem she faults both these parties equally (James for his Catholicism and Marlborough for his ingratitude), Manley is more subtle than that. In a line in which she shifts briefly into free-indirect discourse, Manley draws us into Marlborough's probable thoughts: 'Tis true, he betray'd in this a Master who tenderly lov'd him, but a Master *Indiscreet* and *Bigotted*, that cou'd not in all probability long support himself, and therefore he held it wise to evade a falling Ruin'.[62] Eighteenth-century readers might have been seduced by the logic of this reasoning, until they recalled the age-old law of chivalry according to which a courtier was supposed to offer his own life to protect his monarch rather than betray his monarch to prevent his own 'Ruin'.

In this brief account, Manley satirizes Henriquez (the future William III) for having qualities she also discerns in Marlborough: 'a consummate Courage, deep Dissimulation, under which he conceal'd the most towring Ambition'.[63] As a royalist, Manley was suspicious of William's ambition; as a Tory she was critical of a past regime in which Whigs were favoured over Tories. However, Manley is careful to avoid the touchy issue for Jacobites of whether or not James II abdicated the throne or whether William usurped it. In her condensed account of the upheavals of 1685 and 1688, Manley leaves James II out of the question of William's accession by moving in a single sentence from Monmouth's death to William's succession: '*Caesario*'s [Monmouth's] Enterprize misscarry'd, and his Life fell a Sacrifice to the Laws he had broken. After which *Henriquez* [William III] was consider'd as the Successor'.[64] Although Manley was clearly critical of James II's Catholicism, she does not suggest that he definitely abdicated the throne (either in the language used to justify his replacement with William or the language that Manley's own narrator uses in *Rivella*, written when the return of the Whigs was imminent)[65] or that William was the rightful successor ordained by divine-right succession: he was simply 'consider'd' as such by those who put him on the throne. Here she avoids offending either the Jacobite Tory peer to whom she dedicated the work or the current monarch, James II's Tory daughter, Queen Anne, who would not have acceded to the throne had it not been decided that James had abdicated.

The New Atalantis might be puzzling to modern readers accustomed to more overt political satire because it is clearly a political work, but one in which the strongest political commentary is offered in brief paragraphs almost lost between lengthy, often salacious anecdotes about characters whose actions seem of little consequence compared to those of James, Marlborough, William or Anne. In choosing to entitle her work *Secret Memoirs ... of the New Atalantis*, Manley, of course, signalled that she was writing a secret history, a genre that was, after 1688, supremely important to Whig historiography. As Annabel Patterson has explained, the events of 1688 were recounted and retold in numerous Whig secret histories that justified the interruption of the monarchical line by the suggestion of corruption, dishonesty or tyranny in the regimes of Charles II and James II. Many of these secret histories interwove sexually explicit anecdotes with more serious narratives of actual political events. The anonymous author of *The Secret History of the Reigns of K. Charles II and K. James II* (1690) and *The Secret History of K. James I. and K. Charles I* (1690), according to Patterson, 'showed a prurient interest in the duchess of Portsmouth, the French Louise de Kéroualle, and her sexual manipulation of Charles [II]', but also included 'a long and intense discussion of the trials of Fitzharris, College, Shaftesbury, Russell and Sidney'.[66]

If we compare Manley's work to a nineteenth- or twentieth-century novel, it may seem merely a disjointed sequence of anecdotes. However, Manley's secret histories were not novels, and as Patterson's and Lionel Gossman's studies demonstrate, the structure of many secret histories was intentionally anecdotal: the power of the anecdote or the 'little history' (*la petite histoire*) was that it often contradicted the other side's grand narrative of history. Moreover, as the readers and writers of these anecdotal secret histories well understood, 'sexuality is merely one of the tools of political strategy', and can represent monarchical tendencies that, at least in the minds of Whig writers, 'directly interfere with parliamentary government'.[67]

Whig secret histories routinely deployed salacious anecdotes about either the Duchess of Cleveland or the Duchess of Portsmouth to indicate these powerful women's influence over Charles II, an influence emblematic of the influence of the French monarch, and his purse-strings, over the English sovereign. Manley, by contrast, devoted many pages in *The New Atalantis* to rewriting such stories about the Duchess of Cleveland through a new light: rather than using some illicit scene in Cleveland's bedroom or bath to tarnish the image of Charles II, she uses similar scenes to highlight the ingratitude and disloyalty of the Duke of Marlborough, who not only betrayed the monarch who 'tenderly lov'd him' but who continued, through the reign of Anne, to turn his back on his own party, by pursuing the 'perpetual Foreign War' – i.e. the War of Spanish Succession – the 'Designs' for which '*Henriquez* [William III] had formed'.[68] Unlike the earlier Tory secret history *Queen Zarah and the Zarazians*, probably written by Joseph Browne, which particularly tarnishes the reputation of the Whig Sarah, Duchess of Marlborough, Manley's *New Atalantis* not only touches on the avarice of the duchess, but emphasizes the infidelity and greed of her husband, the powerful Tory peer and military hero John, Duke of Marlborough.

In addition to her first condensed review of the political upheavals of 1685 and 1688–9, Manley subsequently offers a second rewriting of the events so crucial to many Whig secret histories. In this second version Manley turns James II into a woman (Princess Ormia), and turns the problem of Catholic succession into a problem of male succession (which would be a change from the usual female succession in this fictional account). While it is certainly the case that making James II female would be tantamount to calling him a coward (according to traditional gender norms), Manley's focus is not on James II per se but on the ambition of the Marlboroughs and Godolphin, whom she credits with bringing Anne to the throne.

Rather than focusing on the corruption or tyranny of the monarch (or his mistresses) as did Whig secret histories justifying the Revolution of 1688–9, Manley instead suggests that, although Princess Ormia might have shown poor judgement in attempting to change from female to male succession, the real blame lies in the poor judgement of the English people, who 'lov'd Opposition':

> Ormia took it into her Head, to make some Innovations in Utopia, in Favour of her only Son, a Child of but two Years of Age; she would break the Laws and Customs, and make the Succession Masculine. The People as inconstant as possible, lov'd Change, as well as she could do; but it must be a Change of their own, what themselves desired. They oppos'd her, because they lov'd Opposition; and she very well saw through their natural Perverseness, she should find much more Trouble than she expected, before she could be able to effect her Purpose.[69]

The people's capricious and oppositional desire for change, in Manley's version of the Revolution of 1688–9, allowed the ambitious William of Orange to take over. At the moment when William lands in England, Manley's Princess Ormia realizes her mistake in wanting to change the line of succession (a mistake that might correspond in real life to James II's decision to stick by his Catholicism and have his newborn son baptized as a Catholic), but it was too late to compromise because the Duke (William of Orange) 'was concern'd in the Interests of a People, whom one Day he pretended to govern in Right of his Dutchess [his wife Mary, daughter of James II]'.[70]

Meanwhile, the all-consuming ambition of Count Fortunatus (Churchill) caused him to desert Princess Ormia (James II) in her (his) hour of need, as in fact John Churchill had deserted his monarch in the wake of William of Orange's invasion of England in 1688. When Queen Mary dies, in Manley's version, William does not reign alone until his own death. Instead, as would befit a satirist who was devoted to Queen Anne and enough of a royalist Tory (with Protestant Jacobite sympathies) to have had questions about William's legitimacy after Mary's death, Manley claims: 'a malignant Distemper carry'd her [Queen Mary] from her Life, and restor'd the Lady Olimia [Anne] to her Right of Succesion'.[71] Manley here demonstrates her loyalty to the current monarch and her sister (both daughters of James II) even as she implicitly casts some doubt on William's right to rule independently (as he did following Mary's death in 1694 until his own death in 1702), by excising his solo reign from her Tory history of monarchical succession.

Whereas Whig secret histories following the Revolution of 1688–9 frequently focused on the events of the reigns of Charles II and James II, Manley's *New Atalantis* deals in mildly salacious anecdotes from the reign of William and Mary when Whigs dominated the government. William III was unpopular because he surrounded himself with his Dutch favourites, rewarding them with English peerages. His administration also tended to favour the Whigs; not surprisingly anti-Whig and anti-Williamite propaganda of an earlier era had spread rumours about his putative homosexual tendencies. Manley deftly alludes to this propaganda by recounting an anecdote from a period in William's youth when he had smallpox. In fact William did contract smallpox as a young military leader in 1675 and his friend Colonel Hans Willem (later 'William') Bentinck, subsequently first Duke of Portland (who had begun his political career as a page to the young prince), did catch smallpox from nursing him. Manley's emphasis, however, is not only Bentinck's loyalty to his prince, but 'the Pleasure and Boldness' with which he ostensibly threw 'off his Clothes' in a brave offer to help reduce the prince's fever: and 'got into Bed to the *Prince*, embracing closely his Feverish Body, from whence he never stirr'd, 'till the happy Effects of his kind Endeavours, were visible'.[72]

Manley also includes another lengthy anecdote about Portland in the first volume of *The New Atalantis*: his alleged seduction of his deceased wife's niece, Stuarta Werburge Howard (d. 1706), an illegitimate granddaughter of Charles II. This account of Portland's broken promise is corroborated by Narcissus Luttrell's contemporaneous record of political and court news, in which he reports what many believed was true: that Portland had secretly married Howard in 1692.[73] Despite appearances to the contrary, Portland did not marry Howard in 1692 but in 1700 took as his second wife Jane Martha, née Temple (1672–1751), widow of John Berkeley. Manley, however, takes this one item of gossip and invents a lengthy narrative about the innocent young 'Mademoiselle Charlot', deceived both by her guardian and his second wife, who in Manley's narrative is depicted as having been Charlot's friend and confidant. Manley describes in detail the first scene of seduction, which ostensibly took place after her guardian asked her to read certain passages in Ovid about father-daughter incest. Manley's emphasis here, as in her account of her own cousin's seduction of her, is on the deception and disloyalty of a trusted authority figure. This sort of deception and betrayal could be practised by both Whigs and Tories, of course, and Manley records instances of both: the Tory John Manley seducing and betrayed her in her account of Delia; the Tory John Churchill betraying first his cousin-mistress then his sovereign monarch. Portland, however, sided with the Whigs, eventually helping bring the Whig Junto into a position of power within William and Mary's administration.

As part of her project of tarnishing both past and present Whig adminis-trations, Manley also takes on the Whig Cowper family, for reasons that Mary, Lady Cowper was told had to do with a lawsuit Manley lost against John Tilly.[74] Whether or not Manley held a personal grudge against the Cowpers because of such a lawsuit (the details of which have not been found), the anecdotes she recounts about the prominent Whig family – William's adulterous (and pos-sibly bigamous) liaison with Elizabeth Cullen and his brother's trial for the murder of Sarah Stout – are consistent with Manley's depiction of the falseness and deception of the Whigs (and their political allies, including Godolphin and the Marlboroughs).[75] As in the case of the lengthy anecdote about Portland and Howard, both of these items of gossip are based in historical fact. Moreover, Manley develops both incidents into short narratives in which she depicts the characters' ostensible thoughts and motives.

Although she may not have been correct about every detail, some of Manley's characterization rang true to Sarah, Lady Cowper (1644–1720), mother of William and Spencer. As she did with many books she read, Lady Cowper, an assiduous reader and diarist, copied into her diary several passages from *The New Atalantis*, then commented neatly in the margin. Next to a passage about Spencer's relationship with Sarah Stout in which Manley observes 'He was sick at Heart of young Zara [Stout] and did not know how to get rid of Her', Lady Cowper comments: 'I believe it True'.[76] Not surprisingly Lady Cowper disagrees with Manley's characterization of her deceased husband, Sir William Cowper (1639–1706), second Baronet, as an 'Old Debauchee', but Manley's rationale for so characterizing him may have had more to do with the senior Cowper's politi-cal loyalties (he had been an ally of the staunch Whig Anthony Ashley Cooper (1621–83), first Earl of Shaftesbury).[77] Lady Cowper does not comment on Manley's political motives, however, but focuses on the truth or falsity of the depiction of her own family; she appears relieved that, however harsh Manley's treatment of her sons, she herself escapes relatively unscathed: 'Methinks among all this Clatter the Lady Volpone comes off well'.[78]

For all of its power as a secret history, and the concern it brought during the summer of 1709 to the mother of the Lord Chancellor of Britain, the first volume of *The New Atalantis* did not provoke the authorities to arrest Manley or her publisher, who were not arrested until the end of October, presumably shortly after the second volume (for which no newspaper advertisements have been found) appeared in print. Although we cannot be certain why the satire in the first volume did not provoke a governmental response, one reason might be that most of the events about which Manley gossips were old news. As Sarah, Lady Cowper, observed in a July diary entry about Manley's treatment of her family in the first volume of *The New Atalantis*: 'After all, the main matter is but Old Dirt grown so dry it may not stick if it be no mixt with new stuff'.[79] Just as

Whig secret histories supporting the Revolution of 1688–9 recycled court gossip from the 1670s and 1680s, so Manley's anti-Whig *New Atalantis* recycled gossip from the 1690s, particularly concerning the Whigs officials who came into power under William and Mary.

In the second volume of *The New Atalantis*, however, Manley would grow bold: she not only included more recent court gossip, she also reported certain events which had not yet occurred, including the fall of the powerful governmental ministers Godolphin and Marlborough and the death of the latter. Marlborough's son-in-law, who signed the warrants for Manley's and her publishers' arrests, seems to have found these fictitious reports not only offensive but potentially disruptive to the nation's peace.

Libel and Sedition

In the warrant for the arrest of John Morphew and John Woodward, dated 28 October 1709, Sunderland accuses these trade publishers of:

> having printed and publisht divers Books and Pamphlets, wherein are contained many false, malitious and scandalous Reflections upon Several of the Queen's Liege Subjects and highly tending to the Disturbance of the publick Peace and Quiete of her Majesty's Government, particularly two Books Entitled (Secret Memoirs & Manners of Several Persons of Qualtiy of both Sexs from the New Atalntis an Island in the Mediteranean) part the first and the second;[80]

In the subsequent warrant for the arrest of '— Manley & John Barber Printer' (which was probably also issued on 28 October, since Manley's arrest was reported in *The Post Boy* the following day), the author and the printer are 'accused & c. (in the same words of that above)'.[81]

Barber and Manley and their trade publishers were clearly being arrested under the general category of common law libel.[82] The word 'false' was almost always included in such an indictment, and, as Philip Hamburger observes, the idea that a libel 'had to encourage a breach of the peace ... seems to have been accepted in the law of libel of private persons'.[83] Hamburger also suggests that the tendency to breach the peace applied to the emergent category of 'seditious libel', although Sunderland does not specifically use the term 'seditious'. By contrast, the March 1724 warrant, issued by Secretary of State Charles, second Viscount Townshend (1675–1738), to search John Barber's premises on Lambeth Hill (where Manley was living), for the ostensible 'Fifth' volume of 'the New Atalantis', described that work (no copy of which has ever been found by modern scholars) as 'a Seditious and Traiterous Libel'.[84]

Following the lapse of the Licensing Act in May 1695, government officials relied on various aspects of libel law to prosecute the press. When Harley was Secretary of State between 1704 and 1708, the practice of prosecuting for 'seditious libel' expanded the use of traditional libel law (which concerned libels against individuals rather than the government) to include acts of defamation of particular persons as well as the government. As Philip Hamburger has shown, in a detailed history of seditious libel law, precedent was set in 1704 that 'seditious libel', as understood by Chief Justice Holt, 'could bring scandal on the government by reflecting on it as a whole as well as by reflecting on the individuals in it'.[85]

It would appear that the case Sunderland brought against the author and publishers of *The New Atalantis* might fit into the newly expanded category of seditious libel. However, the wording of the warrant does not specify the seditious element but is extremely general, suggesting that Sunderland was casting his net broadly under the general category of common law libel.[86] Hamburger suggests, moreover, that the Whig administration 'brought no seditious libel prosecutions between early 1708 and 1710' for a mixture of ideological and practical reasons.[87] Some Whig writers and officials had been opposed to the prosecution of Whig writers that took place under the Tory ministry of 1704–9. However, Hamburger also notes that 'from October 1709 Sunderland acted independently of his colleagues to harass printers and publishers by threatening to prosecute, and that following Sacheverell's trial he ordered prosecutions'.[88]

Although the second volume of *The New Atalantis* appeared before the impeachment of the High-Tory divine Henry Sacheverell (bap. 1674, d. 1724), which took place in January 1710 (in response to an inflammatory sermon preached on 5 November 1709), the arrest of Manley and her publishers seems to have been part of Sunderland's harassment campaign. On 11 November 1709, six days after Sacheverell's inflammatory sermon and about two weeks after the arrest of Manley and her publishers, Sunderland would issue another warrant for the arrest of John Morphew (along with six other publishers and printers) for other 'Scandalous Libels' including *The Rehearsal Revived*, apparently a revival of Charles Leslie's Jacobite-Tory newspaper *The Rehearsal*.[89] Even though the warrant for apprehending Manley and her publishers suggests a general charge of common law libel, it is clear that Sunderland was concerned about seditious tendencies in all the libels he was investigating during the month that he was interrogating Manley and Barber.

According to contemporary newspaper accounts, Manley sued for habeas corpus on Thursday, 3 November 1709; she was then officially charged and so could be admitted to bail, as she was on Saturday, 5 November. She was released on bail until her trial at the Queen's Bench, scheduled for the next law term – i.e. Hilary, which would begin in mid-January 1710.[90] Unfortunately, neither the writ of Manley's habeas corpus nor the King's Bench indictment records for Anne's reign have survived, so whatever details might have been recorded about her questioning by Sunderland are not available. Some scholars have been confused by a somewhat illegible record of the 11 November arrest warrant for John Morphew and other printers and booksellers for a 'Scandalous' publication, suspecting that Manley might have given information against her publishers and booksellers before she was released on bail. However, that scrap of paper, which does not specifically mention Manley, Barber or *The New Atalantis*, probably refers to the 11 November arrest warrant for *The Rehearsal Revived* mentioned above.[91]

We may wonder why the pseudonyms in this secret history did not work to protect Manley against prosecution for libel, since keys were not included with the first edition. The fact that pseudonyms or blanks or dashes replacing letters in a name were often used to escape legal prosecution is evident in Jonathan Swift's sarcastic 1713 observation, that 'we are careful never to print a Man's Name out at length; but as I do that of Mr. *St—le*: So that although every Body alive knows whom I mean, the Plaintiff can have no Redress in any Court of Justice'.[92] Moreover, Manley, Barber and their trade publishers may have been counting on the fact that in 1700 the attorney general asserted that John Tutchin's poem *The Foreigners*, an attack on the king's Dutch ministers, was immune from prosecution simply because the poet gave the ministers pseudonyms. However, courts were certainly moving away from granting this sort of immunity if the persons meant by the text were comprehensible to most readers.

By 1713, in the case of *R* v. *Hurt* in 1713, the Court of King's Bench would rule that

> a Defamatory Writing expressing only one or two Letters of a Name, in such a Manner, that from what goes before and follows after, it must needs be understood to signify such a particular Person, in the plain, obvious and natural Construction of the whole, and would be perfect Nonsense if strained to any other Meaning, is as properly a Libel, as if it had expressed the whole Name at large.[93]

Steele, so frequently one of Manley's targets, must have welcomed the *Hurt* decision, which decreed, in essence, 'that writing "Mr. St—le" would provide no protection if indeed "every body alive" knew that the writer meant Richard Steele'.[94] In a 1742 case, Lord Chancellor Hardwicke observed that 'All the libellers of the kingdom know now, that printing initial letters will not serve their turn, for that objection has been long got over'.[95] It would appear, from Manley's experience, that by 1709, well before this key judicial decision of 1713, courts had already become suspicious of assuming that blanks or pseudonyms should guarantee protection from prosecution.

The Offending Second Volume

Since the indictment records are not extant for this period, we do not know which specific passages in Manley's work were most troubling to the government, or in particular to Sunderland. As in the first volume of *The New Atalantis*, much of the second volume relates old gossip, especially scandalous sexual intrigues – including accounts of a lesbian cabal involving prominent Whig women, including Manley's former friend the playwright Catharine Trotter, and her patron Lady Sarah Piers – who seems once to have harboured an intense affection for Trotter.[96] Manley also includes a humorous account of an intrigue between Count Biron (Sidney, Earl Godolphin) and the Marchioness de Caria (Sarah, Duchess of Marlborough). In fact, Manley was well aware that rumours about such an intrigue (familiar in anti-Whig propaganda) were unfounded, but she turns the familiar political propaganda into a satire not about sex but about money. Dressed as an innocent country girl, the Marchioness is seduced when the Count offers her a 'purse of Gold', which was 'no Sum to bribe Madam de Caria ... yet it was a very great one for a Country-Girl',[97] and so Biron succeeds in his endeavour. The Marlboroughs were both frequently mocked for their frugality and their avarice; here Manley turns familiar political propaganda about the long-term political allegiance of Marlborough and Godolphin, and their powerful influence on Queen Anne, into an amusing anecdote about greed.

Buried in such amusing accounts are also paragraphs as pointedly serious as the one in which Manley calmly records the imaginary death of the Marquis de Caria (John, Duke of Marlborough) in battle: 'Much about this time the courageous Marquis fought a decisive Battle with the Enemy, which it was not only his Misfortune to lose, but to perish himself'.[98] Marlborough, usually considered the greatest military commander of his era, did not usually lose battles; nor was he dead at the time Manley was writing *The New Atalantis*. However, the Protestant alliance, which Marlborough commanded, lost 24,000 lives in the battle of Malplaquet (September 1709) and, although the Whigs defined it as a victory, it was not clear that the limited strategic advantage that had been won against the French coalition (which probably lost 15,000 lives) was worth the number of lives lost.

Since he did not arrest Manley until after the appearance of the second volume of *The New Atalantis*, Sunderland may have distinguished between anecdotes about adultery and other sexual intrigue (such as are recounted in the first volume) and the announcement of the death of England's greatest military commander (his father-in-law). Manley, in fact, not only reports Marlborough's death but also Queen Anne's death and Godolphin's fall from power. As in the case of 'reporting' Marlborough's death, the suggestion of Godolphin's dismissal is made briefly and in passing. Manley's tour guide simply describes Biron (Godolphin) as 'once Minister to the Princess of Utopia',[99] putting his position as Queen Anne's Lord Treasurer in the past tense. Godolphin, who had served under the regimes of Charles II, James II, William and Mary, as well as Anne, in fact would be dismissed by Queen Anne in August 1710, following Harley's repeated requests to the Queen to do so. However, Godolphin had almost been dismissed in February 1708, but had held on to power after Marlborough had threatened to resign. Manley offers a somewhat different narrative, but one that rather aptly characterizes Godolphin's position in the autumn of 1709. In Manley's version, Anne dies in childbirth before she can choose between Harley and Godolphin, leaving Harley and Abigail Masham as royal regents to her (fictitious) infant daughter and heir. After the ostensible death of Marlborough and Queen Anne, Godolphin's fall from influence is described as follows.

> This was a finishing Stroke to Count Biron's [Godolphin's] Interest in the Cabinet. His Friendship with the General [Marlborough] having still left him a Place there, where under the Power of the Regents, he appear'd but as the Shadow of himself; the Ghost of his own departed Genius![100]

Although neither Marlborough nor Queen Anne was in fact dead in the autumn of 1709, at the time that Manley was writing, Godolphin's diminished influence with the Queen probably did make him seem something of a shadow of his former self. Moreover, the 'false Reflections' Manley reports of the regency of Harley and Masham may have seemed too close to reality for Sunderland's taste.

Manley also describes a scene of a mob uprising against the (in this narrative widowed) Duchess of Marlborough at (the not yet completed but phenomenally costly) Blenheim palace, whose construction was largely being financed at public expense:

> When the Count [Godolphin] was withdrawn, she [the Duchess of Marlborough] was left without Support; all the Particulars of her *rapacious sordid* Life, runing from *Mouth* to *Mouth*, no longer in fear of speaking Truth, since there was now, neither a Princess *Olympia* [Queen Anne] in the Throne! a *Marquis* [Duke of Marlborough] at the Head of Armies, nor a *Count* at the *end* of the *Board* to protect and skreen her from the *Indignation* and *Contempt* of the *Worthy*, from the *Violence* and *Barbarous* Insults of the *Rabble*, who one Morning rush'd altogether like an impetious Torrent upon her *Superbous* Palace, a Palace which had been ostentatiously raised, and adorn'd with the *Spoils* of *many*.[101]

This report of mob violence against Sunderland's mother-in-law – in addition to Manley's prediction of the deaths of Marlborough and the fall of Godolphin – may have struck Sunderland as an open invitation to revolt. This imaginary account might well be classed as not only as 'false, malitious, and scandalous Reflections upon Several of the Queen's Liege Subject', but an invitation to the '*Rabble*' to rise up against the wealthy and powerful Marlboroughs as their imminent descent from power became public news.

In Manley's satire, moreover, the person who valiantly intervenes to save the Duchess of Marlborough from her fate at the hands of the mob is Hilaria (Abigail Masham), a royal bedchamber woman (and a cousin to Sarah, Duchess of Marlborough, who had persuaded Queen Anne to offer her that position) who had become the Queen's closest confidant by about 1707 as the long-standing friendship between the Queen and the Duchess of Marlborough, which had been in decline for several years, continued to deteriorate. The Marlboroughs and the Whig Junto considered Masham's influence dangerous, not only because Masham (a Tory) had replaced the Duchess of Marlborough (a staunch Whig) as Queen Anne's closest confidant, but because Masham was, as well as a cousin of Sarah Churchill, a cousin of Robert Harley, and it was believed that Harley had been using Masham as a conduit to influence the Queen.

The 'false Reflections' that Sunderland was concerned about might have been not only Manley's false reports of Marlborough's death and the attack on his wife by a mob, but also her description of Abigail Masham as

> a new and rising Favourite; who the more alarm'd the Count [Godolphin] and Madam *de Caria* [Duchess of Marlborough], because she was really *wedded* to all those *Virtues*, which the Marchioness but *Woo'd*, and that too but *superficially*, and in *bare* appearance.[102]

Sunderland might likewise have found Manley's description of Don Geronimo de Haro (Robert Harley) a 'false Reflection': 'He was *Honest*! He was *Brave*! Understood the Interest of the Nation, and fearlessly proclaim'd and pursu'd it'.[103] In response to this line in Manley's text, Whig MP Arthur Maynwaring commented in a letter to the Duchess of Marlborough, whom he served as political secretary, mocking Manley's depiction of Harley: 'Could any one but an idiot call him honest, in a good sense?'[104]

Killing Satire

In the preface to the second volume of *The New Atalantis*, Manley signals that she is writing satire, rather than gossip. While there is certainly gossip in both volumes, and while the gossip itself frequently contains her satirical points, Manley's killing off of Marlborough signals a shift into more pointed political satire in the second volume. Manley may be following the lead of her former friend Richard Steele, who had announced in the *Tatler* that he would feel comfortable announcing the premature deaths of those whose conduct he felt authorized such an announcement. Steele justified his having predicted the death of a very much alive Mr Partridge in his *Predictions for the Year 1708* (1707) by suggesting that 'tho' the Legs and Arms, and whole Body, of that Man may still appear and perform their animal Functions; yet, since, as I have elsewhere, observ'd, his Art is gone, the Man is gone'.[105] He ends this first issue of the *Tatler* with the following warning:

> I shall, as I see Occasion, proceed to confute other dead Men, who pretend to be in Being, that they are actually deceased. I therefore give all Men fair Warning to mend

their Manners, for I shall from Time to time print Bills of Mortality; and I beg the Pardon of all such who shall be nam'd therein, if they who are good for Nothing shall find themselves in the Number of the Deceased.[106]

In her dedication to her second volume of *The New Atalantis* (which, like the first volume, she dedicates to the Duke of Beaufort), Manley approvingly cites Steele's published praise of satire for its ability to sanction 'Ingratitude, Avarice, *and those other* Vices, *which the* Law *does not reach*'.[107] Steele, in fact, had not used the term 'satire' in the passage in the *Tatler* that Manley alludes to here. He, however, refers to turning such offenders 'into Ridicule under feign'd Names',[108] very much as Manley did in *The New Atalantis*, but Manley is clearly keen to stake her claim to the tradition of satire as a force for the public good.

In her dedication to the second volume of *The New Atalantis*, Manley locates the precedents for her particular style of satire in 'Ennius, Varro, Lucian, Horace, Juvenal, Persiu, & etc'. Her scholarly authority is Dryden's 'Discourse concerning Satire', the dedication to his translation of Juvenal's satires in which he defines the style of various classical satirists. Manley could not draw directly on Varro as a source since few of his complete works survived to the eighteenth century, but in the dedication she paraphrases Dryden's description of Varro's style of writing in such a way as also describes her own style:

> *The* New Atalantis *seems, my Lord, to be written like* Varonian *Satyrs, on* different Subjects, Tales, Stories *and* Characters *of* Invention, *after the Manner of* Lucian, *who copy'd from* Varro. *In my Opinion nothing can be added to Mr. Dryden's learned Discourse of Satire, in his Dedication of* Juvenal. *He observes thus,* 'What is most essential, and the very Soul of Satire, is scourging of Vice, and Exhortation to Virtue. Satire is of the nature of Moral Philosophy: He therefore who instructs most usefully will carry the Palm. *And again,* 'Tis an Action of Virtue to make Examples of vicious Men. They may and ought to be upbraided with their Crimes and Follies: Both for their own Amendment, if they are not yet incorrigible; and for the Terror of others, to hinder them from falling into those Enormities, which they see are so severely punish'd in the Persons of others. The first Reason was only an excuse for Revenge. But this second is absolutely of the Poet's Office to perform.'[109]

Thus defining her work as serious satire and establishing that she is not merely taking revenge (against former friends and political opponents) for its own sake but working to improve the manners and morals of her country, Manley apparently feels justified in spreading false reports about the death of Marlborough, the dismissal of Godolphin and the mob attack on the Duchess of Marlborough.

Although we do not know which passages Sunderland particularly objected to in *The New Atalantis*, we may infer from the wording of Manley's arrest warrant that he was extremely concerned about the 'false Reflections' or reports Manley was spreading about certain important persons. It seems reasonable to assume that he was prosecuting Manley for her predictions about Godolphin's fall from power. He would also have been concerned about the report of Marlborough's death, since this prediction might not merely have been a satirical critique of Marlborough's behaviour, in the manner threatened by the *Tatler*, but might also have predicted Marlborough's own dismissal from power (which would occur in December 1711, although his influence over the Queen as military commander would already be in decline by 1710). In a letter to his mother-in-law, the Duchess of Marlborough, Sunderland explains his intent to put a stop to the sort of works Manley was publishing:

> I believe Mr Manwaring has given you an account of the Lady I have in Custody for the New Atlantis [*sic*], & of the noble worthy Persons, she Corresponds with, I shall spoil their writing, at least for some time, for I promise them I will push it, as far as I can by law.[110]

In fact, Arthur Maynwaring was not as concerned about Manley's work as Sunderland was. Maynwaring apparently read *The New Atalantis* at the request of the Duchess; he complains in a letter to her: 'I never regretted any pains I took to give your Grace any information you wanted, till this morning, which I have wasted in reading the nauseous book ...'. And while he complains that the 'license of the press is too great' and he hopes for a 'proper way ... to restrain it this winter', he 'would not have the rise taken from this trifling book, which, as you observe truly, would only make it spread more'.[111] Maynwaring even finds amusing the scene in which Sarah, Duchess of Marlborough, is attacked by the mob and is rescued by 'generous Hilaria'; he suggests that the Duchess of Marlborough herself 'could hardly help laughing' at this, were she to read the book (which she does not appear to have done).[112]

Sunderland was clearly concerned about the 'noble persons' encouraging Manley's work, by whom he might have meant the Duke of Beaufort, who appears to have given Manley some sort of monetary reward for the first volume. Sunderland was also convinced (rightly or wrongly) that Manley must have been in contact with some person with inside knowledge of court affairs. During the period when Manley was being held in the custody – i.e. some time between 29 October when she was apprehended and 5 November when she was released on bail until the start of the next court session – Sarah, Duchess of Marlborough, wrote to Queen Anne suggesting (apparently from Maynwaring's account of the book) that 'It has appeared that she [Manley] kept correspondence with two of the favourite persons in the book – my Lord Peterborough and Mr. Harley, and I think it is to be suspected that she may have had some dealing with Mrs. Masham'.[113] From the wording of Manley's subsequent letters to Harley, it does not appear that she wrote to him before her first extant letter to him in 1710. Nor is it necessarily likely that Manley would have been in direct correspondence with Charles Mordaunt (*c.* 1658–1735), Earl of Peterborough, or Abigail, Lady

Masham (*c.* 1670–1734), an attendant to Queen Anne. However, the Duchess of Marlborough was probably correct to believe that *The New Atalantis* was written 'to compliment Abigail [Masham]'.[114]

The second volume of *The New Atalantis* certainly appears to have been written with the hope of currying the favour of Lady Masham, to whom Manley would subsequently dedicate the second volume of *The Memoirs of Europe*, although there is nothing in that dedication that would suggest that Manley had already received any reward from Masham. Nor does her dedication to Peterborough (for the 1713 French translation of *The New Atalantis*) indicate that he had given her any prior recognition or reward. It is, however, testimony to Manley's skill as a satirist that the persons she was satirizing most pointedly believed that she was being fed opinions or information directly by the persons she compliments in her work.

It is, in fact, possible that Manley had some of the 'Intelligence' for which Sunderland felt sure she must have had an inside source from her old acquaintance from the theatre, the Tory MP George Granville, a friend of Henry St John and often an intermediary between St John and Harley. Granville, who would be made secretary of war after Godolphin's dismissal in 1710, probably knew quite a bit about the Continental campaigns (and the bloody battle of Malplaquet at which Manley suggests that Marlborough died); he probably also would have known all the behind-the-scenes gossip about the 1708 power struggle between Harley and Marlborough over Godolphin's position. Whereas Sunderland and his mother-in-law infer that Manley might have been in correspondence with the persons she depicts in such laudatory terms in the second volume of *The New Atalantis*, Manley may, in fact, have been more subtle about concealing her source than Sunderland and his associates suspected. If her source were Granville, her only possible reference to him is as an unnamed friend (not listed in the keys) of St John. While she depicts St John in the first volume as more of a rake than the wit he had pretensions to be, his unnamed friend receives no such satirical treatment or publicity.[115]

We have only Manley's description in *Rivella* of Sunderland's questioning. However, his main concern, as she describes it, was for her to admit her sources for the information she reports in *The New Atalantis*. According to her account, however, Manley seems to have relied on her *own* intelligence and inspiration:

> They us'd several Arguments to make her discover who were the Persons concern'd with her in writing her Books; or at least from whom she had receiv'd Information of some special Facts, which they thought were above her own Intelligence: Her Defence was with much Humility and Sorrow, for having offended, at the same Time denying that any Persons were concern'd with her, or that she had a farther Design than writing for her own Amusement and Diversion in the Country; without intending particular Reflections or Characters: When this was not believ'd, and the contrary

urg'd very home to her by several Circumstances and Likenesses; she said then it must be *Inspiration*, because knowing her own Innocence she could account for it no other Way: The Secretary reply'd upon her, that *Inspiration* us'd to be upon a good Account, and her Writings were stark naught; she told him, with an Air full of Penitence, that might be true, but it was as true, that there were evil Angels as well as good; so that nevertheless what she had wrote might still be by *Inspiration*.[116]

It would appear that Manley held her own in the verbal sparring in court, and successfully clung to her defence against having made scandalous 'Reflections' against any particular person.

Charges against Manley were dropped by the Court of the Queen's Bench on 13 February 1710.[117] Four years later, she would describe their dismissal of her case in *Rivella*:

> Whether the Persons in Power were ashamed to bring a Woman to her Trial for writing a few amorous Trifles purely for her own Amusement, or that our Laws were defective, as most Persons conceiv'd, because she had serv'd her self with Romantick Names, and a feign'd Scene of Action? But after several Times exposing her in Person to walk cross the Court before the Bench of Judges, with her three Attendants, the *Printer* and both the *Publishers*; the *Attorny General* at the End of three or four Terms dropt the Prosecution.[118]

Although we might credit Manley's own cleverness in using 'Romantick Names, and a feign'd Scene of Action', Sunderland may also have had second thoughts about making a martyr of Manley, whose apprehension had attracted widespread attention. The Whig writer Lady Mary Pierrepont (subsequently Wortley Montague), for example, had observed, 'I have five hundred arguments at my fingers' ends to prove the ridiculousness of these creatures that think it worth while to take notice of what is designed only for diversion'.[119] By early 1710, the Whigs probably wanted to avoid further trouble for themselves, since they were already facing public outcry against their impeachment of Henry Sacheverell for a sermon promoting the (Tory) virtue of passive obedience. His impeachment trial began in January 1710, about the time Manley was scheduled to have her case heard at the Queen's Bench.

Manley must have begun writing *Memoirs of Europe* either right after the charges against her for *The New Atalantis* had been dropped or possibly earlier, since the first volume of *Memoirs of Europe* was published in May 1710. In this second secret history, Manley seemed to write from something like a Harleyan position, if such could be said to exist three months before he would be reappointed to the ministry. From Manley's extant letters to Harley it would appear that she wrote both her second secret history and her subsequent pamphlets and periodical issues with the hope of reward, encouragement and direction. However, those same letters suggest that specific direction was not always forthcoming. In other words, as we shall see in the next chapter, even when she was nominally part of the Harley propaganda team, Manley remained through the rest of her career something of a freelance satirist and pamphleteer – relying on her own creativity and inspiration to guide her to how she might best serve her party and her country.

8 WRITING UNDER A TORY MINISTRY: 1710–14

When the Court of the Queen's Bench dropped charges against Manley and her printer and publishers in February 1710, Manley was apparently confident enough that she would be safe from further prosecution to proceed with a sequel to *The New Atalantis*. Lady Mary Pierrepont had expressed concern, in a November 1709 letter to a friend, that Manley's arrest would deter other opposition writers. She observed:

> People are offended at the liberty she [Manley] uses in her memoirs, and she is taken into custody ... Miserable is the fate of writers; if they are agreeable, they are offensive; and if dull, they starve ... After this, who will dare to give the history of Angella [London]? I was in hopes her faint essay would have provoked some better pen to give more elegant and secret memoirs; but now she will serve as a scarecrow to frighten people from attempting any thing but heavy panegyric;[1]

Although we have no epistolary record of Pierrepont's reaction to *Memoirs of Europe*, presumably she would have been pleased that, following the dismissal of the charges against her, Manley was not deterred from writing satire. Pierrepont might also have observed that as Manley's party secured control of Anne's ministry, her second political secret history shifted in tone from satire to panegyric.

The Whigs still retained control of Anne's ministry on 11 May 1710, the day Manley recorded her name as author of the first volume of *Memoirs of Europe* in Stationers Hall.[2] However, Godolphin and Marlborough had been losing ground politically since early that year. Queen Anne had ignored Marlborough's recommendations for two senior military appointments in early January and ignored Sunderland's proposed candidates for bishoprics in February. She had also refused Marlborough's request to be made captain general for life as well as his and the Junto's attempts to have Abigail Masham removed from her court position. Adding a mark of further disregard, Queen Anne proposed Abigail Masham's brother John Hill (d. 1735) be promoted from colonel to general, over Marlborough's objections. Furthermore, rumours began to circulate about Sunderland's imminent dismissal after the Queen replaced the Whiggish Lord Kent as Lord Chamberlain with the Duke of Shrewsbury (a Whig and former ally of Godolphin and Marlborough, who had disagreed with the Whig Junto over

Sacheverell's impeachment) without consulting Godolphin.[3] Although Robert Harley would not be made Chancellor of the Exchequer and second Lord of the Treasury until August 1710 (and would not become Lord Treasurer until his elevation to the peerage in May 1711), his influence on the Queen was apparent in her standing up to Godolphin and Marlborough during the spring of 1710.

Manley's April (or July) 1710 letter to Harley, in which she requests his assistance in securing a lieutenant's position for a young man – who may have been her son by John Manley – suggests not only confidence in herself as a political writer (in assuming that Harley would know who she was and would want to reward her by assisting the young man she mentions) but also confidence in Harley's influence with the Queen before his official return to power.[4] *Memoirs of Europe* itself mirrors the confidence of Manley's letter to Harley. By the spring of 1710, with further Tory appointments to the ministry anticipated by many, *Memoirs of Europe* articulated not merely satirical opposition to the Godolphin-Marlborough ministry but also celebratory confidence that the author would not be writing for an opposition party much longer.

Satire and Celebration

Memoirs of Europe is, like its precursor, a political secret history. Rather than focusing on the Revolution of 1688–9 and William and Mary's reign, as she did in *The New Atalantis*, Manley covers more recent events in her second secret history, including Anne's struggles with her ministers, the trial of Henry Sacheverell (whom Manley depicts in glowing terms as Plato the Patriarch) and the increasingly unpopular War of Spanish Succession. Manley centres the narrative on the Earl of Peterborough, a Whig who, as commander of the Allied troops in Spain, captured Barcelona in 1705.

Although Peterborough was generally applauded for this success, he encountered subsequent difficulties in his military command: he did not cooperate well with the Allies in Spain, and he frequently operated as something of a maverick commander, deploying brilliant but often unorthodox and unapproved strategies for outwitting the Bourbon enemy in Spain, where he was usually badly outnumbered and provided with poor intelligence. By late 1706, Peterborough was found to be troublesome by Marlborough and Godolphin. Sunderland, in his capacity as Secretary of State, sent Peterborough a letter of dismissal in early 1707, which made him an outspoken opponent of the Whig Junto. Peterborough commissioned his military physician, Dr John Freind, to write a pamphlet in his defence (which John Barber printed) that gave him a widespread popular following. The parliamentary investigation against Peterborough never resulted in a conviction for mismanagement of government funds, but no parliamentary vote of thanks for Peterborough's multiple successes in Spain was even proposed.

By 1710, Peterborough was actively cooperating with those attempting to overturn the Godolphin-Marlborough ministry. In *Memoirs of Europe*, Manley depicts Peterborough in exile in Narva, visiting with Charles XII of Sweden, another heroic military commander (who had captured the port of Narva in 1704), listening to visiting courtiers reporting on the situation in 'Constantinople' (i.e. Britain). Manley describes Peterborough, to whom she would dedicate the French translation of this work, as '*Immortal* from his stupendous Conquests in *Iberia*'.[5]

A courtier from England ('the Count de *St. Girronne*', who probably represents Count Anthony Hamilton of the French nobility) appears in Narva and recounts the story of Queen Anne's struggle with her ministers. Marlborough is described as arrogant and controlling, as captain general of the Allied forces, unable to acknowledge the contributions of other subordinate officers. As this courtier explains, addressing himself to Horatio (Peterborough):

> The World under your inimitable Conduct had had *Repose*, the Conquest of *Iberia* [Spain] wou'd have been the finishing Stroak; the Stroak! That at once had shut the Gates of *Janus*'s Temple, and restor'd Peace to the Empire of the East and West. But what then wou'd have become of the invulnerable *Stauracius* [Marlborough]? His Valour had been without Employment, nor had the good Intentions of Fortune avail'd him any thing; all those mighty Conquests he has since gain'd wou'd never have been; it does not suffice to say, there had been no occasion for 'em; think you it is a small thing to take a Hero short in his Course to Glory? No! No! Better a Million of vulgar Lives and Mines of Treasure shou'd be sacrific'd, be exhausted, than he abate the least Grain of that stupendious Reputation he has acquir'd.[6]

Manley is suggesting, in other words, that Marlborough dismissed Peterborough because the latter's future successes in Spain would soon have ended the war (for which the rallying cry was 'No Peace without Spain') and prevented Marlborough from gaining further glory. In the second volume, she goes further by suggesting that it was not just glory but profits from war contracts that enriched the Marlboroughs and the Whigs more generally. Irene (Sarah, Duchess of Marlborough) proclaims, when insisting on Horatio's (Peterborough's) dismissal: 'Our Party is not yet strong and rich enough for Peace'.[7]

The visiting courtiers describe Queen Anne as overly controlled by her ministers and the Marlboroughs. In a clever reconfiguration of actual court and dynastic relations, Manley depicts Queen Anne as Caesar Constantine, the son of Irene (Sarah, Duchess of Marlborough) and Irene's first husband Emperor Leo IV (King William III). John, Duke of Marlborough, is Irene's favourite, Stauracius, with whom she is accumulating wealth and building a palace (i.e. Blenheim); they marry as soon as Leo IV dies. As Ruth Herman has pointed out,

Manley treads a fine line in criticizing the Queen's ministers without denigrating the monarch herself. Other Tory secret histories from the same era, such as the anonymous *Arlus and Odolphus* (1710), depict Anne as generous and tolerant, in contrast to her haughty ministers and advisors. Manley is somewhat bolder, as Herman has pointed out, depicting Anne as indolent – although not by incapacity but by neglect.[8]

Having passed off so many of his royal duties to his mother, the Emperor Constantine (Queen Anne) is shown to be an indolent child whose overbearing mother obstructed his (her) education and development. When faced with a crisis over religion,

> CONSTANTINE's noble Faculties (enfeebled by Neglect and Indolence) presently absconded at a Scene of Terror, and all pale and dastardly, shrunk behind the Representation his Mother had made. The Race of *Leo Isauricus* [James I], was never fam'd for Courage; this *Caesar* did not degenerate; his Education had not taught him to do it, therefore trembling and apprehensive of the future, with Tears he conjur'd *Irene* to advise him for the present.[9]

The cure for Constantine's indolence and neglect, according to Manley's account, will be Herminius (Harley), who, at the end of the second volume, 'appear'd to the Emperor [Anne]' and 'discover'd at large, the Designs of his [her] Favourites'. Herminius persuades Constantine that 'It was only from himself [Anne], that those Men cou'd take leave to destroy himself, and that but 'till *Caesar* [Anne] was pleas'd to exert the Authority of *Caesar*'.[10]

Most importantly, in Manley's narrative, Robert Harley appears as the romance hero who saves Queen Anne by persuading her to rouse herself from the enchanting spell of her ministers and take hold of the reigns of government. Herminius (Harley) artfully 'contriv'd to dispossess *Caesar*' of a certain 'fatal Ring' that put him (Anne) under the control of Stauracius (Marlborough). Having accomplished this,

> *Herminius* beheld the lazy vapour of Indolence breaking from around the easie Emperor slowly it arose, and still ascending, left him at length – strengthen'd – confirm'd – all bright – and all himself – *Herminius* ravish'd to behold his Sovereign Lord returning to his native Vertue, fell at his sacred Feet in Raptures that bespoke his Loyalty; and Transports.[11]

As Harley helps Anne take control of her own country, his cousin and Anne's attendant Abigail Masham (represented as the brave young Leonidas in the second volume), likewise becomes infused with new strength. Manley depicts the young man as refusing to let Godolphin enter the Queen's chambers: '*Leonidas*, with a becoming Boldness, refus'd him the Door'.[12] Manley had already depicted Godolphin as a ghost of his former self in *The New Atalantis*, over a year before he lost his position. However, by the time the second volume of *Memoirs of*

Europe appeared in November 1710, Godolphin had already been dismissed by the Queen (having been asked in August merely to break rather than return to her his staff of office), and Manley apparently felt free to depict a royal chambermaid as a bold youth slamming the door in the face of a peer who had been one of Britain's most powerful ministers under four different monarchs.[13] In this scene Manley moves beyond her continued satire of Marlborough (who retained his offices and military position until December 1711) to triumphant slapstick at Godolphin's expense.

Writing to Harley in April (or July) 1710, Manley suggests that her 'presumption' to believe she deserves some reward 'is held up by many Great and Good'.[14] She had clearly not met Harley or received instructions from him, but she apparently felt certain that her depictions of his role in saving the Queen from the Marlborough-Godolphin ministry would please him. We do not know exactly who of the 'Great and Good' she and her companion John Barber already knew by early 1710. As I suggested in the last chapter, George Granville seems to have known Manley since her first days writing for the theatre. John Barber may have known Dr John Freind, military physician to the Earl of Peterborough, since Barber printed the 1708 edition (and possibly earlier editions) of Freind's popular pamphlet defending Peterborough. Freind could have supplied enough of Peterborough's point of view to explain why Sunderland and the Duchess of Marlborough thought that Manley was in contact with Peterborough while writing *The New Atalantis*.[15] In *Memoirs of Europe*, of course, Manley courts Peterborough as a patron even more openly, although there is no reason to believe that Manley was in contact with him while she was writing her secret histories, or that she ever met him until the morning in early July 1711 when Jonathan Swift met her at Lord Peterborough's, where she 'was soliciting him to get some pension or reward for her service in the cause, by writing her Atalantis, and prosecution, &c. upon it', an effort for which Swift 'seconded her'.[16]

By early 1710 Manley and John Barber may have met Granville's friend Henry St John, formerly an admirer of Marlborough who had sided with Harley and resigned following Harley's forced resignation during the ministerial standoff of February 1708. Manley's depiction of St John – whom she had described as more of a rake than a wit in *The New Atalantis*[17] – as a '*Star*' in the second volume of *Memoirs of Europe*[18] might suggest that she or Barber had already made St John's acquaintance by the time Manley was writing her second secret history. We do not know which other courtiers Manley or Barber may have known at this time. Sarah, Duchess of Marlborough, believed that Manley 'may have had some dealing with Mrs. Masham' and had been given money by Masham for *The New Atalantis*.[19] Of course, the duchess also believed that Manley was in correspondence with both Harley and Peterborough, which was probably not the case. The wording of Manley's dedication of the second volume of *Memoirs of*

Europe does not suggest that Manley personally knew Lady Masham. However, Masham – who was active in arranging back-stairs meetings between Harley and the Queen when Harley returned to London in January 1710 – may neverthe-less have been encouraging opposition writers, including Manley.[20] By 1714 John Barber would know Samuel, Lord Masham (1678/9–1758), Abigail's husband, from the meetings of the 'Society for Rewarding of merit', as Manley describes it, and it is conceivable that Barber had known him earlier.[21]

If Lady Masham did send Manley money after the publication of *The New Atalantis*, Manley certainly rewarded her (and Masham's cousin Harley) with hagiographic treatment in *Memoirs of Europe*. Masham appears as Theodecta in the first volume, the brave youth Leonidas in the second volume, and as Louisa of *Savoy*, Countess of Angoulesm, in Manley's dedication to the second volume. In this dedication, Manley reviews the Duchess of *Beaujou*'s (the Duchess of Marlborough's) resentment of Masham, concluding:

> Because you were still *Loyal*, still *Vertuous*; you must be term'd *Ingrateful*! But if a long
> Train of *Injuries* and black *Aspersions*, can cancel *one* Obligation (as certainly it does)
> How *Innocent* are you, Madam, in respect of the Duchess of *Beaujou*? How *Criminal*
> the Duchess of *Beaujou* in regard to the Countess of *Angoulesm*?[22]

Despite her hagiographic treatment of Masham, Harley and Peterborough in *Memoirs of Europe*, Manley did not dedicate the first volume of it to any of these actual or potential patrons.[23] Instead, she dedicated it to her quondam friend, with whom she was still engaged in a public feud, Richard Steele. In her dedica-tory letter addressed to Isaac Bickerstaff – Richard Steele's pseudonym in the *Tatler* – Manley accuses him of treating her unfairly in the *Tatler*, despite their 'reconcil'd Friendship (promised after my Application to him when under State-Confinement)'.[24] In his *Tatler* of 3 September 1709, Steele included a letter from an ostensible correspondent, accusing *Epicene* (Manley), 'by the Help of some artificial Poisons convey'd by Smells' of bringing 'many Persons of both Sexes to an untimely Fate'.[25] This *Tatler*, of course, appeared before Manley's arrest in late October. However, after she had been released on bail on 5 November 1709, Steele again apparently referred to Manley's (potentially) libellous style of satire in the *Tatler* of 10 November 1709, where he distinguishes between the writer of satire and the writer of libels:

> the Satyrist and Libeller differ as much as the Magistrate and the Murderer. In the
> Consideration of human Life, the Satyrist never falls upon Persons who are not glar-
> ingly faulty, and the Libeller on none but who are conspicuously commendable.

He explains further that the 'true Way of examining a Libel' is to realize 'that no one Man living thinks the better of their Heroes and Patrons for the Panegyrick given 'em, none can think themselves lessen'd by their Invective'. He adds, apparently referring to his own treatment in *The New Atalantis*, 'Had I the Honour to be in a Libel, and had escap'd the Approbation of an Author, I should look upon it exactly in this Manner'. He also notes that while he would not be upset by anything that a libeller wrote about him, he does believe that it is his obligation 'for the Good of my Country ... punish these Wretches' who write such libel.[26]

On the one hand, Steele shows restraint in not referring to Manley by name, or transparent pseudonym. On the other hand, in the second week of November 1709, Manley's arrest was so widely reported and discussed that it would be difficult not to conclude that Manley was the 'Libeller' under consideration. Steele may have been prepared as an old friend to assist Manley when she was in trouble, but as a Whig writer, he insisted on his right to attack Tory libellers 'for the good of [his] Country'. Manley apparently took his comments as insult enough that in her ironic dedication to him she cites a letter he apparently wrote her in early September 1709, in which he protested her treatment of him in *The New Atalantis* but insisted that 'your Sex, as well as your Quality of a Gentlewoman (a Justice you would not do my Birth and Education) shall always preserve you against the Pen of your provok'd, *Most humble Servant*'.[27] Manley clearly feels that he has not been true to this promise in his subsequent *Tatlers*. In including his letter, which she claims to be citing verbatim, she slyly alters it slightly – leaving out Steele's explanation of why he was unable to assist her when she needed money some years earlier and changing the word 'Kindnesses' to 'Services' – so that it appears less gracious and appreciative than the original.[28] Here, Manley engages in a direct attack on a fellow author (and former friend). However, it is an attack that was in some sense justified by Steele's own insistence that attacking those who libel others (and she apparently felt herself libelled by being implicitly accused of being a 'Libeller') was in the best interest of the nation.

Manley's second secret history thus begins with the venom of a satirist under attack, although her attack on Steele paradoxically indicates that she was probably in a stronger position personally and professionally than she was when she began *The New Atalantis* with the obsequious dedication to the wealthy Duke of Beaufort. Had Manley been less successful with *The New Atalantis*, she would have needed to use the dedication to the first volume of *Memoirs of Europe* to secure further patronage. As it was, she seems to have felt secure enough of her work being pleasing to the Tories that she could forgo a potentially profitable dedication in order to continue exchanging barbs with a prominent Whig journalist. By the time she finished the second volume of *Memoirs of Europe* the Tories had secured control of the ministry, and in dedicating the second volume to Abigail Masham, Manley celebrates Masham's victory over Sarah, Duchess of Marlborough.

The Tory victory, of course, would mean that there might not be a great need for many more secret histories denigrating the Whigs who had just lost control of the government. However, Manley, clearly relished her role as a publicly recognized political satirist, and was eager to write more for the cause. Her next publications would take the form of periodical essays and political pamphlets, genres in which she would acquire a rhetorical discipline that was not necessary in her secret histories. Manley's secret histories are necessarily loose collections of historical and personal anecdotes, as appropriate to the style of *la petite histoire* ('little history'), offering a counter-narrative to more chronological works of history from the dominant ideological perspective, which are somewhat difficult for modern readers to follow. In *Memoirs of Europe* Manley writes at times with the dense historical detail of her father's military histories, as her characters relate accounts of the military and political histories of France, Sweden and Turkey in her fictitious translation of these ostensibly eighth-century *Memoirs* written by 'Eginardus, Secretary and Favourite to Charlemagne'.[29]

Manley is skilled at developing rich analytical parallels between the current situation in Britain and other similar moments in the political histories of other countries. Her choice to depict Charles XII of Sweden, imprisoned in Bender, as exchanging stories with Peterborough, is fascinating and complex, since Charles XII was admired by some but not all Jacobites.[30] As Ruth Herman explains, Manley constructs a carefully layered narration that permits Manley to portray contrasting views of Charles XII simultaneously.[31] As in *The New Atalantis*, Manley also includes in *Memoirs of Europe* some steamy scenes of illicit sex involving Whig ministers and courtiers. Although such scenes were standard in political secret histories, as I have already explained, they did contribute to Lady Mary Pierrepont's impression that 'some better pen' might 'give more elegant and secret memoirs'.[32]

In the absence of any hypothetically 'better pen' taking the 'Liberty' Manley took with her subject, Pierrepont (an accomplished epistolary stylist herself) had expressed eagerness in November 1709 for her correspondent to send her 'As soon as possible, the 'second part of the Atalantis' in exchange for the published key that she promised to procure and share.[33] Despite complaints such as Pierrepont's about the quality of the pen responsible for them, *Memoirs of Europe* and *The New Atalantis* (which generally were bound together in four volumes from 1716 onwards and referred to together simply as *The New Atalantis*), went through multiple editions until 1740 and, between printings, were regularly advertised for sale at book auctions, demonstrating the popular appeal of the volumes, long past the time when readers would have had any concerns about the 1708–10 Marlborough-Godolphin ministry.

As popular as they were, Manley's secret histories nevertheless give the impression of having been produced in some haste, as they probably were, given the topicality of the attacks. Despite their frequent allusions to classical satire and European history which suggest Manley's literary pretensions, these works do not give the impression of having been thoroughly revised – either for felicity of phrasing or coherence of narrative. Manley's sentences are often unwieldy even by eighteenth-century standards (as passages cited in this and previous chapters should suggest), the spelling of her characters' names is inconsistent, and plot devices sometimes shift as the narrative develops (the magic ring by which Marlborough controls Queen Anne in *Memoirs of Europe* is introduced as something of an afterthought).[34] When Manley turned to writing periodical essays and pamphlets, however, the results demonstrate that when working with a smaller canvas and taking time to revise, she could produce taut, effective works of satire in the style of the best satirists of her era.

The *Examiner*

The *Examiner*, a Tory periodical designed to counter such Whig periodicals as George Ridpath's *Observator* and Steele's *Tatler*, was begun as a jointly authored effort with the assistance of Francis Atterbury, Dr John Freind, Mathew Prior, Henry St John and probably Delarivier Manley.[35] After the first twelve issues, Robert Harley persuaded Jonathan Swift to take over the periodical, and Swift authored thirty-three weekly issues (averaging about 2,000 words each), from 2 November 1710 (number 14) until 14 June 1711 (number 45). Harley's idea for the *Examiner*, as Swift described it in a pamphlet written in October 1713, was, following the recent change in ministry: 'to keep up the spirit raised in the people, to assert the principles, and justify the proceedings of the new ministers'.[36]

The *Examiner* appeared every Thursday. The Whig periodical the *Medley*, which was designed to respond to the *Examiner*, appeared the following Monday; it was produced by John Oldmixon and often partly conceived or written by Arthur Maynwaring, who had recruited him to produce it. Swift laid down the *Examiner* with issue 46, which he began, but which Delarivier Manley finished. She then wrote the next six issues, laying down her pen when she left London for the country in mid-July 1711, following number 52 (19–26 July). She also may have written one of the pre-Swiftian issues (number 7), which discusses Charles XII of Sweden (1682–1718), a subject she had treated at length in *Memoirs of Europe* and to which she returned in number 49.

Swift and Harley shared a political sensibility that was committed to the Revolution Settlement and the free proceeding of Parliament. They were both distrustful of the Whig Junto. Swift believed strongly that 'a Prince ought not ... to be under the Guidance ... of either [party]'.[37] In his weekly paper, Swift rehearsed these general political principles with a tone of self-confidence and forcefulness that Swift himself described as 'innocent Boldness' but which was perceived by some of his own contemporaries as authoritative, even intimidating.[38] One of Swift's journalistic opponents described him as 'an Author of such a Gigantick Size ... that he is able to crush such Pigmies as you and I with his little finger'.[39] Despite his success at this periodical, Swift ceased writing it after seven months, signalling the change in number 46, for which he claims to have written the first page (and Delarivier Manley finished):

> When a General has conquer'd an Army, and reduc'd a Country to Obedience, he often finds it necessary to send out small Bodies, in order to take in petty Castles and Forts, and beat little straggling Parties, which are otherwise, apt to make head and infest the Neighbourhood ...[40]

If we see Swift as the authoritative General (perhaps of a 'Gigantick Size'), we may interpret the passing of the *Examiner* to Manley as passing the mantle from the official historian to the author of 'small Bodies', or perhaps of 'little' or secret histories (*petites histoires*), a genre at which Manley was obviously experienced.[41] Swift, or whoever asked him to give up writing the *Examiner*, may have believed that he had addressed the main ideological issues of concern to Harley's ministry. Swift explains in number 45, 'the main Design I had in writing these Papers, is fully executed'.[42] Whether or not Swift lay down the journal willingly is a matter of some dispute. He suggests to Stella that it is 'a thousand pities' that another author may be taking it over, but he adds 'who can help it?', suggesting the choice may not have been his own.[43] As J. A. Downie observes, part of the difficulty may have been Swift's 'reassertion of his literary independence' in May 1711 as well as his continuing association with Henry St John, whom Harley increasingly distrusted. Downie speculates that a decision was possibly made during or following Swift's meeting with Harley on 19 May 1711 that seems to have resulted in Swift being told, as Downie puts it: 'if he intended to write without consulting the general policies of the government, then his services were no longer required'.[44]

Swift, of course, continued his work for Oxford's government as a pamphleteer, writing one of the most important and influential pamphlets of his era during the summer and autumn of 1711, *The Conduct of the Allies*, which made the case for the peace being negotiated by Oxford to end the War of Spanish Succession (ultimately the Peace of Utrecht, finalized in March and April 1713). For this sort of work, however, Swift was in frequent discussion with governmental ministers at every stage, even down to circulating the page proofs among 'three or four great people ... to see that there are no mistakes in point of fact', a final effort he found 'troublesome'.[45] It could even be argued that the reason Swift gave up the *Examiner* was to have time and energy to devote to this sort of crucial governmental pamphlet.[46] However, it could also have been, as Ruth Herman argues, that Oxford wanted someone who could help generate party unity, even currying the favour of extreme High-Tories, more directly than Swift had. Herman explains, 'Manley tackled the task of speaking to the potentially dissident Tories in an equally effective, but deliberately less elevated, manner displaying not, as Swift did, a "contempt for party," but merely a contempt for the Whigs'.[47]

Manley probably first met Swift in early 1711 at the home of John Barber. In his *Journal to Stella* for 4 January 1711 Swift mentions: 'I dined with people you never heard of, nor is it worth your while to know; an authoress and a printer'.[48] Although it might appear from this mention that Swift did not think very highly of such dining companions (and although before meeting Manley Swift had referred to Stella's misspelling of 'Rediculous' as the spelling of 'the author of the *Atalantis's*'),[49] he would become good friends with both Barber and Manley. Subsequent *Journal* entries mention regular dinners at Barber's house as well as Swift's seconding of Manley's endeavours at seeking patronage from the Earl of Peterborough, cited above.[50] Interestingly, before having met Manley the 'authoress', Swift was already friendly with the family of Manley's cousin Isaac, brother of Manley's bigamous husband John Manley. Isaac Manley was serving as postmaster general in Ireland and knew Swift's correspondent Esther 'Stella' Johnson, although there is no evidence that Delarivier Manley was in regular contact with Isaac (that branch of the family may have shunned her after her 'marriage' to John Manley). Swift also seems to have met the bigamous John Manley through Isaac.[51]

Expressing concerns about Manley's health to Stella in January 1712, Swift describes her as having 'very generous principles for one of her sort; and a great deal of good sense and invention'. He also describes her in this letter, as has already been mentioned, as 'very homely and very fat'.[52] It is difficult to know exactly what Swift means by 'one of her sort': the mistress of a city printer, a writer of secret histories, the daughter of a Royalist betrayed by her cousin-guardian, or perhaps a competent political writer? As J. A. Downie, has argued, Swift seems genuinely to have respected Manley's abilities (despite her poor spelling) as well as her principles. Moreover, as Downie also shows, Swift almost certainly was not referring to Manley in a denigrating poem entitled 'Corinna', often cited with bewilderment by Manley scholars.[53] In her will, Manley refers to 'my much honoured friend the Dean of St Patrick's Dr. Swift'.[54] Swift himself includes her in his own list of friends, referring to her as 'g[rateful]'.[55] As with so many of his friendships, Swift's connection to Manley had both a literary and a political grounding. Moreover, this friendship apparently resulted in Swift asking her in April 1711 to finish a pamphlet he had begun about the stabbing of Robert Harley. Her success with this pamphlet (which will be discussed in the next section of this chapter) probably explains why she was asked (by whom is not known) to take over the *Examiner* during the summer of 1711.

With her experience as a writer of political secret histories and her ongoing public feud with the Whig journalist Richard Steele, Manley was in many ways well suited to taking over the *Examiner* and continuing the weekly sparring with the *Medley*. Although Swift was not optimistic about Manley's potential for the job (remarking to Stella, 'after this day ... you will hardly find them so good. I prophecy they will be trash for the future'),[56] in fact Manley adapted her style from the diffuse anecdote appropriate for her secret histories to more taut, focused reflections and repartee in her *Examiners*. Although at this point Swift may not have thought highly of her skill as a stylist, Manley seems to have been able to hold her own with the *Medley*. Manley of course did not have the classical education of Swift, Maynwaring or Steele, but she was a quick student and managed to produce the requisite Latin epigraphs to head each issue and appropriate examples from classical history as parallels to the current political situation.

Manley's first partial issue (number 46), for which Swift claims to have written the first page, includes an amusing and ironical petition by Whig writers ostensibly put out of work by the late change in Ministry. This petition was probably written by Swift.[57] However, assuming that the second half of the issue was written by Manley, we see her continuing the mockery of Whig writers in her own style, suggesting that

> the Author of the *Medley*, is a Dunce out of his Element, pretending to intermeddle with *Raillery* and *Irony*, wherein he has no manner of Taste or Understanding ... His *Irony* consists of the Words *MY FRIEND* ... Does he think that when he says, my *impious Friend*, my *stupid Friend*, and the like; says it in every Paper, and often a dozen times in one, that this is either Wit, Humour, or Satyr?[58]

Swift had been perhaps less direct in his reference to his journalistic opponents, but not always any less condescending. He refers, for example, to 'those little barking Pens which have so constantly pursu'd me' in number 45, concluding that 'nothing can well be more mortifying, than to reflect that I am of the same Species with Creatures capable of uttering so much Scurrility, Dulness, Falshood and Impertinence, to the Scandal and Disgrace of Human Nature'.[59]

In number 46, in the paragraph following Swift's mock petition, the author (presumably Manley at this point) lays out her goals for the issues she intends to write over the summer, during the recess of Parliament:

> I have sometimes had it in my Head, to write a particular History of Abuses and Corruptions. As I find my self at leisure this Summer, I shall pursue the Design; where, besides enumerating the gross Defect, not only of Duty and Respect to the most Gracious QUEEN that ever Reign'd: I propose to shew, in every Article, how wrong Things were manag'd under the late M—ry, how right they are now, and according to the Constitution.[60]

As stated here, Manley's plan for the summer issues is not that different from what she had been doing in her secret histories: the only difference is that she would be working in a condensed essay format. As Ruth Herman has pointed out, Manley also seems to have taken on the delicate task of conciliating the more extremist Tory members of the October Club, who would be reading her issues of the *Examiner* at their country estates.[61]

Examiner number 47 includes a précis of the Queen's speech given at the close of the parliamentary session on 12 June, and reiterates the government's success in reducing some portion of the public debt. Manley also responds to the *Medley* of 11 June in taking on the topic of a 1709 act granting indemnity to Whig ministers in case of a change of ministry, a topic Swift had originally treated in *Examiner* number 18. She insists, following a theme apparent in both of her secret histories, that the ministers now dismissed 'had separately and prodigiously enrich'd themselves; to preserve their Wealth and Authority, they must invade the Constitution'.[62] Manley also addresses *The Representation of the State of Religion*, a High-Church assessment of the Church's position, which the House of Commons intended to present to the Queen but which was modified by the more Whiggish bishops in the House of Lords. Manley praises the 'Eloquence of the Argument' and criticizes the quibbling over it in the House of Lords, urging her readers not to provide the 'Enemies of our Holy Religion ... a seeming occasion to deride our Divisions'.[63]

Examiner number 48 gives something of the impression of a miniature version of *The Unknown Lady's Pacquet of Letters*, including excerpts from the letters of putative readers, touching on a range of topics, including one Tory's complaint about the Whigs' embrace of '*Arrians, Socinians, Free-Thinkers*, all sorts of *Christian Sectaries*' as well as the '*Circumcis'd*'. She also prints a plea from an ostensible Whig writer who has 'a Value for your Person and Abilities (but an Aversion to your Cause)', begging the *Examiner* to 'renounce the *Tories*, and come over to *Us*' including a draft of a treatise the writer entitles *The Art of Shifting Sides*.[64] Although Swift had often touched on several different topics in his *Examiners*, this lacks the biting authoritative tone that Swift had cultivated, and reminds us of Manley's earlier more miscellaneous epistolary collections and secret histories. The contrast in style between it and her next issue, her fictitious letter from Bender, a much more focused epistolary essay, nicely demonstrates Manley's continuing development from a writer of miscellaneous letters and anecdotal secret histories to the author of taut, focused pamphlets. However, the post-bag structure of number 48 also allows Manley to tread delicately around the divisive issue of the Church – for example, by putting a High-Church rant about non-Anglicans into the voice of an anonymous correspondent – and give the appearance of welcoming and unifying a disparate range of voices from her own party.

In *Examiner* number 49, the fictitious letter from an officer at Bender takes up the theme pursued in *Memoirs of Europe* and in *Examiner* number 7: recounting the control of the former ministry through the analogy of Charles XII of Sweden (clearly representing Queen Anne) being manipulated by an avaricious Commanding Basha (obviously Marlborough). Rehearsing the depiction of Marlborough's avarice she had already traced in her secret histories, Manley explains, 'when any Person is preferr'd by his Prince's [Queen Anne's] Favour, he learns, first to amass a huge Estate, and then to set an exorbitant Value upon his own Merit'.[65] Although Marlborough was still commanding the Allied forces in the summer of 1711, his power and influence with the Queen was greatly diminished (his wife had already been forced to resign her court offices early in 1711) and he would be dismissed at the end of December that year. Manley also emphasizes the courage of those 'Generous Persons' (presumably including herself) who had the courage to publicize the faults of the previous administration, under whose governance, the national '*Fabrick* [was] tumbling' and the country's '*Foundations Sapped*'.[66] Manley concludes number 49 with the prediction '*that there may come to be a Change in all Things*' since the Commanding Basha was having difficulty finding common ground with 'the *New Superintendant* of the Revenue',[67] i.e. Lord Treasurer Robert Harley, Earl of Oxford.

In *Examiner* number 50, Manley defends herself against the *Medley*'s taunt that the *Examiner* had grown dull by insisting, 'sometimes perhaps, like other Authors of great Reputation, I am Dull by design'. She continues by describing 'This *Medler*' as 'the perfect Reverse of sir *John Falstaffe*; he is not only Dull himself, but he is also the Cause that Dulness is in other Men'.[68] Despite Manley's defence of her writing, this issue does lack the wit and focus of her previous one. Manley cites from some letters she claims are '*real* Letters', refuting the *Medley*'s taunt that the *Examiner* was in correspondence with itself. However, her final attempt at wit on this topic is not particularly effective: 'I differ as much from him [who corresponds with himself] ... as one who steals Mony into his Neighbour's Pocket, does from a Rogue who picks it out'.[69]

Manley's next issue begins with the complaint that she has been drawn into exactly the trivial sparring with the author of the *Medley* that 'himself and his Party desired' and she writes that she had considered leaving off the journal and taking 'leave till the Meeting of the Parliament'. However, she turns from this 'fruitless' exchange, as she describes it,[70] to describe a manuscript entitled *Marcus Antonius*, which she claims to have just discovered. She then offers a 'translation' of the passage about '*Fulvia*'s going to the House of Pride, to implore the Succour of the Goddess towards ruining the Vertue of *Agrippa*', a fable that allows her to review one more time the pride, avarice and boldness of Fulvia (Sarah, Duchess of Marlborough) and Antony (Sarah's husband). Her attack on the duchess, who had already been dismissed from her offices, fits with her stated intent of reminding readers of 'how wrong Things were manag'd under the late M—ry'.[71] She concludes with an appeal for Marlborough's imminent dismissal: '*Antony's* Zeal must languish; let him attempt no farther for the good of the Empire'.[72]

We do not know who asked Manley to take over the *Examiner* for the summer or who decided that her turn should finish at the end of July. In number 46 she indicates that she was asked to manage the periodical during a summer of leisure. In her final issue, number 52, she suggests that she has done what she set out to do: 'I have ... done my Country what Service lay in the Power of an honest, though conceal'd Pen'. She takes her 'Leave of the Town', indicating that she will retire 'from the Fatigue of Politicks and State-Reflections, till some more urgent Occasion again calls forth [her] Endeavours'.[73] It could be simply that she had grown tired of the weekly effort and intended to leave town for the rest of the summer. She indicates in her 19 July letter to Oxford that her 'Infirmities and misfortunes' were 'forcing [her] away into a cheaper part of the Kingdom',[74] but this could just mean that she was going to spend August with her sister in Finchley perhaps, or somewhere else away from the heat of central London.

In the same letter she indicates that 'my Lord Peterborow' (whom she had visited in early July, according to Swift's account) and 'Mr Granvile have promised to recommend me to your Lordship's Protection', clearly hoping for some reward or pension from Oxford.[75] She does not mention her work on the *Examiner* in this letter, but she may have assumed that Oxford knew she was writing it (even if he had not personally requested her to do so) and that this would be one more reason he might want to reward her. There is no evidence that Oxford sent any reward or recognition at this time, although he offered £50 to Swift, who rather than being pleased at the reward, 'affected to be in a rage at the impertinence of the offer'.[76] Manley may have decided that she was not interested in continuing the effort of writing it if no reward was going to be forthcoming, or else John Barber, as printer, may have decided that he was not interested in producing the periodical if Oxford was not more prompt in his payment for the distribution of 100 gratis copies of each issue.[77]

In her final issue of the *Examiner* (number 52), Manley touches on the difficulties she faced in writing the weekly publication. Here she is speaking as the general voice of the *Examiner*, not merely as author of the previous six issues, responding to complaints made as much against Swift as herself:

Notwithstanding the Charge that hath so often been brought against me, with an intent to wound *Great Men* through my Side, of my being a contemptible Hireling, and a little mercenary Fellow, without Probity or Principles; one whose Actions were directed by others, from whence the machine talk'd and mov'd, as conducted by Higher Hands: I solemnly declare, I am still as much unknown to the Leaders of our own Party, as to the others; and very likely to remain so, as long as I please my Self, notwithstanding the wise Remarks of the *Observator*, and the Guesses made by the judicious *Medley*.[78]

Manley is referring to the fact that Oldmixon and Maynwaring had not guessed the identity of the authors of the *Examiner*, whether it was being written by Swift or Manley. However, her larger point, that she is 'unknown to the Leaders of our own Party', is even more accurate in her case than in Swift's and may point to the reason she gave up writing the paper.

In contrast to Manley's position at the margins of the ministry's propaganda machine (although she was expected to write the *Examiner* as if she was at the centre of it), Swift at least was invited to attend the meetings of the Saturday Club at Harley's house and grew to consider Harley a friend, even if Harley did not take him into his confidence about everything or provide specific week-by-week instructions for Swift's *Examiner*.[79] There may have been times when Swift consciously decided to represent St John's more extreme Tory viewpoint rather than Harley's, but he may also not always have known how much of a difference of opinion was developing between Harley and St John during the spring of 1711.[80] Manley, while speaking in the disembodied voice of the *Examiner* (and so in this sense, speaking for Swift's *Examiners* also), is in fact accurate when she says that she is 'unknown' to Oxford, since there is no evidence of her meeting with him until the time that she waited on him in late May 1714.[81] As Ruth Herman has argued, Manley may have been in some respects more flexible than Swift and more willing to adapt her rhetoric to the specific desires of Oxford's policies.[82] However, as Manley indicates in a letter to Oxford written in October 1711 (presumably after she had returned from the country), she could be of more use with more specific direction: 'had I either instructions or incouragement I might succeed better'.[83] As Manley's work as a pamphleteer suggests, when she was given specific instructions about what the ministry wanted, she could usually deliver it.

Stinging Ripostes: Manley's Pamphlets

Whereas Jonathan Swift described Manley's *Examiners* ('the five or six last papers') as 'very silly' in his *Journal to Stella*, he nevertheless apparently considered Manley a capable enough writer to trust her with writing certain political pamphlets he did not have the time or inclination to write himself.[84] By October 1711, he describes, when sending them to Stella, 'five pamphlets, which I have either written or contributed to, except the best, which is the *Vindication of the duke of Marlborough*; and is entirely of the author of the *Atalantis*'.[85] It is not surprising that Swift thought highly of *The D. of M------h's Vindication: In Answer to a Pamphlet Lately Publish'd*, since in that pamphlet Manley achieves an authoritative yet dryly satirical voice that undermines Marlborough under the guise of praising him. The tone and voice bear some similarity to the voice Swift adopts in many of his *Examiners*.

Manley's other pamphlets are also effective and focused works of propaganda, but the voicing is sometimes more personal and the tone sometimes more hyperbolic than in her *Vindication*. In the handful of pamphlets she wrote for the Oxford ministry, Manley was clearly experimenting with different narrative voices, tones and styles of satire. Had the Whigs not returned to power after Queen Anne's death in 1714, Manley might have found further opportunities to develop her own particular style of pamphleteering. On the other hand, had the political situation permitted her to continue her career as a pamphleteer through the last decade of her life, Manley might have maintained her flexible approach – inventing different styles and tones as appropriate for the political exigencies of the moment.

The first pamphlet Manley was asked to write was about the stabbing of Robert Harley, which occurred on 8 March 1711. Initial news accounts reported that the Marquis de Guiscard, a disgruntled military pensioner who was being interrogated by the privy council for treasonous correspondence, stabbed Harley with a penknife during the interview. However, in the *Examiner* number 33, Jonathan Swift told Henry St John's version of the story, reporting that 'The Murderer confessed in *Newgate* that his chief Design was against Mr. *Secretary St. John*'. Unable to reach St John, Guiscard apparently attempted to 'Murder the Person whom he thought Mr. *St. John* loved best'.[86] This account, which angered Harley's family, also prompted the *Medley* to promote the Whig view that 'Truly there was no design at all against Mr *H----y*'.[87] Swift backpedalled slightly from this account in a subsequent *Examiner*, but still defended his initial report, by insisting, 'I relate only what *Guiscard* said in *Newgate*'.[88]

It would appear that Swift struggled to prevent offending either St John or Harley in this matter, and so asked Manley to write the pamphlet he had begun about the topic. *A True Narrative of what Pass'd at the Examination of the Marquis De Guiscard* appeared in mid-April 1711, published by John Morphew and printed by John Barber. Swift explains to Stella, on 14 April 1711, the day after the pamphlet appeared in print:

> I had not time to do it myself; so I sent my hints to the author of the *Atalantis*, and she has cook'd it into a six-penny pamphlet, in her own style, only the first page is left as I was beginning it. But I was afraid of disobliging Mr. Harley or Mr. St. John in one critical point about it, and so would not do it myself.[89]

Even this first mention offers two different reasons for his not writing it: insufficient time and divided loyalties. Two weeks later, he suggests that he may have been responsible for more than just the first page: 'what you will read in the *Narrative*, I ordered to be written and nothing else'.[90] Three years later, in an account of the Harley ministry written after Anne's death and Harley's fall, Swift describes the *Narrative* as an 'account, toward which I furnished the author with some materials'.[91]

Whether or not Swift contributed only 'some materials' or the entire plan for the pamphlet, Manley avoids choosing between Harley and St John for the position of martyred hero by suggesting that the Queen was Guiscard's real target. Further, she suggests that Guiscard would have been happy to have murdered either of these two ministers in her stead. Manley does, however, depict Harley as an example of heroic calm in the face of danger, while showing St John as somewhat more impetuous. Swift seems to agree with her representation of events, since he recommends the pamphlet to Stella: 'It is worth your reading, for the circumstances are all true'.[92] Ruth Herman points out that the introduction of the Queen as Guiscard's main target may have come from Edward Harley, brother to Robert Harley, who mentioned it in a letter to Abigail Harley in late March.[93] Herman suggests that Manley may have been in direct contact with the Harley family at this time.[94] However, it seems equally likely that Edward Harley had made this suggestion to Swift or to someone else who had conveyed the idea either directly to Manley or perhaps through 'hints sent to the printer [John Barber]', as Swift claims to have done in the case of Manley's *Learned Comment*.[95]

The opening of *A True Narrative*, for which Swift has claimed credit, is a meditation on the pleasure and importance of a historian recording 'the minute Passages and Circumstances of such Facts as are Extraordinary and Surprizing'.[96] The pamphlet recounts Guiscard's sordid past life, including his rakishly extravagant lifestyle and his alleged seduction of a nun, paragraphs that sound like passages in Manley's secret histories in their enumeration of his vices and the description of his lack of all 'Principles, or indeed Humanity'.[97] The pamphlet then includes a detailed description of the actual stabbing, including an explanation for why St John was asked by Earl Poulet to switch places with Harley, a detail that would help account for Guiscard's ultimate choice of victim: 'that *Guiscard's* Face might be full in the Light'.[98] We are told that he shuffled and fumbled continually. Then there is a paragraph offering a wonderfully Manleyan description of Guiscard's 'guilty Soul', which resembles paragraphs in her secret histories in which she describes the thoughts or feelings of those she is satirizing or their victims:

> Cou'd one have look'd into *Guiscard's* guilty Soul, how terrible, at that moment, had been the Prospect? His Dread of Conviction, his Ingratitude, his Treachery, his Contempt or Desire of Death, his Despair of Heaven, his Love of his native Country, his Spirit of Revenge, embroil'd this thoughts, fermented his Blood, roused his Shame, and work'd up his Resolution to a pitch of doing all the ... Mischief he cou'd to *England*[99]

This description does not deploy the dryly satirical tone that Swift would so admire in Manley's *The D. of M------h's Vindication*; it resembles much more the fevered pitch of some of the seduction scenes in *The New Atalantis*.[100] However, it probably made quite effective propaganda at the time when it was published, no doubt rousing public sentiment against this putatively libidinous traitor.

The rest of the pamphlet takes a more measured tone, describing who was present, the precise sequence of events, and particularly Harley's presence of mind following the attack. Harley's coolness is described in contrast to Guiscard's treacherous frenzy:

> This is the Man that may truly be said to know himself, whom even Assassination can't surprise; to whom the Passions are in such Obedience, they never contend for Sway, nor attempt to throw him from his Guard. Mr. HARLEY falling back in his Chair, by the redoubled Stroke that was given him, and seeing 'em busie about taking *Guiscard*, by whom he imagin'd himself kill'd, did not call or cry for Help, but getting up as well as he could of himself, apply'd his Handkerchief to the Wound to stop the Blood, and keep out the Air.[101]

This description of Harley's presence of mind not only renders him the hero of this incident (even if the pamphlet also diplomatically suggests that Guiscard's intent was to murder both Harley and St John), but also depicts him, by analogy, as a man of political moderation, a depiction consistent with his own idea of himself as a leader trying to avoid the extremes of factionalism.[102]

Manley then suggests, presumably following a suggestion either from Swift or from some court source, that Guiscard's initial design had been to poison Queen Anne. This monarch, whom Manley describes as 'all merciful and Saint-like', subsequently showed this criminal 'the Goodness (notwithstanding ... his horrible Intentions to destroy her) to appoint two Surgeons and two Physicians, to attend him in *Newgate*'.[103] In order to support Harley's preference for political cooperation rather than the extreme Toryism being pressed by St John and the October Club, Manley then asks: 'Is it not time to redeem our Character, that the World, in applauding our Courage, may no longer object our Division? Tho' we disagree in Religion, yet for common Good, we should, methinks, be glad to *Unite* in Politicks'. She concludes with a plea for 'calming our hearts and Animosities, by taking off the Veil of *Prejudice* and *Party*', a tactic she believes would ensure that '*France* could never be formidable to *England*; nor the Protestant Religion here, under any Apprehension from the restless and encroaching Spirit of the *Roman*'.[104]

As Ruth Herman suggests, Manley 'handled the tricky Guiscard situation with considerable skill', using the incident to create 'a platform for Harley's moderate Toryism'.[105] Her success in this endeavour probably explains why she was chosen to take over the *Examiner* for the summer of 1711. And despite Swift's condescending comments about her issues of the *Examiner*, Manley's skill as a propaganda writer was valued enough that she was asked to write *The D. of M-----h's Vindication* when she returned to London in September. Swift gives Manley entire credit for *The D. of M-----h's Vindication*, but he may have asked her to write it (as he did the pamphlet about Guiscard) or else she may have been asked by some member of Oxford's ministry, either directly or through Barber as intermediary. Swift himself was consumed during most of the months of September and October in composing his lengthy pamphlet *The Conduct of the Allies*, which would justify the peace agreements Oxford's ministry was negotiating to end Britain's involvement in the War of Spanish Succession.

The pressing political reason for a pamphlet about Marlborough in September 1711 was that while the Tories were involved in peace negotiations to end the increasingly unpopular War of Spanish Succession, Marlborough had scored an impressive victory against the French at Bouchain on 12 September. The Whigs wanted to continue the war until the original goal of 'No Peace without Spain' was achieved, and Marlborough's victory, which was followed by celebratory poems and pamphlets, provided a boost to their cause. The Tories, who were determined to end the war without further military involvement in Spain (especially after the death of the Austrian emperor in April 1711, which resulted in King Carlos III of Spain becoming Emperor Karl VI and the European balance of power changing dramatically), found Marlborough's victory awkward. They needed to respond swiftly and effectively to the Whig propaganda. They also needed to do so with caution, since Marlborough was an undeniably gifted military commander and popular war hero, nationally recognized since his famous victory at Blenheim in 1705. In her *Vindication* Manley thus consistently insists on Marlborough's courage, bravery and success, but does so in such a way as to make clear that Marlborough is also avaricious and ungrateful to the monarch who raised him to the greatness he embodies.

Manley's *Vindication*, which appeared on 2 October 1711, was written in response to an anonymous 1711 pamphlet entitled *Bouchain: In a Dialogue between the Late Medley and Examiner* (ascribed to Francis Hare and/or Arthur Maynwaring), which provided a detailed description of the month-long campaign to take Bouchain, a glorified account of Marlborough's brilliance as a general, and a warning against making a peace without Spain.[106] Hare's (and Maynwaring's) *Bouchain* also reanimated the sparring between the anonymous voices of *Medley* and *Examiner*, an exchange which had ended when the two periodicals ceased production after Manley stopped writing the *Examiner* at the end of July. Since the author gives voice to both sides in the fictitious debate in his pamphlet, Manley is obliged to defend Hare's (and Maynwaring's) misleading representation of the *Examiner* (in all its numbers and authors). She is thus speaking not only for herself but is also defending Swift and all previous authors of the *Examiner* when she observes:

> I Was always satisfied of the Stupidity and Disingenuity of the Author, who call'd himself the *Medley*; but never, till now, so thoroughly convinc'd of his Assurance. He (or one who Personates him) appears in a little book call'd, *Bouchain*, as if he were in close Conference, and great Intimacy with the *Examiner*; where, according to the unfair manner of modern Dialogue, he reserves all the Wit and Reasoning for himself, and makes the poor *Examiner* one of the silliest, dullest Rogues, that ever pretended to speak, or hear of Politicks: Nay, he has even treated him worse than the real *Medley* did; who, tho' hir'd by the Party to call him Names by the Week, had still so much Modesty, not to take away his Understanding, tho' he did his Integrity.[107]

Manley maintains this dry irony throughout the narrative as she refutes Hare (and Maynwaring) point by point in his assertions that '*the D. of M— is divested of all Interest and Authority, both at Home and in the Army: Whom so much pains have been taken to mortifie, that he might either in discontent throw up his Command, or continue in it without Honour*'.[108]

In fact, there was some truth to what the author of *Bouchain* suggests: Marlborough's wife had already been removed from her court offices and Marlborough had been warned by the Queen that 1711 would probably be his last military campaign. He had also been excluded from a meeting of Allied leaders in June about the coming campaign. Nevertheless, as Manley observes, when we 'Examin things more cooly' than her pamphleteering opponent had done, we might ask: 'What Hardships has this Great Man to complain of?' She shrewdly points out, 'No Man ever entred upon his Command with greater Encouragement; the Love and Smiles of his Soverign, the good Wishes of the People'. Continuing to insist on his courage and his bravery, just as Shakespeare's Mark Antony reiterates that Brutus is an honourable man, Manley finally asks, 'Is he not the Richest and greatest Subject in *Christendom*?'[109]

Manley defends the *Examiner*'s treatment of Marlborough's avarice by implicitly referring back to Richard Steele's distinction in the *Tatler* between a 'Satyrist' and a 'Libeller' and claiming the high moral ground for the *Examiner*'s classical analogies:

> Cannot a Person treat of the excessive Avaraice and sordid Behaviour, of *Marcus Crassus*, but, because the D. of *M*— is known to be an extream good husband of his Mony, he must needs intend his Grace as Parallel? Indeed! Does this Libeller think there is so near a resemblance between them? Why, where then is the Injustice? To show that there has been many, let him convince us that his Grace is become Generous, or less in love with Richards, and the Comparison will cease.[110]

Manley concludes the pamphlet with a defence of the separate peace Oxford's ministry was secretly negotiating: 'even if a *Separate Peace* should be intended by some of our Allies ... the generality of the People will be easily brought to agree, that 'tis better than no Peace at all'. She insists finally that the members of the current Ministry 'are so well acquainted with the true Interest of the Nation, and are so tender of its Welfare, that they will not consent to take one Step in this Affair, but what makes for the Glory of the QUEEN, and the Happiness of Her Subjects'.[111]

On 27 September 1711, just five days before Manley's *Vindication* appeared in print, a sermon preached by the chaplain general to Marlborough's army, Dr Francis Hare (one of the authors of the pamphlet about Bouchain to which Manley's *Vindication* responded), was published. The published sermon, which criticized the ministerial attempts to make peace, appeared on the very day that preliminary articles for ending the War of Spanish Succession were being signed by England and France.[112] Manley responded quickly, composing a pamphlet that refuted each of Hare's points in turn. This pamphlet, *A Learned Comment upon Dr. Hare's Excellent Sermon Preach'd before the D. of Marlborough*, appeared on 3 October 1711, just ten days before the ministry's preliminary articles would be presented to the Allied diplomats. In refuting Hare's points, Manley is able to reiterate many of the arguments against the war that she had laid out in her *Vindication*. As has already been mentioned, Swift claims to have 'only sent hints to the printer' for Manley's *Learned Comment*.[113] It thus seems reasonable to assume that the words, tone and phrasing are entirely hers.

Manley begins her *Learned Comment* by accusing Hare, who was Bishop of Chichester as well as chaplain-general, of being more of a politician than a churchman: 'His Politicks and his Divinity seem to be much of a size'.[114] In response to his acknowledging God's providence for the victory at Bouchain and his faith that God will bring peace '*If we be content to wait his leisure, and are not by our Impatience and misgiving Fears, wanting to our selves*', Manley protests: 'At this rate when must we expect a Peace? May we not justly enquire, Whether it be God's, or the D. of *M*—'s Leisure, he would have us wait'.[115] She cites and refutes another of Hare's pleas for patience in waiting for God to finish 'by gradual Steps this great Work' by musing 'whether three and twenty Years long will do, or what time he thinks the General and himself may live'.[116] She then enumerates the costs of the war to the British at home: 'the Decay of Trade, Increase of Taxes, Dearness of Necessaries, Expense of Blood, and Lives of our Country-men'. She concludes by suggesting that instead of blessing the generals, the British should be ready 'to bless whoever are the Authors of Peace ... by which we may be freed from those nearer and much more formidable Enemies, Discontent and Poverty at Home'.[117]

Manley's satirical pamphlets about Marlborough were effective enough propaganda that they provoked rebuttals, including *The D. of M-----h's Vindication, in Answer to a Pamphlet Falsely so Called*.[118] They also provoked the Duke of Marlborough himself to complain both to his wife and to Oxford.[119] Oxford somewhat disingenuously replied: 'I do assure your Grace I neither know nor desire to know any of the authors, and I heartily wish this barbarous war was at an end. I shall be very ready to take my part to suppressing them'. He added, somewhat less disingenuously, reporting on new plans for censorship (including schemes that would become the 1712 Stamp Act) being championed by Henry St John, now Viscount Bolingbroke, that 'the queen ordered last Sunday night ... that the authors of all libels shall be impartially sought out and punished'.[120] As J. A. Downie has explained, Oxford almost certainly knew who had been writing the pamphlets in response to the victory at Bouchain. If somehow the fact of Manley's authorship was not already known to him, she made it clear in a letter sent on 2 October 1711, in which she mentions her *Vindication* (which had just appeared) and encloses a copy of her *Learned Comments* (which would be published the following day).[121] It is in this same letter that Manley hints to Oxford that had she could do more for the ministry with 'instructions or incouragement'.

Despite the importance of these two pamphlets in the ministerial propaganda campaign of the autumn of 1711, and despite her obvious desire to continue her work for the Oxford ministry, there is no definite evidence that Manley authored any other pamphlets in 1711 or 1712. It is possible that she was the 'under-strapper' whom Swift asked to write *A True Relation of the Several Facts and Circumstances of the intended Riot and Tumult on Queen Elizabeth's Birth-Day*, in late November 1711, while he was busy finishing his *Conduct of the Allies*.[122] However, as Ruth Herman points out, Swift does not usually refer to Manley as an 'under-strapper' (usually he refers to her as 'Mrs. Manley' or as 'the author of the *Atalantis*'), nor did the late nineteenth- or early twentieth-century editor of Swift's works assume that this 'under-strapper' was Manley, although a subsequent twentieth-century editor did make that assumption.[123] Manley was certainly capable of providing the sort of description of the well-known avarice of the Duchess and Duke of Marlborough included in the pamphlet: 'though her Dexterity in *Getting* be as great as his, he out-does her in *Preserving*'.[124] Unfortunately there is nothing particular in the style or voicing of the pamphlet itself that allows us either to attribute it definitely to Manley or to conclude definitely that she had no hand in it.

Once his *Conduct* appeared, Swift may not have felt the immediate need for Manley's assistance in the propaganda campaign. It would also appear that despite her direct appeal to the Lord Treasurer, Oxford seems not to have responded to Manley with either monetary support or requests for further satirical treatments of Marlborough. By the end of December, Marlborough would be stripped of his command and court positions. One month later, in late January 1712, Swift would write to Stella: 'Poor Mrs. Manley the author is very ill of dropsy and sore leg; the printer [Barber] tells me he is afraid she cannot live long'. He adds 'I am heartily sorry for her'.[125]

Fame and Uncertain Ascriptions, 1712–14

Manley did not die of dropsy in 1712, but she apparently struggled with the chronic condition for the rest of her life, and she refers to her poor health in several of her begging letters to Oxford. Despite her physical ailments, Manley kept writing – although not at the furious pace she maintained during the years from 1709 to 1711. She may have written other pamphlets for the Oxford, printed for 'John Morphew', the trade publisher whom John Barber usually employed, although it is not possible to verify these possible attributions to her with certainty.

The Honour and Prerogative of the Queen's Majesty Vindicated and Defended Against the Unexampled Insolence of the Author of the Guardian in a Letter from a Country Whig to Mr. Steele, which was published on 13 August 1713, has sometimes been attributed to Manley and sometimes to Daniel Defoe.[126] This pamphlet was part of a broader propaganda war between the Whigs and the Tories over the planned demolition of the port of Dunkirk.[127] The Whigs considered this demolition, of a port from which the Jacobite invasion of 1708 had been launched, vital to the peace treaties signed at Utrecht in March and April 1713. The Queen and the ministry, however, seemed in no hurry to demolish the port or to have it demolished by the French. Richard Steele attacked the Oxford ministry about this matter in the *Guardian* for 7 August 1713, asserting the great importance of the matter to Britain. *The Honour and Prerogative* is written from the point of view of an 'Old Whig' rebuking Steele for the way he has represented 'all [his] Friends the *Whigs*, that they should be supposed to approve of [his] Conduct [i.e. his dictatorial approach to the Queen] in this Matter'.[128]

The case for ascribing this pamphlet to Manley is somewhat slender. Manley does not refer to herself as an 'Old Whig' in any of her other pamphlets, although Swift sometimes characterizes himself as an 'Old Whig' in the *Examiner*, especially when objecting to the strife of partisan conflict, and, if she wrote this pamphlet, Manley might have been following Swift's lead in adopting this persona. The narrative voice of *The Honour and Prerogative*, however, does not particularly resemble either the detached ironic narration of Manley's *The D. of M------h's Vindication* or the biting tone of Manley's attack on Steele in her dedication of the first volume of *Memoirs of Europe*. Nowhere does this pamphlet refer to him as 'ungrateful', Manley's usual complaint against him, although the author does make some aspersions on his character, alluding to 'the Article of your Morals'.[129] There is also a reference to the distinguishing 'Dulness' the author has come to expect from 'Mr. *Steele*' when he is writing in his own voice and not putting his name on the works of others.[130]

The Whig journalist Abel Boyer reported in September 1713 that *The Honour and Prerogative* 'is said to be written by the Author of the *New Atalantis*', although he also notes that the author of a subsequent pamphlet, *Reasons Concerning the Immediate Demolishing of Dunkirk* (1713), is 'generally guess'd to be the same' as the author of *The Honour and Prerogative*.[131] This subsequent pamphlet has recently been attributed with strong probability to Defoe.[132] The same modern scholars who believe the second pamphlet is probably Defoe's, however, do not believe there is adequate evidence to attribute *The Honour and Prerogative* to him.[133] I would argue that, despite Boyer's hearsay report, there is hardly adequate external or internal evidence to attribute it to Manley either.[134] Steele's article in the *Guardian*, after all, won him many critics and enemies.

It is possible that Manley wrote some numbers of the *Examiner* after 1711, since Barber's Tory biographer suggests that Manley 'often shined in the EXAMINER, without the World's knowing that she had any Hand in it'.[135] It is also possible that she had some hand in the John Bull pamphlets usually ascribed to John Arbuthnot.[136] The title page for the third part of the published collections of John Bull pamphlets suggests that it was 'Publish'd, (as well as the two former Parts) by the Author of the NEW ATALANTIS'.[137] The title page also indicates that it was printed for John Morphew, the trade publisher whom Barber employed for all of the Oxford ministries pamphlets and periodicals. It is not clear whether Manley is referenced here merely because she lodged at Barber's printing house (and because the association with her might increase sales) or whether Manley in fact paid the costs of publishing this pamphlet and stood to share in the profits. The author of the *Observator* responds to the title page by suggesting that *John Bull* was 'poison'd with ... the Practices of such Persons as the Author of *The New Atalantis*'.[138] The fable-like stories in these pamphlets, with characters such as John Bull and Nicholas Frog, do not resemble Manley's narrative style in any of her other known works, and scholars who have made thorough studies of the pamphlets usually ascribe them to John Arbuthnot.[139] Ruth Herman suggests, however, that Manley might possibly have written some of the prefaces to the published collections of these pamphlets.[140]

Since Manley was lodging within the premises of Barber's printing shop, it seems plausible that she might have assisted with other pamphlets published by Barber under Morphew's imprint. Manley may have been the author whom John Barber asked to add two final pages to Jonathan Swift's *A New Journey to Paris: Together with some Secret Transactions between the Fr---h K---g, and an Eng--- Gentleman. By the Sieur du Baudrier*, a fictitious letter about Mathew Prior's recent secret trip to Paris to pursue secret peace negotiations (ostensibly written by the French manservant who accompanied Prior in Paris), which appeared in September 1711. Swift complained to Stella that the final pages 'are so romantick, they spoil all the rest'.[141] These last few paragraphs (which Swift claims not to have written) offer an anecdote about Prior giving a coin in charity to a beggar dressed in rags who had the 'Mien' of a man 'of a good House' and who declared himself to be '*the Marquis* de Sourdis'. The correspondent records Prior as wondering aloud whether that creature really was a marquis and concluding 'if it were so, surely the Miseries of our Country must be much greater than even our very Enemies could hope or believe'.[142] Although Swift does not suggest directly that he believes the pamphlet was finished by Manley, her proximity to the printing house and his suggestion that final pages were 'romantick' may suggest that he believed they were hers.

There is some evidence to suggest, as Calhoun Winton has argued, that Manley may have contributed to *The Ecclesiastical and Political History of Whig-Land of Late Years* (1714), whose title page identifies John Lacy as the author (an attribution Winton disputes).[143] This pamphlet contains some description of Steele's early years, years to which Manley also refers in *The New Atalantis*, using phrases similar to those Manley used to describe Steele's life at that time, such as his 'Pursuit of the *Philosophers Stone*'.[144] Of course, Lacy (or whoever the author really was) could simply have borrowed such descriptions from Manley's *New Atalantis*. The rest of the pamphlet does not seem Manleyan either in style, topic or length: at almost a hundred pages, it is a very different sort of work than Manley's other sixteen-page pamphlets.

There is no specific evidence, either external or internal, to ascribe to Manley *A Modest Enquiry into the Reasons of the Joy Expressed by a Certain Sett of People upon the Spreading of a Report of her Majesty's Death* (1714), although the Swift scholar John Nichols believed it was hers.[145] Similarly, there is no evidence that Manley wrote *The Representation of the Loyal Subjects of Albinia* (1712), although John Barber's modern biographer makes this claim.[146] The lengthy pamphlet *The Conduct of the Duke of Ormonde* (1715) is often catalogued with Manley as author, even though it includes detailed military accounts and is written in a style unlike any of Manley's other publications.[147] A *Memorial* of Ormond's wife, published in 1735, over a decade after Manley's death, has likewise been ascribed to Manley. These last two ascriptions may perhaps be explained by Manley's mention of the Duke of Ormond in *The New Atalantis*, but such a rationale would be tenuous at best, since Manley's treatment of him is highly satirical.[148]

The success Manley had achieved as a political writer between 1709 and 1714 meant that her name might get used to increase sales of a work. She may have willingly allowed Morphew and Barber to suggest on the title page of the *John Bull* pamphlets that she was the 'publisher' (especially if in fact she had some hand in their publication). However, as has already been mentioned, Manley publicly objected to the appearance of *Court Intrigues*, an unauthorized reissue of her *Unknown Lady's Pacquet of Letters*, and she publicly disclaimed authorship of *The New Atalantis for the Year 1713*. Coincidentally, however, *Court Intrigues* was published by Manley's usual trade publishers, Woodward and Morphew, who brought out her *Remaining Part of the Unknown Lady's Pacquet*. It is conceivable, then, that if Manley truly objected to this publication, she might have had the possibility of intervening before it appeared, especially if John Barber were the printer, as has been speculated.[149] However, someone other than Barber may have been the printer and *Court Intrigues* may in fact have been produced without her knowledge.

Although not ascribed to her either in her own lifetime or by the eighteenth-century biographer of Barber, *The Female Tatler*, a periodical that appeared for twenty-five issues in 1709, has sometimes been attributed to Manley. Aside from the obvious fact that Manley was probably too busy finishing the second part of *The New Atalantis* in the summer of 1709 to have much time to write anything else, the periodical treats the affairs of London citizens, whom Manley never otherwise mentions, not the members of court and Parliament whom she usually makes the topic of her satire. This work was originally attributed to the lawyer Thomas Baker. The reasons that Paul Bunyan Anderson gave for suggesting that Manley wrote it have been refuted by Walter Graham; the reasons Fidelis Morgan offers for reasserting Manley's authorship do not refute Graham's points and are otherwise unconvincing. For example, simply asserting that 'Mother Mab' and 'Scandalosissima Scoundrella' definitely refer to 'Mrs. Manley' does not establish Manley's authorship. Susannah Centlivre's reference to 'Delia's' desire to 'make a noise for reformation' in response to Bickerstaff might well refer to Manley's complaints about Steele in *The New Atalantis*, but in no way proves Manley's authorship of *The Female Tatler*.[150] Moreover, Steele himself certainly believed the author of *The Female Tatler* and the author of *The New Atalantis* were two distinct persons, since he refers to the former and then to the latter as 'another': 'I was ... scolded at by a *Female Tatler*, and slandered by another of the same Character, under the Title of *Atalantis*'.[151]

Manley's success as a Tory writer not only meant that her name or the name of her most famous work would be invoked by other authors and publishers to help market their books, it also meant that she could be vulnerable to those trying to denigrate her, as Charles Gildon and Edmund Curll were apparently trying to do with their intended *Adventures of Rivella*. Of course, Manley's fame as a best-selling author also meant that she was apparently able to persuade Curll to let her write the work in her own way.[152] Although *The Adventures of Rivella* gives the impression of having been written quickly (as indeed it was according to the account in Curll's 1724 preface), it nevertheless saw three editions between 1714 and 1717. Manley would not have profited from its success if Curll bought the copyright from her for a lump sum, as was usual in this era (unless the author employed a trade publisher or sold the work by subscription). However, its relative success demonstrated Manley's appeal in yet another genre: autobiographical secret history 'interspersed with Memoirs and Characters of several Persons Cotemporary with the said Author', as it is described on the title page of the first edition.[153] A contemporary reader of the work, who described himself as 'No Worshipper' of 'the Famous De la Riviere Mrs. Manley', nevertheless found them diverting enough to recommend to his sister 'Some Memoirs Relating ... to her'.[154]

Manley's success as a writer of political secret histories, periodicals and pamphlets, of course, made her so renowned as a writer for the Tory cause that she would have had difficulty writing for the government after the death of Queen Anne and the return of the Whigs. Although she may only have been paid once by Oxford, Manley nevertheless had apparently enjoyed writing for the Oxford ministry and would probably have liked an opportunity to continue writing on the side of those in power, secure from further governmental prosecution. As she suggests in *Rivella*, it might have been more profitable to have written for the Whigs, but having staked out her place on Oxford's team, along with Swift, Barber and the rest of the authors of the *Examiner*, she would have to be content with Oxford's bill of £50 and the patent for future profits from Barber and Tooke which she mentions in her will (but from which she had apparently not yet seen any profits) and which may have been granted to her because of her work for the Oxford ministry.[155] Her moment of triumph as a political writer, however, probably occurred when John Barber rode out from London (presumably to her sister's house in Finchley), in June 1714, to deliver her the monetary reward from Oxford.[156]

9 A CELEBRATED 'MUSE': 1714-24

After the death of Queen Anne, the Whigs returned to power under George I, and life changed dramatically for the coterie of writers and publishers on Oxford's propaganda team. Oxford himself, of course, had gone into a decline even before Anne's death. He had lost the Queen's trust in favour of Bolingbroke and Anne dismissed him as Lord Treasurer in late July 1711, only a few days before she died. Despite Oxford's efforts on behalf of the Hanoverian succession, the new administration did not show him any gratitude, but stripped him of the rest of his offices and began impeachment proceedings against him in 1715.

Meanwhile, at the instigation of some Scottish members of the House of Lords, John Barber had been apprehended on a charge of libel for printing Swift's pamphlet *The Public Spirit of the Whigs*, which had appeared on 23 February 1714. Barber, however, 'insisting not to answer any Questions the Answer to which might tend to accuse himself or to corroborate the Accusation against him', never dropped any hint that Swift was the author of the pamphlet.[1] Swift was therefore not prosecuted for libel, and Barber, although charged with printing a libel (and so probably fined), was not yet removed as the printer of the governmental *Gazette*. Swift, however, became increasingly frustrated in his inability to reconcile Bolingbroke and Oxford and, after he was overlooked for the vacant office of historiographer royal in the summer of 1714, returned to Ireland. After Harley's fall and Swift's departure, Barber would no longer be at the centre of governmental propaganda production, but he would remain a successful printer and publisher, retaining the profitable position of printer to the South Sea Company, which he had held since the company's inception in 1711, and which may have facilitated his subsequent success as an investor.

We do not know exactly how Manley occupied her time after she ceased writing political periodicals and pamphlets and before the production of her most successful dramatic work, *Lucius, the First Christian King of Britain*, in 1717. She seems to have continued to live at John Barber's residence and printing house, with regular visits to her widowed sister Cornelia Markendale in Finchley; Cornelia also seems to have frequently stayed with Manley at Lambeth Hill.[2] After she took a house in Beckley, Oxfordshire, probably in about 1717, Manley spent time there as well; her will, which she wrote in October 1723, describes her as 'Delarivier Manley, of Beckley in the County of Oxford'. A new edition of *The New Atalantis*, issued together with *Memoirs of Europe*, in two volumes, was published for Barber's trade publisher, John Morphew, in 1716, and a four-volume edition, labelled 'the sixth edition', also with Morphew's imprint, appeared in 1720.[3]

When Manley negotiated with Richard Steele, then governor of the Drury Lane Theatre, for his company's right to produce *Lucius*, she was apparently negotiating from a position of strength, as a famous writer whose *New Atalantis* was still selling copies in its third edition, seven years after its initial appearance. Some twentieth-century scholars have assumed that the generous sum of 600 guineas Steele agreed to pay her for *Lucius* was a deliberate act of reconciliation.[4] This assumption makes sense if we follow Robert D. Hume's carefully reasoned observation that 'no one was making a living by writing plays in the mid-1720s';[5] nor, presumably, for the same reasons, in the previous decade. However, Brean Hammond has subsequently shown that a few early eighteenth-century plays did produce substantial profits. Steele's own *The Conscious Lovers*, for example, grossed £2,536 3s. 6d. for the theatre over an eighteen-night run in 1722 and also brought Steele £600 and £329 5s. from his own benefit nights.[6]

Manley's *Lucius*, her most polished dramatic production and the most likely to please an audience, was, according to Barber's Tory biographer, 'acted fifteen Nights successively; and to a crowded House every Night'.[7] This same source describes the ostensible negotiations between Manley and the managers at the Drury Lane:

> she could not bear the Thought of cringing for a Crown or a Guinea; as her Circumstances, *as she said*, made begging none of her Business, so she would have nothing to do with the Author's third Night; or trust to Chance or Caprice or her Benefit: She would not bear the Fatigue of a Moment's Expectation or Uncertainty as to the Fate of the Play; she knew it was a good one, and would not therefore put any Part of its Reputation upon the just or injudicious Performancces of those who were to act it ...[8]

Barber's biographer notes that 'she judged right upon this Occasion', adding as a compliment both to her sense of business and to her literary judgment, 'to be just to her Memory, we might add, that she was seldom or never known to do otherwise upon any Occasion'. He then continues: 'She made her Demand and 'twas readily complly'd with ... Instead of Benefit Nights, she asked six hundred Guineas, which they gladly agreed to'.[9]

This same biographer reports that the managers included an author's benefits every third night, 'on which, according to Custom they raised their Prices; but it was themselves, and not Mrs *Manley* who received the Benefit of their doing so'.[10] This biography of Barber, published in 1741, several decades after this play was produced, may be incorrect in some of these details. The authors of *The London Stage* do not confirm that it was produced on fifteen nights, but record evidence that it was produced on three nights, 11 May, 13 May and 18 May, with the third performance announced as an author's benefit.[11] Manley's own gracious description of Steele as her 'Patron'[12] in her dedication to him suggests that he certainly might have bought the play from her for some generous sum and then covered those costs by the profits from the author's benefit on the third night. If Barber's biographer was incorrect about the prepayment, then it is possible that Manley simply made a tidy profit from the benefit, as Steele himself would by his author's benefits for *The Conscious Lovers*. Although it would appear that the play may not have run as many days as reported by Barber's biographer, it may well have been the case that the author's benefit was a success and produced several hundred (if not the reported six hundred) guineas for Manley, either as a result of the benefit or in some form of prepayment.

Lucius was printed for (and possibly by) John Barber on 19 June 1717, although it appears from an earlier advertisement that Edmund Curll had brought out a pirated edition almost six weeks earlier.[13] Barber's Tory biographer suggests that the play sold well:

> Mr. BARBER printed this Play; and 'tis almost needless to say, that the Profits by the Sale of so celebrated a Tragedy must be far from inconsiderable; so far that the Demand was exceeding large; and in Proportion to the Value, the universal Approbation of those who had seen it had stamp'd upon it; and in Proportion to the Curiostiy excited by common Report of those who had not seen it, to read it; so that (and we have it upon good Authority) there was as much Money got by the printing and Sale of this Play, as the Writer got for allowing it to be acted.[14]

Of course, this estimate that someone made a profit of about six hundred guineas for the sales of the printed play does not tell us what portion of that went to Barber and what portion to Manley, although her mention of his 'many favours' to her in her will does not give the impression that she felt cheated from her share of the profits of this or any other of her works that he published.[15] This statement by Barber's Tory biographer may also be an exaggeration, however, since Barber's 1720 edition of *Lucius*, with the exception of a new title page claiming to be the 'Second Edition Corrected', so closely resembles the 1717 printed version that it could in fact be composed of leftover sheets from that earlier edition.[16] It is hard to determine how well Curll did with his pirated 1717 edition. He continued to advertise it – along with his third edition of *Rivella*, which he also brought out in 1717 – regularly in *The Post Boy* during much of the year 1718, which means that it either continued to sell well or that it was selling slowly enough that he still had inventory to clear a year later.[17]

By contrast with Manley's first two plays, produced over two decades earlier, *Lucius* does not express particular cynicism either about men, politics or the future of the nation. Rather, its plot might be viewed as a celebration of Britain's Protestant monarchy. Lucius, does not know that King Vortimer, the tyrannical usurper whom he believes to be his father, is really his father's murderer. When the truth is revealed to him, Lucius kills the usurper, saves his bride from being raped by Vortimer and triumphantly regains the British throne. Before accomplishing all this, Lucius had converted to Christianity and married Rosalind, the widow of the defeated King of Aquitaine, in a Christian ceremony. Borrowing elements of Hamlet's tragic predicament, but incorporating a hero who does not doubt either the woman he loves or his right to avenge his father, the play was clearly designed to be a crowd-pleaser. The play also alludes to *Richard III*, whose Tudor hero likewise restored England to its legitimate monarchical line. Lucius's reference to the 'six Otharios' he has slain clearly echoes Richard's 'I think there be six Richmonds in the field; Five have I slain to-day, instead of him'.[18]

Although this play seems to celebrate the successful Protestant Hanoverian succession (and possibly the triumph over the failed Jacobite rising in 1715), it could also be argued that *Lucius* expresses a dream of an idealist and Protestant style of Jacobitism, a desire for a Stuart restoration only if the Stuart claimant would convert to (an acceptably British form of) Christianity. Of course, the play was not so overtly Jacobite that either Barber or Curll were reluctant to include their own names as publishers in their advertisements for it. However, in the midst of his public battle legal with Thomas Pelham Holles (1693–1768), Duke of Newcastle and Lord Chamberlain, in February 1720, Steele apparently added the following more overtly Hanoverian closing lines to his spoken prologue for the 1720 revival of the play (which took place on 27 April 1720):

> – In wanton East – ye *Britons*, learn to know,
> Nor slight, in present Welfare, distant Woe!
> Rescu'd from foreign Bonds, the happy Age
> Sees no Abuse of power, but on the Stage:
> The *Briton* here, beholds the Tyrant bleed,
> The Just thro' all the Mazes of their Fate succeed;
> Our opening Earth, and our descending Sky,
> Our Bowl, our Dagger, ready Wrath supply,
> And, at the Poet's Nod, Kings reign, or die.
> On such dire forms, long shall this happy Isle,
> As only Stage-Events, in Safety Smile:
> While her great King magnificently spares,
> Conquers, and wins, and Deeds of Grace prepares!
> On *Dungeon*-Guilt, *He* Gleams of Mercy throws,
> And his each Action, Heav'n's Vicegerent shows.[19]

In case Lucius's conversion to Christianity and ultimate triumph might be seen as suggesting that James Edward Stuart should convert to Protestantism and save the British from the fate of being ruled by Hanoverian foreigners, these added lines make it clear that the Hanoverians have saved Britain from the tyranny of a royal family that, if not exactly foreign, was not only Catholic but had been residing for the last three decades in France.

Whatever Steele's motivation for producing Manley's *Lucius* (in addition to the possibility that it would produce a profit for his company), Manley seems to have found his production of her play a signal of reconciled friendship. In her dedication to Steele, she not only refers to him as her 'Patron' but she also confesses to have regretted her previous public criticism of him:

> I have not known a greater Mortification than when I have reflected upon the Severities which have flow'd from a Pen, which is now, You see, dispos'd as much to celebrate and commend You. On Your Part, Your sincere Endeavour to promote the Reputation and Success of this TRAGEDY, are infallible Testimonies of the Candour and Friendship you retain For Me.[20]

By the time *Lucius* was produced on stage, Steele and Manley (who were very close in age) were both approaching fifty. Each enjoyed a level of financial comfort neither had enjoyed in younger years, and the partisan conflicts from the last years of Anne's reign, which had fuelled their duel as pamphleteers and periodical writers, had taken a different form under the new monarch and new Whig ministry. Steele and Manley would no longer spend evenings together with Manley acting as Steele's literary and alchemical muse, but Steele certainly compliments Manley warmly in his prologue:

> *But the Ambitious Author of these Scenes,*
> *With no low Arts, to court your Favour means:*
> *With Her Success, and Disappointment, move,*
> *On the just Laws of Empire, and of Love!*[21]

Significantly, although other friends such as the Earl of Bristol would acknowledge Manley's talent as a writer about love, Steele acknowledges Manley's achievement as a writer both of love and politics.

Manley refers in her will to 'one Tragedy called the Duke of Somerset and one Comedy named the double Mistress ... which may perhaps turn to some amount' (these texts have never been found). Her point in mentioning these plays in her will seems to have been to give her executors permission to publish them if they chose, while the rest of her letters and papers she requested be destroyed so that not 'the least from them' could be published.[22] It is possible that one of these two plays was the play that was originally scheduled to be produced, presumably by Steele's Drury Lane Theatre, in the spring of 1720, but was 'Through Ld Chamberlains wize management ... deferrd till next season' as Manley ironically puts it in a letter to Matthew Prior, who had written the epilogue to *Lucius* and whom the actress Anne Oldfield wanted to consult about her planned performance of the epilogue for Manley's *Lucius* benefit.[23] It would appear, from Manley's reference to the Lord Chamberlain's interference, that Steele's apparent plans to produce another play of hers in the spring of 1720 were foiled when Newcastle stripped Steele of his managerial power at the Drury Lane Theatre in January 1720 by revoking the licence of the Drury Lane managers and then issuing a new royal licence for Colly Cibber, Robert Wilkes (1665–1732) and Barton Booth (1681–1733), leaving Steele with 'his patent but ... no voice in the company'.[24] Because of this deferral of her new play (a production that never seems to have seen the light of day), Manley explains to Prior that 'To make some amends, they [presumably the new theatre managers] have promised me to revive Lucius for my Benefit'.[25]

Although the two plays mentioned in her will were not produced in her lifetime, Manley's career as a playwright ended on a note of triumph with the revival of *Lucius* in 1720. We do not know how much money she made from this benefit performance, which was advertised in several newspapers between 21 and 25 April, but from her will we do know that she purchased £500 of South Sea stock in 1721, a purchase perhaps made possible in part by this author's benefit. However, given that she had made her first attempt to break into the world of the theatre over two decades earlier, the fact that she was still interested in writing plays at this point in her life might suggest that just as important to her as the money she might have made from this benefit or the 1717 production of the play was the public recognition of her as a successful playwright. Although this 1720 revival was only for one night, Manley was being honoured again with Richard Steele's prologue and Matthew Prior's epilogue, which the well-connected Anne Oldfield apparently took the care to rehearse with particular attention. Given the mockery with which she was treated in *The Female Wits*, following her first season on stage over two decades earlier, Manley might well feel, as she enjoyed her success in her final years of life, that she had finally achieved the public recognition as a playwright that she had long sought.

Years of Leisure

If we are to judge by the report, already cited, of Barber's Tory biographer, who appears to have possibly known and certainly admired Manley (and so may not be the most objective of observers), Manley was comfortable enough in 1717 that 'begging [was] none of her Business'. Negotiating from a position of confidence, and probably benefiting from the kindness of an old friend, she seems to have earned a profit from *Lucius* (whether or not Steele's company saw a profit from it). It may have been from this profit that she was able to lease the house in Beckley. Extant court rolls for the Beckley area do not offer any information about which house Manley leased; nor do we know what sort of contract was made, or what it cost her.[26] Since there is no mention of the house in her will, other than as her current place of residence, the lease presumably extended only for her lifetime. We likewise do not know why Manley chose Beckley, outside of Oxford, as her country residence. However, some clues are provided by an extant letter written to Manley (addressed to her 'near Oxford') in mid-December 1717 by John Hervey, Earl of Bristol and an old family friend:

> Had your nine neighbouring sisters clubbd their joint assistance, they could not have produced a piece so finishd in its kind as this unequal one comes to thank you for; Oxford being reinforced with the inspiration of such a tenth Muse may not surpass her learned corrivals in all polite performances throughout the world.[27]

The 'piece' that Manley sent could possibly have been a copy of *Lucius* (five months after it was first published) or else perhaps a poem in compliment to some member of his family (she would send one praising his wife the following year).[28] Hervey's description of her as a 'tenth Muse' joining forces with other muses already established in Oxford gives the impression that she had arrived there relatively recently; the timing of this letter suggests that she might have acquired this country residence as a result of the 1717 production of *Lucius* at the Drury Lane Theatre.

Hervey's letter appears to refer back to Manley's earlier collection of poems *The Nine Muses*, reminding us that Hervey seems have known Manley since her earliest years as a writer (and possibly earlier).[29] It also suggests that Manley's reasons for choosing a residence near Oxford may have been for its connections to the world of letters. This connection would be to literary society in general, rather than to the other nine muses of the collection, since, judging from her satirical references to Mary Pix and Catharine Trotter in *The New Atalantis*, Manley was no longer on good terms with all of her fellow muses. Bristol further compliments Manley on her intellectual achievements and counters her concerns (probably made in a gesture of authorial humility) about her lack of formal education: 'The complaint you make of a barren education only serves to sett the force & fruitfulness of your natural genius in ye strongest light, which ... I had the pleasure & advantage of being early acquainted with.'[30] Interestingly, Bristol, a staunch Whig MP, does not mention Manley's Tory pamphlets or her published attacks on the Marlboroughs, his political patrons. Bristol's letters to Manley focus entirely on her literary, rather than on her political, talent.

Bristol's references to Manley's intellectual life and to her skill as a writer suggest that Manley chose Beckley as a residence where she would have an independent literary life, quite separate from her life at John Barber's house in London. Beckley was substantially further from London than the village of Finchley, on the outskirts of London, where Manley used to visit her sister, a village close enough to London that John Barber was able to 'ride over' to deliver the much-awaited payment from Oxford in 1714.[31] Manley's choice of Beckley thus also indicates that she had the financial independence to travel there at will, incurring costs much greater than a journey to Finchley.

We do not know when Barber began his purported liaison with Manley's servant Sarah Duffkin, but if it had begun by 1717, this would be further reason why Manley would have desired a social life separate from Barber's. However, since Manley maintained her lodgings at his residence on Lambeth Hill until her death (in fact, she probably died there), we might assume that, despite Barber's biographer's insinuations to the contrary, Manley was not overly troubled by Barber's affair with Duffkin. The putative romantic element of Manley's own relationship with Barber may in fact have already ended by 1717. Whatever the precise nature of their relationship then or previously, Manley and Barber, who would be elected alderman for the Tory ward of Castle Baynard in 1722 and was a strong City critic of Robert Walpole (1676–1745), still apparently remained friends and business associates, since Barber continued to publish her literary work, and since Manley mentions him in her will with gratitude rather than resentment.

Despite Manley's early years of shame and loneliness following her marriage to her bigamous first cousin, she seemed to have regained some portion of respectability during her later years. Her friendship with Jonathan Swift was one mark of this, as was her public reconciliation with Steele and the Earl of Bristol's continued friendship. In Manley's letter to Matthew Prior, who wrote the epilogue to *Lucius*, she thanks him for his recent letter, which suggests that she stayed in touch with this fellow Tory writer. She also thanks Prior for 'Lord Harley and Lady Harrietts Bounty', suggesting that while she might not have been in direct contact with the current Lord Harley (Robert Harley's son and heir), since the 'bounty' was sent through Prior as intermediary, she had not been forgotten by the Harley family.[32] Although she was apparently not visited by Lord or Lady Harley themselves, Lord Bristol mentions, in his 1718 letter, his intention of waiting on Manley in London (in order to convey his family's appreciation of the poem she wrote about his wife), suggesting that Manley was certainly visited by some members of 'good' society. The poem for which Bristol intends to convey his gratitude mentions 'Titian's colours', a reference alluding to a painting 'at my Lord Bristol's' and so suggests that Manley might have known of the painting because she had visited the Bristols at their estate in Ickworth, Suffolk.[33]

Manley also seems to have served as something of a mentor for at least one young Hervey relation, for which Bristol thanks her in a letter of 12 July 1710:

May that part of it [the Hervey family] which you have thought worthy of interesting
your self so zealously for, (& who for that reason I shall take more particularly into
my protection,) live to deserve but half the trouble you have give your self for him, &
then I shall think all the cares of his education thoroughly repaid ... [34]

The poem that Manley wrote to Lady Bristol was published in a 1720 collection
of poems that also included a poem by Manley to 'J. M—e, *Esq*; *Of* Worcester-
College, OXON' as well as a lengthy poem of appreciation by 'J. Moore, *Esq*' to
'Mrs. *Manley. On the foregoing* STANZAS', which may identify either the young
man to whom Bristol refers or else some other young Oxonian whom Manley
mentored.

Moore's verses of appreciation to Manley help us understand that, while she
may have begun her career as the outcast daughter of an 'Ancient' family, she had
earned her place as a revered muse:

> Whilst the sad Heavens replenish *Charwell's* Urns,
> And *Lambeth-Hill* exults, tho' *Oxford* mourns,
> Forgive an Infant Muse, whose lowly Strain,
> Molests the Fav'rite of *Apollo's* Train;
> A Muse, not polish'd by the Courtier's Art,
> To speak a Language Foreign to her Heart;
> That spight of Envy's Force, or Criticks Rage,
> Owns and adores the *Sappho* of our Age. [35]

Moore also refers to Manley's 'Immortal LUCIUS' which 'By Pious Themes'
would 'fix an Erring Stage, / Revive dead Heroes and reform an Age'. This verse
to Manley also acknowledges the continuing popularity of her *Atalantis* (popularity already ironically acknowledged in Pope's *Rape of the Lock*), but here the
work is described neither as offensive nor difficult to read, as Arthur Maynwaring had described it to the Duchess of Marlborough, but as a serious work of
literature that will endure until '*Albion* Burns, and Nature fades away'. [36] This
poem, of course, may have been written by a fawning undergraduate who probably saw an advantage in flattering someone as famous as Manley: if nothing
else, it might have helped him to hospitality at Manley's home in Beckley, and
it seems to have helped him find a publisher for his verses. Manley was probably
not involved in the publishing process herself, since the *Miscellany* was brought
out by T. Jauncy (a regular publisher of plays and poems), [37] rather than John Barber, but the pair of poems to and by her must have been attractive to Jauncy since
he chose to list 'Mrs. Manley' on the title page, along with 'Mr. Prior', 'Mr. Pope'
and 'Lady M. W. M—'. Thus from having been viewed in 1709 by Lady Mary
Pierrepont as an author somewhat lacking in elegance, [38] by 1720, Manley found
her own politely stylish occasional verses featured alongside those of Lady Mary,
now Wortley Montague. This apparent transformation in Manley's reputation is

worth remarking, because it suggests that despite the initial anger of her political enemies against her, it is almost certain that not every reader would have read these works politically; many would have read them simply for diversion. Even a reader as partisan as Arthur Maynwaring nevertheless found some of the scenes quite diverting.[39]

Manley of course helped to shape her own reputation for the Hanoverian era (and subsequent centuries) by suggesting at one point in *Rivella* that *The New Atalantis* represented merely 'a few amorous Trifles [written] purely for her own Amusement'.[40] Of course, in that work, written a few months before Queen Anne died and the Tories fell from power (although both events would have been predicted as imminent at the time she was writing), Manley also reminds readers of her political courage for 'throwing the first Stone' and acknowledges her cleverness in escaping prosecution for libel 'because she had serv'd her self with Romantick Names, and a feign'd Scene of Action'.[41] Yet, she ends *Rivella* with a description of herself (always through the voice of her admiring narrator, Lovemore) that paints her as a writer (and a woman) more interested in love than politics. Lovemore explains to his interlocutor that rather than having provided 'that part of *Rivella*'s History, which has made the most Noise against her' he might have:

> brought you to her Table well furnish'd and well serv'd; have shown you her sparkling Wit and easy Gaiety, when at Meat with Persons of Conversation and Humour: From thence carried you (in the Heat of Summer after Dinner) within the Nymphs Alcove, to a Bed nicely sheeted and strow'd with *Roses, Jessamins* or *Orange-Flowers*, suited to the variety of the Season; her Pillows neatly trim'd with Lace or Muslin, stuck round with *Junquils*, or other natural Garden Sweets, for she uses no Perfumes, and there have given you leave to fancy your self the happy Man, with whom she chose to repose her self, during the Heat of the Day, in a State of Sweetness and Tranquility: From thence conducted you towards the cool of the Evening, either upon the Water, or to the Park for Air, with a Conversation always new, and which never cloys ...[42]

Here Manley ends her autobiographical description of herself as both writer of and participant in the pleasures of the 'softer Passions', a description that apparently did not damage her reputation in her own time, so much as encourage young men to flatter her with poems of love and aspiring writers to dedicate their works to her.[43]

Manley's attempt to brand herself in *Rivella* as a writer and conversationalist (as well as something of a courtesan) whose 'softer Passions have their Predominancy in Her Soul' is also evident in *Lucius*, in which true love assists the hero's conversion to Christianity as well as his overthrow of the tyrant usurper.[44] This portrayal of Manley as a literary expert on the 'softer Passions' is also evident in the title of her collection of novellas, *The Power of Love in Seven Novels*, which appeared in late 1719. This final published work, by its very title, would help secure her name in history (for better and worse) as a literary expert on love.

The Power of Love in Seven Novels

Although the title of Manley's final prose publication would resonate with readers who thought her an expert on love, the seven 'novels' (really novellas) themselves, many of which have fifteenth-century Continental sources, bear very little resemblance to Manley's other writings about love, politics or anything else. None of these tales makes any mention of Manley herself, her contemporaries, or even her own country. The stories often lack the wit and the frequent literary allusions of Manley's earlier works, and they do not treat the topic of love with anything approaching the tolerant attitude Manley usually conveys. Several of Manley's novels in *The Power of Love* represent women as violently revengeful (as in the example of Violenta who murders and mutilates the body of the man who betrayed her) or as having revenge violently taken against them (as in the case of the woman locked in the chamber with the rotting carcass of the man with whom she committed adultery). Although in her earlier works Manley often depicts women betrayed by the men who seduced them, as well as some women who initiate acts of betrayal, in her usual depictions of gender relations she does not include anything like these scenes of violence and revenge.

As previous scholars have discovered, five of the seven novels in *The Power of Love* appear to be based on novellas in William Painter's *Palace of Pleasure* (1566–7), a collection of novellas translated from Greek, Latin, Italian and French sources.[45] Manley's use of the term 'novel' also appears to borrow from Painter, who probably takes it from his Continental sources. The term does not refer to what we would consider a 'novel' by modern standards, but derives from the French *nouvelle* (an item of news or a short tale or history), the term used by Marguerite de Navarre in *L'Heptaméron* (1559); its Italian equivalent, as used by Matteo Bandello, is *novella* (*novelle* in the plural). Painter's term in sixteenth-century typography (where u also serves as v), is 'nouell'. Five of Manley's 'novels' are similar to 'nouells' included in Painter's *Palace of Pleasure*. Two of the tales that Manley appears to adapt from Painter originally derive from Boaistuau de Launay's French translations of two *novelle* by Bandello; a third is based on François de Belleforest's French translation of another Bandello *novella*. Two other novellas that Manley may have adapted from Painter originated as *nouvelles* in Navarre's *L'Heptaméron*.[46]

The source for Manley's second novel, 'The Physician's Stratagem', has not been identified. It might be an entirely original tale, although it is written in the style of the tales translated by Painter, and there were similar Continental tales available in collections and translations other than Painter's by the end of the sixteenth century. Manley's final novel, 'The Perjur'd Beauty', is probably based on the life of a sixteenth-century Benedictine nun, Donna Virginia Leyva, whose story had passed into histories and legends. However, the precise text (if there was one), from which Manley may have adapted her own story about Leyva has not been discovered.

In Manley's earlier works, her female characters, while not always morally perfect, are drawn with empathy and nuance. Manley shows particular empathy in her depictions of young women seduced and betrayed by smooth-talking men: Charlot in *The New Atalantis*, Belira in *The Lost Lover*, Delia in *The New Atalantis*, and Rivella in *The Adventures of Rivella* (the last two are characters representing Manley herself). In *The Power of Love*, of course, Manley is depicting the mores of earlier Continental aristocratic cultures – or at least as these are represented in the traditional tales that she adapts for her collection. Manley not only adapts these tales, however, she also makes certain that her readers understand the morals of her stories. For example, we might consider the conclusion of the fourth novel in *The Power of Love*. It ends with a husband finally feeling compassion for the woman against whom he has exacted a grotesque but not fatal form of punishment, and Manley concludes with a cautionary dogmatism, which she makes far more explicit than does the narrator in Painter's fifty-seventh nouell (her probable source):

> If there be any Wives who pursue false Pleasure, as did this wretched Lady, it will be well if they take Warning, and forego their Delights, that they may return again into the Path of Vertue, so as to preserve their Lives from Death, and their Reputation from what is much worse than Death, an infamous Report![47]

This sort of didactic interjection not only is not found in Painter, but it is quite the opposite sort of ending to Painter's own source, *nouvelle* 32 in Navarre's *L'Heptaméron*, in which the story ends with a handful of voices offering a range of commentary about the tale, none of them the monolithic didacticism that Manley interjects.[48] In fact, it is hard to know how Manley, whose own reputation had presumably suffered numerous 'infamous Reports' (following her marriage to her bigamous cousin and her subsequent romantic relationships with Tilly and probably Barber), thought her readers would respond to such warnings, especially in a text with her name on the title page.

We are a long way here from Lovemore's suggestion to the Chevalier d'Aumont at the end of *Rivella*, that to better know Rivella he should spend the afternoon in her flower-strewn chamber. Still, some hint of Manley's usual wit occasionally emerges in *The Power of Love*. She begins her fourth novel, for example, with a reference back to the revengeful Violenta from her third novel:

> That we may not leave upon the Minds of our Readers too great an Impression of the Cruelty of Woman-kind, from the vindictive and revengeful temper of *Violenta*,

I have thought fit, out of ten thousand Histories, where even a Million might be produced, to bring two Examples, that a Husband dishonoured is a no less terrible Animal, than a Wife jealous, injur'd, and betray'd.[49]

Although in Painter's *Palace of Pleasure*, and in the original source for this story in Navarre's *L'Heptaméron*, there are examples of both husbands and wives guilty of adultery, in neither Painter's version nor the Bandello tale that was his source does this story begin with such a statement.[50]

There is no reason to assume that Manley attempted her own translation of any of these originally Continental stories, since her knowledge of French, the only foreign language with which she describes an acquaintance, was probably not adequate to produce a sustained translation of a lengthy work.[51] In fact the occasional foreign footprints in her prose (the word *advertise* as 'to warn', in a way that sounds like a literal translator's rendition of *advertir*, and the word *sollicite* written as if it were French rather than English)[52] are better explained by some carelessness in adapting someone else's translation than by any awkwardness in her own use of English, had she been the translator. Moreover, in describing her adaptation of these antiquated tales in the dedication to Lady Lansdowne, Manley does not claim to have translated them herself but merely to have drawn 'them out of Obscurity':

THESE Novels, Madam, have Truth for their Foundation; several of the Facts are to be found in Ancient History: To which, adding divers new Incidents, I have attempted, in Modern *English*, to draw them out of Obscurity, with the same Design as Mr. *Dryden* had in his Tales from *Boccace* and *Chaucer*. Though with a far, far unequal Performance![53]

Manley's insistence that her work be viewed in the same light as Dryden's adaptation of Chaucer helps to explain why she would have been comfortable putting her name on stories so violent, rigidly didactic and otherwise uncharacteristic of her work. Exactly how much adaptation Manley effected on these works is not always possible to know, since we do not have precise evidence for exactly which sources or translations she used. However, if we assume she was working directly from Painter's *Palace of Pleasure*, at least for the five novellas that can be traced to tales in his collection, we may glean some sense of the sort of changes she made by comparing some of his passages to corresponding passages in her adaptation.

Painter's 'nouell' forty-two, the story of Violenta, who takes revenge on the nobleman who had secretly married her and then abandoned her to marry a noblewoman, concludes with a description of Violenta's suicide, the escape of the maid who helped her take revenge, and a reflection on the historical sources used for this account:

Thus infortunate Violenta ended her life, her mother and brethren being acquitted: and was executed in the presence of the duke of Calabria, the sonne of king Frederic of Aragon: which was that time the Viceroy there, and afterwards died at Torry in Fraunce: who incontinently after caused this historie to be registered, with other thinges worthy of remembraunce, chaunced in his time at Valencia. Bandell doth wryte, that the mayde Ianique was put to death with her maistres: but Paludanus a Spaniard, a lieu at that time, writeth an excellent historie in Latine, wherin he certainly declareth that she was neuer apprehended, which opinion (as most probable) I haue followed.[54]

Manley's ending to her third novel, 'The Wife's Resentment', is remarkably similar to Painter's ending, although she tellingly includes a phrase not found in Painter reminding readers how vigorously Violenta had defended her chastity (before agreeing to a secret marriage with the unfaithful nobleman, whom she subsequently murders): 'She dy'd with the same Spirit and Resolution with which she had defended her Chastity'.[55]

While the ending of her version of this story closely resembles Painter's ending, Manley adds some observations in the opening of the tale about the hapless nobleman's attitude towards women that are not included in Painter's version:

He did not love his Studies; and there being no War at that time to employ an active Mind, for want of better Business, according to the Custom of *Spain*, he walked up and down the City, wasting his Youth in Trifles, Musick, Masquerades, courting of Ladies, a Form of Devotion which was very common, and fit for such Pilgrims, designing only to conquer, not to be conquered; for as yet all Women were equally indifferent to him, he had no more Esteem or Tenderness for one than another; his Business was meer Gallantry, he knew not what it was to love; provided he could but triumph, he valued not the Conquest.[56]

This description of Roderigo's careless gallantry certainly resonates with Manley's description of other unfaithful men (her own cousin John Manley or the Duke of Portland in his alleged seduction of Stuarta Howard), although it is also conceivable that some of this description derived from a different, and as yet undiscovered, source for or translation of this story.

The stories in *The Power of Love* mention certain European monarchs (Louis XIII of France, Frederick of Aragon) and noblemen (the Count de St Severin, the Duke of Calabria). However, these references to specific monarchs or nobles, which appear in earlier versions of these tales by Painter and his Continental source, do not appear to be offering any direct commentary on the current situation in England. Manley's tales are clearly not intended to function as political secret histories where, for example in *Memoirs of Europe*, the events ostensibly taking place during the reign of Charlemagne offer obvious commentary on the last years of Queen Anne's reign. We might conclude, then, that the seven tales in *The Power of Love* should be taken as apolitical. However, there is a possible political resonance to Manley's decision to dedicate the work to Lady Mary Landsowne, the wife of George Granville, Baron Lansdowne, whom Manley had apparently known in the mid-1690s during her first foray into the world of theatre.[57]

Arrested for high treason in 1715 and held in the Tower for two years, Baron Lansdowne was still a vigorous Jacobite in 1719. He would travel to Paris in the summer of 1720, accompanied by his wife, where he would become an eloquent negotiator and spokesman for the Jacobite cause. Whether Manley intended *The Power of Love* to have any Jacobite resonance is difficult to know. Certainly, she would have long known of, and quite possibly been sympathetic to, Lansdowne's staunch Jacobite sympathies. Manley even refers in her dedication to Lady Lansdowne's devotion to her husband during the 'painful Hours of [Lord Lansdowne's] Confinement' in the Tower of London, recognizing Lady Lansdowne's decision to join her husband in the Tower during part of his imprisonment.[58]

However, Manley herself, having the instructive legacy of her father's own frustrating decades in exile, never expressed directly her possible Jacobite sympathies (although many of her works have a political resonance that could be read by Jacobites as expressing solidarity with them). Moreover, since *The Power of Love* appeared in late December 1719 and the Lansdownes did not leave for Paris until the following summer, Manley may have dedicated her last work to Lady Lansdowne without any knowledge of the Lansdownes' travel plans. Of course, it could be argued that adapting novellas set during earlier eras of European monarchies and nobility might represent an aristocratic mindset inherently in sync with the romantic elements often associated with Jacobite ideology.[59] And Manley's possible sympathy for a Protestant Jacobite restoration probably extended little further than such an ideological resonance: she certainly did not accompany John Barber on his risky trip to Italy in 1722, when he reputedly carried bills of exchange from English Jacobites.[60] However, when adapting the didactic, old-fashioned Continental novellas for what would be her final publication, Manley was probably thinking less about the Jacobite cause than about the commercial success of Eliza Haywood's three-part *Love in Excess*, the first two parts of which had appeared respectively in January and June 1719.[61]

Eliza Haywood, as a Tory playwright and novelist whose depictions of romantic intrigue often had Tory, and sometimes Jacobite overtones, obviously knew Manley's works. Haywood's *Memoirs of a Certain Island, Adjacent to Utopia* (1724–5), *The Secret History of the Present Intrigues of the Court of Caramania* (1727) and *The Adventures of Eovaai* (1736, 1741) are works of coded political satire clearly inspired by Manley's earlier political secret histories. However, in 1719, it was Haywood, not Manley, who produced a novel the first two parts of which, 'in terms of books sales' share with *Gulliver's Travels* and the first two parts of *Robinson Crusoe* 'distinction of being the most popular English fiction of the eighteenth century before *Pamela*'.[62] Haywood's *Love in Excess*, like much of her subsequent prose fiction, depicts love as an overwhelming passion or desire.

Her novels from the 1720s frequently describe women – particularly those in the care of guardians, uncles or someone other than their genuine father – as vulnerable to the advances of ambitious unscrupulous seducers.[63] *Love in Excess*, as one modern critic has described it, 'is a cautionary young-adult novel tracing the love-lives of impressionable young women in a violent, male-dominated world' in which women are punished for expressing their sexual desire.[64] Quite possibly attempting to compete with Haywood in this genre, Manley begin the first novel in *The Power of Love* with an opening line similar to Painter's forty-fifth 'nouell': 'Of all those Passions which may be said to tyrannize over the Heart of Man, Love is not only the most violent, but the most persuasive'.[65]

Haywood's *Love in Excess*, which ostensibly takes place in France and concerns aristocratic characters such as the 'Count D'elmont', shows the influence of the stories and novels of Aphra Behn, which in turn, were often based on earlier Continental models. Haywood's works were also clearly inspired by the descriptions of passion and desire in Manley's own secret histories. Manley's apparent decision to respond to Haywood's success with adaptations of sixteenth-century Continental tales demonstrates a certain strategic logic, but her adaptations do not usually include the sort of subjective descriptions of inner thoughts and emotions that Haywood describes with such intensity and that Manley herself had often described so effectively in her own earlier works. Nowhere in *The Power of Love* is there a description equivalent to Manley's own depiction in *The New Atalantis* of John Churchill's thoughts when planning to deceive the Duchess of Cleveland, or of Charlot's emotions as she falls in love with her guardian, or of her guardian's passionate plotting to seduce her. Manley occasionally offers very brief descriptions of a character's emotions, but without the intensity of passion she conveys in her other works. For example, in describing the nobleman who secretly marries the innocent Violenta in her third novel, Manley depicts his emotions as an act of exchange: 'He, whose Busines had hitherto been to give Love, rather than to take it, was in a moment reduc'd to be one of the Order of Lovers; to wish, sigh and desire, in return of those Sighs and Desires he had caus'd in others'.[66] This matter of fact reference to a character experiencing an emotion he had previously effected in others does not express the intensity of emotion conveyed in Manley's descriptions of Charlot's or her seducer's passion in *The New Atalantis* or Guiscard's violent desire for revenge in her pamphlet on the assassination attempt on Harley.[67] Not surprisingly, *The Power of Love*, which was successful enough to appear in a second edition in April 1720, did not achieve the phenomenal success either of Manley's own *New Atalantis* or Haywood's *Love in Excess*, which saw six editions between 1719 and 1725.

Posthumous Reputation

In *The Adventures of Rivella* Manley simultaneously presents two apparently contrasting images of herself: as a writer of love who knows something of the life of a
courtesan (as in Lovemore's description of her in the final scene) and secondly as
a canny political strategist who had the courage to cast 'the first Stone' and outwit
the authorities by disguising her political satire with fake names and scenes of
romance. Of course, these two descriptions of herself – as both physically alluring and as politically powerful – were not at all incompatible in her own era. The
Duchess of Cleveland, former mistress to Charles II, with whom Manley spent six
months in 1694, was described in secret histories such as *Hattigé* as dangerously
alluring and dangerously powerful (as well as an emblem of the sway that France
held over the susceptible Charles II). The Duchess of Marlborough, the Duke of
Marlborough's strikingly attractive wife, had so much apparent political influence
over Lord Treasurer Sidney Godolphin that she was rumoured (by Manley and
others) to have been his mistress; she was also depicted in secret histories such as
Queen Zarah as emblematic of the power of the Whig Junto.

In other words, it was taken for granted in Manley's era that women's sexual
power could both stand for and be turned into actual political power. Given
Manley's role as an influential writer of political secret histories and pamphlets,
it is not surprising that, in *Rivella*, the physical description Manley provides of
herself (through the voice of her admiring male narrator) echoes the description
of the powerful, ambitious and lustful Queen Homais from the novel (really a
secret history) she uses as the basis of the plot for her tragedy *The Royal Mistress*.[68] It is also not hard to imagine, as I suggested in an earlier chapter, that had
Manley been granted the position at court that in *Rivella* she claims was promised to her (and had she not had her complexion ruined by smallpox), she might
well have made as advantageous a marriage as Sarah Jenyns, or else become an
influential royal mistress, like John Churchill's sister Arabella (mistress to James
II) or Barbara, née Villiers, subsequently Duchess of Cleveland.

Although nineteenth- and twentieth-century critics and historians (including Winston Churchill in his defence of the Duke of Marlborough) have
described Manley as disreputable or notorious, this is not an accurate description of how she was viewed her in her own time. Because of her unfortunate
early marriage to her bigamous cousin and her subsequent relationships with
Tilly and then Barber, Manley was no doubt excluded from much of respectable
society – but not from all of it. Epistolary evidence (both her own and Swift's)
suggests that Manley waited on the Earl of Oxford and the Earl of Peterborough
at least once; the Earl of Bristol apparently did not flinch from visiting her at
her home in Lambeth Hill; Jonathan Swift considered her a friend, as did Rich-

ard Steele, among probably many other writers and playwrights and members of Tory political circles.

Manley was also generally treated with respect when others described her in print. Steele refers to her 'Quality of a Gentlewoman' while chiding her for not always acknowledging his 'Birth and Education'.[69] Although certain Whig writers, such as Abel Boyer who described her as a 'poor Whore in Petticoats and tawdry Ribbons', subjected her to partisan attacks during her years as a Tory pamphleteer, in general, as Ruth Herman has shown, 'contemporary comments about Manley's personal life were markedly circumspect'.[70] Newspapers often made note of Manley's activities – as they did of other well-known society figures; for example, *The Weekly Post or Saturday Journal* reported on 29 February 1724 that 'Mrs. De la Manley, Author of the *New Atalantis*, is dangerously ill'. When she died, on 11 July 1724, after having been seized five days earlier 'with a Fitt of the Cholick', at least seven newspapers reported her death.[71] The obituary most often reprinted or abridged in other newspapers described her as follows

> Mrs. Manley, Author of several celebrated Pieces: She was the Daughter of Sir Roger Manley, formerly Governor of the Isle of Jersey; and as her Father was esteem'd a Gentleman of the finest Taste, most excellent Understanding, and Author of one of the brightest Pieces of that Age; so she inherited from him all that polite Genius, and uncommon Capacity, which made her Writings so naturally delicate, and easy, and her Conversation so agreeably entertaining.[72]

This and the other published obituaries thus follow Manley's own lead in *Rivella*, referring to the legacy of her father's published works and describing her own wit and conversational skills. From the obituaries, readers would have no clue as to Manley's importance as a political writer. Nevertheless the very term *Atalantis* had already become synonymous with political critique. In March 1724, just four months before Manley died, Secretary of State Charles Townshend had issued a warrant to search Barber's (and his neighbour's) house in order to seize copies of a 'Seditious and Traiterous Libel entitled the new Atalantis Vol. yᵉ Fifth or with some like Title'. It is not certain that such a work actually existed. However, apparently without Townshend's having yet seen the work, the very title, or 'some like Title', including the key term *Atalantis* seems to have suggested to him that the work was a seditious libel.[73]

The possibility that Manley had continued writing potentially seditious political critique until the time of her death apparently also prompted the Duke of Newcastle to take John Barber (who had recently been permitted to return from the Continent) into custody for questioning about six weeks after Manley died:

> 'Tis said, that Alderman Barber, after he had been examined in two or three Questions last Saturday at Windsor, by his Grace the Duke of Newcastle, was remanded into Custody. Tis said that no Papers were found upon him of any Consequence:

> That he gave Notice to the Government of his coming hither: That the Motive of which, was the News of the Death of Madam Manley ... [74]

At the time of her death, therefore, government officials were still concerned about the potential satirical power of any of her unpublished political writings (although if any existed, Barber and her executors may already have destroyed them, following the instructions in her will). At the same time, of course, the standard accounts in obituaries and the continued sales of *Rivella*, which was produced in Curll's fourth edition in September 1724, emphasized her reputation as a witty conversationalist whose narrator insisted that she now agreed that 'Politicks is not the Business of a Woman'.[75]

Although Manley herself was obviously proud of the contributions she made as a Tory political writer, her simultaneous promotion of herself as a witty and sensual conversationalist probably did not help her retain her status as serious political satirist in subsequent eras, when women's wit and sensuality would not necessarily be assumed to have political significance. Furthermore, as the novel started to become a dominant literary genre in the mid to late eighteenth century, Manley's secret histories, which she never referred to as novels, began to be described as such. For example, in 1735 *The New Atalantis* was serialized in *The Weekly Novellist*, a publication described as 'Containing a select Collection of the best Novels, Moral, Political, &c. with other Pieces of Love and Gallantry'.[76] Manley's secret histories, as I have already shown, very much fit the mould of the anecdotal *petites histoires*, or intentionally anecdotal histories written to challenge the grand narrative of historians scripting the dominant view of history. When read through the lens of the much less anecdotal and much more tightly organized structure of the late eighteenth- and early nineteenth-century British novel, however, Manley's secret histories naturally appear deficient.

It is not surprising that Anna Letitia Barbauld, in her 1810 'On the Origin and Progress of Novel Writing', the canon-shaping introduction to her fifty-volume edition *The British Novelists*, ironically observes that 'Mrs. Manley lives only in that line of Pope which seems to promise it immortality', i.e. 'As long as *Atalantis* shall be read'.[77] Nor is it surprising that Manley's reputation as a Tory satirist (often anonymously published) did not flourish during the Whig regimes of the rest of the eighteenth century or under the Whig versions of history familiar to most nineteenth- and twentieth-century scholars. The early twentieth-century critical tendency to conflate a woman's works with her life story did not improve her reputation, nor did Winston Churchill's reductive dismissal of her in his biography of the first Duke of Marlborough. Now that we may view Manley without the blinders of Victorian morality, Whig historiography or the weighty literary tradition of the nineteenth-century British novel, however, it should be possible to judge her, as insistence on her skills as a witty and politically savvy conversationalist suggests, as one of the important wits of her age.

NOTES

Introduction

1. Canto III, ll. 161, 165, cited from A. Pope, *The Rape of the Locke and Other Poems*, ed. G. Tillotson (London: Methuen; New Haven, CT: Yale University Press, 1962), pp. 180–1.

2. See her preface to the second volume of *The New Atalantis*, in *The Selected Works of Delarivier Manley*, ed. R. Carnell and R. Herman, 5 vols (London: Pickering & Chatto, 2005), vol. 2, p. 152. Subsequent references to those works of Manley included in our *Selected Works* will be to this edition by volume and page number.

3. Hertfordshire Archives, DE/P/F211. This item is cited and discussed in R. Carnell, 'Delarivier Manley's Possible Children by John Tilly', *Notes and Queries*, n.s. 54:4 (December 2007), pp. 446–8.

4. John Manley, son of 'John and Dela Manley', was born on 24 June and christened on 13 July 1691, according to parish records for St Martin-in-the-Fields, Westminster.

5. See my 'Delarivier Manley's Possible Children by John Tilly'.

6. W. Churchill, *Marlborough: His Life and Times*, 2 vols (1933–8; London: George G. Harrap, 1947), vol. 2, p. 795, vol. 1, p. 53.

7. *The Dictionary of National Biography*, especially the first edition, cites so extensively from *The New Atalantis* in its entries on the social and political figures of Manley's era, that in the process of annotating Manley's work for *Selected Works*, I often had the circular experience of attempting to locate the 'real story' behind Manley's object of satire, only to find that the exact passage that I was trying to explicate was itself cited as fact about that person in the *DNB*.

8. Anna Letitia Barbauld, in her 'On the Origin and Progress of Novel Writing', the introductory essay to her fifty-volume edition *The British Novelists* (London: F. C. and J. Rivington, 1810), ironically observes that 'Mrs. Manley lives only in that line of Pope which seems to promise it immortality'. See *The Selected Poetry and Prose of Anna Letitia Barbauld*, ed. W. McCarthy and E. Kraft (Peterborough, Ontario: Broadview Press, 2002), p. 400. Ian Watt groups Manley with Aphra Behn and John Lyly, faulting them all for giving their characters 'foreign, archaic or literary connotations which excluded any suggestions of real and contemporary life'. See *The Rise of the Novel: Studies in Defoe, Richardson, and Fielding* (Berkeley and Los Angeles, CA: University of California Press, 1957), p. 19. He is probably here referring to *The Power of Love*, which, unlike Manley's other works, refers to no contemporary persons or events.

9. For an interesting discussion of Manley's use of Menippean/Varronian satire, see M. Aliker Rabb, 'The Manl(e)y Style: Delariviere Manley and Jonathan Swift', in *Pope, Swift, and Women Writers*, ed. D. C. Mell (Newark, DE: University of Delaware Press; London: Associated University Press, 1996), pp. 125–53.

10. 'Mary Manly Ap 7:63 H 3:30 PM ♀ Londini'. British Library (hereafter BL), Sloane MS 1708, f. 117, and Prerogative Court of Canterbury Wills Register, PROB 11/391, PROB 11/599. One basic problem with the assumption that the Sloane manuscript item refers to Manley (first ascribed to her in the 1904 errata list to the 1893 edition of the *DNB*), aside from the fact that it refers to 'Mary' not 'Delarivier', is that the subscription of 'Londini' appears to indicate that the birth took place in London, whereas Roger Manley was still stationed in the United Provinces in 1663. This mistake was repeated in the works of scholarship most often used as source material for Manley's life: P. Bunyan Anderson, 'Mistress Manley's Biography', *Modern Philology* (February 1936), pp. 261–78; and D. D. C. Duff, 'Materials toward a Biography of Mary Delariviere Manley' (unpublished PhD dissertation, Indiana University, 1965). Although most scholarship in the last twenty years has acknowledged that there are flaws in the ascription, even the recent Broadview edition of *The Adventures of Rivella* follows the Sloane manuscript date in the chronology of Manley. See *The Adventures of Rivella*, ed. K. Zelinsky (Peterborough, Ontario: Broadview Press, 1999), pp. 21–2, 37. On Jersey, where Manley is claimed as part of the literary heritage, her birth date is assumed by archivists to be 7 April 1673, presumably following what appears to be G. R. Balleine's mis-transcription of the Sloane Manuscript in his *A Biographical Dictionary of Jersey* (London and New York: Staples Press, 1948), p. 472.

11. This effort was begun by Patricia Köster in her 'index' to her facsimile edition of Manley's 'novels', *The Novels of Delarivier Manley*, ed. P. Köster, 2 vols (Gainesville, FL: Scholars' Facsimiles and Reprints, 1971), and continued by Ruth Herman in *The Business of a Woman: The Political Writings of Delarivier Manley* (Newark, DE: University of Delaware Press and London: Associated University Press, 2003).

12. See item TB 1/2/-22 in the Badminton Archives. I cite this letter and discuss it further in note 44 to Chapter 7, below.

13. See J. A. Downie, 'What if Delarivier Manley did *Not* Write *The Secret History of Queen Zarah*?', *The Library*, 7th series, 5:3 (September 2004), pp. 247–64.

14. See Lucyle Hook's Introduction to her edition of the anonymous comedy *The Female Wits: or The Triumvirate of Poets at Rehearsal. A Comedy* (1704), ed. L. Hook, Augustan Reprint Society publication 124 (facsimile reproduction, Los Angeles, CA: William Andrews Clark Memorial Library, 1967), p. vi.

15. See M. A. Doody, *The True Story of the Novel* (New Brunswick, NJ: Rutgers University Press, 1996), pp. 284–6. See also my discussion of how Whig realism emerged as aesthetically and politically dominant during the first half of the eighteenth century, when it was in constant competition with now less canonical styles of Tory and Jacobite realism, in *Partisan Politics, Narrative Realism, and the Rise of the British Novel* (New York: Palgrave, 2006), pp. 8–10.

1 'A Long Untainted Descent'

1. *The Adventures of Rivella*, vol. 4, p. 13. A handwritten pedigree of the Manley family starting with 'Rogerus de Manley' who married Lucie, daughter of Sir Piers Thornston, in 1316, is included in Sir Peter Leycester's *Book of Pedigrees*, Cheshire and Chester Archives, DLT/2173/145. The Manley coat of arms is also reproduced on Delarivier Manley's gravestone in the Church of St Benet Paul's Wharf.

2. P. Bunyan Anderson, 'Mrs. de la Rivière Manley: A Cavalier's Daughter in Grub Street' (PhD thesis, Harvard University, 1931).
3. 'Lectorem nec ambio, nec arceo'. See 'Ad Lectorem', unpaginated preface to Roger Manley's *Commentariorum de Rebellione Anglicana ab Anno 1640, Usque ad Annum 1685* (London: L. Meredith and T. Newborough, 1686). I am grateful to Clive Cheesman for his assistance in interpreting this preface. The lines about satire are from Juvenal's Satire 1, l. 30.
4. See R. Herman, 'An Exercise in Early Modern Branding', *Journal of Marketing Management*, 19:7 (September 2003), pp. 709–27.
5. *The New Atalantis*, vol. 2, p. 254.
6. See N. Tucker, *Royalist Officers of North Wales 1642–1660* (Denbigh: Gee & Son, 1961), p. 42. Tucker mentions that Francis Manley's 'home' was 'taken by Brereton, April, 1645' (p. 42) but offers no information about the extent or value of this property. The date for the death of Francis Manley comes from Clive Cheesman's research for the Manley family tree.
7. PROB 11/391.
8. This information was conveyed to me in a conversation with Clive Cheesman, Rouge Dragon Pursuivant at The College of Arms, who prepared the most recent Manley family pedigree.
9. J. Foster (ed.), *The Register of Admissions to Gray's Inn, 1521–1889* (London: Hansard Publishing Union, 1889), p. 235.
10. *The Adventures of Rivella*, vol. 4, p. 13.
11. Tucker, *Royalist Officers of North Wales*, p. 42; *ODNB*, s.v. John first Baron Byron (1598– 1652).
12. In a description of Charles II's visit to Portsmouth, Samuel Pepys refers to Sir Roger Manley as 'the deputy governor there'. S. Pepys to [Joseph] Williamson, 3 July 1675, Portsmouth, in National Archives, Kew, Public Record Office (hereafter PRO), SP 371/215; cited from the transcription in *Calendar of State Papers, Domestic Series, March 1st 1675 to February 20th 1676*, ed. F. H. B. Daniell (London: His Majesty's Stationery Office, 1907), p. 197. The church record for the death of Manley's wife (12 November 1675, St Thomas Cathedral, Portsmouth) lists her as 'Lady Manly [*sic*], wife of Sir Roger Manly, Lt. Governor'. However, the official list of governors and lieutenant governors in the Portsmouth Records Office does not include Roger Manley, so deputy governor or 'deputy to Governor Legge' is probably accurate, which is how Philip Sergeant refers to him in *Rogues and Scoundrels* (New York: Brentano's Publishers, [1927]), p. 172. Mundane letters written by Manley, including one to Secretary Coventry in August 1678 about conflicting watch signals between the admiralty and the town (Bodleian MS, University of Oxford, Tanner 39, f. 83), indicate that Manley seems to have been in a position of command at Portsmouth.
13. Manley's section comprises pages 275–338 of R. Knolles and P. Rycaut, *The Turkish History, from the Original of that Nation to the Growth of the Ottoman Empire. With a Continuation to this Present Year. Whereunto is Added the Present State of the Ottoman Empire* (London: Jonathan Robinson et al., 1687). See Patricia Köster's 'The Correspondence of Sir Roger Manley', *Bulletin of Bibliography*, 42:4 (1985), pp. 179–86, on p. 180. In Carnell and Herman's edition of Manley's *Selected Works*, there is a mistake in the annotation about this matter (vol. 4, p. 242, n. 31). Although no mention of Manley's name is given on the title page or table of contents, Köster is correct in her ascription to Roger Manley of the section that begins on p. 275.
14. No other translator is listed, and Patricia Köster, who has made the most thorough study of Roger Manley's letters and published works to date, believes that it might have been his translation. See 'The Correspondence of Sir Roger Manley', p. 179.

15. *The New Atalantis*, vol. 2, p. 256.
16. See note 4 to Introduction, above.
17. *The Adventures of Rivella*, vol. 4, p. 56.
18. Both the original *DNB* entry for John Tidcomb and the updated *ODNB* cite Manley's account in *Rivella* as evidence that Tidcomb once offered her refuge at his country house. Conveniently, for Manley's purposes, if he did not know her, he was not only dead at the time she was writing, but had no wife or children who might dispute her account.
19. *The Adventures of Rivella*, vol. 4, p. 7.
20. Ibid., p. 56.
21. Ibid., p. 54.
22. Ibid., p. 235.
23. The *Daily Courant* for Monday, 1 June 1714, announces the publication 'This Day' by Roberts; the second edition with 'a compleat Key' was advertised as published 'This Day' in *The Post Man and the Historical Account* for Thursday, 2 September 1714.
24. I am drawing on Michael Treadwell's definition of 'trade publisher'; see 'London Trade Publishers 1675–1730', *The Library*, 6th series, 4:2 (June 1982), pp. 99–134.
25. See P. Baines and P. Rogers, *Edmund Curll, Bookseller* (Oxford: Clarendon Press, 2007), p. 15.
26. The third edition, entitled *Memoirs of the Life of Mrs. Manley*, published for E. Curll and J. Pemberton, was first advertised in the *Evening Post* for Saturday, 19 January 1717; Roberts advertised a third edition in the *Post Boy* on Tuesday, 26 March 1717. These advertisements, which both include a verse about Manley ('The God of Love and it inspire her Pen, / And Love and Beauty is her glorious Theme'), should not be seen as competing. Curll may simply have employed Roberts for the third edition but afterwards realized that there was no risk to having the work appear with his own name on it as well, and for the copies he sold with his own name on the title page, he presumably would not need to pay the publishing fees to Roberts. Roberts brought out a fourth edition (possibly unauthorized by Curll) one year before Curll, using the title of the third edition. Curll's fourth edition, *Mrs. Manley's History of Her Own Life and Times*, printed for E. Curll and John Pemberton, was advertised in the *Daily Post* for Wednesday, 14 October 1724.
27. *The Adventures of Rivella*, vol. 4, p. 56.
28. Ibid., p. 19.
29. Ibid., p. 56.
30. Ibid., p. 54.
31. Ibid., p. 56.
32. Ibid., p. 56.
33. Ibid., p. 56.
34. See note 6 to Introduction, above.
35. See Churchill, *Marlborough*, vol. 1, pp. 31–2.
36. *The Adventures of Rivella*, vol. 4, p. 19.
37. *The New Atalantis*, vol. 2, p. 254. I have changed 'emply' (as in our *Selected Works*) to 'employ' (following our copy-text).

2 Roger Manley

1. *The New Atalantis*, vol. 2, p. 254.
2. *The Adventures of Rivella*, vol. 4, p. 13.
3. As the second of three sons, Roger Manley would have been born before 1622 since his father is believed to have died in 1623 (according to the date of death listed for Cornelius

in the *ODNB*, s.v. Roger Manley); he therefore would have been at least twenty in 1642 when John Byron became colonel of the regiment Manley joined, and probably in his early twenties when he was captured at Powys.

4. Roger Manley to John Lord Byron, Baron of Rochdale, 3 October 1644, Bala, BL, Add. MS 18981, f. 281. For a discussion of the way that writers of Renaissance military memoirs intermixed 'lifestory' and 'history', see Y. N. Harari, *Renaissance Military Memoirs: War, History, and Identity, 1450–1600* (Woodbridge, Suffolk: Boydell Press, 2004).

5. Manley to Byron, 3 October 1644, Bala, BL, Add. MS 18981, f. 281.

6. In the preface to his translation of *A True Description of the Mighty Kingdoms of Japan and Siam* (1663), he excuses any awkwardness in his written English by reference to 'a Fourteen years Exile'. See F. Caron and J. Schorten, *A True Description of the Mighty Kingdoms of Japan and Siam*, trans. R. Manley (1663), ed. C. R. Boxer (London: Argonaut Press, 1935), p. 3.

7. See ibid., p. 115, for Boxer's biographical note about Manley, which is cited by most modern sources, including the recent *ODNB* article.

8. Boxer may simply have taken the 'fourteen years' from the old *DNB* entry; again, however, there is no source in that entry that definitively establishes the date Manley left England.

9. In his *ODNB* entry on Roger Manley, Clive Cheesman suggests that Manley left England after Lord Byron's defeat at Chester in February 1646. None of the sources Boxer lists provide concrete evidence that Roger Manley left England as early as this. The original *DNB* entry cites a line 'from the preface to his English "History of the Rebellion"' that he played his part in the war until, in his own words, he was, 'upon the rendition of one of the king's garrisons in 1646, obliged by his articles to depart the kingdom', and provides in the parenthetical reference: 'translation of CARON, *Japan*, 1663, Dedication, pp. 1–2', but this dedication does not mention the year 1646.

10. All of this information is taken from the recent *ODNB* article on Byron, written by Ronald Hutton.

11. Boxer provides this information, without qualification, in his biographical note to Caron and Schorten, *A True Description*, trans. Manley, p. 115, and most subsequent scholars have not questioned this assumption.

12. None of Boxer's sources provide this information. The earliest extant letter from Manley to Dorislaus, from August 1653, is printed in *A Collection of the State Papers of John Thurloe, esq; Secretary, First to the Council of State, and Afterwards to the Two Protectors, Oliver and Richard Cromwell*, ed. T. Birch, 7 vols (London: Thomas Woodward and Charles Davis, 1742).

13. Patricia Köster assumes that Manley left after the surrender of Denbigh Castle in October 1646. See 'The Correspondence of Sir Roger Manley', p. 179. Although she cites no specific source for this information, she may well be drawing on Manley's claims in his letter from Brussels of 15 July [1654] to Isaac Dorislaus, in which Manley asks Dorislaus to help him procure a passport to England. Manley insists in that letter: 'I have acted nothing directly nor indirectly' for the Stuart cause 'since my coming out of Denbigh-castle'. Bodleian MS, Rawl.A.16, ff. 82–3; cited from the transcribed version printed in *State Papers of John Thurloe*, vol. 2, p. 425. All the information about the date and place of these letters, when it is not marked specifically on the letters themselves, is drawn from Patricia Köster's painstakingly prepared list of Roger Manley's letters in 'The Correspondence of Sir Roger Manley'. As Köster explains, the dates on Roger Manley's letters written from the Continent are New Style, whereas subsequent letters from England are Old Style dates; Köster modernizes the dating slightly, by having the year begin

in January. Following Köster, I put dates and places in square brackets when they are not listed on the letters themselves.

14. Roger B. Manning offered this insight in comments on a previous draft of this chapter.

15. Information about Manley's wife was collected from the herald's visitation of Hampshire (College of Arms, London, K8, Church Notes, f. 28). Since the gravestone inscription cited in this material is in Latin, we have the Latin version of her name, Maria Catherina. Since she was French-speaking, I give her name in the French form, Marie-Catherine. As Clive Cheesman (author of the recent article on Roger Manley in the *ODNB*) has pointed out to me in conversation, the seraphic description of her as *natu nobilis* would indicate, were she English, that she was the daughter of a peer. Roger B. Manning points out, in comments on a draft of this chapter, that 'the armigerous gentry of England were assumed to be the equivalent of the lesser nobility of mainland European countries'.

16. Boxer provides this information in his note about Manley to his edition of Caron and Schorten, *A True Description*, trans. Manley, p. 115. Although I disagree with Boxer's assumption that Manley sought patronage with the older Isaac Dorislaus, Boxer provides a very specific citation for Manley's employment (*Resolutien v.d. Staaten-Feneraal*, 8. v. 1659), which I see no reason to doubt, although I have not been able to check this source myself. Roger B. Manning has kindly reviewed his own notes about English, Irish and Scots regiments in the States' Army, from F. J. S. ten Raa and F. De Bas, *Het Staatsche Leger*, 8 vols (Breda, 1911–80); since Manley's name is not on these lists, Manning surmises that Manley may have held his commission in a Dutch or Frisian regiment.

17. Roger B. Manning explains further in comments on a draft of this chapter: 'The regiment of Dutch marines which landed at Sheerness and Landguard in 1665 during the Second Anglo-Dutch War were mostly English and were led by Col. Thomas Dolman'. See also his *An Apprenticeship in Arms: The Origins of the British Army, 1585–1702* (Oxford: Oxford University Press, 2006), pp. 328–9.

18. The source for the claim that Manley had been employed by the envoys Van Slagelands and De Huybert is given in most scholarship as located in his letters to de Witt from 1658 in *Brieven aan Johan de Witt Eerste Deel 1648–1660*, ed. R. Fruin and N. Japikse (Amsterdam: Johannes Müller, 1919). However, there is in fact no mention of these envoys or Manley's involvement in such an expedition in those letters.

19. N. A. M. Rodger, *The Command of the Ocean* (London: Penguin Books with National Maritime Museum, 2004), p. 29.

20. John Manley had apparently purchased the office of Postmaster General in 1653 for £8,260 'with good securities' (see *Calendar of State Papers, Domestic Series, 1649–60*, ed. M. A. E. Green, 13 vols (London: Her Majesty's Public Record Office, 1875–86), vol. for 1652–3, p. 450), but sold it in 1655 to Thurloe, then secretary to the council of state, because of 'security considerations' (*ODNB*, s.v. John Manley).

21. Following a diplomatic mission to the United Provinces in 1751, Thurloe apparently concluded 'that the Dutch seemed to have learned from the Scots and the French to profess much but perform nothing except as to their own advantage' (*ODNB*, s.v. John Thurloe; this appears to be a paraphrase by the author of the *ODNB* article rather than an exact quote from Thurloe).

22. Roger Manley (signed 'RM') to Isaac Dorislaus ('Ant Rogers'), 23 August [1653], Bodleian MS, Rawl.A.5, f. 167, cited here from the transcription published in *State Papers of John Thurloe*, vol. 1, p. 421. According to comments from Roger B. Manning, The States' Army paid 'substantial recruiting bonuses'.

23. Manley to Dorislaus, 23 August [1653], in *State Papers of John Thurloe*, vol. 1, p. 422.

24. Ibid., vol. 1, p. 421.
25. Roger Manley (unsigned) to Isaac Dorislaus ('Ant Rogers'), [April 1654], [Maastricht], Bodleian MS, Rawl.A.13, f. 149.
26. Ibid.
27. Manley to Dorislaus, 23 August [1653], in *State Papers of John Thurloe*, vol. 1, p. 422.
28. Roger Manley (signed 'T. Smith') to Isaac Dorislaus (Monsieur Upton), 30 May [1657], Coningsb[erg], although Patricia Köster assumes the letter in fact might have been sent from 'Danzig', Bodleian MS, Rawl.A.50, p. 167; cited from *State Papers of John Thurloe*, vol. 6, p. 293. See item 25 in 'The Correspondence of Sir Roger Manley', p. 182.
29. Roger Manley (unsigned) to Isaac Dorislaus ('An[tonio Rogers]'), 20 September [1653], Bodleian MS, Rawl.A.6, pp. 209–10; cited from *State Papers of John Thurloe*, vol. 1, p. 471.
30. Manley to Dorislaus, 15 July [1654], in *State Papers of John Thurloe*, vol. 2, p. 425.
31. Ibid.
32. Ibid.
33. Roger Manley (unsigned) to Isaac Dorislaus ('Antonio Rogers'), 21 August [1654], Bodleian MS, Rawl.A.5, ff. 91–2; cited from *State Papers of John Thurloe*, vol. 2, p. 534.
34. *State Papers of John Thurloe*, vol. 7, p. 787.
35. Roger Manley (signed 'N. Tibs') to Isaac Dorislaus ('D[eare] Br[other]'), 31 January 1657, [Danzig], Bodleian MS, Rawl.A.46, pp. 269–72; cited from *State Papers of John Thurloe*, vol. 6, p. 8.
36. Roger Manley (unsigned) to Isaac Dorislaus ('An[tonio Rogers]'), 20 September [1653], Bodleian MS, Rawl.A.6, pp. 209–10; cited from *State Papers of John Thurloe*, vol. 1, p. 472.
37. Roger Manley (signed 'David Fitty') to Isaac Dorislaus ('[Antonio] Rogers'), [1?] November 1656, [Danzig], Bodleian MS, Rawl.A.43, pp. 221–2.
38. Roger Manley (signed 'Jos. Thompson') to Isaac Dorislaus ('Antonio Rogers'), 13 December 1656, Bodleian MS, Rawl.A.45, ff. 82–3; cited from *State Papers of John Thurloe*, vol. 5, p. 676.
39. Roger Manley (signed 'RM') to Isaac Dorislaus ('Antonio Rogers'), 10 January 1657, [Danzig], Bodleian MS, Rawl.A.45, pp. 336–7; cited from *State Papers of John Thurloe*, vol. 5, p. 743. Patricia Köster modernizes the date to 10 January 1657, although the printed transcription lists 10 January 1656. See item 18 in 'The Correspondence of Sir Roger Manley', p. 182.
40. Roger Manley (signed 'RM') to Isaac Dorislaus (to 'Jacob Jacbobson' on the envelope, but 'Deare A[ntonie]' inside), 4 April 1657, Bodleian MS, Rawl.A.49, ff. 4–5.
41. Roger Manley (signed 'RM') to Isaac Dorislaus ('Jacob Jacobson'), 11 April 1657, directed to Monsieur Jacob Jacobson à Londre on the envelope, but the letter is addressed 'Dear Sir' (i.e. Anthony Rogers, aka Isaac Dorislaus), Bodleian MS, Rawl.A.49, ff. 4–5.
42. Roger Manley (signed 'DB') to Isaac Dorislaus ('Antonie Rogers'), 2 May [1657], [Danzig?], Bodleian MS, Rawl.A.37, pp. 590–2; cited from *State Papers of John Thurloe*, vol. 4, p. 725. Birch assumes this was written in 1656 in editing Thurloe's *State Papers*, but Köster corrects this date to 1657. See item 23 in 'The Correspondence of Sir Roger Manley', p. 182.
43. Roger Manley (signed 'T. Smith') to Isaac Dorislaus ('Monsieur Upton'), 30 May [1657], Conigsb[erg], Bodleian MS, Rawl.A.50, ff. 243–4; cited from *State Papers of John Thurloe*, vol. 6, p. 293.

44. Roger Manley (signed 'RM') to Isaac Dorislaus ('Antonio Rogers'), 6 June 1657, [Danzig], Bodleian MS, Rawl.A.50, ff. 243–4; cited from *State Papers of John Thurloe*, vol. 6, p. 314.

45. Roger Manley (signed 'Ti: Roberts') to Isaac Dorislaus ('Antonio Rogers'), 11 July 1657, Conigsberg, Bodleian MS, Rawl.A.52, ff. 32–3; cited from *State Papers of John Thurloe*, vol. 6, p. 378.

46. Roger Manley (signed 'Jos. Thompson') to Isaac Dorislaus ('Antonio Rogers'), 13 December 1656, [Danzig], Bodleian MS, Rawl.A.45, ff. 82–3; cited from *State Papers of John Thurloe*, vol. 5, p. 409.

47. Ibid., p. 410.

48. Roger Manley (unsigned) to Isaac Dorislaus ('Antonio Rogers'), 4 October [1656], Danzig, Bodleian MS, Rawl.A.42, pp. 631–2; cited from *State Papers of John Thurloe*, vol. 5, p. 443.

49. Roger Manley (signed 'B') to Isaac Dorislaus ('Antonio Rogers'), 11 October [1656], Bodleian MS, Rawl.A.43, ff. 9–10; cited from *State Papers of John Thurloe*, vol. 5, p. 487.

50. Roger Manley (signed 'PB') to Isaac Dorislaus ('Antonio Rogers'), 8 [November] 1656, [Danzig], Bodleian MS, Rawl.A.43, pp. 337–8; cited from *State Papers of John Thurloe*, vol. 5, p. 531.

51. Manley is referring to a 'proposition' that he had M. le Rheingraeff make to de Witt, which he describes here as 'le plus beau et le plus util secret, principlalement pour un minister d'Etat, qui fut jamais' (the most beautiful and useful secret, principally for a minister of state, that ever was). Roger Manley to Johan de Witt, 17 April 1658, [Maastricht], in *Brieven aan Johan de Witt*, p. 244.

52. Ibid., p. 245.

53. Roger Manley (signed 'JW') to Isaac Dorislaus ('Monsieur Upton'), 27 June 1657, [Danzig], Bodleian MS, Rawl.A.51, ff. 150–1; cited from *State Papers of John Thurloe*, vol. 6, p. 353.

54. Manley to de Witt, 17 April 1658, in *Brieven aan Johan de Witt*, p. 244.

55. Manley to Dorislaus, 6 June 1657, in *State Papers of John Thurloe*, vol. 6, p. 314.

56. Ibid.

57. Roger Manley (signed 'GB') to Isaac Dorislaus ('Antonio Rogers'), 12 November [1657], Wismar, Bodleian MS, Rawl.A.55, ff. 225–6; cited from *State Papers of John Thurloe*, vol. 6, p. 598.

58. PRO, SP 77/32, ff. 146–7.

59. Roger Manley (signed 'RM') to Isaac Dorislaus ('Antonio Rogers'), 9 October [1654], Rotterd[am], Bodleian MS, Rawl.A.18, pp. 434–7; cited from *State Papers of John Thurloe*, vol. 2, p. 634.

60. Roger Manley (unsigned) to Isaac Dorislaus ('Antonio Rogers'), 17 October 1654, Maestricht [*sic*], Bodleian MS, Rawl.A.19, pp. 141–2; cited from *State Papers of John Thurloe*, vol. 2 p. 655.

61. This is cited from the transcript in the *Calendar of State Papers, 1649–60*, vol. for 1656–7, p. 345. The question mark, possibly noting the illegibility of the name 'Manley', is in the transcription. I have not seen the original of this document.

62. I am relying on Patricia Köster's summary of Manley's letter to Harald Oxe, sent from the Hague in 'mid-February, 1658', Stockholdm. Riksarkivet. Coyeska Samling (5:149), vol. E3401, as cited in item 37 in Köster's 'The Correspondence of Sir Roger Manley', p. 183.

Köster does not identify, and I have been unable to identify, who Oxe was or for what Manley was thanking him in this letter.

63. The testimony of Thomas Topham, in *State Papers of John Thurloe*, vol. 7, p. 147.
64. Ibid.
65. Ibid., p. 148.
66. *State Papers of John Thurloe*, vol. 7, p. 787.
67. This cousin, John Manley, was 'a great Ingeneer', according to Randle Holme's pedigree of the Manley family, cited by Clive Cheesman in a preliminary draft of his *ODNB* entry on Roger Manley, which he was kind enough to share with me.
68. The precise family connection between Manley and this 'cousin' has not been traced.
69. R[oger] Manley to Lord [Arlington], [25 July 1665] [the Hague], PRO, SP 29/127/161.
70. Ibid.
71. Ibid.
72. Ibid.
73. This is an annotation to Edward Manley, brother of Cornelius (father of Elizabeth, Catharine, Francis, Roger and John) in the handwritten pedigree in the Sir Peter Leycester's *Book of Pedigrees*, Cheshire and Chester Archives, DLT/2173/145. It is not clear whether this 'breach of Maastricht' refers to Maastricht being taken by the Spanish in 1579 or by Prince Frederick Henry of Orange in 1632, although the latter siege would have been of more recent memory. In the pedigree, no dates are given for Edward or Cornelius Manley; the latter died in 1623 shortly after the birth of his youngest son John, but we do not know how old he was then, how much younger his brother Edward was, or at what age the latter died in battle; therefore it is hard to know to which of these battles the note refers.
74. Manning, *An Apprenticeship in Arms*, pp. 62, 263.
75. R. M[anley] to R. Francis, 13 July 1668, Old Castle [Jersey], PRO, SP 29/243/8–9. Cited from the abstract in *Calendar of State Papers, Domestic Series, November 1667–September 1668*, ed. M. A. E. Green (London: Her Majesty's Stationery Office, 1893), p. 483.
76. Roger Manley (signed 'RM') to Isaac Dorislaus, 4 July 1675, PRO, SP 29/371/297.
77. C. Dalton (ed.), *English Army Lists and Commission Registers, 1661–1714*, 6 vols (1892–1904; London: Francis Edwards, 1960), vol. 1, pp. 50, 55, 99, 270, 315; vol. 2, p. 19.
78. Dalton's *English Army Lists* does not ever list Roger Manley as anything other than captain, even in the entry indicating his commission in the First Regiment of Foot, 9 February 1685. John Henry Leslie indicates in his *The History of Landguard Fort* (London: Eyre and Spottiswoode, 1898) that Manley 'had attained the rank of Lieut. Colonel' at the time of James II's accession (p. 100; he cites the *Domestic Entry Book*, vol. 69, p. 148). However, the ranks of 'major' or 'lieutenant-colonel' were not permanent ranks, but positions held by senior captains of a particular regiment only so long as that captain served in that regiment and only so long as the colonel in that regiment wished.
79. Samuel Pepys to Colonel Legge at Portsmouth, Derby House, 10 February 1679, in *The Further Correspondence of Samuel Pepys, 1662–1679*, ed J. R. Tanner (London: G. Bell and Sons, 1929), p. 344.
80. R. Manley to John Cooke, 25 March 1684, Landguard Fort, PRO, SP 29/437/97–8. Cited from the abstract in *Calendar of State Papers, Domestic Series, October 1, 1683–April 30, 1684*, ed. F. H. Blackburne Daniell and F. Bickley (London: His Majesty's Stationery Office, 1938), p. 324.
81. The first stanza of *Hudibras* ends: 'Then did Sir *Knight* abandon dwelling, / And out he rode a Colonelling'. See S. Butler, *Hudibras*, ed. J. Wilders (Oxford: Clarendon Press, 1967), p. 1. Clive Cheeseman noticed this detail, which he mentions in his *ODNB* entry on Roger Manley.

82. This work is cited as a source for rules regarding the striking of naval flags in Commonwealth maritime orders. See PRO, SP 18/202/30–1.

83. Patricia Köster gives a list of these references in 'The Correspondence of Sir Roger Manley', p. 179.

84. As Harari explains, such memoirs might include accounts of battles at which the narrator was present, but without providing any mention of the narrator's own role. While such memoirs were a mixture of 'lifestory' and more objective 'history', the mixture is not what modern readers would expect. See *Renaissance Military Memoirs*, pp. 1–63. Many of the histories Manley writes, of course, were not necessarily intended as memoirs at all.

85. R. Manley, *The History of the Rebellions in England, Scotland and Ireland: Wherein the Most Material Passages, Sieges, Battles, Policies and Stratagems of War, are Impartially Related on Both Sides; from the year 1640 to the Beheading of the Duke of Monmouth in 1685* (London: L. Meredith and T. Newborough, 1691), p. 2.

86. Ibid., sig. A3v.

87. Ibid., p. 2.

88. Ibid., p. 4. For a detailed discussion of how political pamphleteers humanize themselves and render their opponents inhuman extremists, see my *Partisan Politics*, pp. 17–43.

89. Manley, *The History of the Rebellions*, p. 40.

90. Ibid., p. 97.

91. Ibid., p. 49.

92. Ibid., p. 81.

93. Ibid., p. 87.

94. Ibid., p. 155.

95. Ibid., p. 333.

96. Ibid., pp. 333, 335.

97. Ibid., p. 333, 335.

98. Ibid., p. 316.

99. [R. Manley], *The Russian Impostor: or, The History of Muskovie, under the Usurpation of Bortis and the Imposture of Demetrius, Late Emperors of Muskovy* (London: Thomas Basset, 1674), sig A2r–v.

100. The 1677 reissue includes the appendix and a new title page with the author's initials: 'by Sir R. M.'.

101. Harari argues that Renaissance military memoirs narrated collections of 'memorable things', whether or not such events were of national importance or personal interest. See *Renaissance Military Memoirs*, p. 18.

102. *The Adventures of Rivella*, vol. 4, p. 58.

3 A 'Liberal Education'

1. *The Adventures of Rivella*, vol. 4, p. 13.

2. Margaret Edwards at the Priaulx Library in Guernsey helpfully pointed this out to me.

3. G. Langbaine, *The Lives and Characters of the English Dramatick Poets* (London: William Turner, 1699). The title page gives credit to Gerard Langbaine (1656–92) for having begun the work and suggests that it was 'improv'd and continued' by 'a Careful Hand', generally believed to be Charles Gildon. The entry on Manley must have been written by Gildon, since both of her plays postdate Langbaine's decease.

4. Dolores Duff assumes that Morgan was a friend of Roger Manley (who went into exile in his early twenties) prior to Manley's posting to Portsmouth in 1664; see 'Materials toward a Biography', p. 13. Duff also believes that Delarivier Manley was born in 1663

(following the Sloane manuscript dating – see note 10 to Introduction, above), and so she needs to explain the rationale behind the name Delarivier. I do not assume that Roger Manley had known Thomas Morgan before 1665 or that their families would necessarily have been on friendly terms; Morgan, after all, served in Cromwell's army, while Manley was a royalist. Morgan might plausibly have met Manley upon his setting out to Jersey (quite likely from Portsmouth, where Manley was a commanding officer of a regiment of foot) in 1665, but it seems more likely that Manley would decide to name a daughter Delarivier once he had joined Morgan on Jersey.

5. '18/9/1672. Roger Maneley [*sic*] fils Roger Esqr. Liet. Gouverneur sous Messier Thomas Morquin [*sic*]'. Typescript of original baptismal record for the parish of Grouville, the town just adjacent to Mont Orgueil Castle (although the castle itself, where Roger Manley would probably have resided, was not in Grouville parish).

6. F. Morgan, *A Woman of No Character: An Autobiography of Mrs. Manley* (London: Faber and Faber, 1986), p. 37. I do not agree with her conclusion that because the son was named after his father he was necessarily the first son. Three sons had been born by 1668 (twins on Jersey and a son born earlier and left behind in Liège). It is conceivable that an earlier born (and presumably deceased) son had been named Roger, but Cornelius and Francis were also important Manley family names (the eldest living son in 1687 was Francis, and there may have been a son Cornelius who died before daughter Cornelia was born).

7. *The Adventures of Rivella*, vol. 4, p. 14.

8. J. Swift, *Journal to Stella*, ed. H. Williams, 2 vols, *Swift's Prose Works*, ed. H. Davis, vols 15–16 (Oxford: Basil Blackwell, 1974), 28 January 1712, vol. 2, p. 474.

9. Duff, 'Materials toward a Biography', p. 14, n. 44. See note 10 to Introduction, above, for a discussion of the problems in the Sloane manuscript item so often associated with Manley.

10. See note 15 to Chapter 2, above.

11. Roger Manley to [Joseph Williamson], [30] September 1666, Mont Orgueil, Jersey, PRO, SP 29/173/211.

12. Roger Manley to [Robert Francis], 25 March 1668, Jersey, PRO, SP 29/237/98–9. As Patricia Köster points out, there is a mistake in the transcript in the *Calendar of State Papers, November 1667–September 1668*, p. 307, which transcribes 'my Dearest' (i.e. Manley's wife) as 'my Daughter', thus giving the mistaken impression that Manley had a daughter old enough to travel to France without either parent. See item 50 in 'The Correspondence of Sir Roger Manley', p. 183.

13. R[oger] Manley to R[obert] Francis, 25 August 1668, Jersey, PRO, SP 29/245/87–8.

14. *The Adventures of Rivella*, vol. 4, p. 14.

15. Raleigh wrote to Elizabeth 'It is a stately fort of grat capacity and I consider it a pity to cast it down'; this is cited – without any bibliographic details – in D. Ford, *Mont Orgueil Castle: A Souvenir Guide* (St Helier: Jersey Heritage Trust, 2007), p. 63.

16. R[oger] Manley to R[obert] Francis, 18 March 1669, Jersey, PRO, SP 29/257/195.

17. The letter explaining Manley's recanting of his accusation of Richard Bourke is from Ralph Hope to Williamson, 2 August 1669, Coventry, PRO, SP 29/263/158. Manley's letter full of bravado to his cousin Robert Francis is also dated 2 August, from Wrexham, PRO, SP 29/263/160. Both are transcribed in the *Calendar of State Papers, Domestic Series, October 1668–December 1669*, ed. M. A. E. Green (London: Her Majesty's Stationery Office, 1894), p. 438.

18. R[oger] Manley to Christopher Hatton, 26 February 1672, BL, Add. MS 29553, f. 389.

19. [E. Curll], *Mr. Pope's Literary Correspondence*, 3 vols (London: E. Curll, 1735), vol. 3, p. 56. It makes sense to view this claim with some caution since it appears in a work published a decade after Manley's death; no such claim was published during her own lifetime. This does not exclude the possibility that she once told a story to this effect and that Curll recalled it, but it also may be one of Curll's fictional embellishments.

20. I am indebted to Margaret Edwards, of the Priaulx Library, Guernsey, for her kindness in checking the available records for Guernsey.

21. R[oger] Manley to Joseph Williamson, 20 January 1673, Southampton, PRO, SP 29/332/264–5; cited from the abstract in *Calendar of State Papers, Domestic Series, November 1st, 1673, to February 28th, 1675*, ed. F. H. B. Daniell (London: His Majesty's Stationery Office, 1904), p. 462. Patricia Köster corrects the mistaken transcription of the date from 22 to 20 January in 'The Correspondence of Sir Roger Manley', item 68, p. 184.

22. See note 15 to Chapter 2, above.

23. J. Charnock, *Biographia Navalis; or Impartial Memoirs of the Lives and Characters of the Officers of the Navy of Great Britain from 1660 to the Present Time*, 6 vols (London: R. Faulder, 1794–8), vol. 2, pp. 400–1. The document certifying him as a member of the Church of England (a requirement for becoming an officer) is dated 3 December 1688, issued in Portsmouth. The presiding minister was Thomas Heather and the church-warden Anthony Stratton, according to the transcriptions of sacrament certificates in the Portsmouth Records Office.

24. All of the information about naval careers comes from N. A. M. Rodger, *The Wooden World: An Anatomy of the Georgian Navy* (1986; London and New York: W. W. Norton, 1996), pp. 15–137.

25. Francis was defending the mackerel fishery when he was mortally wounded and taken by the French on 15 (or 17) June 1693. See W. L. Clowes, *The Royal Navy: A History from the Earliest Times to the Present*, 7 vols (London: S. Low, Marston, 1897–1903), vol. 2, p. 472, who gives 17 June as the date of his capture; Charnock lists the capture as 15 June in *Biographia Navalis*, vol. 2, pp. 400–1. Francis Manley's will was proved 28 July 1693; PROB 11/415. The journal, or log book, kept by Francis Manley (from October 1688 to May 1690) when he was lieutenant of the York, contains no personal information about himself or his family. See Bodleian MS, Rawl.C.968.

26. There is a mistake in an annotation about this brother in our *Selected Works* (vol. 4, p. 245, n. 54); the younger brother was in fact Edward (d. 1688).

27. The Lloyd (Floyd) cousins were presumably relations of Roger Manley's mother, Mary, née Lloyd, wife of Cornelius Manley (d. 1623). Edward's will was signed on 11 April and proved on 30 June 1688; PROB 11/391. He appears to have been living in London at the time that he made his will, since one of his witnesses was Dr Robert Midgley, who was also living in London. The burial register for St Michael's Bassishaw indicates that Edward was buried on 15 June 1688 and 'wrapped in woolen onely'. Being buried in a woollen shroud was required by an act of Charles II (in order to aid the English wool industry), but being buried *only* in such a shroud might suggest he died in poverty. In his will, however, Edward leaves bequests of up to £20 each to his sisters, cousins and family friends totalling less than £100 but not indicating impoverishment; since he requested only that he be 'decently buried' the other family members presumably decided not to spend money on an extravagant funeral or coffin. See PROB 11/391.

28. *The Adventures of Rivella*, vol. 4, p. 13.

29. Ibid.

30. See p. 10 and note 13 to Chapter 1, above.

31. R. Manley to Sir Lionel Jenkins, 13 March 1684, Landguard Fort, PRO, SP 29/437/54, cited from the abstract in *The Calendar of State Papers, October 1, 1683–April 30, 1684*, p. 325. Roger Manley would bequeath this house to his eldest daughter; it originally belonged to his cousin Arthur, brother of the other 'Captain Manley' living in the United Provinces in the 1650s; Roger Manley did not inherit it directly from Arthur (who died in 1661), but seems to have acquired it later, possibly as a bequest from another family member.

32. *The Adventures of Rivella*, vol. 4, p. 17.

33. This description is cited from an email (sent 5 November 2007) from Paul Pattison, who has extensively documented the ground plan layout of Landguard Fort during this period; he kindly shared with me his detailed drawing, recreating the grounds, which will be part of a forthcoming article in *Post-Medieval Archaeology*.

34. *The Adventures of Rivella*, vol. 4, p. 16.

35. As Fidelis Morgan points out, Carlisle, an actor and budding playwright as well as a soldier, was in the Drury Lane Company in 1682 and again in 1687; his play *The Fortune Hunters* was performed at Drury Lane in 1689. He died in the battle of Aughrim in July 1691. See *A Woman of No Character*, p. 38, nn. 6, 7. See also Dalton, *English Army Lists*, vol. 2. p. 33; E. A. H. Webb, *The History of the 12th (the Suffolk) Regiment 1685–1913* (London: Spottiswoode, 1914), pp. 3–4; W. Van Lennep (ed.), *The London Stage 1660–1800: A Calendar of Plays, Part 1: 1660–1700* (Carbondale, IL: Southern Illinois University Press, [1965]), pp. 370, 385; and P. H. Highfill, K. A. Burnim and E. A. Langhans, *A Biographical Dictionary of Actors, Actresses, Musicians, Dancers, Managers, and other Stage Personnel in London, 1660–1800*, 16 vols (Carbondale, IL: Southern Illinois University Press, 1973–93).

36. One of the companies in the Duke of Norfolk's Regiment of Foot was ordered to Landguard Fort on 11 July 1685; by 3 August, this company had rejoined headquarters (at the Tower of London). See Webb, *The History of the 12th Regiment*, pp. 3–4. Morgan assumes that the regiment therefore stayed 24 days at Landguard Fort (see *A Woman of No Character*, p. 38), but the visit must have been briefer, since days must be allotted for the company to have marched from Yarmouth to Landguard (a distance of about 240 km) on or shortly after 11 July and for the company to have marched from Landguard to central London (a distance of about 110 km) before 3 August.

37. *The Adventures of Rivella*, vol. 4, p. 16.

38. Ibid., p. 12.

39. *OED*, s.v. liberal.

40. *The New Atalantis*, vol. 2, pp. 130, 131.

41. *The Adventures of Rivella*, vol. 4, p. 29.

42. F. A. Inderwick (ed.), *A Calendar of the Inner Temple Records*, 3 vols (London: Henry Sotheran & Co., Stevens and Haynes; Stevens and Sons, by order of the Masters of the Bench, 1896–1901), vol. 3 (1660–1714), p. 291.

43. François, sixth duc de La Rochefoucauld (1613–80), was the author of *Réflexions ou sentences et maximes morales* (1665). Manley is probably referring here to the popular English translation, *Moral Maxims and Reflections* (London: M. Gillyflower, R. Sare, and J. Everingham, 1694; 2nd edn, 1706), from which she cites verbatim several times in *The New Atalantis*.

44. *The Adventures of Rivella*, vol. 4, p. 35.

45. Ibid., p. 12.

46. Ibid., p. 56.

47. Ibid., p. 58.

48. For a discussion of the gendered politics in classical and neoclassical political philosophy, see my '"It's Not Easy Being Green": Gender and Friendship in Eliza Haywood's Political Periodicals', *Eighteenth-Century Studies*, 32:2 (Winter 1998–9), pp. 199–214.

49. *The Lady's New Year's Gift, or Advice to a Daughter* (London: D. Midwinter, 1707), pp. 136–7; the first edition of this work appeared in 1688 but Manley may well have been citing from the 1707 edition. Manley refers to 'excelling in a Mistake' in *The New Atalantis*, vol. 2. p. 50.

50. *The New Atalantis*, vol. 2. p. 50.

51. *The Adventures of Rivella*, vol. 4, p. 58.

52. Manley may be citing from the 1707 edition, *Politeuphuia, Wits Commonwealth. Or a Treasury of Divine, Moral, Historical, and Political Admonitions, Similes, and Sentences* (London: W. Freeman, 1707). The first extant edition of this work was published by in London by Nicholas Ling in 1598.

53. See *Selected Works*, vol. 1, p. 273, n. 5. The author of *Queen Zarah* also borrowed extensively from Bellegarde elsewhere in the text; see R. Carnell, 'More Borrowing from Bellegarde in Manley's *Queen Zarah and the Zarazians*', *Notes and Queries*, 249 (December 2004), pp. 377–9.

54. See Downie, 'What if Manley did *Not* Write', p. 258.

55. Most other scholars have presumed that the Huguenot minister was living in France, following Manley's description of the place as 'on the other Side of the Sea' and as about 'eighteen Miles farther from *London*' (*The Adventures of Rivella*, vol. 4, p. 18). This presumption, however, seems to rely on somewhat mistaken geography. Landguard Fort, Suffolk, is across the channel from the Netherlands (and modern-day Belgium); the distance to Oostende is about 130 km. It is possible that this Huguenot minister was living in exile from France in the prosperous coastal port of Aldeburgh, which is 30 km further along the Suffolk coast from London. It may have been easiest, in those days, to travel there from Landguard by boat, along the coast, which may explain why Manley refers to it as 'on the other Side of the Sea'.

56. *The Adventures of Rivella*, vol. 4, p. 18.

57. Manley's father may have been reluctant to leave his daughter in this minister's family during the winter months, which he would probably spend in Kew, especially if the minister were living in or near a port, such as Aldeburgh, given that Delarivier (at about age fifteen) had already developed an infatuation for one young army officer.

58. See *Selected Works*, vol. 2, p. 339, n. 340.

59. *The New Atalantis*, vol. 2. p. 255.

60. *The Adventures of Rivella*, vol. 4, p. 14.

61. Ibid., p. 11.

62. Ibid.

63. Ibid., p. 19.

64. PROB 11/391; PRO, SP 44/164, p. 381; cited from *Calendar of State Papers, Domestic Series, James II, Volume II, January, 1687–May, 1687* (London: Her Majesty's Stationery Office, 1964), p. 393.

65. See note 36 above.

66. *The New Atalantis*, vol. 2. p. 255.

67. Duff, 'Materials toward a Biography', p. 32.

68. I agree with Dolores Duff about Delarivier's possible resentment of perceived favouritism; see ibid., p. 42.

69. For the will of Mary Elizabeth Brathwaite, a widow living in Ipswich, see PROB 11/700. No will has been discovered for Cornelia Markendale.

70. *The New Atalantis*, vol. 2. p. 255.

71. Leslie, *The History of Landguard Fort*, p. 101.

72. Morgan suggests that Ellis Lloyd died in 1687, shortly after Roger Manley (but presumably before Eyton); she does not give a source, and I have been unable to verify this information. She also interprets Edward's will as listing 'uncle Edward' as 'Edward Lloyd', whereas I read it as 'Floyd', but the spellings may have been interchangeable, following Welsh pronunciation. See *A Woman of No Character*, pp. 46–8. Roger Manley's will assigns 'Ellis Lloyd' (not spelled Floyd) as executor, but these are quite possibly members of the same family (PROB 11/391).

73. *The New Atalantis*, vol. 2. p. 255.

74. Morgan, *A Woman of No Character*, p. 46; Wrexham Parish Registers (microfilm of original): '10 July 1686, The Lady Doro' Manly [*sic*]'.

75. According to the Manley family pedigree in the Sir Peter Leycester's *Book of Pedigrees*, Cheshire and Chester Archives, DLT/2173/145, Francis, Roger and John Manley had two older sisters, Elizabeth and Catharine. Morgan suggests that the aunt might be Mary Manley (d. 1701), the second wife of John Manley (*A Woman of No Character*, p. 46), but since Delarivier's uncle John Manley (d. 1699) was not listed as an executor or beneficiary in Roger Manley's will, it seems that the families were not on close enough terms that Delarivier and Cornelia would have gone to live with him and his second wife in London. In any case, Manley's description of these events in *The New Atalantis* suggests that the aunt was a widow and living in the country, not London.

76. *The New Atalantis*, vol. 2. p. 255.

77. See p. 19 and note 35 to Chapter 1, above.

78. *ODNB*, s.v. John Manley. Dolores Duff's discussion of the 'Major Manley' suspected of treason in 1685 most likely refers to Major John Manley rather than to Roger as she assumes ('Materials toward a Biography', pp. 29–33).

79. On 17 January 1679, 'John Manley of Gray's Inn, Middlesex, bachelor, about 24' married 'Mrs. Ann Grosse, St. Martin-in-the-fields, spinster, about 23, her parents dead'. See J. Foster (ed.), *London Marriage Licenses* (London, 1889), p. 879. This source spells 'Ann' without a final 'e', as do the original birth records from St Mary, Truro (on microfilm), for her daughter Jane (25 August 1680) and her son Francis (9 August 1694); occasionally her name is spelled 'Anne' in some of the legal documents pertaining to mortgages and in some secondary sources.

80. *The New Atalantis*, vol. 2. p. 254.

81. Ibid.

82. Ibid., p. 257.

83. Ibid., p. 256.

84. Foster (ed.), *The Register of Admissions to Gray's Inn*.

85. *The New Atalantis*, vol. 2. p. 255.

86. Ibid.

87. Ibid., pp. 255, 256.

88. Ibid., p. 255.

89. Ibid., p. 257.

90. *The Adventures of Rivella*, vol. 4, p. 19.

91. Ibid., p. 36.

92. *The New Atalantis*, vol. 2. p. 256.

93. *The Adventures of Rivella*, vol. 4, p. 19.
94. Ibid., p. 10.
95. This account in Lady Cowper's papers is cited and discussed further in Chapter 6, see pp. 132–5.
96. *The New Atalantis*, vol. 2. p. 255.
97. Dolores Duff makes this argument in 'Materials toward a Biography', p. 70.
98. *The New Atalantis*, vol. 2. p. 255.
99. Ibid.
100. *The Adventures of Rivella*, vol. 4, p. 10. I disagree with Katherine Zelinsky's assumption that this awkwardly worded line in Manley's text somehow indicates that Manley remarkably recovered from or 'reversed' the effects of smallpox; see *Rivella*, ed. Zelinsky, p. 47, n. 2. I see the line as meaning 'given the condition in which the disease left her face, Rivella now (as an adult) has scarcely any claim to beauty'.
101. *The Adventures of Rivella*, vol. 4, p. 10.
102. Swift, *Journal to Stella*, 28 January 1712, vol. 2, p. 474. Ros Ballaster refers to two possible likenesses in her *ODNB* entry on Manley. However, as she has explained to me in an email of 19 May 2008, the engraving of a woman between pp. 8–9 of a 1714 edition of *The Adventures of Rivella* held at the Bodleian Library (12 THETA 1893) is 'unlikely' to be Manley.
103. *The Rival Princesses: or, the Colchian Court: A Novel* (London: R. Bentley, 1689), p. 9. The textual connections to Manley's *Royal Mischief* are discussed at more length in Chapter 4, pp. 102–3.
104. *The Rival Princesses*, p. 10; *The Adventures of Rivella*, vol. 4, p. 11.
105. *The Rival Princesses*, p. 9; *The Adventures of Rivella*, vol. 4, p. 10.
106. *The Rival Princesses*, p. 11.
107. *The New Atalantis*, vol. 2. p. 255.
108. A. H. Dodd, *A History of Wrexham* (Wrexham: Hughes & Son, 1957), pp. 69–70. The house had originally been owned by (the regicide) John Jones and then by his heirs; Major Manley leased it (possibly after Llwyd's death), and retained the lease of it even when he moved to London.
109. Ellis Sutton to Rich. Earl of Carbery, Wrexham, 17 February 1665; cited from *Calendar of State Papers, Domestic Series, 1664–1665*, ed. M. A. E. Green (London: Her Majesty's Public Record Office, 1863), p. 205.
110. Dodd describes one Lady Eyton who was 'steadfast till her death', although 'a number of Morgan Llwyd's wealthier disciples had conformed' after the Restoration; he also believes that Lady Eyton helped to provide employment and protection for the Nonconformist preacher John Evans (*A History of Wrexham*, p. 71). Dodd does not provide Lady Eyton's first name, so we cannot be certain whether this is Dorothea Eyton, related to the Manleys by marriage, but it may well be.
111. *Calendar of State Papers, November 1667–September 1668*, p. 467. Dolores Duff makes the suggestion about Llwyd in 'Materials toward a Biography', p. 69.
112. Devon Record Office, 1262M/TC/135; Cornwall Record Office, T/51, DD/CM/1045, and DD/CD/1046. John Manley's avarice is also evident in a 1696 complaint by tenants (Cornwall Record Office, KL/21/3).
113. *The New Atalantis*, vol. 2. p. 258.
114. He would represent Bossiney (1695–8, 1701–8, 1710–13) and Camelford (1708–10).
115. *The New Atalantis*, vol. 2. p. 254.
116. Ibid., p. 257.

117. Ibid., p. 258.

118. Ibid., pp. 257–8.

119. Ibid., p. 257. Dolores Duff suggests that the Markendale whom Cornelia married may have been John Markendale, who was listed as second lieutenant in Roger Elliot's regiment of foot in 1703. See 'Materials toward a Biography', p. 24. See also Dalton's *English Army Lists*, vol. 5, p. 175. Even if this is correct, we do not know when they were married nor where Cornelia would have been living following the marriages of her sister and cousin marriage but before her own marriage. We know Cornelia was still single in 1691 at the time that her brother Francis had made his will, since he refers to her under her maiden name.

120. D. Manley, *The Lost Lover; or The Jealous Husband: A Comedy* (London: R. Bentl[e]y et al., 1696); cited from *Eighteenth-Century Women Playwrights*, ed. D. Hughes, 6 vols (London: Pickering & Chatto, 2001), vol. 1, ed. M. Rubik and E. Mueller-Zettlmann, p. 5.

121. *The New Atalantis*, vol. 2. p. 258.

122. Ibid.

123. Ibid.

124. Correspondence (dated 9 October 1685) about a petition that John Manley made to be granted a cottage in the borough of Fowey mentions that 'since ye Death of Mr. Richard Hoblin' John Manley 'hath been appointed by ye Rt Honoble Ye Earle of Bath Steward of ye Mannor wthin ye Dutchy and in ye County of Cornwall'. See PRO, T 54/15, p. 59. Although this correspondence is dated late in 1695, it seems as if John Manley was involved in what would appear to be official duchy business; he is listed, for example, on correspondence about the surveying of Pendennis Castle in 1694. See *Calendar of Treasury Books, vol. 10: January 1693 to March 1696*, ed. W. A. Shaw, (London: His Majesty's Stationery Office, 1935), part 2, p. 728. The entry on John Manley in *The History of Parliament* suggests that he 'may have been the "Mr. Manley" reported by Secretary Trenchard ... to be living at Brussels, apparently engaged "on a project of making all sorts of apparel proof against water" but in fact keeping "a constant correspondence with the Jacobites here"'. The article is citing here from a letter from Trenchard to Portland, 19 August 1693 (Nottingham University Library, Bentinck MSS, PwA 1418). However, since John Manley was so busy assisting Lord Bath, it seems more likely that the Mr Manley in Brussels was another Manley, possibly a relation (perhaps a son) of the royalist Captain John Manley who had been living in the Netherlands in the 1650s.

125. *The New Atalantis*, vol. 2. pp. 258–9.

126. See p. 192 below.

127. *The Adventures of Rivella*, vol. 4, p. 20.

128. Ibid., p. 21.

129. Ibid., p. 22.

130. Ibid.

131. Ibid.

132. Ibid., p. 24.

133. *ODNB*, s.v. Barbara Palmer.

134. *The Adventures of Rivella*, vol. 4, p. 21.

135. The original *DNB* entry on Marlborough cites Manley about Churchill having enriched himself through Palmer's generosity; Leslie Stephen, the author, notes, 'Mrs. Manley is also responsible for the assertion, repeated in Pope's "Sober Advice from Horace," that he

afterwards behaved ungratefully to his mistress' (*DNB*, s.v. John Churchill). This citation is not included in the most recent edition of the *ODNB*.

136. See note 23 to Chapter 1, above.

137. Parish records for St Mary, Truro. Dolores Duff makes the suggestion that this might have been John and Delarivier's child ('Materials toward a Biography', p. 72).

138. S. E. Gay, et al. (eds), *The Register of Marriages, Baptisms and Burials of the Parish of St. Mary, Truro, Co. Cornwall, A.D. 1597 to 1837*, 2 vols (Exeter: Devon and Cornwall Record Society, 1940), vol. 1, p. 243.

139. *The Adventures of Rivella*, vol. 4, p. 24.

4 A 'Female Wit'

1. *The Post Man and the Historical Account,* Thursday, 20 February 1696. The work was listed in *The Term Catalogues* for April to June 1696. See E. Arber (ed.), *The Term Catalogues, 1668–1709*, 3 vols (London: Edward Arber, 1903–6), vol. 2, p. 591.

2. Since *The Lost Lover* was advertised in *The London Gazette*, no. 3177, 20–3, April 1696, it was probably first performed no later than March 1696. Since *The Royal Mischief* was advertised in *The Post Man*, 4–6 June 1696, it was probably acted in late April or May. See Van Lennep (ed.), *The London Stage 1660–1800, Part 1*, pp. 460–1.

3. *The Adventures of Rivella*, vol. 4, p. 24.

4. See H. Crane, *Playbill: A History of the Theatre in the West Country* (Plymouth and London: McDonald and Evans, 1980), pp. 30–7.

5. See Hook's Introduction to her facsimile edition of *The Female Wits*, p. xiv. Hook suggests that the actor-writer who had the main hand in writing the play was probably Joseph Haynes (d. 1701), whose friend and patron William Mann may have been the 'Mr. W. M.' on the title page of the 1704 edition and the author of the preface to that edition in which he refers to this play as written by someone now deceased.

6. *The Female Wits*, ed. Hook, p. 22.

7. Ibid., p. 24.

8. *History of Parliament*, s.v. Thomas Skipwith.

9. *The Adventures of Rivella*, vol. 4, p. 24.

10. See *Selected Works*, vol. 1, p. 271, n. 18.

11. D. Manley, 'To the Author of Agnes de Castro' [Catharine Trotter], in *Agnes de Castro, A Tragedy* (London: H. Rhodes, R. Parker, S. Briscoe, 1696), sig A2r; cited from a facsimile reproduction in *Catharine Trotter's The Adventures of a Young Lady and Other Works*, ed. A. Kelley (Aldershot, Hampshire: Ashgate, 2006).

12. *Letters Writen by Mrs. Manley*, vol. 1, p. 74.

13. *The Lost Lover*, in *Eighteenth-Century Women Playwrights*, vol. 1, p. 5.

14. *Letters Writen by Mrs. Manley*, vol. 1, p. 73.

15. The description of Manley as a Deist is Letter XV, allegedly from Steele, included in *The Unknown Lady's Pacquet*, vol. 1, p. 191.

16. *Letters Writen by Mrs. Manley*, vol. 1, p. 59.

17. *Selected Works*, vol. 1, p. 269, n. 5. Some scholars have assumed that Manley was writing these letters to her spouse John Manley, which seems unlikely, given that he was probably in Cornwall not London in June 1694 and given that Manley's feelings towards her bigamous husband were far from romantic at this point.

18. Letter to Mrs. De la Riviere Manley, near Oxford, 11 December 1717, in *Letter-Books of John Hervey, First Earl of Bristol*, 3 vols (Wells: Ernest Jackson, 1894), vol. 2, p. 48,

item 507. In a subsequent letter 'To Mrs. M. on ye verses she made of dear wife & our family' (undated but by the sequence of the letter books probably written in December 1718), he thanks Manley for the poem, for which Bristol's expense books indicate that he probably sent her 20 guineas. See ibid., vol. 2, p. 68, item 529 and unnumbered footnote about the expense books; and Appendix 1 to *The Diary of John Hervey, First Earl of Bristol, with Extracts from his Book of Expenses, 1688–1742* (Wells: Ernest Jackson, 1894), p. 195 unnumbered footnote.

19. *The Adventures of Rivella*, vol. 4, p. 26.
20. Herman, *The Business of a Woman*, p. 20.
21. This is the first stanza of the 'Song' in Act 1, scene 1 of *The Lost Lover*. See *Eighteenth-Century Women Playwrights*, vol. 1, p. 11.
22. *The Adventures of Rivella*, vol. 4, p. 26.
23. Ibid., p. 26. This other mistress is identified in the keys as 'Mrs. Pym'; Skipwith's wife is Margaret, née Brydges; see *Selected Works*, vol. 4, p. 250, nn. 94, 95.
24. *The Adventures of Rivella*, vol. 4, p. 27.
25. Ibid., pp. 28–9.
26. Ibid., p. 29.
27. *The Lost Lover*, in *Eighteenth-Century Women Playwrights*, vol. 1, p. 5.
28. Citing John Manley's June 1695 petition for 'a small burage and garden' within the borough of Fowey (*Calendar of Treasury Books*, vol. 10, part 3, p. 1134), Dolores Duff speculates that this may have been 'part of an attempt to make Delia's retirement more comfortable' ('Materials toward a Biography', p. 76). In fact, it seems likely that Delarivier Manley had already returned to London by June 1695. Nor is she likely to have been interested in taking up residence in the small fishing village of Fowey, a location much more remote than her original destination, in June 1694, of Exeter. More likely, having recently become Steward of the Earl of Bath's Manors within the Duchy of Cornwall, Manley was simply reviewing the holdings for properties for which the tenancy had lapsed; this particular piece of property does not seem to have been particularly desirable. As explained in decision to grant the parcel to Manley, the 'Burgage or Cottage discovered by ye person with a Little garden and a small piece of wast ground in ye Borrough of Fowey ... being so inconsiderable no person has desired a Lease thereof since 1660' (PRO, T 54/15, p. 59).
29. *The Remaining Part of the Unknown Lady's Pacquet*, vol. 1, p. 257.
30. *The Royal Mischief*, in *Eighteenth-Century Women Playwrights*, vol. 1, p. 52. See also *Eighteenth-Century Women Playwrights*, vol. 1, p. 220, n. 3, p. 221, n. 16. The editors do not offer specific evidence for why they believe Devonshire was Manley's patron for *The Lost Lover* as well as *The Royal Mischief*.
31. Herman, *The Business of a Woman*, p. 20.
32. Dalton, *English Army Lists*, vol. 2, p. 34.
33. See Herman, *The Business of a Woman*, pp. 19–20.
34. For a discussion of the publishing history of the keys to her secret histories, see Chapter 7, pp. 173, 182, below.
35. Because this was advertised in *The Post Boy* for 27–9 February 1696, it was probably not produced later than January of that year, according to Van Lennep (ed.), *The London Stage 1660–1800, Part 1*, p. 457.
36. D. Hughes, *English Drama 1660–1700* (Oxford: Clarendon Press, 1996), p. 377.
37. *The Lost Lover*, in *Eighteenth-Century Women Playwrights*, vol. 1, p. 5.

38. *ODNB*, s.v. William Congreve, Catharine Trotter.

39. Maureen Sullivan, Introduction to *Colly Cibber: Three Sentimental Comedies*, ed. M. Sullivan (New Haven, CT, and London: Yale University Press, 1973), p. xxix.

40. For a discussion of William and Mary's ostensibly moralizing effect on theatre and society, see ibid., pp. xxxvi–xxxvii.

41. *The Man of Mode*, V.ii.313–16, cited from J. D. Canfield (ed.), *The Broadview Anthology of Restoration and Early Eighteenth-Century Drama* (Peterborough, Ontario: Broadview Press, 2003).

42. *The Lost Lover*, in *Eighteenth-Century Women Playwrights*, vol. 1, p. 37.

43. *The Man of Mode*, V.ii.323.

44. *The Lost Lover*, in *Eighteenth-Century Women Playwrights*, vol. 1, p. 29.

45. Ibid., pp. 8, 13.

46. Herman, *The Business of a Woman*, p. 184.

47. For a thorough discussion of the ways in which Manley refutes the convention of the jilted lover, see C. B. Katz, 'The Deserted Mistress Motif in Mrs Manley's *Lost Lover*', *Restoration and Eighteenth-Century Theatre Research*, 16 (1977), pp. 27–39.

48. *The Lost Lover*, in *Eighteenth-Century Women Playwrights*, vol. 1, p. 6.

49. See Hughes, *English Drama*, p. 387.

50. *The Lost Lover*, in *Eighteenth-Century Women Playwrights*, vol. 1, p. 5.

51. Ibid.

52. *The Royal Mischief*, in *Eighteenth-Century Women Playwrights*, vol. 1, p. 47. Hook suggests that Devonshire was responsible for the play being produced so promptly by Betterton's company in the Introduction to her edition of *The Female Wits*, although she offers no other evidence for the Duke's intervention than Manley's dedication, p. iv.

53. *The Works of John Dryden*, ed. E. N. Hooker, H. T. Swedenberg, Jr, and A. Vinton, 20 vols (Berkeley and Los Angeles, CA: University of California Press, 1956–94), vol. 13, p. 231.

54. *All for Love*, V.I.510–11, in ibid.

55. My analysis of Behn and Southerne and the gender politics of Tory Restoration tragedy is developed more fully in my 'Revising Tragic Conventions: Aphra Behn's Turn to the Novel', *Studies in the Novel*, 31:2 (Summer 1999), pp. 133–51. Southerne's plays from the 1680s, including *The Loyal Brother*, articulate a standard pro-Stuart ideology, according to Susan J. Owen; see her *Restoration Theatre and Crisis* (Oxford: Clarendon Press, 1996), p. 122n. Southerne's politics, however, seem to shift after 1688, according to his patrons; see Robert Jordan and Harold Love's Introduction to *The Works of Thomas Southerne*, ed. R. Jordan and H. Love (Oxford: Oxford University Press, 1988), pp. xi–xliv. This fact does not change the way he depicts female characters.

56. See Kelley's Introduction to *Catharine Trotter's The Adventures of a Young Lady*, p. ix.

57. See my 'Revising Tragic Conventions', pp. 133–5.

58. See C. Lowenthal, 'Portraits and Spectators in the Late Restoration Playhouse: Delariviere Manley's *Royal Mischief*, *Eighteenth Century*, 35:2 (1994), pp. 119–34.

59. *The Royal Mischief*, in *Eighteenth-Century Women Playwrights*, vol. 1, p. 103.

60. Hook's Introduction to her edition of *The Female Wits*, p. viii.

61. *The Adventures of Rivella*, vol. 4, p. 24.

62. Herman, *The Business of a Woman*, p. 188.

63. *The Rival Princesses*, p. 8. Ruth Herman cites this passage in *The Business of a Woman*, p. 188.

64. *The Royal Mischief*, in *Eighteenth-Century Women Playwrights*, vol. 1, p. 49.

65. Ibid., vol. 1, p. 102.
66. *The Rival Princesses*, pp. 160–1.
67. *The Royal Mischief*, in *Eighteenth-Century Women Playwrights*, vol. 1, p. 49.
68. Ibid., p. 96.
69. R. Ballaster, *Fabulous Orients: Fictions of the East in England, 1662–1785* (Oxford: Oxford University Press, 2005), p. 55.
70. E. Settle, *The Female Prelate: Being the History of the Life and Death of Pope Joan, A Tragedy* (London: W. Cademan, 1680), p. 44.
71. Herman, *The Business of a Woman*, p. 189.
72. *The Royal Mischief*, in *Eighteenth-Century Women Playwrights*, vol. 1, p. 103.
73. Herman, *The Business of a Woman*, p. 192.
74. *Letters Writen by Mrs. Manley*, vol. 1, p. 57.
75. See note 1 above.
76. See notes 1 and 2 above.
77. *The Post Boy*, Tuesday, 23 June 1696.
78. See note 24 to Chapter 1, above.
79. This was first published as part of the miscellany *Familiar Letters of Love, Gallantry, and Several Occasions* (London: S. Briscoe, 1718).
80. I am citing from Anne Kelley's facsimile edition of Trotter's *Letters of Love and Gallantry and Several other Subjects* (London: S. Briscoe, 1693), sig A 5r, in *Catharine Trotter's The Adventures of a Young Lady*.
81. Ibid.
82. *Letters Writen by Mrs. Manley*, vol. 1, p. 60.
83. Ibid., p. 61.
84. Ibid., p. 69. I have corrected 'Farigue' (as it appears in our *Selected Works*) to 'Fatigue' (as it appears in the original copy-text).
85. Ibid., p. 64.
86. Ibid., p. 72.
87. [G. J. de Lavergne, vicomte de Guilleragues], *Five Love-Letters from a Nun to a Cavalier: Done out of French into English by Sir Roger L'Estrange* (London: Henry Brome, 1678); subsequent English editions appeared in 1680 and 1693.
88. *Letters of Love and Gallantry*, in *Catharine Trotter's The Adventures of a Young Lady*, p. 129. I follow Anne Kelley in assuming that the final two passionate and angry letters ostensibly written by Orinda directly to Cleander were not part of Trotter's original narrative, since the style and substance is so contrary to the rest of Trotter's narrative. See Kelley's Introduction *Catharine Trotter's The Adventures of a Young Lady*, p. viii.
89. *Letters Writen by Mrs. Manley*, vol. 1, p. 65.
90. See for example, R. Foulché-Delbosc's Introduction to a twentieth-century reissue of the 1691 English translation: Madame D'Aulnoy, *Travels into Spain* (1691), ed. R. Foulché-Delbosc (London: George Routledge & Sons, [1930]), pp. xii–xiv.
91. Dalton, *English Army Lists*, vol. 2, p. 227, n. 1; *ODNB*, s.v. Thomas Tollemache.
92. *Letters Writen by Mrs. Manley*, vol. 1, p. 69.
93. Ibid., p. 59.
94. *The Genuine Works in Verse and Prose of the Right Honourable George Granville, Lord Lansdowne*, 3 vols (London, J. and R. Tonson, L. Gilliver, J. Clarke, 1736), vol. 1, p. 15.
95. *The Adventures of Rivella*, vol. 4, p. 12.
96. *The Female Wits*, sig. A1r. Ruth Herman speculates that Manley may already have cultivated 'wealthy and powerful, perhaps Tory, friends' (*The Business of a Woman*, p. 21),

but it seems more likely to have been the influential Whig theatre patron Devonshire, to whom Manley had dedicated her most recent play.

97. Robert D. Hume observes of a later decade what was largely true in the 1690s: 'no one was making a living by writing plays in the mid-1720s'. See *Henry Fielding and the London Theatre, 1728–1737* (Oxford: Clarendon Press, 1988), p. 27. Brean Hammond's subsequent research into this matter suggests that there were a few, but not many, exceptions to this rule. Manley's first three plays had such short runs that she would not have made much money from them. However, Hammond reports that Thomas Southerne, also writing plays in the 1690s, apparently managed to make a living from his efforts (reputedly earning more than Dryden from a single play), largely because he went to the effort of approaching important and wealthy persons individually and selling them tickets at a steep price. See *Professional Imaginative Writing in England 1670–1740* (Oxford: Clarendon Press, 1997), p. 56. (Hammond's citation for the line in Hume that I cite above gives an incorrect page reference to Hume).

98. *ODNB*, s.v. William Congreve.

99. *The Female Wits*, sig. A1v–A2r.

5 'Some More [and Less] Profitable Employ'

1. *The Adventures of Rivella*, vol. 4, p. 34. This inquiry came about because of a petition by Baldwin Leighton; see R. L. Brown, *A History of the Fleet Prison, London: The Anatomy of the Fleet*, Studies in British History, 42 (Lewiston, NY: Edwin Mellen Press, 1996), p. 36. According to the report of the House of Commons for 30 December 1696, Tilly had been examined at length by the investigating parliamentary committee and it was ordered that '*John Tilly* Esquire be taken into the Custody of the Serjeant at Arms attending this House'. In the record for 27 January 1697, he was described as (still) 'being in Custody of the Serjeant at Arms attending this House' (*Journal of the House of Commons*, 11), accessed through www.british-history.ac.uk on 2 February 2008; this method of access does not provide page numbers.

2. *The Adventures of Rivella*, vol. 4, p. 34.

3. We have no knowledge of Cornelia's whereabouts at this time. In August 1714, Manley seems to have visited her near Finchley (following the directions she gives to the Earl of Oxford for replying to her; Delarivier Manley to Earl of Oxford, 30 August 1714, BL, Add. MS 70033, unfoliated). Markendale seems also to have taken up residence with Manley, at the home of John Barber, possibly as early as 1714 (since Manley mentions her sister accompanying her on her visit to Curll to discuss taking over from Gildon the writing of *Rivella*; see *Selected Works*, vol. 4, p. 236).

4. See note 43 to Chapter 3, above, for details about the work she is carrying.

5. *The Adventures of Rivella*, vol. 4, p. 35.

6. Ibid., pp. 35–6.

7. Ibid., p. 29.

8. PRO, SP 44/272, ff. 46–7; cited in Brown, *A History of the Fleet Prison*, p. 36.

9. *The Adventures of Rivella*, vol. 4, p. 38.

10. Brown, *A History of the Fleet Prison*, p. 33.

11. This information about Tilly is included in the description of the proceedings documented in note 1 above.

12. *Journal of the House of Commons*, 11, p. 643; cited in Brown, *A History of the Fleet Prison*, p. 256. This information was reported on by the investigating committee during the 30

December discussion of Tilly's case; see *Journal of the House of Commons*, 11, www.brit-ish-history.ac.uk.

13. See London Metropolitan Archives, Middlesex Sessions of the Peace, MJ/SP 1708/8/68.

14. In the report for 30 December, the House of Commons assigned Manley and four others to write a bill to redress the grievances (caused by Tilly's behaviour); see *Journal of the House of Commons*, 11, www.british-history.ac.uk.

15. *The Adventures of Rivella*, vol. 4, p. 36.

16. According to reports of the House of Commons, Tilly petitioned for his release on 2 February 1697 and was reprimanded and ordered to be fined and released on 3 February. See *Journal of the House of Commons*, 11, www.british-history.ac.uk.

17. Brown, *A History of the Fleet Prison*, pp. 40–1.

18. *The Adventures of Rivella*, vol. 4, p. 36.

19. Ibid., pp. 36–7.

20. Following the *ODNB*, I use the conventional, but inconsistent, spellings John Grenville but George Granville for his nephew, Delarivier Manley's friend (actually the *ODNB* inconsistently refers to George's uncle as John Granville in the entry on George Granville).

21. *The Adventures of Rivella*, vol. 4, p. 37.

22. Ibid.

23. Ibid., p. 43.

24. *ODNB*, s.v. John Grenville, citing Luttrell, vol. 4, p. 443. At the time that Bath died in 1701, he was struggling to remain solvent,

25. *The Adventures of Rivella*, vol. 4, p. 38.

26. Ibid., p. 49.

27. Ibid., pp. 49, 50.

28. Ibid., p. 53.

29. 'Dela Manley' to [the Duke of Montagu], n.d., in Historical Manuscripts Commission, *Report on the Manuscripts of The Duke of Buccleuch and Queensberry, Preserved at Montagu House, Whitehall*, 3 vols (London: Her Majesty's Stationery Office, 1899), vol. 1, p. 357. This report offers a summary, not an exact transcription of the letter. Although the editor of the report suggests a date of '*c.* 1710', Manley's reference to her just published 'Tragedy' (which had been 'acted in the past winter' and a copy of which she is enclosing) allows us to date the letter as 1707, following the publication of her tragedy *Almyna: or, The Arabian Vow*, which had been produced in December 1706 and whose publication was advertised in the *Daily Courant* of 16 May 1707.

30. *The Adventures of Rivella*, vol. 4, p. 51.

31. *The New Atalantis*, vol. 2, p. 116. Dolores Duff points out that Manley's 'knowledge of Steele's life before the date of *The Procession*' might have come 'to her afterward from Steele's own account' ('Materials toward a Biography', p. 113).

32. Although the date for the *Remaining Part* has previously been given as 1708, following the date on the title page, recently discovered advertisements for this work indicate that the *Remaining Part* was published in September 1707 (mentioned in the advertisement for d'Aulnoy's *Memoirs of the Court of England*, which was announced as 'Just published' in *The Post Man and the Historical Account* for Thursday, 11 September 1707), while the first part of *The Unknown Lady's Pacquet* appeared in early January 1707 (listed in the advertisement for d'Aulnoy's *The History of the Earl of Warwick* in *The Daily Courant* for Tuesday, 31 December 1706, announcing 'To Morrow will be publish'd').

33. There are no dates given on the letters, but Rae Blanchard follows Paul Bunyan Anderson's suggestions that because of their references to Manley's 'husband' – presumed to be Tilly – they must have been written before 1702. See *The Correspondence of Richard Steele*, ed. R. Blanchard (Oxford: Clarendon Press, 1968), p. 429, n. 1, and Bunyan Anderson, 'Mistress Manley's Biography', p. 271.

34. *The Unknown Lady's Pacquet*, vol. 1, p. 190.

35. Ibid., p. 191.

36. Ibid., pp. 191–2.

37. *The New Atalantis*, vol. 2, p. 117.

38. Ibid., pp. 117–18.

39. Ibid., p. 118.

40. Ibid., p. 119.

41. Ibid.

42. 6 September 1709 (draft), in *The Correspondence of Richard Steele*, p. 29. See BL, Add. MS 5145B, f. 190 (per catalogue, but f. 290 on item). The sentence that Blanchard cited over half a century ago is currently missing; only a fragment of the letter she cites from is bound in the relevant volume of Additional Manuscripts. The issue of the *Tatler* that provoked Manley was number 63 from Saturday, 3 September 1709. Cited from *The Tatler*, ed. D. F. Bond, 3 vols (Oxford: Clarendon Press, 1987), vol. 1, pp. 439–40.

43. This originally appeared in Charles Gildon's *Examen Miscellaneum* (London: B. L., 1702), pp. 10–11 (the lines cited here are from p. 10); it is reprinted in *The Occasional Verse of Richard Steele*, ed. R. Blanchard (Oxford: Clarendon Press, 1952), p. 63.

44. The poem originally appeared in *The Muses' Mercury*, April 1707; it is cited here from *Occasional Verse*, ed. Blanchard, p. 63–4. I draw here on Blanchard's suggestion for the date of composition in her notes to this poem (pp. 101–2).

45. Duff, 'Materials toward a Biography', p. 116.

46. *Guardian*, 53 (Tuesday, 12 May 1713), in *The Guardian*, 2 vols (London: printed by J. Nichols, 1789), vol. 1, p. 360.

47. *Guardian*, 63 (Saturday, 23 May 1717), in *The Guardian*, vol. 1, p. 426.

48. She mentions 'having begged Mr Steels interest that I may be brought to a speedy Examination' in a letter to Secretary Thomas Hopkins following her apprehension for libel in October 1709. Delarivier Manley to Sir Thomas Hopkins, Wednesday, [2 November 1709], Pierpont Morgan Library, New York, MA 4695; reprinted in Herman, *The Business of a Woman*, p. 252. In her transcription of this letter, Herman has mistakenly transcribed 'John' Hopkins for Thomas Hopkins.

49. Identifications have not yet been made for 'Euterpe: The Lyrick Muse', 'Terpsichore: A Lyrick Muse' or 'Polimnia: Of Rhetorick'. The *ODNB* entry on Susanna Centlivre identifies her as 'Polumnia' [*sic*], although the tag 'By Mrs. D. E.' does not necessarily support this identification. In a letter to Catharine Trotter, dated 28 October [1]700, Lady Sarah Piers asks Trotter to 'give my thanks to mistress Manely [*sic*] for her discharge of the late trouble I gave her, and let her know my illness has prevented me hitherto'. See BL, Add. MS 4264, ff. 292–3. Since *The Nine Muses* was advertised in *The Post Boy* on Saturday, 19 October 1700, it would appear that Lady Piers only just managed to finish her poems in time for the publication of the work.

50. *The Nine Muses, or Poems upon the Death of the Late Famous John Dryden, Esq.* (London: Richard Basset, 1700), p. 1.

51. Ibid., p. 2.

52. Ibid., pp. 11, 13.

53. *The New Atalantis*, vol. 2, p. 113.
54. *The Nine Muses*, sig. A1v.
55. *ODNB*, s.v. Charles Montagu.
56. *The Unknown Lady's Pacquet of Letters*, vol. 1, pp. 242, 243.
57. Paul Bunyan Anderson gives a date of 1704 for the visit to Bristol; see 'Mistress Manley's Biography', p. 271, and other scholars seem to have accepted this date without question.
58. *The Unknown Lady's Pacquet of Letters*, vol. 1, p. 183. The first performance of *Abra-Mule* took place about 13 January 1704; its publication was advertised in the *Daily Courant* of 27 January. *Liberty Asserted* was first performed on 24 February 1704 and advertised for publication in the *Daily Courant* of 24 March 1704. See Judith Milhouse and Robert D. Hume's 2001 'Draft of the Calendar for Volume 1', in J. Milhouse and R. D. Hume (eds), *The London Stage 1660–1800: A Calendar of Plays, Part 2, 1700–1729* ('A New Version of Part 2') (Carbondale, IL: Southern Illinois University Press, forthcoming), pp. 138, 150–1. Accessed on 22 January 2007, http://www.personal.psu.edu/users/h/b/hb1/London%20Stage%202001/.
59. *The Unknown Lady's Pacquet of Letters*, vol. 1, p. 183.
60. Ibid., p. 243.
61. *The New Atalantis*, vol. 2, pp. 99–102.
62. Ibid., p. 101.
63. *The Epistolary Correspondence of Sir Richard Steele*, ed. J. Nichols, 2 vols ([London]: J. Nichols, 1787), vol. 2, pp. 456–7.
64. See pp. 15–16 and notes 23 and 26 to Chapter 1, above, for a discussion of the publishing history of this work and the reasons his account might be true. The third editions of the work (one with Robert and one with Curll listed on the title page) were published under the title *Memoirs of the Life of Mrs. Manley*.
65. *The Adventures of Rivella*, vol. 4, pp. 235, 236.
66. See pp. 162, 180 in Chapter 7, below, for a discussion of the warrant Sunderland issued for Manley's arrest.
67. *The New Atalantis*, vol. 2, p. 258.
68. *The Adventures of Rivella*, vol. 4, p. 43.
69. *The New Atalantis*, vol. 2, p. 117.
70. *The Adventures of Rivella*, vol. 4, p. 50.
71. Hertfordshire Archives, DE/P/F211. See also my 'Delarivier Manley's Possible Children by John Tilly', p. 447.
72. See W. Blackstone, *Commentaries on the Laws of England* (1765–9), 4 books in 2 vols (Chicago, IL: Callaghan and Cockcroft, 1871). Bigamy is covered in book 4, pp. 162–4 (vol. 2, pp. 395–6); benefit of clergy is discussed in book 4, pp. 365–71 (vol. 2, pp. 521–5). Robert Feilding, who bigamously married Barbara Palmer, Duchess of Cleveland, in 1705 – a scandal that Manley herself refers to in *The Unknown Lady's Pacquet* – was found guilty of bigamy at the Old Bailey, but escaped the death penalty by pleading benefit of clergy; he would have been burnt in the hand, except that he obtained a warrant from Queen Anne suspending the execution of the sentence (*ODNB*, s.v. Robert Feilding).
73. Hertfordshire Archives, DE/P/F211.
74. Likewise Sir Winston Churchill would dismiss Manley two centuries later as 'a woman of disreputable character' when defending his ancestor, John Churchill, first Duke of Marlborough, from Manley's attacks on his character and military policies. Churchill, *Marlborough*, vol. 1, p. 53.

75. London Metropolitan Archives, MJ/SP/1705.
76. London Metropolitan Archives, MJ/SP/1708/8/68.
77. *The Adventures of Rivella*, vol. 4, pp. 51, 52.
78. *OED*, s.v. 'gossip'.
79. *The New Atalantis*, vol. 2, p. 117.

6 Not Yet a Propaganda Writer

1. The reason *Queen Zarah* is included in our *Selected Works* is that J. A. Downie's article de-attributing it ('What if Manley did *Not* Write') was published two and a half years after our plan and contents were finalized.
2. For a discussion of such depictions, see *Selected Works*, vol. 1, p. 275, n. 27, p. 277, nn. 44, 47; and Herman, *The Business of a Woman*, p. 42.
3. *ODNB*, s.v. William Cowper.
4. *Queen Zarah*, vol. 1, p. 96.
5. Ibid., p. 97. I have corrected two typographical errors in this passage (changing 'begin' to 'being' and deleting a stray hyphen), which appear in our *Selected Works* but not in the copy-text we used for that edition.
6. *The New Atalantis*, vol. 2, p. 24.
7. Ibid. I have corrected 'Superfluons' (as it appears in our *Selected Works* and in the copy-text we used for that edition) to 'Superfluous'.
8. Downie, 'What if Manley did *Not* Write', pp. 256–8.
9. Downie succinctly summarizes the trajectory of scholarly misapprehensions about Manley's authorship of *Queen Zarah* in ibid., pp. 258–62.
10. See, for example, *Selected Works*, vol. 2, p. 321, n. 156, p. 396, n. 365, p. 397, n. 374. On *Politeuphuia*, see note 52 to Chapter 3, above.
11. The title page of the work states 1705. Ruth Herman suggests that it probably did not appear before July of that year, since it makes no references to the 'Tack' (the controversial attempt of the Tories to tack a measure outlawing the practice of Occasional Conformity to a money bill), which had been a key issue in the parliamentary elections which took place in May 1705 but which lost momentum when the 1705 elections brought in a Commons almost evenly balanced between Whigs and Tories; see Herman, *The Business of a Woman*, p. 41. The dating of the second part is based on its having been listed in the Term Catalogues under Michaelmas Term (i.e. before November) 1705. See Arber (ed.), *The Term Catalogues*, vol. 3, p. 481: 'Mich. [Nov.] 1705'. This dating is also consistent with the reports of Harley's press spy; see H. L. Snyder, 'The Reports of a Press Spy for Robert Harley: New Bibliographical Data for the Reign of Queen Anne', *Library*, 5th series, 22:4 (1967), pp. 326–45, on p. 333. As Downie points out, other evidence also indicates that the second part of *Queen Zarah* appeared in September 1705: Thomas Hearne's diary for 17 September (*Remarks and Collections*, vol. 1, p. 45, cited in Downie, 'What if Manley did *Not* Write', p. 256).
12. The French translation of both parts of *Queen Zarah*, which claimed to be the 'Seconde Edition Corrigée', was published, according to the title page, in Oxford by Alexandre le Vertueux in 1708. It included an explanatory preface to the political events in England at the time and a key. This text, in fact, could not have been based on the second English edition, since none had then appeared; subsequent French editions are dated 1711, 1712 and 1713. A French continuation, or third part, of the tale, for which there is no English equivalent, appeared in 1712 and 1713, with the same Oxford imprint, as *Suite*

de L'Histoire Secrette de la Reine Zarah et des Zaraziens; ou la Duchesse de Marlborough demasquée.

13. Downie, 'What if Manley did *Not* Write', p. 247, n. 3.

14. *The Adventures of Rivella*, vol. 4, p. 53. As Downie points out, Patricia Köster was the first modern scholar to cite this line as evidence that Manley may not have written *Queen Zarah*; see *The Novels of Manley*, ed. Köster, vol. 1, p. xi; and Downie, 'What if Manley did *Not* Write', p. 259.

15. *An Impartial History of the Life, Character, Amours, Travels, and Transactions of Mr. John Barber, City-Printer, Common-Councilman, Alderman, and Lord Mayor of London. Written by Several Hands* (London: E. Curll, 1741), p. 24.

16. [G. Jacob], *The Poetical Register; or, The Lives and Characters of All the English Poets. With an Account of their Writings*, 2 vols (London: E. Curll, 1723), vol. 1, p. 167; this passage is mentioned by Downie, 'What if Manley did *Not* Write', p. 248.

17. Advertisements in the *Examiner*, 14 June 1711 and 12 April 1714; cited in Herman, *The Business of a Woman*, pp. 63, 64.

18. The French introduction is likewise very helpful to modern scholars attempting to understand the partisan arguments of 1705.

19. I would need more evidence to agree with Ruth Herman's suggestion that the 1711 reissue necessarily provides 'evidence' for the work's 'popularity' (*The Business of a Woman*, p. 65).

20. Anon., *The Secret History, of Queen Zarah, and the Zarazians Wherein the Amours, Intrigues, and Gallantries of the Court of Albigion (during her Reign) are pleasantly expos'd, and as surprising a Scene of Love and Politicks, represented, as perhaps this, or any other Age or Country, has hitherto produc'd* (London: J. Huggonson, 1743).

21. *State Tracts: Containing many Necessary Observations and Reflections on the State of Our Affairs at Home and Abroad ... By the Author of the Examiner* (London: George Sawbridge et al., 1715).

22. Correspondence from Foxon to Downie, 4 December 1978, cited in 'What if Manley did *Not* Write', p. 251. Herman claims not to find Browne's authorship plausible, but she does not refute the evidence that Foxon and Downie use to argue for it (*The Business of a Woman*, pp. 63–5).

23. Downie, 'What if Manley did *Not* Write', p. 251.

24. Duff, 'Materials toward a Biography', p. iii; cited in Downie, 'What if Manley did *Not* Write', p. 258. In his summary of twentieth-century Manley scholarship that has taken Duff's unsubstantiated assertion as fact, Downie acknowledges that Patricia Köster and Catherine Gallagher were more careful than Duff to acknowledge that Manley's authorship of *Queen Zarah* was not certain. See *The Novels of Manley*, ed. Köster, vol. 1, p. xi; and C. Gallagher, *Nobody's Story: The Vanishing Acts of Women Writers in the Marketplace, 1670–1820* (Oxford: Oxford University Press, 1994), p. 88, 96. Both of these cautionary references are cited in Downie, 'What if Manley did *Not* Write', p. 261.

25. Downie, 'What if Manley did *Not* Write', p. 258.

26. J. L. Sutton, 'The Sources of Mrs. Manley's Preface to Queen Zarah', *Modern Philology*, 82 (1984), pp. 167–72; and F. Deloffre, *La Nouvelle en France à l'âge classique* (Paris: Didier, 1967), p. 57; P. Hourcade (ed.), Introduction to *Sentiments sur les lettres et sur l'histoire avec des scrupules sur le style* (Geneva: Droz, 1975).

27. Downie, 'What if Manley did *Not* Write', p. 259; Swift, *Journal to Stella*, vol. 1, p. 154.

28. PRO, SP 44/78, p. 65.

29. Gallagher, *Nobody's Story*, p. 103, n. 29. R. Herman, 'Similarities between Delarivier Manley's *Secret History of Queen Zarah* and the *English Translation of Hattigé*', *Notes and Queries*, 47 (2004), pp. 193–6.

30. See my 'More Borrowing from Bellegarde in Manley's *Queen Zarah*'. When I wrote this article, I had not yet made up my mind about the authorship of the work; I therefore followed Herman's scholarship on *Queen Zarah* and treated Manley as the author of the work.

31. Herman, 'Similarities between *Queen Zarah* and *Hattigé*', p. 195.

32. Downie, 'What if Manley did *Not* Write', p. 264.

33. [A. Varillas], *Medicis. Written Originally by that Fam'd Historian, the Sieur de Varilles. Made English by Ferrand Spence* (London: R. Bentley and S. Magnes, 1686), 'Epistle Dedicatory', sig. A4v–5r, A6r; translated from the French version (La Haye: A. Leers, 1685); cited in M. McKeon, *The Secret History of Domesticity: Public, Private, and the Division of Knowledge* (Baltimore, MD: Johns Hopkins University Press, 2005), p. 808, n. 5.

34. J. Richetti, *Popular Fiction before Richardson* (Oxford: Clarendon Press, 1969), p. 121.

35. L. Gossman, 'Anecdote and History', *History and Theory*, 42 (May 2003), pp. 143–68, on p. 143.

36. Herman, *The Business of a Woman*, p. 51.

37. Performances were advertised for 'this day' in *The Daily Courant* for 17 and 18 December 1706.

38. See note 97 to Chapter 4, above.

39. *Almyna*, vol. 5, p. 97.

40. Ibid.

41. *Almyna* ran for three nights, Monday, 16 December through Wednesday, 18 December; *Camilla* played at Drury Lane on the same nights, before an interruption in its performances for Christmas. As Milhouse and Hume observe, Manley's reference to the 'Eunuch' might refer to the Castrato Valentini, although his performance in *Camilla* was not advertised for his role in that production until March 1707'. See their 2001 'Draft of the Calendar for Volume 1', in *The London Stage 1660–1800*, 'A New Version of Part 2', p. 329. Accessed on 13 January 2007, <http://www.personal.psu.edu/users/h/b/hb1/London%20Stage%202001/>.

42. *Almyna*, vol. 5, p. 97.

43. The *ODNB* entry on Bracegirdle offers the following explanation from 'The anonymous life of Ann Oldfield published in 1730': 'Mrs. Oldfield's benefit, being allowed by Swiney [Swiny] to be in the season before Mrs. Bracegirdle's, added so much to the affront that she quitted the stage immediately' (Genest, 2.375)'.

44. See note 29 to Chapter 5, above.

45. *Arabian Nights Entertainments: consisting of One Thousand and One Stories, told by the Sultaness of the Indies … Translated into French from the Arabian MSS. By M. Galland … and now done into English*, 2 vols (London: Andrew Bell, 1706).

46. Ros Ballaster provides the information about the Umayyad caliphate in *Fabulous Orients*, p. 85, n. 28.

47. See, for example, G. B. Needham, 'Mrs. Manley: An Eighteenth-Century Wife of Bath', *Huntington Library Quarterly*, 14 (1950–1), pp. 259–84, on p. 266.

48. Of course, we do not know whether the published version is exactly the version that Manley wrote or whether it was revised by the actors or director and, if so, whether this revised version would have been the one printed.

49. Ballaster, *Fabulous Orients*, p. 83.

50. Pix explains in her preface that she began the play while working from a recollection of Rycaut's work; only after publication did she realize that Ibrahim was the twelfth not the thirteenth emperor. M. Pix, *Ibrahim, the Thirteenth Emperour of the Turks* (London: John Harding and Richard Wilkin, 1696), sig. A3r.

51. *The Turkish History, from the Original of that Nation to the Growth of the Ottoman Empire* lists Richard Knolles as the primary author. Sir Paul Rycaut is listed as author of *The Present State of the Ottoman Empire* (London: Jonathan Robinson, 1687), Roger Manley also contributed to this work but was not listed on the title page; see Chapter 1 above, p. 10. Ballaster observes in *Fabulous Orients* (p. 84) that Rycaut draws an analogy between Ibrahim and Charles I.

52. Ballaster, *Fabulous Orients*, p. 84.

53. Ibid., p. 89.

54. For a discussion of the politics of Behn's representations of vow-breakers, see my *Partisan Politics*, pp. 57–73.

55. [J. Toland], *The Jacobitism Perjury and Popery of High-Church-Priests* (London: J. Baker, 1710), p. 14.

56. *Almyna*, vol. 5, pp. 110, 111.

57. Herman, *The Business of a Woman*, p. 196. Herman is citing here from coronation oaths (old and new), 1685 and 1689, reproduced in E. N. Williams (ed.), *The Eighteenth-Century Constitution 1688–1815, Documents and Commentary, 1688–1815* (Cambridge: Cambridge University Press, 1970), p. 37.

58. As Leopold Legg explains, 'Since 1689 a few verbal alterations have been made' to the coronation ceremony, but none of particular importance; see L. G. W. Legg (ed.), *English Coronation Records* (Westminster: A. Constable, 1901), p. xix. For the quote from Anne's subsequent speech to Parliament, See J. A. Downie, *To Settle the Succession of the State: Literature and Politics, 1678–1750* (Houndmills, Basingstoke, Hampshire and London: Macmillan, 1994), p. 63.

59. This speech was her farewell address to the Parliament that was prorogued in May 1705. See *Journal of the House of Lords*, 17, p. 150, cited in Downie, *To Settle the Succession of the State*, p. 66.

60. Downie, *To Settle the Succession of the State*, p. 66.

61. *Almyna*, vol. 5, p. 145.

62. Herman, *The Business of a Woman*, p. 197.

63. In her annotations to *Almyna*, Herman incorrectly suggests that 'there was no Earl of Sandwich' alive in 1707 (*Selected Works*, vol. 5, p. 277). In 1707, the (third) Earl of Sandwich was Edward Montagu (1670–1729), husband of Manley's dedicatee.

64. For a detailed summary of such arguments, see my *Partisan Politics*, pp. 19–27.

65. After the change in government of 1710, Harley entered into 'secret negotiations with the French secretary of foreign affairs, the marquis de Torcy, suggest[ing] that James's restoration was his ultimate goal, "if he thinks like us in matters of religion"' (cited in *ODNB*, s.v. James Francis Edward).

66. *ODNB*, s.v. Edward Montagu, first Earl of Sandwich.

67. *Almyna*, vol. 5, p. 97.

68. Gildon's knowledge of *Il Corriere* seems to have come from Jean de Préchac's French adaptation of it, *La Valize ouverte* (1680); see McKeon, *The Secret History of Domesticity*, p. 825, n. 48.

69. McKeon, *The Secret History of Domesticity*, p. 568.

70. See note 32 to Chapter 5, above, for evidence about the dates of publication.

71. Gossman, 'Anecdote and History', p. 143.

72. *The Unknown Lady's Pacquet*, vol. 1, p. 159.

73. An advertisement in *The Daily Courant* for Tuesday, 31 December 1706, indicates that the work would be published 'To morrow'.

74. M. D. Palmer, 'Madame d'Aulnoy in England', *Comparative Literature*, 27:3 (1975), pp. 237–53.

75. For smaller works, trade publishers would generally have expected to be paid something in advance, to help defray the initial investment. For larger works, the author would have run up an account, but for large print runs, he or she would have been expected to have made 'progress payments in respect of both paper and print'. See K. Maslen, 'Printing for the Author: From the Bowyer Printing Ledgers, 1710–1775', *Library*, 5:27 (1972), pp. 302–9, on p. 305. We do not know how large a print run was made of *Memoirs of England*, nor whether Manley (who seems to have been quite short of money in 1707) might have been able to append her work onto a project whose initial costs might have been defrayed by d'Aulnoy or her translator.

76. Edward Wilson (d. 1694), 'the son of one who had not above 200 pounds per Annum'; he was living, according to Narcissus Luttrell 'at a rate of 4000l. per annum'. See *The Diary of John Evelyn*, 6 vols (Oxford: Clarendon Press, 1955), vol. 5, pp. 175–6; and N. Luttrell, *A Brief Historical Relation of State Affairs: from September 1678 to April 1714*, 6 vols (Wilmington, DE: Scholarly Resources, 1974), vol. 3, pp. 291, 299, 308.

77. A different account of the 'Beau' Wilson affair, which appeared a decade and a half later in fact, suggested that he was engaged in a homosexual affair; see *Love Letters Between a certain Late Nobleman and the famous Mr. Wilson: Discovering The True History of the Rise and Surprising Grandeur of that Celebrated Beau* (London: A. Moore, [1723]). Whether rumours to this effect were circulating when Manley wrote her version is not known; nor is it known whether Manley's suggestion about the 'She-Favourite' was an original one, or whether such rumours had already been in circulation.

78. See PRO, SP 44/78, pp. 64–5, and PRO, SP 34/11, f. 69.

79. See PRO, SP 44/78, p. 65.

80. Charles A. Rivington cites this in *'Tyrant': The Story of John Barber: Jacobite Lord Mayor of London, and Printer and Friend to Dr. Swift* (York: William Sessions, 1989), p. 16. He found this quote in the manuscript Minutes of the House of Lords (see House of Lords MS Minutes, 49) for the March 1714 investigation of Barber for *The Public Spirit of the Whigs* (Barber not only printed this tract but owned the copyright). The manuscript minutes apparently contain this quote and other information not included in the relevant section of the *Journal of the House of Lords*, 19, pp. 624–35.

81. *The Remaining Part of the Lady's Pacquet*, vol. 1, p. 217.

82. John Morphew brought out a pamphlet about the trial, *The Arraignment, Tryal, and Conviction of Robert Feilding, Esq; for Felony, in Marrying her Grace, the Dutchess of Cleaveland; His First Wife Mrs. Mary Wadsworth, being then Alive* (London: John Morphew, 1708). See *Selected Works*, vol. 1, pp. 224–5, p. 319, n. 12, p. 320, n. 17; for a discussion of Feilding's punishment for bigamy, see note 72 to Chapter 5, above.

83. See p. 44 and note 81 to Chapter 2, above.

84. Charles Spencer, third Earl of Sunderland, to Sarah Churchill, Duchess of Marlborough, 4 November 1709, BL, Add. MS 61443, f. 35.

7 '[T]hrowing the First Stone'

1. Delarivier Manley to Earl of Oxford, 30 August 1714, BL, Add. MS 70033, unfoliated; reprinted in Herman, *The Business of a Woman*, p. 260.

2. J. A. Downie, *Robert Harley and the Press: Propaganda and Public Opinion in the Age of Swift and Defoe* (Cambridge: Cambridge University Press, 1979), p. 2.

3. On 14 April 1711 Swift wrote to Stella of having asked 'the Author of the *Atalantis*' to write the pamphlet on Guiscard's assassination attempt on Harley because of time constraints as well as some concern about 'disobliging Mr. Harley or Mr. St. John in one critical point about it'. See *Journal to Stella*, vol. 1, p. 245.

4. Manley refers to the 'Second Vol. of his [Damier's] travails [i.e. travels]' (see Herman, *The Business of a Woman*, p. 260). The second part of William Dampier's *A New Voyage Around the World* (London: James Knapton, 1697) was entitled *Voyages and Descriptions* (London: James Knapton, 1699).

5. Manley refers to having waited on Harley 'three weeks ago' in her letter to Oxford of 3 June 1714, BL Add. MS 70032, unfoliated; reprinted in Herman, *The Business of a Woman*, p. 257.

6. Delarivier Manley to Robert Harley, 12 May 1710, BL Add. MS 70026; reprinted in Herman, *The Business of a Woman*, p. 254.

7. Delarivier Manley to Robert Harley, Sunday, 16 [April or July] 1710, BL Add. MS 70290; reprinted in Herman, *The Business of a Woman*, p. 253. The letter written 'about a month later' refers to the letter of 12 May cited in note 6'.

8. Delarivier Manley to Earl of Oxford, 19 July 1711, BL, Add. MS 70028, unfoliated; reprinted in Herman, *The Business of a Woman*, p. 255.

9. Manley to Oxford, 3 June 1714, in Herman, *The Business of a Woman*, p. 257.

10. See the letter from Delarivier Manley to Earl of Oxford, 14 June 1714, in which she thanks him for his 'goodness'. BL, Add. MS 70032, unfoliated; reprinted in Herman, *The Business of a Woman*, p. 259.

11. See pp. 15–16 and notes 23 and 26 to Chapter 1, above, for the publication dates of *Rivella*; see *Rivella*, vol. 4, p. 54, for Manley's comments.

12. Manley to Oxford, 3 June 1714, in Herman, *The Business of a Woman*, p. 257.

13. Harley, who was drinking heavily at this point and often not in attendance on the Queen, was being out manoeuvred by Bolingbroke, who was ingratiating himself with Anne in late 1713 and early 1714 (*ODNB*, s.v. Robert Harley).

14. *Journal to Stella*, 7 March 1711, vol. 1, p. 208, n. 23. See also Downie, *Robert Harley and the Press*, p. 131.

15. The first volume of *The New Atalantis* was advertised as being published 'Next week' in *The Post Boy* for 19 May 1709. It was advertised in *The Post Man and the Historical Account* for the following week and advertised again in *Bickerstaff's Lucubrations* for Saturday, 4 June 1709.

16. PRO, SP 44/78, pp. 64–5.

17. See note 75 to Chapter 6, above.

18. See note 29 to Chapter 5, above.

19. Ruth Herman makes a convincing case for Manley's authorship of this poem in *The Business of a Woman* (pp. 207–12); she includes the poem as an appendix in that work. Its publication was advertised in *The Daily Courant* for Thursday, 24 February 1709. Abigail Baldwin was the widow of the printer, publisher and bookbinder Richard Baldwin and was known for her careful business and accounting practices. See H. R. Plomer, *A Dic-*

tionary of the Printers and Booksellers who were at Work in England, Scotland and Ireland from 1668–1725 (London: Bibliographical Society, 1968), p. 15 (Plomer gives her first name as Ann, but Treadwell gives it as Abigail, which I follow as the more recent scholarly source). According to Michael Treadwell, Abigail Baldwin was generally a Whig trade publisher. See his 'London Trade Publishers', p. 108.

20. See note 80 to Chapter 6, above.

21. *An Impartial History*, p. 24.

22. In fact, after this initial investment success in 1720, Barber subsequently lost money in the bubble, but he nevertheless ended up a wealthy man. See Rivington, *Tyrant*, pp. 80–7.

23. This annotation suggests the sum Barber may have earned from Manley's works in contrast to the stinginess of his leaving only £50 to Manley's sister, Cornelia Markendale, 'to be paid to her at such Times, and at such Proportions as my Executors shall think proper'. The annotator observes, 'the Legacy was very *mean* and the Manner of paying it very *Scandalous*, considering *how many Thousand Pounds* he got by Mrs. Manley's writings'. See *An Impartial History*, p. xxvii–xxviii.

24. Ibid., p. 24.

25. PROB 11/599.

26. Rivington, *Tyrant*, p. 23.

27. *The Life and Character of John Barber, Esq; Late Lord-Mayor of London* (London: T. Cooper, 1741), p. 9.

28. Only on the third edition of this pamphlet (dated 1708), does the title page indicate the printer's name: printed by J. B. for John Boyer. Obviously, Barber may have printed the first two editions, which appeared in 1707, without putting his name on the title page. See Rivington, *Tyrant*, p. 241.

29. *The Life and Character of John Barber*, p. 10.

30. Ibid., p. 13.

31. Ibid., p. 12.

32. Ibid.

33. Ibid., pp. 15–16.

34. *Journal to Stella*, 23 December 1710 and 4 January 1711, vol. 1, pp. 140, 154.

35. *Journal to Stella*, 21 June 1711, vol. 1, p. 294.

36. The 14 June letter does not specify that Manley was in Finchley, although it does suggest that, wherever she was, Barber was able to 'ride over' to deliver the payment to her. Since her next letter to Oxford later that summer (30 August) gives a return address via her sister at Finchley Common, I am assuming that Barber 'rode over' to Finchley in June. See Manley to Oxford, 14 June and 30 August 1714, in Herman, *The Business of a Woman*, pp. 259, 260.

37. *An Impartial History*, p. 45.

38. Ibid., p. 46. This account suggests that Markendale lived there until she died in 1731, but she must have lived at least ten years longer than this, since Barber left her £50 in his will in 1741. She was also listed as a beneficiary of her older sister, Mary Brathwaite, who died in 1740. See PROB 11/700.

39. *The Life and Character of John Barber*, p. 26. We do not know if she began living with him openly in the house in Queen Square before Barber left for the Continent, therefore before Manley's death.

40. *The Adventures of Rivella*, vol. 4, p. 53.

41. *The New Atalantis*, vol. 2, pp. 12–13.

42. Herman, *The Business of a Woman*, p. 77.

43. M. G. H. Pittock, *Jacobitism* (New York: St Martin's Press, 1998), p. 71.

44. Lord Arthur Somerset (1671–1743; uncle to Henry Somerset, second Duke of Beaufort) to his sister, Lady Anne Somerset (1673–1763), undated letter possibly written some time after the appearance of either the third or fourth edition of Manley's *The Adventures of Rivella*, since the writer refers to her *Memoirs*, i.e. *Memoirs of the Life of Mrs. Manley*, the title for the third edition of *Rivella* (which appeared in January 1717). See Badminton Archives, TB 1/2/-22, item 12.

45. Beaufort's chaplain from 1706 was Thomas Yalden (1670–1736), High-Church poet, fellow and Dean of Divinity at Magdalen College, Oxford, whom Manley refers to in *The New Atlantis* as the 'Household grand Druid'. He was said to have given Manley 'a Certificate of Virtue and Honour, which she exposes on all Occasions'. See *The Court of Atalantis* (London: J. Roberts, 1714), p. 87. Some scholars have been puzzled about why Manley apparently depicts her dedicatee in an adulterous liaison shortly after his wife's death; this scene, however, is not about the Duke but about someone else Manley's deities pass on their way to Beaufort's London mansion. For a clarification of the misunderstanding, see *Selected Works*, vol. 2. p. 244, p. 381, n. 229.

46. *The New Atalantis*, vol. 2, p. 18.

47. For a discussion of this power struggle and the reasons for Harley's resignation at this time, see G. S. Holmes and W. A. Speck, 'The Fall of Harley in 1708 Reconsidered', *English Historical Review*, 79 (1965), pp. 673–98.

48. *The New Atalantis*, vol. 2, p. 18.

49. Ibid., p. 118. See p. 136 above.

50. Manley to Hopkins, Wednesday, [2 November 1709], in Herman, *The Business of a Woman*, p. 252. See note 48 to Chapter 5, above.

51. *The New Atalantis*, vol. 2, p. 152.

52. J. Gordon, *Gossip and Subversion in Nineteenth-Century British Fiction* (New York: St Martin's Press, 1996), p. 59.

53. *The New Atalantis*, vol. 2, p. 120.

54. Herman, *The Business of a Woman*, p. 80.

55. *The Adventures of Rivella*, vol. 4, p. 55.

56. The 'Key at the Bottom of each Page' is mentioned in an advertisement in *The Daily Journal* for 10 December 1735. A similar claim is made for the seventh edition in *The London Evening Post* for Saturday, 2 August 1740

57. See pp. 138–40 above.

58. *The New Atalantis*, vol. 2, p. 30.

59. During the week when I was writing this chapter, the governor of New York resigned after a routine governmental phone-tap recorded him making arrangements for meeting a 'call girl'. By contrast, the illegitimate child born to the Duchess of Cleveland fathered by John Churchill (which Manley does not even mention) does not seem to have hindered Churchill's impressive political ascent.

60. *The New Atalantis*, vol. 2, p. 30.

61. Ibid., p. 31. See pp. 000–000 above.

62. *The New Atalantis*, vol. 2, p. 31.

63. Ibid.

64. Ibid.

65. See *The Adventures of Rivella*, vol. 4, p. 19.

66. A. Patterson, *Early Modern Liberalism* (Cambridge: Cambridge University Press, 1997), p. 193.

67. Ibid., pp. 194–5. See also Gossman, 'Anecdote and History'.
68. *The New Atalantis*, vol. 2, pp. 31, 32.
69. Ibid., p. 219.
70. Ibid., p. 228.
71. Ibid., p. 232.
72. Ibid., p. 33.
73. Narcissus Luttrell mistakenly concluded that the marriage had taken place in December 1692, and reported Mrs Howard as having brought a fortune of £20,000. See *A Brief Historical Relation of State Affairs*, vol. 2, p. 644.
74. See p. 115 and note 13 to Chapter 5, above.
75. See pp. 132–3, 138, 179 above for details of these incidents, both of which were widely reported.
76. Hertfordshire Archives, DE/P/F33, p. 11. This passage appears in Cowper's diary entry for 19 July 1709. See *Selected Works*, vol. 2, p. 138, for the passage Cowper is citing from *The New Atalantis*.
77. Hertfordshire Archives, DE/P/F33, p. 10 (also from 19 July 1709); *Selected Works*, vol. 2, p. 130. Whether or not Sir William Cowper was in fact an 'Old Debauchee' is difficult to ascertain; the entry on him in *The History of Parliament* cites this description of him from *The New Atalantis* as if it were fact, without offering other evidence either to support or deny its validity.
78. Hertfordshire Archives, DE/P/F33, p. 10.
79. Ibid.
80. PRO, SP 44/78, p. 64.
81. PRO, SP 44/78, p. 65.
82. I had originally believed that Sunderland was attempting to prosecute Barber and Manley on a charge of *scandalum magnatum* – and I mentioned this theory in a paper given at the American Society for Eighteenth-Century Studies in March 2008 (Portland, Oregon). However, I have subsequently been persuaded that the category of 'Liege Subject' is too broad for the charge of *scandalum magnatum*, since it does not specifically mention 'prelates, dukes, earls, barons, and other nobles, and great men of the realm' or specific royal ministers. See F. L. Holt, *The Law of Libel* (London: W. Reed, 1812), p. 150. I am indebted for my change in thinking to Gary Dyer's careful comments on a previous draft of this chapter and to several extremely helpful conversations with him about the history of libel.
83. P. Hamburger, 'The Development of the Law of Seditious Libel and the Control of the Press', *Stanford Law Review* 37:661 (1985), pp. 661–755, on p. 701.
84. PRO, SP 44/81, p. 389.
85. Hamburger, 'The Development of the Law of Seditious Libel', p. 735.
86. Following this logic before having discovered the actual warrant for her arrest or studied Hamburger's research, I previously assumed that Manley was in fact arrested for seditious libel and mistakenly made this assertion in the General Introduction to our *Selected Works* (vol. 1, pp. 1, 22, 23, 35, 51).
87. Hamburger, 'The Development of the Law of Seditious Libel', p. 746.
88. Ibid., p. 747.
89. PRO, SP 44/78, p. 63.
90. This information was reported in *The Post Boy* for Saturday, 5 November 1709. Manley mentions having 'sued for Habeus Corpus' in *Rivella*, vol. 4, p. 55.

91. See PRO, SP 34/11, f. 69, for the scrap of paper; and Herman, *The Business of a Woman*, p. 73, for the suggestion that Manley had implicated others rather than attempting to protect them, as she claims in *Rivella*. The discovery of legible copies in Sunderland's warrant book for the two warrants of 28 October as well as the separate warrant of 11 November, however, seem to suggest that Manley was not guilty of bringing information against her trade publishers, whose arrest warrant for *The New Atalantis* was apparently issued on the same day as that for Manley and Barber.

92. [J. Swift], *A Friend of Mr. St—le. The Importance of the Guardian Considered, in a Second Letter to the Bailiff of Stockbridge* (London: John Morphew, 1713), p. 24.

93. W. Hawkins, *A Treatise of the Pleas of the Crown: or A System of the Principal Matters Relating to that Subject, Digested under their Proper Heads*, 2 vols (London: J. Walthoe and J. Walthoe, Jr, 1716–21), vol. 1, p. 194.

94. G. R. Dyer, 'The Truth of the Innuendos and the Generality of Readers', paper given at the Midwest Modern Language Association meeting in Cleveland, Ohio, October 2007. I am indebted to Dyer for this citation and for his references to Hawkin and the *Hurt* decision.

95. Cited in J. T. Atkyns, *Reports of Cases Argued and Determined in the High Court of Chancery, in the Time of Lord Chancellor Hardwicke* (London: J. Wenman, 1781), p. 485.

96. The intensity of this affection (which seems to have made Trotter somewhat uncomfortable) is evident in the letters from Piers to Trotter in the Birch manuscript collection at the British Library: BL, Add. MS 4264, ff. 284–332. It is possible that while Trotter and Manley were still friends, she discussed Piers with Manley.

97. *The New Atalantis*, vol. 2, p. 226.

98. Ibid., p. 238.

99. Ibid., p. 177.

100. Ibid., p. 238.

101. Ibid., p. 239.

102. Ibid., p. 234.

103. Ibid., p. 235.

104. Mr Maynwaring to the Duchess of Marlborough, Saturday, past one o'clock [the editor dates this as 'end of October 1709'], reprinted in *Private Correspondence of Sarah, Duchess of Marlborough*, 2nd edn, 2 vols (1838; New York: Kraus Reprint, 1972), p. 238.

105. *Tatler*, 1 (12 April 1709), in *The Tatler*, ed. Bond, vol. 1, p. 23.

106. Ibid.

107. *The New Atalantis*, vol. 2, p. 152. Manley is paraphrasing here from Steele's *Tatler*, 61 (Tuesday, 30 August 1709), in *The Tatler*, ed. Bond, vol. 1, p. 421, although in fact Steele does not specifically mention avarice in his discussion of satire.

108. *Tatler*, 61 (Tuesday, 30 August 1709), in *The Tatler*, ed. Bond, vol. 1, p. 421.

109. *The New Atalantis*, vol. 2, p. 152. See Dryden's dedicatory preface to *The Satires of Decimus Junius Juvenalis*, trans. J. Dryden, N. Tate, W. Congreve, S. Hervey and T. Creech et al. (1693), 6th edn (London: Jacob Tonson, 1735), pp. liv–lix.

110. BL, Add. MS 61443, f. 35.

111. Mr Maynwaring to the Duchess of Marlborough, [October 1709], in *Private Correspondence of Sarah, Duchess of Marlborough*, p. 237.

112. See *Private Correspondence of Sarah, Duchess of Marlborough*, p. 236.

113. Duchess of Marlborough to Queen Anne, [between 29 October and 5 November 1709], reprinted in *Private Correspondence of Sarah, Duchess of Marlborough*, p. 244.

114. This note is added in the Duchess's handwriting to a copy of the letter she wrote to Queen Anne (see note above). See *Private Correspondence of Sarah, Duchess of Marlborough*, p. 246.

115. See *Selected Works*, vol. 2, pp. 109–10, pp. 338–9, nn. 331–42.

116. *The Adventures of Rivella*, vol. 4, p. 55.

117. According to Narcissus Luttrell, in a report for 14 February, 'Yesterday, being the last of the [Hilary] term, Mrs. Manley, under prosecution for being author of a book entituled, the New Atlantis [*sic*], appeared at the queens bench court, and was discharged'; *A Brief Historical Relation of State Affairs*, vol. 6, p. 546.

118. *The Adventures of Rivella*, vol. 4, p. 55.

119. Lady Mary Pierrepont to Mrs Frances Hewet, 12 November [1709], in *The Complete Letters of Lady Mary Wortley Montague*, ed. R. Halsband, 3 vols (Oxford: Clarendon Press, 1965), vol. 1, p. 18.

8 Writing under a Tory Ministry

1. Mary Pierrepont to Frances Hewet, 12 November [1709], in *The Complete Letters of Lady Mary Wortley Montague*, vol. 1, p. 18.

2. The Copyright Act of 1709 vested the rights to a work in an author's name for 14 years, renewable for a second 14 years if the author was still alive at the end of the first term. Manley was the earliest woman to sign her name as author under the new copyright act, which took effect in April 1710. It is not clear, however, whether Manley owned the work outright and so saw its profits herself, or whether John Barber financed the publication (as I have speculated that he did for *The New Atalantis* – see pp. 156–62 above) and so shared in the profits.

3. *ODNB*, s.v. Charles Spencer.

4. See p. 160 and note 7 to Chapter 7, above.

5. *Memoirs of Europe*, vol. 3, p. 14.

6. Ibid., pp. 142–3.

7. Ibid., p. 282.

8. Herman, *The Business of a Woman*, p. 122.

9. *Memoirs of Europe*, vol. 3, p. 96.

10. Ibid., p. 304.

11. Ibid., p. 307.

12. Ibid.

13. The second volume of *Memoirs of Europe* was advertised in the *Examiner* as published on 16 November 1710. The Queen advised Godolphin in her 8 August 1710 letter of dismissal: 'instead of bringing the staff to me, you will break it, which I believe will be easier to us both'. BL, Add. MS 61118, ff. 47–8, cited in *ODNB*, s.v. Sidney Godolphin.

14. This letter is reprinted in Herman, *The Business of a Woman*, p. 253.

15. See pp. 187–8 above.

16. *Journal to Stella*, 3 July 1711, vol. 1, p. 306. Swift adds that he hopes 'they will do something for the poor woman'.

17. See p. 188 above.

18. *Memoirs of Europe*, vol. 3, p. 310.

19. *Private Correspondence of Sarah, Duchess of Marlborough*, vol. 1, pp. 238, 244.

20. *ODNB*, s.v. Abigail Masham.

21. See Manley's 3 June 1714 letter to Harley in Herman, *The Business of a Woman*, p. 257, cited on p. 160 above.
22. *Memoirs of Europe*, vol. 3, p. 170.
23. *L'Atalantis de Madame Manley, Traduit de l'Anglais* (The Hague: Henry Scheurleer, 1713).
24. See p. 124 and note 48 to Chapter 5, above, for her appeal to Steele for assistance after her arrest.
25. *Tatler*, 63 (Saturday, 3 September 1709), in *The Tatler*, ed. Bond, vol. 1, pp. 339–40.
26. *Tatler*, 92 (Thursday, 10 November 1709, in *The Tatler*, ed. Bond, vol. 2, p. 74.
27. *Memoirs of Europe*, vol. 3, p. 8.
28. See *The Correspondence of Richard Steele*, p. 29.
29. *Memoirs of Europe*, vol. 3, p. 5.
30. For a discussion of the difficulties most Hanoverians and many Jacobites had with Charles XII, see H. D. Weinbrot, 'Who Said He Was a Jacobite Hero?: The Political Genealogy of Johnson's Charles of Sweden', *Philological Quarterly*, 75:4 (Fall 1996), pp. 411–50.
31. Herman, *The Business of a Woman*, pp. 106–7.
32. Mary Pierrepont to Frances Hewet, 12 November [1709], in *The Complete Letters of Lady Mary Wortley Montague*, vol. 1, p. 19.
33. Ibid.
34. Herman discusses this inconsistent development of plot in *The Business of a Woman*, p. 99.
35. The author of the *Medley* suggests in number 21 (19 February 1711) that he believed the authors of the *Examiner* included 'a Poet [probably Matthew Prior] ... a Priest [probably Francis Atterbury] ... a Physician [probably Dr John Freind] ... a silly academick [probably William King], and sometimes even an old Woman [probably Manley]'. Manley's name was not always included in subsequent lists of the authors of the first *Examiners*, but many modern scholars have been persuaded that she probably wrote number 7, which is continued in number 49, which she is known to have written. See G. B. Needham, 'Mary de la Riviere Manley: Tory Defender', *Huntington Library Quarterly*, 12 (1948–9), pp. 271–2.
36. *Memoirs Relating to that Change which Happened in the Queen's Ministry in the Year 1710*, written in October 1714, first printed in 1765 in Hawkesworth's edition of Swift's works (London: W. Johnston), vol. 8, part 1 (this volume edited by Swift); reprinted in *Prose Works of Jonathan Swift*, 14 vols, ed. H. Davis (Oxford: Basil Blackwell, 1941–68), vol. 8: Political Tracts 1713–1719, ed. H. Davis and I. Ehrenpreis, p. 123.
37. Frank Ellis, Introduction to *Swift vs. Mainwaring: The Examiner and The Medley*, ed. F. Ellis (Oxford: Clarendon Press, 1985), p. xxvii. Ellis asserts that Harley shared this viewpoint, which he cites from Swift's *The Sentiments of a Church-of-England Man*, in *Prose Works*, ed. Davis, vol. 2, p. 24.
38. *Examiner*, 42 (17 May 1711), reprinted in *Swift vs. Mainwaring*, ed. Ellis, p. 427.
39. George Ridpath, *Observator*, 4–8 (18–22 November 1710), cited in *Swift vs. Mainwaring*, ed. Ellis, p. xxxvii.
40. *Selected Works*, vol. 5, p. 7.
41. Ruth Herman appropriately suggests that previous critical speculation that Swift was ungallantly commenting on Manley's corpulence through his reference to 'small Bodies' is improbable (*The Business of a Woman*, p. 137), since Swift would probably not have been impertinent about a gentlewoman and a friend of his. Herman believes that Manley

may have written this line herself, since she was open about her size in *Rivella*; however, this does not explain away Swift's claim to have written the first page of this number (and this line is early in the first paragraph). However, given opposition banter to the size of Swift as a then still anonymous author, it makes sense to read this as a comment about writing style and genre rather than the bodies of particular authors. Furthermore, Manley's style was generally less authoritative than Swift's.

42. Reprinted in *Swift vs. Mainwaring*, ed. Ellis, p. 470.
43. *Journal to Stella*, 7 June 1711, vol. 1, p. 291, n. 38. See also Downie, *Robert Harley and the Press*, p. 216, n. 21.
44. Downie, *Robert Harley and the Press*, p. 137. Downie has also suggested, in an email comment to me (sent 17 May 2008), that Oxford's reason for giving the *Examiner* to Manley when he did may have been that 'he wanted to run it down with the end of the parliamentary session'.
45. *Journal to Stella*, 10 November 1711, vol. 2, p. 408.
46. *Swift vs. Mainwaring*, ed. Ellis, p. xxxiii; and R. Quintana, *The Mind and Art of Jonathan Swift* (London: Oxford University Press, 1953), p. 185.
47. *The Business of a Woman*, p. 149; Herman is citing Herbert Davis's Introduction to his edition of Swift's *Prose Works*, vol. 3, p. xiii.
48. *Journal to Stella*, 4 January 1711, vol. 1, p. 154. His first mention of having dined with Barber was about a week earlier, in the entry for 26 December 1710: 'I went to-day by water into the city, and dined with no less a man than the city printer' (vol. 1, pp. 140–1).
49. Ibid., 14 December 1710, vol. 1, p. 123.
50. See note 16 above.
51. See, for example, *Journal to Stella*, 9 September, 1 October and 16 November 1710, vol. 1, pp. 11, 37, 97.
52. *Journal to Stella*, 28 January 1712, vol. 2, p. 474.
53. J. A. Downie, 'Swift's "Corinna" Reconsidered', *Swift Studies*, 23 (2007), pp. 161–8.
54. PROB 11/599.
55. *The Correspondence of Jonathan Swift*, ed. H. Williams, 5 vols (Oxford: Clarendon Press, 1965), vol. 5, p. 271 (Appendix XXX).
56. *Journal to Stella*, 7 June 1711, vol. 1, p. 291.
57. *Swift vs. Maynwaring*, ed. Ellis, p. 478, n. 23.
58. *Selected Works*, vol. 5, p. 9.
59. *Examiner*, 45 (7 June 1711), reprinted in *Swift vs. Maynwaring*, ed. Ellis, p. 470.
60. *Selected Works*, vol. 5, p. 8.
61. Herman, *The Business of a Woman*, pp. 136–9.
62. *Selected Works*, vol. 5, p. 12.
63. Ibid., p. 14.
64. Ibid., p. 19.
65. Ibid., p. 21.
66. Ibid., p. 22.
67. Ibid., p. 24.
68. Ibid., p. 25.
69. Ibid., p. 28.
70. Ibid., p. 29.
71. Ibid., p. 8.
72. Ibid., p. 33.

73. Ibid., p. 35.
74. Delarivier Manley to Earl of Oxford, 19 July 1711, BL, Add. MS 70028, unfoliated; reprinted in Herman, *The Business of a Woman*, p. 255.
75. Ibid.
76. Downie, *Robert Harley and the Press*, p. 138.
77. Evidence for this arrangement, for which Oxford's payments may have been delinquent, is offered by a printer's bill that Barber sent Oxford when the latter was in the Tower, following his impeachment in 1715, for issues 5 to 50. See J. A. Downie, 'Swift and the Oxford Ministry', *Swift Studies*, 1 (1986), pp. 4–5. Downie is not certain why the bill did not cover numbers 51 and 52, but believes perhaps that Barber may simply have decided to work in round numbers. As Downie has added in a subsequent email comment to me (sent 17 May 2008), given that the bill was sent long after the event, Barber may have been 'willing to take anything he could get'.
78. *Selected Works*, vol. 5, p. 36.
79. *Swift vs. Mainwaring*, ed. Ellis, pp. xxix–xxxi.
80. Downie, *Robert Harley and the Press*, p. 135.
81. See note 5 to Chapter 7, above.
82. Herman, *The Business of a Woman*, p. 148.
83. Delarivier Manley to Earl of Oxford, 2 October [1711], BL, Add. MS 70028, unfoliated, reprinted in Herman, *The Business of a Woman*, p. 256.
84. *Journal to Stella*, 24 August 1711, vol. 1, p. 340.
85. Ibid., 22 October 1711, vol. 2, pp. 390–1.
86. Reprinted in *Swift vs. Mainwaring*, ed. Ellis, p. 303.
87. Ibid., pp. 312–13.
88. *Examiner*, 34 (21 March 1711), reprinted in *Swift vs. Mainwaring*, ed. Ellis, p. 320.
89. *Journal to Stella*, 16 April 1711, vol. 1, pp. 244–5.
90. Ibid., 28 April 1711, vol. 1, p. 254.
91. *Memoirs relating to that Change which Happened in the Queen's Ministry*, in *Prose Works*, ed. Davis, vol. 8, p. 127. See also R. Herman, 'Swift, Manley, and the Commissioning of *A True Narrative*', *Swift Studies*, 15 (2000), pp. 88–103.
92. *Journal to Stella*, 16 April 1711, vol. 1, p. 245.
93. Edward Harley to Abigail Harley, 22 March 1711, BL, Add. MS 70144, unfoliated, cited in Herman, *The Business of a Woman*, p. 285, n. 54.
94. Herman, *The Business of a Woman*, p. 162.
95. *Journal to Stella*, 3 November 1711, vol. 2, p. 402.
96. *A True Narrative*, vol. 5, p. 43.
97. Ibid., p. 45.
98. Ibid., p. 47.
99. Ibid.
100. The description of the Duke of Portland's putative seduction of Charlot (i.e. Stuarta Howard) in *The New Atalantis* portrays the frenzied heat of emotion in language very similar to the description of Guiscard's desire for revenge: 'He could neither eat or sleep! love and restlessness rais'd Vapours in him to that degree, he was no longer Master of his Business! Wearied with all things, hurry'd by a secret Principle of *Self-Love*, and *Self-Preservation*, the Law of Nature! He orders his Coach to carry him down once more to his *Villa*, there to see his Dear! this dangerous *Charlot*! that little innocent Sweetness! (vol. 2, p. 42).
101. *A True Narrative*, vol. 5, p. 49.
102. See note 37 above.

103. *A True Narrative*, vol. 5, p. 51.

104. Ibid., pp. 53, 54.

105. Herman, *The Business of a Woman*, p. 165.

106. *Bouchain: In a Dialogue between the Late Medley and Examiner* (London: A. Baldwin, 1711). This appeared on 20 September 1711 and was originally believed to be by Hare, but John Oldmixon subsequently gave Maynwaring credit for revising and publishing it. See R. D. Horn, *Marlborough: A Survey; Panegyric, Satires, and Biographical Writings, 1688–1788* (New York: Garland Publishers, 1975), p. 322.

107. *The D. of M------h's Vindication*, vol. 5, p. 57.

108. Ibid., p. 58. Manley is citing directly from *Bouchain*, p. 35. She italicizes the citation and changes 'D. of M.' to 'D. of M------'. She omits 'to the D. of M.' before the 'whom' and adjusts the punctuation from a semi-colon to a colon.

109. *The D. of M------h's Vindication*, vol. 5, pp. 58, 59.

110. Ibid., p. 62.

111. Ibid., p. 65.

112. F. Hare, *The Charge of God to Joshua: In a Sermon Preach'd before his Grace the Duke of Marlborough at Avennes le Sec September 9. 1711* (London: n.p., 1711).

113. See note 95 above.

114. *A Learned Comment upon Dr. Hare's Excellent Sermon*, vol. 5, p. 69.

115. Ibid. In the published version of Hare's sermon, the line Manley cites appears on p. 3. Manley italicizes Hare's words and omits to capitalize 'Leisure', as Hare does.

116. *A Learned Comment upon Dr. Hare's Excellent Sermon*, vol. 5, p. 74.

117. Ibid., pp. 75, 76.

118. *The D. of M------h's Vindication, in Answer to a Pamphlet Falsely so Called* (London: A. Baldwin, 1712).

119. The letters of complaint are cited in Churchill, *Marlborough*, vol. 2, pp. 868–9.

120. Longleat, Portland MSS, v., ff. 253–4: 30 October 1711 (copy); cited in Downie, *Robert Harley and the Press*, p. 152.

121. Downie, *Robert Harley and the Press*, p. 153; Manley to Oxford 2 October [1711], cited in Herman, *The Business of a Woman*, p. 256.

122. *Journal to Stella*, 29 November 1711, vol. 2, p. 421 and p. 415, n. 1.

123. Herman, *The Business of a Woman*, p. 223; *Journal to Stella*, vol. 2, p. 421 and p. 415, n. 1.

124. *A True Relation of the Several Facts and Circumstances of the Intended Riot and Tumult on Queen Elizabeth's Birth-Day* (London: John Morphew, 1711), p. 4.

125. *Journal to Stella*, 28 January 1712, vol. 2, p. 474.

126. This was advertised as 'Just published' in the *Mercator, or, Commerce Retrieved* for Thursday, 13 August 1713. The attribution to Manley was first made by Abel Boyer in September 1713; see note 131 below; it was challenged by some Defoe scholars, including John Robert Moore and Maximillian E. Novak, who claimed it for Defoe, although without offering specific internal or external evidence. See J. R. Moore, *A Checklist of the Writings of Daniel Defoe*, 2nd edn (Hamden, CT: Archon Books, 1971) and Novak's list in *The New Cambridge Bibliography of English Literature*, ed. G. Watson, 5 vols (London: Cambridge University Press, 1969–77), vol. 2: 1660–1800. The pamphlet does appear in our *Selected Works* (see note 134 below).

127. Defoe wrote at least one other pamphlet on this subject and several of his biographers have felt he probably wrote this one. However, Furbank and Owens have shown that there is no definite evidence linking it to Defoe; see P. N. Furbank and W. R. Owens,

Defoe De-Attributions: A Critique of J. R. Moore's Checklist (London and Rio Grande, OH: Hambledon Press, 1994), p. 61.

128. *The Honour and Prerogative of the Queen's Majesty*, vol. 5, p. 86.

129. Ibid., p. 86.

130. Ibid., p. 89.

131. A. Boyer, *Quadriennium Annae Postremum; or The Political State of Great Britain*, 8 vols (London: for the author, 1718–19), vol. 5, pp. 141, 144.

132. P. N. Furbank and W. R. Owens, *A Critical Bibliography of Daniel Defoe* (London: Pickering & Chatto, 1998), p. 141.

133. Furbank and Owens, *Defoe De-Attributions*, p. 61.

134. Ruth Herman, who cites Boyer's attribution as evidence that Manley 'probably' wrote it (*The Business of a Woman*, p. 152), made the decision to include it in vol. 5 of our *Selected Works*. The headnote, however, to the text in our edition could make clearer that this attribution is not as definite as are the attributions to her of the other pamphlets included (vol. 5, pp. 270–1).

135. *The Life and Character of John Barber*, p. 16.

136. Herman explores this possibility in *The Business of a Woman*, pp. 214–23.

137. *John Bull Still in his Senses: Being the Third Part of Law is a Bottomless-Pit*, 3rd edn (London: John Morphew, 1712).

138. *Observator*, 24 May 1712.

139. See, for example, H. Teerink, *The History of John Bull for the First Time Faithfully Re-Issued from the Original Pamphlets, 1712, together with an Investigation into its Composition, Publication and Authorship* (Amsterdam: H. J. Paris, 1925), pp. 1–133.

140. Herman, *The Business of a Woman*, pp. 216–17.

141. *Journal to Stella*, 13 September 1711, vol. 1, p. 359.

142. Swift, *Prose Works*, ed. Davis, vol. 3, pp. 217–18. In the original sixteen-page publication, this anecdote comprises pp. 15–16.

143. C. Winton, 'Steele, Mrs. Manley, and John Lacy', *Philological Quarterly*, 62:2 (1963), pp. 272–5.

144. This phrase appears in *The New Atalantis* (vol. 2, p. 116). See also J. Lacy, *The Ecclesiastical and Political History of Whig-Land of Late Years* (London: J. Morphew, 1714), p. 14.

145. See Herman's refutation of Nichols's ascription in *The Business of a Woman*, p. 223.

146. See Herman's refutation of Charles Rivington's assertion in ibid., p. 223.

147. The English Short Title Catalogue ascribes the 1748 edition to Manley.

148. Ruth Herman discovered this 1735 *Memorial* ascribed to Manley in the Huntington Library catalogue (*Business of a Woman*, p. 224), although the current version of the Huntington catalogue online does not make that ascription. See our *Selected Works*, vol. 2, p. 334, n. 304, for Manley's treatment of Ormond.

149. See note 17 to Chapter 6, above, for Manley's published objections to the appearance of these two works. Charles Rivington includes *Court Intrigues* in a lists of works he believes John Barber may have printed (*Tyrant*, p. 243), but marks it as one of the works for which he is not certain of Barber's involvement (and Rivington probably did not know about Manley's published disavowal). In our *Selected Works* we included the preface to *Court Intrigues* (long attributed to Manley) and Letter XLI, added to Manley's original collection for *Court Intrigues* (vol. 1, pp. 259–68). These items either should not have been included in our edition or should have been included along with information about her disavowal.

150. Walter Graham convincingly argues that the *Female Tatler* was probably not written by Manley and may have been written by Thomas Baker. See 'Thomas Baker, Mrs Manley and the *Female Tatler*', *Modern Philology*, 34 (1936–7), pp. 267–72. Fidelis Morgan, who makes the points listed above, does not actually refute Graham's arguments. See her Introduction to *The Female Tatler* (London: J. M. Dent & Sons, 1992), pp. vii–ix.

151. *Tatler*, 63 (Tuesday, 26 September 1710), in *The Tatler*, ed. Bond, vol. 3, p. 188.

152. See pp. 15–16, 130–1 above for a discussion of why Curll's account of the origin of this narrative might well be plausible.

153. See note 23 to Chapter 1.

154. Lord Arthur Somerset to Lady Anne Somerset, n.d., Badminton Archives, TB 1/2/-22, item 12.

155. See p. 164 above for her reference to the patent in her will. We do not know why she was granted this patent, although it may well have been as acknowledgement for her work for the Tories; it could have been granted to her as a result of her requests to Peterborough and Harley for a pension.

156. See note 36 to Chapter 7, above.

9 A Celebrated 'Muse'

1. The description of Barber is taken from the address by the House of Lords to the Queen about this matter on 11 March 1714; *Journal of the House of Lords*, 19, p. 635, cited in Rivington, *Tyrant*, p. 46.

2. Jonathan Swift apparently knew her well enough from dinners at Barber's residence to write the following rebus on her name: 'What few Men can hit, tho' most can spy / At the Foot of a Hill or from Mountain on High, / Is that fair Lady's Name, with a Black rolling Eye'. See Curll's *An Impartial History*, p. xxviii. Curll also mentions, in his possibly credible account in his preface to the fourth edition of *Rivella*, that 'Mrs. Manley and her Sister' called on him when Manley sought to negotiate with him about writing *Rivella* (vol. 4, p. 236).

3. PROB 11/599. The 1716 edition (which would have been the third edition of *The New Atalantis* although the first edition issued together with *Memoirs of Europe*) excised the elegy for Edward Coke, but otherwise it would be difficult to assert that there was a definitive 'corrected' version of this text, since some of the variants of the 'second edition' are more carefully corrected (fixing minor errors in punctuation and capitalization) than the 'sixth edition'. While the English Short Title Catalogue lists many extant copies (in many different variants) of the second edition of *The New Atalantis*, there are no extant library holdings for either a 'fourth' or a 'fifth' edition, which suggests that there may not have been any such editions and that the claim for status as 'sixth' on the 1720 edition may be a slight exaggeration.

4. Calhoun Winton suggests that Swift was 'working hard to restore some of the relationships' with his former Tory friends. *Sir Richard Steele, M. P.* (Baltimore, MD: Johns Hopkins University Press, 1970), p. 118.

5. Hume, *Henry Fielding and the London Theatre*, p. 27.

6. Hammond, *Professional Imaginative Writing in England*, pp. 62–3.

7. See *The Life and Character of John Barber*, p. 15.

8. Ibid., p. 14.

9. Ibid.

10. Ibid., p. 15.

11. E. L. Avery (ed.), *The London Stage 1660–1800: A Calendar of Plays, Part 2: 1700–1729*, 2 vols (Carbondale, IL: Southern Illinois University Press, 1960), vol. 1, pp. 450–1.

12. *Lucius*, vol. 5, p. 171.

13. In *The Evening Post* for Tuesday, 7 May 1717, the play was advertised as 'Printed for E. Curll', announcing its appearance '*Next Saturday*'. The advertisement for Barber's edition in *The Post Boy* of 18 June 1717 announces that it will appear 'To Morrow'.

14. *The Life and Character of John Barber*, p. 15.

15. PROB 11/599.

16. See note 19 below.

17. No copies with Curll's imprint are listed in the English Short Title Catalogue.

18. V.iv.11–12; see *The Riverside Shakespeare*, ed. G. Blakemore Evans (Boston, MA: Houghton Mifflin, 1972). Herman first noticed the echo of *Richard III* (*The Business of a Woman*, p. 204).

19. The 1720 'Second Edition Corrected' of the play, also printed for Barber, does not show this difference (or any other obvious sign of correction); in fact the epilogue included in the 1720 version (it is missing from the 1717 version of the play to which I have had access) suggests that it was 'Spoken by Mrs. *Horton*', as it may have been in 1717. However, in 1720, the epilogue was going to have been spoken by Mrs Oldfield, as Manley explains in a letter to Matthew Prior, in which she attempts to make arrangements for Oldfield to discuss her planned performance of said epilogue with Prior (see note 23 below). Steele prints this (expanded) version of his prologue in the issue for Tuesday, 2 February 1720 of his periodical the *Theatre*. See *Richard Steele's The Theatre 1720*, ed. J. Loftis (Oxford: Clarendon Press, 1962), p. 47.

20. *Lucius*, vol. 5, p. 171.

21. *Lucius*, vol. 5, p. 176.

22. PROB 11/599.

23. Delarivier Manley to Matthew Prior, 19 March 1719/20. Institute of Historical Research, Prior Papers, vol. 7, f. 127; reprinted in Herman, *The Business of a Woman*, p. 261.

24. Winton, *Sir Richard Steele*, p. 170.

25. Manley to Prior, 19 March 1719/20, in Herman, *The Business of a Woman*, p. 261.

26. I searched all the available court rolls covering Beckley in the Bertie Papers at the Bodleian Library.

27. Bristol to Manley, near Oxford, 11 December 1717, in *Letter-Books of John Hervey*, vol. 2, p. 48, item 507.

28. In an undated letter, probably written in December 1718, Bristol promises to wait on Manley 'to bring you ye joint thanks of the whole House of Hervey' for a poem 'so perfect', *Letter-Books of John Hervey*, vol. 2, p. 68. The editor of these letters observes that Bristol's expense books indicate that he sent Manley 20 guineas for these verses 'of dear wife & our family'. See ibid., vol. 2, p. 68, item 529 and unnumbered footnote.

29. See p. 88 above.

30. See *Letter-Books of John Hervey*, vol. 2, p. 48.

31. See note 36 to Chapter 7, above.

32. See note 23 above.

33. The poem believed to have been written by Manley (the copy in Hervey's collection has a pencil marking, '*By Mrs. Manley*') is included in an appendix to *The Diary of John Hervey*, pp. 195–9. The annotation explaining the reference is on p. 197.

34. Bristol to Mrs Manley, 12 July 1720, from Ickworth, in *Letter-Books of John Hervey*, vol. 2, p. 125.

35. *A New Miscellany of Original Poems* (London: T. Jauncy, 1720), p. 193.

36. Ibid., p. 196. See p. 187 above for Maynwaring's comments.

37. In Plomer's *Dictionary of Printers and Booksellers*, T. Jauncy is listed as the publisher of only two items, one of which is this miscellany (p. 171). However, a search of the English Short Title Catalogue (computerized since Plomer compiled his *Dictionary*) indicates that Jauncy's name appeared on ninety-three items (often published jointly with several publishers), many of them works of poetry or drama.

38. See p. 191 above.

39. See p. 187 above.

40. *The Adventures of Rivella*, vol. 4, p. 55.

41. Ibid., pp. 53, 55.

42. Ibid., pp. 57–8.

43. The dedication to Mrs Manley by the author of *Lover's Week* is mentioned in this advertisement for this work in *The Evening Post* for Saturday, 12 July 1718. Michael McKeon offers an interesting interpretation of the '"pornographic" frame' of *Rivella* in *The Secret History of Domesticity*, pp. 614–15.

44. *The Adventures of Rivella*, vol. 4, p. 11. Ruth Herman first suggested the idea of Manley as a marketer of her own 'brand' (in a business sense). See her 'An Exercise in Early Modern Branding'.

45. Duff, 'Materials toward a Biography', p. 343.

46. See our General Introduction to *Selected Works* for further details about the specific sources for each of these (vol. 1, pp. 40–1).

47. *The Power of Love*, vol. 4, p. 190.

48. See M. de Navarre, *L'Heptaméron* (1559; Paris: Garnier Frères, 1967), pp. 245–6.

49. *The Power of Love*, vol. 4, p. 171.

50. See Matteo Bandello's *novella* 42, in *Tutte le Opere di Matteo Bandello*, ed. F. Flora, 2 vols ([Milan]: Arnoldo Mondadori Editore 1966), vol. 1, pp. 496–508.

51. See pp. 56, 61–2 above.

52. *The Power of Love*, vol. 4, pp. 101, 113.

53. Ibid., p. 65.

54. W. Painter, *The Palace of Pleasure* (1566–7), ed. J. Jacobs, 3 vols (1890; New York: Dover Publications, 1966), vol. 1, p. 239.

55. *The Power of Love*, vol. 4, p. 170.

56. Ibid., p. 147.

57. See p. 84 above.

58. For a reference to this joint confinement, see M. G. Delaney, *The Autobiography and Correspondence of Mrs. Delaney*, 6 vols (London: Richard Bentley, 1861–2), vol. 1, p. 20.

59. See Pittock, *Jacobitism*, pp. 68–73, for a discussion of the romantic elements of Jacobite literature; and my *Partisan Politics*, pp. 129–38, for a discussion of the difference between Whig and Jacobite versions of novelistic realism (and romance).

60. Rivington, *Tyrant*, pp. 100–2.

61. For the publication history of *Love in Excess*, see P. Spedding (ed.), *A Bibliography of Eliza Haywood* (London: Pickering & Chatto, 2004), pp. 91–3.

62. W. H. McBurney, 'Mrs. Penelope Aubin and the Early Eighteenth-Century English Novel', *Huntington Library Quarterly*, 20 (1957), pp. 245–67, on p. 250.

63. See chapter 5 of my *Partisan Politics* for a discussion of the politics of Haywood's novels.

64. D. Oakleaf, Introduction to *Love in Excess; or, The Fatal Enquiry*, ed. D. Oakleaf, 2nd edn (Peterborough, Ontario: Broadview Press, 2000), p. 23.

65. *The Power of Love*, vol. 4, p. 67. Painter's forty-fifth 'nouell' begins: 'Love commonly is counted the greatest passion amongs all the most greuous, that ordinarily do afflict the spirits of men', (*The Palace of Pleasure*, vol. 1, p. 285).

66. *The Power of Love*, vol. 4, p. 149.

67. All of these scenes, except the description of Charlot's passion for the Duke, have already been discussed: see p. 149 above for the description of Churchill's thoughts and desires and pp. 208–9 above for the comparison between Portland's plans to seduce his ward and Guiscard's plans to assassinate Harley. In Manley's description of Charlot's passion for the Duke, she describes 'that new and lazy Poison stealing to her Heart, and spreading swiftly and imperceptibly thro' all her Veins' (*The New Atalantis*, vol. 2, p. 42).

68. See pp. 73, 102 above.

69. Steele to Manley, [6 September 1709], printed in *The Correspondence of Richard Steele*, p. 29.

70. Herman, *The Business of a Woman*, p. 229; she is citing Boyer from *Quadriennium Annae Postremum*, vol. 6, pp. 253–4.

71. This report of her death was in *The Evening Post* for Tuesday, 14 July 1724. There were also reports in *The Daily Post*, *The Daily Journal*, *The Impartial Intelligencer*, *The British Journal*, *The Universal Journal*, *The British Gazeteer*, and *The Saturday Post*, and probably in other newspapers which do not happen to be preserved in the Burney collection.

72. This originally appeared *The Daily Journal* for Monday, 13 July 1724.

73. PRO, SP 44/78, p. 63.

74. *Newcastle Courant*, Saturday, 29 August 1724.

75. *The Adventures of Rivella*, vol. 4, p. 56.

76. This information is taken from an advertisement in *The Newcastle Courant* for Thursday, 18 September 1735.

77. See *The Selected Poetry and Prose of Anna Letitia Barbauld*, p. 400, referring to Canto III, ll. 161, 165, in Pope, *The Rape of the Locke and Other Poems*, pp. 180–1.

WORKS CITED

Manuscripts

Badminton Archive

    Correspondence of Lord Arthur Somerset

    Correspondence of Henry, second Duke of Beaufort

Bodleian Library

    Bertie Papers and Manorial Records

    Clarendon State Papers

    Tanner Manuscripts

    Rawlinson Manuscripts

    Thurloe State Papers

British Library

    Additional Manuscripts

    Sloane Manuscripts

Canterbury, Prerogative Court of and Related Probate Jurisdictions, Will Registers

Cheshire and Chester Archives, Sir Peter Leycester's Book of Pedigrees

College of Arms, Heralds' Visitations

Cornwall Record Office, Parish Records, Title Deeds

Devon Record Office, Parish Records, Title Deeds

Guildhall Library, City of London Parish Records

Hertfordshire Archives, Records of the Earls Cowper

Jersey Archive, Parish Records

London Metropolitan Archives, Middlesex Sessions of the Peace, Session Papers

National Archives (formerly PRO)

    Secretary of State Papers

    State Papers Domestic

Anne

Charles II

Commonwealth Papers

James II

William III

William and Mary

Treasury Books and Warrants

Portsmouth Record Office, Parish Records, Sacrament Certificates

Suffolk Record Office, Parish Records

Westminster City Archives, Parish Records

Wrexham Local Records Office, Parish Records

Newspapers and Journals

Bickerstaff's Lucubrations

The British Gazeteer

The British Journal

The Daily Courant

The Daily Journal

The Daily Post

The Evening Post

The Examiner

The Female Tatler

The Impartial Intelligencer

The London Evening Post

The Medley

The Mercator, or, Commerce Retrieved

The Newcastle Courant

The Observator

The Post Boy

The Post Man and the Historical Account

The Saturday Post

The Universal Journal

State Papers

Calendar of State Papers, Domestic Series, 1649–60, ed. M. A. E. Green, 13 vols (London: Her Majesty's Stationery Office, 1875–86).

Calendar of State Papers, Domestic Series, 1664–1665, ed. M. A. E. Green (London: Her Majesty's Public Record Office, 1863).

Calendar of State Papers, Domestic Series, November 1667–September 1668, ed. M. A. E. Green (London: Her Majesty's Stationery Office, 1893).

Calendar of State Papers, Domestic Series, October 1668–December 1669, ed. M. A. E. Green (London: Her Majesty's Stationery Office, 1894).

Calendar of State Papers, Domestic Series, November 1st, 1673, to February 28th, 1675, ed. F. H. B. Daniell (London: His Majesty's Stationery Office, 1904).

Calendar of State Papers, Domestic Series, March 1st 1675 to February 20th 1676, ed. F. H. B. Daniell (London: His Majesty's Stationery Office, 1907).

Calendar of State Papers, Domestic Series, October 1, 1683–April 30, 1684, ed. F. H. Blackburne Daniell and F. Bickley (London: His Majesty's Stationery Office, 1938).

Calendar of State Papers, Domestic Series, James II, Volume II, January, 1687–May, 1687 (London: Her Majesty's Stationery Office, 1964).

Calendar of Treasury, vol. 10: January 1693 to March 1696, ed. W. A. Shaw, (London: His Majesty's Stationery Office, 1935).

A Collection of the State Papers of John Thurloe, esq; Secretary, First to the Council of State, and Afterwards to the Two Protectors, Oliver and Richard Cromwell, ed. T. Birch, 7 vols (London: Thomas Woodward and Charles Davis, 1742).

Journal of the House of Commons, at www.british-history.ac.uk.

Primary Sources

Anon., *The Rival Princesses: or, the Colchian Court: A Novel* (London: R. Bentley, 1689).

—, *The Female Wits: or The Triumvirate of Poets at Rehearsal. A Comedy* (1704), ed. L. Hook, Augustan Reprint Society publication 124 (facsimile reproduction, Los Angeles, CA: William Andrews Clark Memorial Library, 1967).

—, *Arabian Nights Entertainments: consisting of One Thousand and One Stories, told by the Sultaness of the Indies ... Translated into French from the Arabian MSS. By M. Galland ... and now done into English*, 2 vols (London: Andrew Bell, 1706).

—, *The Lady's New Year's Gift, or Advice to a Daughter* (London: D. Midwinter, 1707).

—, *Politeuphuia, Wits Commonwealth. Or a Treasury of Divine, Moral, Historical, and Political Admonitions, Similes, and Sentences* (London: W. Freeman, 1707).

—, *The Arraignment, Tryal, and Conviction of Robert Feilding, Esq; for Felony, in Marrying her Grace, the Dutchess of Cleaveland; His First Wife Mrs. Mary Wadsworth, being then Alive* (London: John Morphew, 1708).

—, *The Female Tatler* (1709–10), ed. F. Morgan (London: J. M. Dent & Sons, 1992).

—, *A True Relation of the Several Facts and Circumstances of the Intended Riot and Tumult on Queen Elizabeth's Birth-Day* (London: John Morphew, 1711).

—, *John Bull Still in his Senses: Being the Third Part of Law is a Bottomless-Pit*, 3rd edn (London: John Morphew, 1712).

—, *The D. of M—h's Vindication, in Answer to a Pamphlet Falsely so Called* (London: A. Baldwin, 1712).

—, *The Court of Atalantis* (London: J. Roberts, 1714).

—, *State Tracts: Containing many Necessary Observations and Reflections on the State of Our Affairs at Home and Abroad ... By the Author of the Examiner* (London: George Sawbridge et al., 1715).

—, *Familiar Letters of Love, Gallantry, and Several Occasions* (London: S. Briscoe, 1718).

—, *A New Miscellany of Original Poems* (London: T. Jauncy, 1720).

—, *Love Letters Between a certain Late Nobleman and the famous Mr. Wilson: Discovering The True History of the Rise and Surprising Grandeur of that Celebrated Beau* (London: A. Moore, [1723]).

—, *An Impartial History of the Life, Character, Amours, Travels, and Transactions of Mr. John Barber, City-Printer, Common-Councilman, Alderman, and Lord Mayor of London. Written by Several Hands* (London: E. Curll, 1741).

—, *The Life and Character of John Barber, Esq; Late Lord-Mayor of London* (London: T. Cooper, 1741).

—, *The Secret History, of Queen Zarah, and the Zarazians Wherein the Amours, Intrigues, and Gallantries of the Court of Albigion (during her Reign) are pleasantly expos'd, and as surprising a Scene of Love and Politicks, represented, as perhaps this, or any other Age or Country, has hitherto produc'd* (London: J. Huggonson, 1743).

Bandello, M., *Tutte le Opere di Matteo Bandello*, ed. F. Flora, 2 vols ([Milan]: Arnoldo Mondadori Editore 1966).

Barbauld, A. L., *The Selected Poetry and Prose of Anna Letitia Barbauld*, ed. W. McCarthy and E. Kraft (Peterborough, Ontario: Broadview Press, 2002).

Boyer, A., *Quadriennium Annae Postremum; or The Political State of Great Britain*, 8 vols (London: for the author, 1718–19).

Caron, F., and J. Schorten, *A True Description of the Mighty Kingdoms of Japan and Siam*, trans. R. Manley (1663), ed. C. R. Boxer (London: Argonaut Press, 1935).

Churchill, S., *Private Correspondence of Sarah, Duchess of Marlborough*, 2nd edn, 2 vols (1838; New York: Kraus Reprint, 1972).

Cibber, C., *Colly Cibber: Three Sentimental Comedies*, ed. M. Sullivan (New Haven, CT, and London: Yale University Press, 1973).

[Curll, E.], *Mr. Pope's Literary Correspondence*, 3 vols (London: E. Curll, 1735).

Dampier, W., *A New Voyage Around the World* (London: James Knapton, 1697).

—, *Voyages and Descriptions* (London: James Knapton, 1699).

d'Aulnoy, M., *Travels into Spain* (1691), ed. R. Foulché-Delbosc (London: George Routledge & Sons, [1930]).

de Witt, J., *Brieven aan Johan de Witt Eerste Deel 1648–1660*, ed. R. Fruin and N. Japikse (Amsterdam: Johannes Müller, 1919).

Dryden, J., *The Works of John Dryden*, ed. E. N. Hooker, H. T. Swedenberg, Jr, and A. Vinton, 20 vols (Berkeley and Los Angeles, CA: University of California Press, 1956–94).

Evelyn, J., *The Diary of John Evelyn*, 6 vols (Oxford: Clarendon Press, 1955).

Granville, G., *The Genuine Works in Verse and Prose of the Right Honourable George Granville, Lord Lansdowne*, 3 vols (London, J. and R. Tonson, L. Gilliver, J. Clarke, 1736).

The Guardian, 2 vols (London: printed by J. Nichols, 1789).

[Guilleragues, G. J. de Lavergne, vicomte de], *Five Love-Letters from a Nun to a Cavalier: Done out of French into English by Sir Roger L'Estrange* (London: Henry Brome, 1678).

Hare, F., *The Charge of God to Joshua: In a Sermon Preach'd before his Grace the Duke of Marlborough at Avennes le Sec September 9. 1711* (London: n.p., 1711).

[Hare, F., and A. Maynwaring], *Bouchain: In a Dialogue between the Late Medley and Examiner* (London: A. Baldwin, 1711).

Hawkins, W., *A Treatise of the Pleas of the Crown: or A System of the Principal Matters Relating to that Subject, Digested under their Proper Heads*, 2 vols (London: J. Walthoe and J. Walthoe, Jr, 1716–21).

Haywood, E., *Love in Excess; or, The Fatal Enquiry*, ed. D. Oakleaf, 2nd edn (Peterborough, Ontario: Broadview Press, 2000).

Hervey, J., *Letter-Books of John Hervey, First Earl of Bristol*, 3 vols (Wells: Ernest Jackson, 1894).

—, *The Diary of John Hervey, First Earl of Bristol, with Extracts from his Book of Expenses, 1688–1742* (Wells: Ernest Jackson, 1894).

Historical Manuscripts Commission, *Report on the Manuscripts of The Duke of Buccleuch and Queensberry, Preserved at Montagu House, Whitehall*, 3 vols (London: Her Majesty's Stationery Office, 1899).

[Jacob, G.,] *The Poetical Register; or, The Lives and Characters of All the English Poets. With an Account of their Writings*, 2 vols (London: E. Curll, 1723).

Juvenal, *The Satires of Decimus Junius Juvenalis*, trans. J. Dryden, N. Tate, W. Congreve, S. Hervey and T. Creech et al. (1693), 6th edn (London: Jacob Tonson, 1735).

Lacy, J., *The Ecclesiastical and Political History of Whig-Land of Late Years* (London: J. Morphew, 1714).

Langbaine, G. [and C. Gildon], *The Lives and Characters of the English Dramatick Poets* (London: William Turner, 1699).

Luttrell, N., *A Brief Historical Relation of State Affairs: from September 1678 to April 1714*, 6 vols (Wilmington, DE: Scholarly Resources, 1974).

Manley, D., *The Lost Lover; or The Jealous Husband: A Comedy* (1696), in *Eighteenth-Century Women Playwrights*, ed. D. Hughes, 6 vols (London: Pickering & Chatto, 2001), vol. 1, ed. M. Rubik and E. Mueller-Zettlmann.

—, *L'Atalantis de Madame Manley, Traduit de l'Anglais* (The Hague: Henry Scheurleer, 1713).

—, *The Adventures of Rivella* (1714), ed. K. Zelinsky (Peterborough, Ontario: Broadview Press, 1999).

—, *The Novels of Delarivier Manley*, ed. P. Köster, 2 vols (Gainesville, FL: Scholars' Facsimiles and Reprints, 1971).

—, *The Selected Works of Delarivier Manley*, ed. R. Carnell and R. Herman, 5 vols (London: Pickering & Chatto, 2005).

[Manley, D., et al.], *The Nine Muses, or Poems upon the Death of the Late Famous John Dryden, Esq.* (London: Richard Basset, 1700).

Manley, R., *Commentariorum de Rebellione Anglicana ab Anno 1640, Usque ad Annum 1685* (London: L. Meredith and T. Newborough, 1686).

—, 'The History of the Turkish Empire continued from the Year 1676 to the Year 1686', in R. Knolles and P. Rycaut, *The Turkish History, from the Original of that Nation to the Growth of the Ottoman Empire. With a Continuation to this Present Year. Whereunto is Added the Present State of the Ottoman Empire* (London: Jonathan Robinson et al., 1687), pp. 275–338.

—, *The History of the Rebellions in England, Scotland and Ireland: Wherein the Most Material Passages, Sieges, Battles, Policies and Stratagems of War, are Impartially Related on Both Sides; from the year 1640 to the Beheading of the Duke of Monmouth in 1685* (London: L. Meredith and T. Newborough, 1691).

[Manley, R.], *The Russian Impostor: or, The History of Muskovie, under the Usurpation of Bortis and the Imposture of Demetrius, Late Emperors of Muskovy* (London: Thomas Basset, 1674).

Navarre, M. de, *L'Heptaméron* (1559; Paris: Garnier Frères, 1967).

Painter, W., *The Palace of Pleasure* (1566–7), ed. J. Jacobs, 3 vols (1890; New York: Dover Publications, 1966).

Pepys, S., *The Further Correspondence of Samuel Pepys, 1662–1679*, ed J. R. Tanner (London: G. Bell and Sons, 1929).

Pix, M., *Ibrahim, the Thirteenth Emperour of the Turks* (London: John Harding and Richard Wilkin, 1696).

Pope, A., *The Rape of the Locke and Other Poems*, ed. G. Tillotson (London: Methuen; New Haven, CT: Yale University Press, 1962).

Rycaut, P., *The Present State of the Ottoman Empire* (London: Jonathan Robinson, 1687).

Settle, E., *The Female Prelate: Being the History of the Life and Death of Pope Joan, A Tragedy* (London: W. Cademan, 1680).

Shakespeare, W., *The Riverside Shakespeare*, ed. G. Blakemore Evans (Boston, MA: Houghton Mifflin, 1972).

Southerne, T., *The Works of Thomas Southerne*, ed. R. Jordan and H. Love (Oxford: Oxford University Press, 1988).

Steele, R., *Richard Steele's The Theatre 1720*, ed. J. Loftis (Oxford: Clarendon Press, 1962).

—, *The Epistolary Correspondence of Sir Richard Steele*, ed. J. Nichols, 2 vols ([London]: J. Nichols, 1787).

—, *The Occasional Verse of Richard Steele*, ed. R. Blanchard (Oxford: Clarendon Press, 1952).

—, *The Correspondence of Richard Steele*, ed. R. Blanchard (Oxford: Clarendon Press, 1968).

—, *The Tatler*, ed. D. F. Bond, 3 vols (Oxford: Clarendon Press, 1987).

Swift, J., *Prose Works of Jonathan Swift*, 14 vols, ed. H. Davis (Oxford: Basil Blackwell, 1941–68).

—, *Journal to Stella*, ed. H. Williams, 2 vols, Swift's *Prose Works*, ed. H. Davis, vols 15–16 (Oxford: Basil Blackwell, 1963).

—, *The Correspondence of Jonathan Swift*, ed. H. Williams, 5 vols (Oxford: Clarendon Press, 1965).

[Swift, J.], *A Friend of Mr. St—le. The Importance of the Guardian Considered, in a Second Letter to the Bailiff of Stockbridge* (London: John Morphew, 1713).

[Swift, J., A. Maynwaring and J. Oldmixon], *Swift vs. Mainwaring: The Examiner and The Medley*, ed. F. Ellis (Oxford: Clarendon Press, 1985).

[Toland, J.], *The Jacobitism Perjury and Popery of High-Church-Priests* (London: J. Baker, 1710).

Trotter, C., *Catharine Trotter's The Adventures of a Young Lady and Other Works*, ed. A. Kelley (Aldershot, Hampshire: Ashgate, 2006).

Wortley Montague, M., *The Complete Letters of Lady Mary Wortley Montague*, ed. R. Halsband, 3 vols (Oxford: Clarendon Press, 1965).

Secondary Sources

Aliker Rabb, M., 'The Manl(e)y Style: Delariviere Manley and Jonathan Swift', in *Pope, Swift, and Women Writers*, ed. D. C. Mell (Newark, DE: University of Delaware Press; London: Associated University Press, 1996), pp. 125–53.

Arber, E. (ed.), *The Term Catalogues, 1668–1709*, 3 vols (London: Edward Arber, 1903–6).

Atkyns, J. T., *Reports of Cases Argued and Determined in the High Court of Chancery, in the Time of Lord Chancellor Hardwicke* (London: J. Wenman, 1781).

Avery, E. L. (ed.), *The London Stage 1660–1800: A Calendar of Plays, Part 2: 1700–1729*, 2 vols. (Carbondale, IL: Southern Illinois University Press, 1960).

Baines, P., and P. Rogers, *Edmund Curll, Bookseller* (Oxford: Clarendon Press, 2007).

Ballaster, R., *Fabulous Orients: Fictions of the East in England, 1662–1785* (Oxford: Oxford University Press, 2005).

Balleine, G. R., *A Biographical Dictionary of Jersey* (London and New York: Staples Press, 1948).

Blackstone, W., *Commentaries on the Laws of England* (1765–9), 4 books in 2 vols (Chicago, IL: Callaghan and Cockcroft, 1871).

Brown, R. L., *A History of the Fleet Prison, London: The Anatomy of the Fleet*, Studies in British History, 42 (Lewiston, NY: Edwin Mellen Press, 1996).

Bunyan Anderson, P., 'Mrs. de la Rivière Manley: A Cavalier's Daughter in Grub Street' (PhD thesis, Harvard University, 1931).

—, 'Mistress Manley's Biography', *Modern Philology* (February 1936), pp. 261–78.

Butler, S., *Hudibras*, ed. J. Wilders (Oxford: Clarendon Press, 1967).

Canfield, J. D. (ed.), *The Broadview Anthology of Restoration and Early Eighteenth-Century Drama* (Peterborough, Ontario: Broadview Press, 2003).

Carnell, R., '"It's Not Easy Being Green": Gender and Friendship in Eliza Haywood's Political Periodicals', *Eighteenth-Century Studies*, 32:2 (Winter 1998–9), pp. 199–214.

—, 'Revising Tragic Conventions: Aphra Behn's Turn to the Novel', *Studies in the Novel*, 31:2 (Summer 1999), pp. 133–51.

—, 'More Borrowing from Bellegarde in Manley's Queen Zarah and the Zarazians', *Notes and Queries*, 249 (December 2004), pp. 377–9.

—, *Partisan Politics, Narrative Realism, and the Rise of the British Novel* (New York: Palgrave, 2006).

—, 'Delarivier Manley's Possible Children by John Tilly', *Notes and Queries*, n.s. 54:4 (December 2007), pp. 446–8.

Charnock, J., *Biographia Navalis; or Impartial Memoirs of the Lives and Characters of the Officers of the Navy of Great Britain from 1660 to the Present Time*, 6 vols (London: R. Faulder, 1794–8).

Churchill, W., *Marlborough: His Life and Times*, 2 vols (1933–8; London: George G. Harrap, 1947).

Clowes, W. L., *The Royal Navy: A History from the Earliest Times to the Present*, 7 vols (London: S. Low, Marston, 1897–1903).

Crane, H., *Playbill: A History of the Theatre in the West Country* (Plymouth and London: McDonald and Evans, 1980).

Dalton, C. (ed.), *English Army Lists and Commission Registers, 1661–1714*, 6 vols (1892–1904; London: Francis Edwards, 1960).

Delaney, M. G., *The Autobiography and Correspondence of Mrs. Delaney*, 6 vols (London: Richard Bentley, 1861–2).

Deloffre, F., *La Nouvelle en France à l'âge classique* (Paris: Didier, 1967).

Dodd, A. H., *A History of Wrexham* (Wrexham: Hughes & Son, 1957).

Doody, M. A., *The True Story of the Novel* (New Brunswick, NJ: Rutgers University Press, 1996).

Downie, J. A., *Robert Harley and the Press: Propaganda and Public Opinion in the Age of Swift and Defoe* (Cambridge: Cambridge University Press, 1979).

—, 'Swift and the Oxford Ministery', *Swift Studies*, 1 (1986), pp. 4–5.

—, *To Settle the Succession of the State: Literature and Politics, 1678–1750* (Houndmills, Basingstoke, Hampshire and London: Macmillan, 1994).

—, 'What if Delarivier Manley did *Not* Write *The Secret History of Queen Zarah*?', *The Library*, 7th series, 5:3 (September 2004), pp. 247–64.

—, 'Swift's "Corinna" Reconsidered', *Swift Studies*, 23 (2007), pp. 161–8.

Duff, D. D. C., 'Materials toward a Biography of Mary Delariviere Manley' (unpublished PhD dissertation, Indiana University, 1965).

Dyer, G. R., 'The Truth of the Innuendos and the Generality of Readers', paper given at the Midwest Modern Language Association meeting in Cleveland, Ohio, October 2007.

Ford, D., *Mont Orgueil Castle: A Souvenir Guide* (St Helier: Jersey Heritage Trust, 2007).

Foster, J. (ed.), *London Marriage Licenses* (London, 1889).

— (ed.), *The Register of Admissions to Gray's Inn, 1521–1889* (London: Hansard Publishing Union, 1889).

Furbank, P. N., and W. R. Owens, *Defoe De-Attributions: A Critique of J. R. Moore's Checklist* (London and Rio Grande, OH: Hambledon Press, 1994).

—, *A Critical Bibliography of Daniel Defoe* (London: Pickering & Chatto, 1998).

Gallagher, C., *Nobody's Story: The Vanishing Acts of Women Writers in the Marketplace, 1670–1820* (Oxford: Oxford University Press, 1994).

Gay, S. E., et al (eds), *The Register of Marriages, Baptisms and Burials of the Parish of St. Mary, Truro, Co. Cornwall, A.D. 1597 to 1837*, 2 vols (Exeter: Devon and Cornwall Record Society, 1940).

Gordon, J., *Gossip and Subversion in Nineteenth-Century British Fiction* (New York: St Martin's Press, 1996).

Gossman, L., 'Anecdote and History', *History and Theory*, 42 (May 2003), pp. 143–68.

Graham, W., 'Thomas Baker, Mrs Manley and the *Female Tatler*', *Modern Philology*, 34 (1936–7), pp. 267–72.

Hamburger, P., 'The Development of the Law of Seditious Libel and the Control of the Press', *Stanford Law Review* 37:661 (1985), pp. 661–755.

Hammond, B. S., *Professional Imaginative Writing in England 1670–1740* (Oxford: Clarendon Press, 1997).

Harari, Y. N., *Renaissance Military Memoirs: War, History, and Identity, 1450–1600* (Woodbridge, Suffolk: Boydell Press, 2004).

Herman, R., 'Swift, Manley, and the Commissioning of *A True Narrative*', *Swift Studies*, 15 (2000), pp. 88–103.

—, 'An Exercise in Early Modern Branding', *Journal of Marketing Management*, 19:7 (September 2003), pp. 709–27.

—, *The Business of a Woman: The Political Writings of Delarivier Manley* (Newark, DE: University of Delaware Press and London: Associated University Press, 2003).

—, 'Similarities between Delarivier Manley's *Secret History of Queen Zarah* and the *English Translation of Hattigé*', *Notes and Queries*, 47 (2004), pp. 193–6.

Highfill, P. H., K. A. Burnim and E. A. Langhans, *A Biographical Dictionary of Actors, Actresses, Musicians, Dancers, Managers, and other Stage Personnel in London, 1660–1800*, 16 vols (Carbondale, IL: Southern Illinois University Press, 1973–93).

Holmes, G. S., and W. A. Speck, 'The Fall of Harley in 1708 Reconsidered', *English Historical Review*, 79 (1965), pp. 673–98.

Holt, F. L., *The Law of Libel* (London: W. Reed, 1812).

Horn, R. D., *Marlborough: A Survey; Panegyric, Satires, and Biographical Writings, 1688–1788* (New York: Garland Publishers, 1975).

Hourcade, P. (ed.), *Sentiments sur les lettres et sur l'histoire avec des scrupules sur le style* (Geneva: Droz, 1975).

Hughes, D., *English Drama 1660–1700* (Oxford: Clarendon Press, 1996).

Hume, R. D., *Henry Fielding and the London Theatre, 1728–1737* (Oxford: Clarendon Press, 1988).

Inderwick, F. A. (ed.), *A Calendar of the Inner Temple Records*, 3 vols (London: Henry Sotheran & Co., Stevens and Haynes; Stevens and Sons, by order of the Masters of the Bench, 1896–1901).

Katz, C. B., 'The Deserted Mistress Motif in Mrs Manley's *Lost Lover*', *Restoration and Eighteenth-Century Theatre Research*, 16 (1977), pp. 27–39.

Köster, P., 'The Correspondence of Sir Roger Manley', *Bulletin of Bibliography*, 42:4 (1985), pp. 179–86.

Legg, L. G. W. (ed.), *English Coronation Records* (Westminster: A. Constable, 1901).

Leslie, J. H., *The History of Landguard Fort* (London: Eyre and Spottiswoode, 1898).

Lowenthal, C., 'Portraits and Spectators in the Late Restoration Playhouse: Delariviere Manley's *Royal Mischief*', *Eighteenth Century*, 35:2 (1994), pp. 119–34.

McBurney, W. H., 'Mrs. Penelope Aubin and the Early Eighteenth-Century English Novel', *Huntington Library Quarterly*, 20 (1957), pp. 245–67.

McKeon, M., *The Secret History of Domesticity: Public, Private, and the Division of Knowledge* (Baltimore, MD: Johns Hopkins University Press, 2005).

Manning, R. B., *An Apprenticeship in Arms: The Origins of the British Army, 1585–1702* (Oxford: Oxford University Press, 2006).

Maslen, K., 'Printing for the Author: From the Bowyer Printing Ledgers, 1710–1775', *Library*, 5:27 (1972), pp. 302–9.

Milhouse, J., and R. D. Hume (eds.), 'Draft of the Calendar for Volume 1, A New Version of Part 2', for *The London Stage 1660–1800: A Calendar of Plays, Part 2, 1700–1729*, 2nd edn (Carbondale, IL: Southern Illinois University Press, forthcoming), http://www.personal.psu.edu/users/h/b/hb1/ London%20Stage%202001/.

Moore, J. R., *A Checklist of the Writings of Daniel Defoe*, 2nd edn (Hamden, CT: Archon Books, 1971).

Morgan, F., *A Woman of No Character: An Autobiography of Mrs. Manley* (London: Faber and Faber, 1986).

Needham, G. B., 'Mary de la Riviere Manley: Tory Defender', *Huntington Library Quarterly*, 12 (1948–9), pp. 271–2.

—, 'Mrs. Manley: An Eighteenth-Century Wife of Bath', *Huntington Library Quarterly*, 14 (1950–1), pp. 259–84.

The New Cambridge Bibliography of English Literature, ed. G. Watson, 5 vols (London: Cambridge University Press, 1969–77).

Owen, S. J., *Restoration Theatre and Crisis* (Oxford: Clarendon Press, 1996).

Palmer, M. D., 'Madame d'Aulnoy in England', *Comparative Literature*, 27:3 (1975), pp. 237–53.

Patterson, A., *Early Modern Liberalism* (Cambridge: Cambridge University Press, 1997).

Pittock, M. G. H., *Jacobitism* (New York: St Martin's Press, 1998).

Plomer, H. R., *A Dictionary of the Printers and Booksellers who were at Work in England, Scotland and Ireland from 1668–1725* (London: Bibliographical Society, 1968).

Quintana, R., *The Mind and Art of Jonathan Swift* (London: Oxford University Press, 1953).

Richetti, J., *Popular Fiction before Richardson* (Oxford: Clarendon Press, 1969).

Rivington, C. A., '*Tyrant': The Story of John Barber: Jacobite Lord Mayor of London, and Printer and Friend to Dr. Swift* (York: William Sessions, 1989).

Rodger, N. A. M., *The Wooden World: An Anatomy of the Georgian Navy* (1986; London and New York: W. W. Norton, 1996).

—, *The Command of the Ocean* (London: Penguin Books with National Maritime Museum, 2004).

Sergeant, P., *Rogues and Scoundrels* (New York: Brentano's Publishers, [1927]).

Snyder, H. L., 'The Reports of a Press Spy for Robert Harley: New Bibliographical Data for the Reign of Queen Anne', *Library*, 5th series, 22:4 (1967), pp. 326–45.

Spedding, P. (ed.), *A Bibliography of Eliza Haywood* (London: Pickering & Chatto, 2004).

Sutton, J. L., 'The Sources of Mrs. Manley's Preface to Queen Zarah', *Modern Philology*, 82 (1984), pp. 167–72.

Teerink, H., *The History of John Bull for the First Time Faithfully Re-Issued from the Original Pamphlets, 1712, together with an Investigation into its Composition, Publication and Authorship* (Amsterdam: H. J. Paris, 1925).

ten Raa, F. J. S., and F. De Bas, *Het Staatsche Leger*, 8 vols (Breda, 1911–80).

Treadwell, M., 'London Trade Publishers 1675–1730', *The Library*, 6th series, 4:2 (June 1982), pp. 99–134.

Tucker, N., *Royalist Officers of North Wales 1642–1660* (Denbigh: Gee & Son, 1961).

Van Lennep, W. (ed.), *The London Stage 1660–1800: A Calendar of Plays, Part 1: 1660–1700*, (Carbondale, IL: Southern Illinois University Press, [1965]).

Watt, I., *The Rise of the Novel: Studies in Defoe, Richardson, and Fielding* (Berkeley and Los Angeles, CA: University of California Press, 1957).

Webb, E. A. H., *The History of the 12th (the Suffolk) Regiment 1685–1913* (London: Spottiswoode, 1914).

Weinbrot, H. D., 'Who Said He Was a Jacobite Hero?: The Political Genealogy of Johnson's Charles of Sweden', *Philological Quarterly*, 75:4 (Fall 1996), pp. 411–50.

Williams, E. N., (ed.), *The Eighteenth-Century Constitution 1688–1815, Documents and Commentary, 1688–1815* (Cambridge: Cambridge University Press, 1970).

Winton, C., 'Steele, Mrs. Manley, and John Lacy', *Philological Quarterly*, 62:2 (1963), pp. 272–5.

—, *Sir Richard Steele, M. P.* (Baltimore, MD: Johns Hopkins University Press, 1970).

INDEX

Works by Manley (DM) appear directly under title; works by others under author's name.